RULES AND UNRULINESS

Rules and Unruliness

Canadian Regulatory Democracy, Governance, Capitalism, and Welfarism

G. BRUCE DOERN, MICHAEL J. PRINCE,
AND RICHARD J. SCHULTZ

McGill-Queen's University Press
Montreal & Kingston • London • Ithaca

© McGill-Queen's University Press 2014

ISBN 978-0-7735-4332-4 (cloth)
ISBN 978-0-7735-4333-1 (paper)
ISBN 978-0-7735-9040-3 (ePDF)
ISBN 978-0-7735-9041-0 (ePUB)

Legal deposit first quarter 2014
Bibliothèque nationale du Québec

Printed in Canada on acid-free paper that is 100% ancient forest free
(100% post-consumer recycled), processed chlorine free

This book has been published with the help of a grant from the Canadian
Federation for the Humanities and Social Sciences, through the Awards to
Scholarly Publications Program, using funds provided by the Social
Sciences and Humanities Research Council of Canada.

McGill-Queen's University Press acknowledges the support of the Canada
Council for the Arts for our publishing program. We also acknowledge the
financial support of the Government of Canada through the Canada Book
Fund for our publishing activities.

Library and Archives Canada Cataloguing in Publication

Doern, G. Bruce, 1942–, author
    Rules and unruliness: Canadian regulatory democracy, governance,
    capitalism, and welfarism / G. Bruce Doern, Michael J. Prince, and
    Richard J. Schultz.

    Includes bibliographical references and index.
    Issued in print and electronic formats
    ISBN 978-0-7735-4332-4 (bound). – ISBN 978-0-7735-4333-1 (pbk.). –
    ISBN 978-0-7735-9040-3 (ePDF). – ISBN 978-0-7735-9041-0 (ePUB)

    1. Administrative agencies – Canada. 2. Administrative procedure –
    Canada. 3. Canada – Economic policy. 4. Industrial policy – Canada.
    5. Social legislation – Canada. 6. Canada – Politics and government –
    1945–. I. Prince, Michael John, 1952–, author II. Schultz, Richard J.
    (Richard John), 1945–, author III. Title.

    KE5019.D63 2014   342.71'066   C2013-908496-7
    KF5407.D63 2014   C2013-908497-5

This book was typeset by Interscript in 10.5/13 Sabon.

In memory of the late Professor Peter Aucoin, our friend, teacher, colleague, lifelong inspiration, and a great Canadian and international scholar and advocate of renewed parliamentary democracy

Contents

Chart and Tables

CHART

TABLES

Preface

This book is the product of the authors' individual and collaborative work on regulation in Canada and internationally over the past four decades. During this extensive period of reading, discussion, and interviews, we owe numerous debts of thanks, gratitude, and learning to many individuals and to many agencies and institutions involved directly and indirectly with the story of Canada's regulatory democracy and governance.

We are indebted to the two McGill-Queen's University Press peer reviewers for their constructive and insightful comments on an earlier version of the manuscript. They have helped us strengthen the overall conceptual and empirical coherence of the book. We are also grateful to many academics and practitioners from across Canada and internationally. We have drawn on their scholarly research, which we cite and debate throughout the book.

A continuing intellectual and personal set of thanks are owed to colleagues and staff at our respective academic institutions, the School of Public Policy and Administration at Carleton University, the Politics Department, University of Exeter in the United Kingdom, the Faculty of Human and Social Development, University of Victoria, in particular, the Studies in Policy and Practice Program, and the Department of Political Science at McGill University in Montreal.

G. Bruce Doern, Michael J. Prince, and Richard J. Schultz

Abbreviations

AANDC	Aboriginal Affairs and Northern Development Canada
AHRA	Assisted Human Reproduction Act
AHRC	Assisted Human Reproduction Agency of Canada
AHRT	assisted human reproduction technologies
AIT	Agreement on Internal Trade
BCNI	Business Council on National Issues (now the Council of Chief Executives)
BQ	Bloc Québécois
BSE	bovine spongiform encephalopathy
CBC	Canadian Broadcasting Corporation
CBSA	Canada Border Services Agency
CDRM	Cabinet Directive on Regulatory Management
CDSR	Cabinet Directive on Streamlining Regulation
CEO	chief executive officer
CEPA	Canadian Environmental Protection Act
CESD	Commissioner of Environment and Sustainable Development
CFI	Canada Foundation for Innovation
CFIA	Canadian Food Inspection Agency
CFIB	Canadian Federation for Independent Business
CHT	Canadian Health Transfer
CHST	Canada Health and Social Transfer
CIC	Citizenship and Immigration Canada
CIHR	Canadian Institutes of Health Research
CIPO	Canadian Intellectual Property Office
CMA	Canadian Manufacturing Association
CORE	Centre for Regulatory Expertise

CPP	Canada Pension Plan
CRA	Canada Revenue Agency
CRTC	Canadian Radio-television and Telecommunications Commission
CSIS	Canadian Security Intelligence Service
CST	Canadian Social Transfer
CTA	Canadian Transportation Agency
CTC	Canadian Transport Commission
CUFTA	Canada-US Free Trade Agreement
DOC	Department of Communications
DPP	Director of Public Prosecutions
DTH	direct to home
EACSR	External Advisory Committee on Smart Regulation
EI	Employment Insurance
EMR	Energy, Mines, and Resources
EU	European Union
FCAC	Financial Consumer Agency of Canada
FDA	Food and Drug Administration (US)
FISC	Financial Institutions Supervisory Committee
FPAC	Forest Products Association of Canada
FSB	Financial Stability Board
FTA	Free Trade Agreement (Canada-US)
GATT	General Agreement on Tariffs and Trade
GST	Goods and Services Tax
HRSDC	Human Resources and Skills Development Canada
HST	harmonized sales tax
ICT	information and communication technology
IMF	International Monetary Fund
INAC	Indian and Northern Affairs Canada
IP	intellectual property
IRBD	Immigration and Refugee Board of Canada
MI	Ministerial Instruction
MOT	Ministry of Transport
MOU	memorandum of understanding
NAFTA	North American Free Trade Agreement
NDP	New Democratic Party
NEB	National Energy Board
NEP	National Energy Program
NGO	non-governmental organization

NRTEE	National Round on Environment and Economy
NTA	National Transportation Act
OECD	Organization for Economic Cooperation and Development
OSFI	Office of the Superintendent of Financial Institutions
PBO	parliamentary budget officer
PMO	Prime Minister's Office
R&D	research and development
RAS	Regulatory Affairs Sector
RCMP	Royal Canadian Mounted Police
RIAS	regulatory impact assessment system
RSA	related science activities
SEIA	Socio-Economic Impact Analysis
SMES	small and medium-sized enterprises
SOA	special operating agency
TSB	Transportation Safety Board of Canada
UK	United Kingdom
US	United States
WIPO	World Intellectual Property Organization
WTO	World Trade Organization
WTO TRIPS	World Trade Organization Trade-Related Intellectual Property System

RULES AND UNRULINESS

Introduction

Rules and Unruliness is mainly for academics and students interested in the developments, strengths, and weaknesses of Canadian rule making and regulation. We also have in mind governmental and business leaders who follow regulatory issues and those citizens and interest group participants who too often feel they are caught up in a bewildering regulatory maze. The book provides an in-depth historical and comparative examination of Canadian regulation and how, with regard to both enforcement and preventative mandates, state regulation has evolved in regimes of multilevel rule making, compliance, and non-compliance that over the years have become more complex.

To better appreciate the context and nature of both rules and unruliness, the book covers Canada's regulatory politics and governance changes over four to five decades during the Stephen Harper, Jean Chrétien–Paul Martin, Brian Mulroney, and Pierre Trudeau prime ministerial eras. We also raise questions about the near term future and about longer-term issues regarding Canadian regulatory democracy, governance, capitalism, and welfarism.

There are many levels and many types of rule making. Regulation refers to "rules of behaviour backed up by the sanctions of the state" (Doern, Hill, Prince, and Schultz 1999, 1). Such state-sanctioned rules are variously expressed through laws, delegated legislation (or the "regs"), guidelines, codes, and standards, alongside judicial decisions and rulings by tribunals and courts. Regulation making occurs, and rules derive from, and are interpreted by (1) legislative, (2) executive/administrative, and (3) judicial branches, as well as in (4) the intergovernmental arena of executive federalism in the form of fiscal arrangements, policy accords, and other agreements. All four are institutional sources of public powers and rule making but traditional regulatory and related administrative law scholarship has tended to focus on the first two (Jones and de Villars 1999).

Guidelines and codes, moreover, are often seen as realms of "soft law" or rule making in the shadow of the law that can be several steps removed from parliamentary or executive-level central agency scrutiny as well as scrutiny by other arenas of democracy. Rules are central to our historical account, and unruliness as a concept must be examined in relation to such increasingly embedded and complex rules.

Public regulation involves decisions by state authorities about *regulatory flows*; that is, the most recent regulatory measures, which typically are more visible and often publicly contentious. Public regulation also involves the continuing existing *regulatory stock* of rules and policies made by previous governments, sustained by popular support and the backing of interest groups, institutional inertia, and the power of the status quo. Public regulation further involves the realities and rhetorical layers of red flags and red tape, risks and benefits, safety and health, regulatory capture, the so-called nanny state, the paper burden – and the cumulative regulatory weight of intervention and other images humorously and critically depicted in Charles Dickens' account of the legendary government office of circumlocution.

UNRULINESS

Our analytical approach is anchored in the notion that rules and regulation are increasingly exhibiting diverse kinds of *unruliness* defined as challenges in effectively developing and enforcing rules in both parent laws and delegated regulations because of any number of policy and mandate conflicts, gaps, and weaknesses. To some people, the notion of unruliness may evoke a picture of chaos or mob rule or abject failure. It has not been hard to conjure up such examples of unruliness in the period since 2008 during which time the world has witnessed the debacle of failed bank and related sovereign debt regulation; Japan's nuclear reactor regulatory collapse in the face of both human error and an earthquake and a tsunami: the massive US oil spill in the Gulf of Mexico and the regulatory failures that revealed; the UK's media regulatory black hole regarding newspaper hacking into private lives; and the tragic consequences caused by the weaknesses and failures of American gun control laws.

At first glance, Canada would seem to have been a relative sea of tranquillity, a bastion of peace, order, and good government on each of these fronts of unruliness. This self-congratulatory instinct, we contend, is presumptuous and misleading. Canada has its own regulatory unruliness. Some episodes and failures include the following: Quebec student demonstrations over university fee increases and subsequent rules regarding the right to protest, both policies being subsequently cancelled after a change in government; abject regulatory failure with regard to climate change at the national level under both Liberal and Conservative governments; the unravelling of some aspects of federal environmental assessment regulation; lapses regarding the provision of medically essential radio isotope products; and the laxity and incompetence of more than one parliamentary watchdog agency.

Some regulatory unruliness involves more than one episode of major failure. The 2008 crisis regarding deaths caused by listeriosis in the food system led to a major review via the 2009 Weatherill Report (Canada 2009) that recommended major changes to Canada's food regulatory system centred on the Canadian Food Inspection Agency (Doern 2010a). Then a major *E. coli* outbreak in the fall of 2012 focused on an Alberta slaughterhouse led to illness in several people, yet the detection of it was slow and heavily criticized. The Harper government promised change after the listeriosis crisis but did not address the overall set of Weatherill recommendations regarding the number of inspectors needed or the systems of information required (Curry 2012; Mahoney and Wingrove 2012). This lack of regulatory action was because of the government's pursuit of other priorities including government-wide budget and staff cuts and because of its regulatory plans of weakening environmental rules so that they better favoured the growth of energy exports. In essence, these two food safety crises were cases where regulatory reach exceeded regulatory grasp and where agenda setting and priorities were leisurely and significantly missing the mark.

A second recent example of unruliness if not regulatory failure occurred in the July 2013 railway accident and disaster in Lac-Mégantic, Quebec, in which forty-seven persons were killed by an out-of-control train carrying a shipment of oil in seventy-two tanker cars. The resulting derailment, explosions, and fire also destroyed the town centre. The accident seemed almost unbelievable to have happened in the way it did. It involved hazards and risks related to transportation and to dangerous goods cargo, and thus immediately raised issues about what risk regulation means, an issue to which we return throughout this book. Questions have been raised about longer-term federal transport regulation but also about the immediate peculiarities of the accident itself and whether it proved, as a single case, the inadequacies of past and current regulatory policies (Bishop 2013; Mackrael 2013).

At another level of observation, in Canada and elsewhere, a search through daily newspapers, blogs or other social media yields reports of rules gone awry and the stories of individuals or communities caught up adversely in the regulatory maze. Examples such as rules or the absence of rules regarding assisted suicide or aspects of health such as tackling obesity show up repeatedly in such coverage. Media exposure, of course, is more likely to focus on things that go wrong or are patently unjust than things that are right or just. Nonetheless, there is a formidable array of anecdotal evidence to use as a further entry point for the analysis of unruliness.

More difficult to examine empirically is unruliness that may result from a variety of human characteristics and diverse levels and degrees of misbehaviour in an imperfect, uncertain, and unjust world. Unruliness relates to earlier theories and empirical analyses that showed how various kinds of impairment, caused by systematic indoctrination of many kinds, tends to reinforce the current social and political order but also reduces the underlying intelligence needed for democratic problem solving (Lindblom 1992; Lindblom and Woodhouse 1993). Unruliness can include the non-compliance with rules due to strategies of overt disobedience and wilful ignorance but also conflicts within regulatory agency cultures regarding both what is required behaviour and also what to do when no one is looking. For example, the global pharmaceutical industry has incurred fines of more than $11 billion in three recent years "for criminal wrongdoing, including withholding safety data and promoting drugs for use beyond their licensed conditions" (Laurance 2012). Seemingly, such costs/fines are treated as part of the cost of doing business (Goldacre 2012). A further example is the Internet industry, which usually presents itself as both economically efficient and environmentally friendly. The unruliness, in this case, concerns the vast and wasteful use of electrical power to maintain the industry's huge data centres. Pollution from data centres is growing to the extent that "many data centers appear on state government's Toxic Contaminants Inventory, a roster of the area's top stationary diesel polluters" (Glanz 2012, 2).

Unruliness can be linked analytically to established versions of regulatory capture theory as laws and rules – especially in the US political system with its separation of powers – are changed and redrafted by industries and interests being regulated, and by other strategies of pressure and tactical politics (Etzioni 2012a). This need not involve some sense of total capture of the regulator by the interests it is regulating. Capture can involve partial kinds of pressure that weaken parent laws or enforcement penalties and fines in the name of both profit making for firms and industries and regulatory peace, legitimacy, and tranquillity for regulators dealing with complex mandates. For regulators, too, there is the practical reality, almost regardless of how large an inspection staff it has, of not being able to be in all of the right places at the right times to identify and deal with offences that occur across Canada's huge geographical/ spatial terrain and that extends further internationally in other complex ways. Indeed, almost as soon as new rules and regulations are promulgated, some regulated interests, and even the regulators themselves, immediately start to find ways around the rules, especially those they define or perceive as irksome.

Our analysis shows that Canada's regulatory system is rife with unruliness and that key types of actual and potential unruliness, as set out below, are growing and need to be better understood in regulatory scholarship and practice. Our hope is that citizens and policy makers alike can then better appreciate why multiple types of unruliness are occurring and how, and to what extent they can or should be addressed. The analytical challenges of examining unruliness need to be stressed from the outset. Different entry points exist in current literature and commentary that may reveal unruliness without it being the initial focus of analysis. For example, some observers have examined the growth of "blame game" politics and spin as a feature of politics for some time but now practised in a system of complex rules and risks and in an era of permanent attack politics and campaigning (Hood 2011; Fletcher and Blais 2012; Smith and Baier 2012). In the July 2013 federal Cabinet shuffle, for example, ministers were introduced and announced partly in the normal way, but media coverage also showed how some new minister guidance briefings and checklists included an "enemies" list of people, organizations, and public service projects to avoid in their new jobs (Berthiaume 2013; Delacourt 2013) supplied by the Prime Minister's Office. Given past Harper-era attack politics, instincts, and practices, this revelation was seen as even more profoundly undemocratic.

In the pervasive hothouse context of the banking and sovereign debt crisis, analysts point to how banks and financial institutions are now "blindly reliant on computers, on algorithms, [and] on high-frequency, trading" and that "for a trader relying on an algorithm, the 'long term' is an hour" (Nocera 2012, 1). And analysts of the Internet and social networks argue that as a pervasive technology, socially, economically, and culturally, standard systems of regulation are in their wake easily rendered obsolete (Pager and Candeub 2012; Rainie and Wellman 2012; Smith, Rhea, and Meinrath 2012).

Unruliness of three main types is the focus in our analysis: namely, (1) unruliness that is related to regulatory agencies; (2) unruliness that is related to regulatory regime complexity; and (3) unruliness that is related to agenda setting. Unruliness is always in relation to the nature of rules and rule making. The regulatory world and, therefore, the previewed kinds of unruliness need to be analysed with a full appreciation of the complex nature of what good or better regulatory performance might involve. At a minimum, this means a recognition that some rules and even regimes of rules are focused on securing compliance regarding undesirable behaviour, including criminal behaviour that has already occurred, while other rules are focused more on preventative missions to ensure that various kinds of undesirable behaviour do not occur in the first place (Salomon 2002; OECD 2010). Other regimes of rules entail establishing positive goals for the regulated to meet, an example being Canadian content rules in the broadcasting sector. Many regulatory agencies do all three.

Regulatory performance needs to be calibrated with some kind of "degree of difficulty" score, as in certain sports competitions. The previously mentioned example of obesity easily comes to mind in this regard with elements of individual health, family genetics, lifestyle choices, and socio-economic factors combining in various ways. Without doubt, there are different temporal dimensions to regulatory performance including concepts of regulatory life cycles and regulatory institutional learning across the medium term and longer-term periods (Sparrow 2008).

These separate and combined notions of unruliness and how to treat them analytically are further defined and assessed in later empirical chapters. A more detailed discussion of unruliness as a conceptual paradigm in our analytical framework is presented in chapter 1 following our discussion of three key literature streams on which we build and to which we contribute: (1) the political economy of regulation, (2) regulatory governance in a complex networked world, and (3) conceptions of safety, risk, uncertainty, and risk-benefit.

PURPOSES AND CONTRIBUTION

The book's overall contribution centres on our presentation of a comprehensive historical and contemporary account of the evolution of both change and inertia in the Canadian regulatory system. Chart I.1 previews the basic nature of the analytical journey involved beginning with a sense of the contextual background (see Part I chapter profiles below). Next is the development and use of an *analytical framework* that consists of examining (1) the above main types of unruliness, (2) six changing regulatory regimes, and (3) their three key attributes as relevant factors in understanding the nature and causes of change and inertia within and across the regulatory regimes.

Regulatory regimes are defined as integrated and interacting systems of ideas, institutions, interests, policies, rules, and compliance systems. The broader concept of regimes is, of course, used often in political, policy, and governance scholarship and is applied mainly to highlight more complex mezzo-level institutional realms including types of democracy, political executive structures, international relations, and budgetary systems, but also more particular cross-governmental policy areas such as risk, safety, and science and technology (Harris and Milkis 1989; Krasner 1983).

The six regulatory regimes examined are the following:

1 Macro regulatory governance regime
2 Economic sectoral regulatory regime
3 Regulatory regime of social sectors
4 Marketplace framework regulatory regime
5 Societal framework regulatory regime
6 Parliamentary democracy regulatory regime.

Chart 1.1 Analysing Rules and Unruliness in the Evolution of the Canadian Regulatory System: Regulatory Democracy, Governance, Capitalism, and Welfarism

Context

Conceptual Foundations and Literature Streams
- Political Economy of Regulation
- Regulatory Governance in a Complex Networked World
- Conceptions of Safety, Uncertainty, Risk, and Risk-Benefit

Canadian Regulatory Democracy in Liberal and Conservative Prime Ministerial Eras and in a Global Context

The Changing Ecosystem of Ministerial-Agency Relations and Expanding Interests

Analytical Framework

Unruliness
- Regulatory Agency-Related
- Regulatory Regime Complexity-Related
- Agenda-Setting Related

Regulatory Regimes
- As Middle-Level Realities
- As Vertical and Horizontal in Direction and Scope
- With Economic and Social Intent and Intended and Unintended or Ill-Considered Social and Economic Impacts

Regime Attributes
- Ideas, Discourses, and Agendas
- Public and Private Power in Regulation Making and Compliance
- Science, Evidence, Knowledge

Six Regulatory Regimes

Change, Inertia, and Unruliness across 40–50 Years of Rule Making and Implementation in the:

- Macro-Regulatory Regime
- Economic Sectoral Regime
- Regime of Social Sectors
- Marketplace Framework Regime
- Societal Framework Regime
- Parliamentary Democracy Regime

Table I.1 The Six Regulatory Regimes and Case Realms Examined

Policy Scope	*Sectoral Framework*	
ECONOMIC	INDUSTRIES/SECTORS (CHAPTER 5) • Energy • Transportation • Telecommunications	MARKETPLACE CROSS-ECONOMY RULES (CHAPTER 7) • Competition • Banking and financial services • Intellectual property
SOCIAL/ SOCIETAL/ COMMUNITY	SOCIAL SECTORS (CHAPTER 6) • Charities • Citizenship and immigration • Assisted human reproduction	SOCIETAL RULES (CHAPTER 8) • Law and order • Morality and sexuality • Welfare state
OVERALL POLICY AND GOVERNANCE	MACRO REGULATORY GOVERNANCE (CHAPTER 4) • Cabinet Directive on Regulatory Management • Statutory Instruments Act • *Canada Gazette* consultation processes • Consultation and quasi-constitutional provisions	PARLIAMENTARY DEMOCRACY (CHAPTER 9) • Elections and political parties • Responsible government • Parliamentary watchdog agencies

We look at the content of each regime and build on and extend considerably our earlier work on the interactions among such regimes (Doern and Wilks 1998; Doern, Hill, Prince, and Schultz 1999).

Table I.1 previews the eighteen case study areas and realms that provide both policy scope and depth to the overall forty- to fifty-year empirical story. The above regimes are also defined in relation to whether they are primarily horizontal and framework oriented intended to reach out across the economy or across society or whether they tend to be more sectoral or confined in nature and scope. We further draw out the ways in which horizontal framework regime development is driven by the power of some sectoral interests. We are alert to complex ideas, power plays, and gaming as the six regimes have been developed, criticized, and amended across time. We show that while some regulatory regimes are anchored in economic, market-based, and public interest ideas, they also produce social and community effects of diverse and often unintended kinds. In addition, we show that while other regulatory regimes are societally oriented and motivated they also produce economic effects, good, bad, and indifferent.

Examining the six regimes compels us to look contextually at the changing overall ecosystem of regulatory governance and interests including the following: foundational concepts in economic regulation linked to policing versus planning modes and aspirations in regulation; the relationship between independent regulators and elected, especially Cabinet authorities; the much more complicated nature of the structure of interests involved in regulatory politics and power than was previously the case; and finally, frequent exogenous factors and forces including technological ones and periodic crises.

Our analytical framework allows each regulatory regime to be examined in terms of three attributes that help propel and explain change or inertia within and across regimes, and also help us probe the nature of unruliness, namely:

1 Ideas, discourses, and agendas
2 Public and private power in regulation making and compliance
3 Science, evidence, and knowledge.

We introduce these analytical attributes initially in chapter 1, and they are a key feature of each of the regulatory regime chapters as we examine both regime change and inertia.

A second basic contribution of the analysis presented in this book is our deliberate and systematic extension of the analysis of regulatory scholarship to what we call *regulatory welfarism*. This refers to relatively distinct rules related to governing relationships among institutions and actors for managing social sectors and societies. We do this through an examination of the societal framework and social sectoral regulatory regimes, aspects of which have been previously labelled as *civic regulation* (Prince 1999a). Social regulatory regimes are both of the sectoral kind, such as the regulation of charities, citizenship and immigration, and assisted human reproduction technologies, and of an even broader and diverse societal framework regulation kind, such as rules entrenched in law and order, morality and sexuality, and the social welfare state (Rice and Prince 2013; Levi-Faur 2012a; Wincott 2012; Prince 2012).

No mere conceptual counterpoint to regulatory capitalism as discussed below, regulatory welfarism has its own historical elements and relatively distinct relationships among institutions and actors for managing particular social groups and overall societies. Moreover, regulatory welfarism is not restricted to a recent period in economic affairs, political developments, or social trends; regulatory welfarism spans centuries.

Rules and Unruliness provides a crucially needed discussion of the regulatory regime for Canadian parliamentary democracy itself, a regime that includes rules regarding political parties and elections, and the practice of responsible government (Aucoin, Jarvis, and Turnbull 2011; Bakvis and Jarvis 2012). This regime includes Parliament's many watchdog agencies that deal with access to information, privacy, lobbying, and ethics, as well as other accountability values and ideas. This ultimate and crucial regime in a liberal democratic setting is often simply left out of conventional regulatory scholarship even though it profoundly impacts the roles and relative legitimacy of the other five regulatory regimes.

The book's research methodology involves the above three-part analytical framework deployed in a central way to explore Canadian regulatory unruliness, democracy, governance, capitalism, and welfarism. Across the six regimes, we examine the above-mentioned eighteen regulatory case study fields, drawing empirically on numerous reports and studies of Canadian and international regulation, academic, think tank, and governmental, complemented by our own research including a large number of interviews with regulatory officials and players across the six regimes. The historical content of the empirical chapters broadly covers a forty- to fifty-year period, sometimes in a basic chronological manner but more often by moving back and forth between earlier periods to more recent developments in the Harper and also Chrétien-Martin prime ministerial eras.

MAIN QUESTIONS AND ARGUMENTS

The six principal questions addressed in this book are as follows: (1) What kinds of regulatory unruliness, as defined above, have been evident or addressed in the Canadian regulatory system overall? (2) How has Canadian regulatory democracy and governance changed in the past four decades? (3) How does Canada's system of public regulatory democracy and governance need to be reformed to deal democratically with rule making, compliance, and unruliness in a globalized context? (4) How and why has Canadian regulatory capitalism emerged in the past two decades in particular, and is it different from regulatory capitalism in other competitor countries? (5) Why does regulatory welfarism in social policy need a greater presence and understanding in mainstream regulatory scholarship? (6) Can Canada achieve an effective adherence to regulatory agendas and to a multiple-points-in-time full life cycle system of regulatory governance as envisaged in the federal Cabinet Directive on Regulatory Management (CDRM), the main set of macro-rules about federal rule making and in related health and environmental regulatory policy positions?

Throughout the analysis, we advance several arguments. Our first overall argument is that regulatory unruliness is growing in Canada and internationally. This growing unruliness is related to (1) regulatory agencies, (2) regulatory regime complexity, and (3) agenda setting. The range of core regulatory reform ideas of the past four decades have not so much replaced or succeeded each other, but rather have been placed beside or layered on top of each other. This mix of change and inertia has also contributed to unruliness and its challenges.

Second, we contend that Canadian regulatory democracy must be seen in the context of all of its many forms and arenas of democracy. We argue that there is a compelling need for greater democratic governance of regulation, in all of its actual and potential arenas of debate and accountability, in a way that more readily scrutinizes regulatory programs over longer time frames. These governance reforms should relate to internal Cabinet debate in an era of excessive prime ministerial power and to parliamentary scrutiny, including wider reporting by Parliament's regulatory watchdogs. In this context, it is especially crucial that the regulation of parliamentary democracy itself achieve renewed and urgent attention. If the regulation of parliamentary democracy does not garner fundamental public trust, then the legitimacy of other regulatory regimes suffers accordingly.

Third, like that in other countries, we show that Canada's system of regulatory governance has exhibited increasingly varied forms of delegated governance and degrees of independence (Krawchenko 2012: Rosenau 2007; Eliadis, Hill, and Howlett 2005). We argue, however, that regulatory independence by arm's-length commissions and watchdog agencies needs reinforcement to cement the reputation and authority of these commissions and agencies (Carpenter 2010). Regulatory independence, as a constitutional convention in Canada's Cabinet-parliamentary system of government, has been harmed unnecessarily and unwisely by seemingly random ministerial incursions and by weakening the evidence-based resources that crucially underpin such delegated governance. These ministerial interventions have been present regarding decisions of the regulators of nuclear energy (which included the dismissal of the agency head), telecommunications and broadcasting, and foreign investment. Arguably, the greatest threat of this kind has come from efforts to muzzle scientists in federal regulatory departments by subsuming the public advice they provide under the shackles of government communications strategies.

Fourth, we argue that a Canadian version of regulatory capitalism has emerged, in concert with countries elsewhere and that regulatory capitalism is fast overlaying the 1980s and earlier deregulatory and market liberalism era, which was itself considerably overplayed as an accurate descriptor of what was happening to regulation overall. Market liberalism in Canada is advancing in some respects but is accompanied not by fewer rules but, rather, by more rules and also more complex kinds of interwoven and often colliding rules under the auspices of both Liberal and Conservative governments. The main evidence for this regulatory analytical argument does not come from industry interests themselves advocating "regulatory capitalism" as part of their overt policy discourse; it emerges, rather, from their own recognition of, and direct and indirect support for, forms of co-regulation with the state and with non-governmental organizations (NGOs) as opposed to the state doing the regulating on its own.

Fifth, we argue that compared with regulatory capitalism, which fundamentally has international and global dimensions, regulatory welfarism is primarily anchored in domestic relations of power; in the Canadian federation, this is most notably so in national and subnational governance arrangements in the realms of both the state and civil society. Furthermore, regulatory welfarism does not necessarily signify a decentering of the state itself. At the same time, there is no single centre to managing society. With regard to regulatory capitalism, Braithwaite (2005) claims that "more of the governance that shapes the daily lives of most citizens is corporate governance than state governance" (2) and that, in part, regulatory capitalism involves "using markets as regulatory mechanisms, as opposed to the neoliberal schema of markets as the antithesis of regulation" (7). In liberal market societies, social entities and relationships have always been fundamental shapers of most people's existence.

For regulation in the regime of social sectors and in the societal framework regime, we show that there are several different sites that shift over time and restructure equally within and across jurisdictions. These sites are the federal and provincial states and local public bodies; professions, health disciplines, and occupational associations; myriad N G O s, civil society interests and entities; and individuals and families. Corresponding in exemplar form with these sites is command-and-control regulation, delegated regulation, co-regulation, and self-regulation or governance of the self.

Our sixth main argument is that Canada's regulatory governance system needs a far greater focus on democratic and policy needs related to social and civic regulation in both a sectoral sense and in terms of societal framework regulation. This includes social welfare program spending embedded with more and more rules in health care, education, housing, charities, and assisted human reproduction, to point out some examples. It also ultimately includes regulation related historically and at present to law and order, morality, sexuality, and national security in the age of heightened terrorism and fears of terrorism.

Seventh, we make the case that Canada's regulatory system as a system of governance has features that are more aspirational than real. This applies to the issues of regulatory agendas and to the implementation of life cycle approaches. The system still focuses to a great extent on a "one regulation at a time" and has, therefore, reduced chances of dealing successfully with many contemporary regulatory challenges. Unless it moves towards a regulatory agenda-centred approach that addresses broader notions and groups of rules with common risk, uncertainty, and risk-benefit characteristics, Canada's system of regulatory democracy and governance will remain deficient. Some aspects of a regulatory agenda-centred approach do happen within independent regulatory agencies and their mandate changes but not in the system as a whole.

The desirable overall policies for more comprehensive life cycle regulation, from pre-market to post-market, in many regulatory regimes and product, project, and process activities is also largely aspirational. To have a higher probability of achieving such multiple points in time and often extended intergenerational regulatory capacities will depend on all the elements of Canadian regulatory democracy and governance. It will also require underlying extended investments in regulatory capacity, including science, evidence, and knowledge in a much more networked set of players, especially regarding post-market monitoring.

THE DEFINITIONAL CORE

In addition to the previous definitions of regulation, unruliness, and regulatory regimes, the further definitional core for the book gives attention to the concepts of regulatory democracy, governance, capitalism, and welfarism.

Regulatory democracy we identify broadly to include all the main values, criteria, and arenas of democracy in existence in the Canadian political system. These include elected representative Cabinet-parliamentary democracy, federalist democracy, interest group pluralist democracy, civil society democracy, and direct democracy including burgeoning Internet-based social networks (Pal 2013; Bickerton and Gagnon 2009; Williams 2009; Rainie and Wellman 2012).

Regulatory governance is a subset of the broader concept of overall governance that emerged in the literature on politics, policy, and public administration over the past thirty years (Aucoin 1997, 2008; Rhodes 1997). In one sense, governance can be expressed simply as an effort to recognize more explicitly that governing is more than government, more than the state, and more than public policy pronounced and implemented by the state and its bureaucracies. Governance implies the state playing a role characterized at times more by steering than rowing and by more explicit efforts to improve service delivery, while it still implies the continued need for a strong state and state-led capacities (Bell and Hindmoor 2009).

Regulatory governance refers to the deployment of softer instruments of governing such as guidelines and codes of behaviour rather than just harder command-and-control direct regulatory ones, in part out of recognition of the need to regulate and serve different kinds of entities being regulated but also other clients who are the beneficiaries of regulation (Jordana and Levi-Faur 2004). The boundaries of regulatory governance extend to the rules embedded in taxation and in spending, two basic policy instruments traditionally seen as separate from regulation. In most policy and program fields and realms, citizens and interests are caught up in rules that are tax- and spending-centred as well as rules emanating from traditional realms and definitions of regulation. This is because all taxes, at their core, are rules of behaviour regarding the acquisition by the state of private income and wealth. All forms of spending always come with rules about how monies are to be spent, who is an eligible versus ineligible recipient of such funds, and who may suffer when such funds are cancelled under budgetary and austerity measures. This growing intermingling dynamic creates processes and outcomes that are themselves a form of unruliness for any number of players, including regulatory bodies.

Regulatory governance theory has always recognized that state-centred regulatory bodies almost always do more than regulate. These bodies are typically multifunctional in nature. In addition to regulation as such, they are planning entities; they exhort, persuade, and provide information; they adjudicate, negotiate, and network; they conduct research; they utilize different kinds of science, evidence, and knowledge; and the rules they deploy mandate large amounts of mainly private spending by businesses and citizens (Roman 1978; Schultz and Alexandroff 1985; Hill 1999a; Doern 2007).

Regulatory capitalism is a characterization of regulation that seeks to differentiate it from the 1970s and 1980s era of neo-liberalism. It seeks to capture the fact that regulation is growing markedly but is less a feature of state rule and enforcement and much more a system of co-regulation between the state and business interests and firms, as well as other non-state social interests and networks (Levi-Faur 2005; Braithwaite 2005, 2008). Regulatory capitalism is a crucial feature for understanding regulation as it co-mingles with modern capitalism.

Regulatory welfarism refers to relatively distinct rules related to governing relationships among institutions and actors for managing social sectors and societies. In political developments and social trends, but also in economic affairs, regulatory welfarism spans centuries – not just recent decades. There is a continual pattern of change and inertia in formal and informal rules coupled with hybrid networks of regulation making, implementation, and compliance. Regulatory welfarism is chiefly attached to domestic relations of power in the realms of both the state and civil society, with important effects in formulating identities of ethical conduct and valued roles in public and private realms.

STRUCTURE OF THE BOOK

Part I of *Rules and Unruliness* examines the Canadian regulatory system and its analysis conceptually and in a historical context and sets out our analytical framework and methodological approach. It examines key prime ministerial eras and maps the changing interests and power structure that underpin regulatory governance and its varied forms of ministerial and agency relations. Part II provides the complementary empirical analysis of the six regulatory regimes including their basic historical features and the manner in which the three attributes help us understand change and inertia and to probe the three types of unruliness.

Chapter 1 provides an analysis of the conceptual foundations needed to understand the nature of rules and unruliness and sets out in detail our analytical framework previewed above. The academic conceptual foundations draw on three main streams of literature: the political economy of regulation; regulatory governance in a complex networked world; and conceptions of safety, risk, uncertainty, and risk-benefit.

Chapter 2 presents an initial historical view of Canadian regulatory democracy and governance set in a global context. This provides a basic account of the regulatory approaches of prime ministerial and political party eras beginning with the Trudeau Liberals in the late 1960s and extending through the Mulroney Conservative, Chrétien and Martin Liberal, and Harper Conservative eras. It also examines the contending arenas and criteria of regulatory democracy. Key impacts and aspects of multilevel regulation, governance, and democracy are previewed as a crucial context for the book as a whole.

Chapter 3 examines contextually the changing overall ecosystem of the Canadian regulatory system centred on ministerial-agency relations and expanding interests. These two interacting features help us capture preliminary insights into unruliness, especially unruliness related to regulatory agencies, one of the three types being examined in this book. These strategic realities have been forged in the field of economic sectoral regulation, which lies at the heart of traditional regulatory scholarship. The chapter surveys some of the central exogenous forces that have disrupted the regulatory system such as the impact of economic disruptions, technological change of various kinds and magnitudes, and international factors. Each of these brings new ideas, new demands, new crises, and new relationships to bear on existing systems of ministerial-agency relations and the structure of interests.

As the analysis proceeds in Part II, we show why a broader set of regimes in the twenty-first century are also part of the Canadian regulatory system and now need to be at the heart of regulatory scholarship. We demonstrate that these regimes have their own versions of even broader and more complex ministerial-agency relations, expanding interests, and exogenous forces. These complex changes anchor our arguments regarding the need to examine regulatory capitalism and regulatory welfarism as revealed in a wider array of core regulatory regimes in Canada.

The chapters in Part II provide the empirical analysis of regulatory regimes and the application of the three regime attributes previewed above. It includes the eighteen case study regulatory realms and areas. Chapter 4 analyses the *macro-regulatory governance regime*, the regime that makes rules about rule making. It is centred at present on the Cabinet Directive on Regulatory Management (CDRM) but also extends to other key pillars of both constitutional and Cabinet-parliamentary government. The different newer life cycle aspirations of regulatory policy loom large in this macro-regime as does the question of regulatory agendas.

Chapter 5 focuses on the *economic sectoral regulatory regime*, often seen historically as public utility regulation but shifted and reshaped by technology and other forces that reconfigured sectoral mandates across the past forty years. The chapter focuses on the core regulators in the energy, transportation, and telecommunications sectors, the National Energy Board, the Canadian Transportation Agency and its predecessor agency the Canadian Transport Commission, and the Canadian Radio-television and Telecommunications Commission, respectively. They are examined in relation to challenges and pressures for regulatory space and power from their parent ministries and ministers and other federal departments in the face of changing regulatory values and economic forces, including environmental and consumer interests. The chapter portrays their transformation from agencies that were initially "governments in miniature" to the "mere miniatures" that they mainly are now.

Chapter 6 maps and examines the *regulatory regime of social sectors* treated as a regime needing greater and belated academic and practitioner regulatory governance recognition among traditional regulatory scholars. Conceptually, it begins by focusing on regulatory welfarism as a model and as one of the book's central arguments. Empirically, three sample sectors are profiled: registered charities, citizenship and immigration, and assisted human reproduction technologies. The analysis draws out the changing nature of what a social sector is and also the diverse notions of both social intent and economic impacts. The regulators here include the

Department of Finance, Citizenship and Immigration Canada, and also highly dispersed entities involved in the regulation of assisted human reproduction technologies, including Health Canada and the short-lived agency Assisted Human Reproduction Canada. In concert with the analysis of the societal framework regulatory regime in chapter 8, the chapter points to the long-standing historical nature of regulatory welfarism.

Chapter 7 shifts and extends the regime focus to the *marketplace framework regulatory regime* and, hence, to more economic *horizontal* framework rules regarding markets composed of both businesses and consumers of diverse kinds and set in both a Canadian and international context. Three selected market framework realms are explored: competition, banking and financial markets, and intellectual property with a focus on patents – again, with economic framework intent and social impacts both fully in mind. The regulators here include the Competition Bureau, the Department of Finance, the Bank of Canada, several financial services regulatory bodies, Industry Canada, and the Canadian Intellectual Property Office.

Chapter 8 provides a parallel effort, not usual in mainstream regulatory literature, to understand the crucial and long present *societal framework regulatory regime*. As such, it is a further key realm of regulatory welfarism. Here the focus is on broad horizontal societal coverage of three realms: law and order, morality and sexuality, and the welfare state. Regarding the welfare state, rules are often embedded in taxation, in public spending conditions and levered spending related to health care, employment, pensions and education, as well as in other aspects of detailed governance in these combined but diverse social welfare areas. The regulatory departments and ministries in these three realms include Justice Canada, Health Canada, the Department of Finance, and numerous related agencies, including those dealing with border safety and security. In many respects, this regime includes the oldest kind of state regulation begun under historic notions of the night watchman state and their modern variants, reinvented with new political vigour and theoretical interest.

Chapter 9 completes our empirical study of regulatory regimes with an analysis of the *parliamentary democracy regulatory regime*. It examines the rules, laws, regulations, and conventions governing political parties, elections, and responsible government as both a constitutional and partisan political matter regarding the relations between elected members of Parliament, the Cabinet, and the prime minister.

This regulatory regime also involves the growing number of parliamentary watchdog regulatory agencies that act as agents of Parliament's House of Commons, the elected representatives of the people. These include watchdog agencies, often referred to euphemistically as "gotcha agencies" regarding elections, lobbying, access to information, privacy, conflict of interest and ethics, and public sector integrity.

Chapter 10 provides our overall conclusions about the purposes and contribution of the book, our analytical framework, and our main arguments. We discuss here the future of rules and unruliness in Canadian regulatory democracy and governance in the context of needed democratic reform and global imperatives.

PART ONE

Regulatory Democracy and Governance: Analytical Framework and Historical Context

1

Conceptual Foundations
and Analytical Framework

The purpose of this chapter is to delineate the conceptual and analytical elements that inform our study of public rule making in the contemporary age of networked governance, innumerable risks, and growing unruliness. We first discuss the conceptual foundations of rule making and rules which, along with our empirical research, led to the development of the book's analytical framework centred on *unruliness, regulatory regimes*, and *regime attributes*. This conceptual review and the resulting framework draw on a range of academic, governmental, and other studies that are both historical and contemporary as well as Canadian and comparative. The literature emerges from diverse social science disciplines and fields, including political science, economics, sociology, public policy, governance, and public administration. The regulatory regime analysis in Part II of the book also draws on other more particular policy relevant literature. In the second part of the chapter, we then discuss further our analytical framework by elaborating on the different types of unruliness, the basic nature of regulatory regimes and the six regimes being examined, and the three regime attributes used to help understand regime change and inertia in Canada over the past four decades. Conclusions then follow.

CONCEPTUAL FOUNDATIONS

Three conceptual literature streams provide a crucial theoretical and applied regulatory policy, politics, and governance foundation. These streams are the political economy of regulation, regulatory governance in a complex networked world, and conceptions of safety,

Table 1.1 Conceptual Foundations in Brief

THE POLITICAL ECONOMY OF REGULATION
• Night watchman and law and order state as regulator
• Self-regulation for entrenched and new professions
• Public interest regulation
• Monopoly and rate of return regulation
• Regulatory capture and related concepts of policy impairment, inadequacy, and failure
• The regulatory state and regulatory capitalism vs. the social welfare state and the developmental state
• French-European "regulation theory" and varieties of capitalism in Canadian political economy

REGULATION AND REGULATORY GOVERNANCE IN A COMPLEX NETWORKED WORLD
• Command-and-control regulation
• Deregulation and re-regulation
• Incentive-based economic regulation
• Cap and trade
• Performance-based regulation
• Management-based regulation
• Governmentality
• Post-regulatory state
• Voluntary codes and private standards
• Risk assessment and risk management concepts
• Precautionary approach and the precautionary principle
• Smart regulation paradigm and the innovation economy and society
• Regulatory cooperation and harmonization
• The life cycle approach
• Regulation as "nudge"
• Networks, regulation, and meta-governance

CONCEPTIONS OF SAFETY, UNCERTAINTY, RISK, AND RISK-BENEFIT
• Safety as an absolute mandate and standard
• Uncertainty, risk, and its varieties
• Risk-benefit as the real world of regulation?

uncertainty, risk, and risk-benefit. We explore each briefly and comment on ways in which they are linked and overlap and also how we extend them to help produce both our analytical framework and the discussion of our complementary themes of Canadian regulatory capitalism, welfarism, democracy, and governance. The following list of conceptual foundations previews the content at a glance.

The Political Economy of Regulation

The political economy of regulation literature refers to broad interpretations of stages in regulatory development where the focus is on
the macro-relations of regulatory power between the state and capitalism and between the state and society. The presentation is broadly
chronological but it must be stressed that most of the issues and
arguments are still in play as various interests debate and characterize the ideas and power structures involved.

The *night watchman* and *law and order state as regulator* refer to
arguably the earliest form of regulation but were rarely given the
label of "regulation." Predating regulatory developments after the
Second World War and also the expansion of the welfare state, and
extending back to the eighteenth and nineteenth centuries, this related
to classic law and order rules that included the poor laws in the
United Kingdom but also in Canada and elsewhere, and to rules dealing with capital punishment, abortion, marriage, limited voting rights,
and invasive cradle-to-grave arrangements imposed on Aboriginal
populations. Concerns for issues of morality, immorality, limited
rights for workers, and early worker compensation legislation were
part of this night watchman law and order era, which some might
argue is being reborn to some extent in the current Stephen Harper
era (Prince 2012). Many of these rules were and still are mainly
embedded in statute law rather than in delegated law (the "regs"). In
addition, there were particular bursts of draconian forms of law and
order and security rules during both the First and Second World wars
and after the post-9/11 and continuing anti-terrorism period.

Self-regulation for entrenched and new professions has both historic and continuing relevance as a form of regulation and power. Its
earliest forms in Canada and elsewhere centred on the powers of
self-regulation granted by the state (the provinces) to the legal and
medical professions. In exchange for their delegated control of entry
to the profession and basic qualifications, these two dominant professions had to maintain core professional values anchored as well
around lawyer-client and doctor-patient privilege and confidentiality
(Competition Bureau 2007; Dewees 1983; Doern 1995a; Goode
1969). Few, if any, later professions have matched the power structure won by doctors and lawyers historically, but many subsequent
knowledge groups and occupations, including nurses, particular
medical specialists, and professional advisers, have sought and

partially achieved similar but more limited powers and rights. Some key professions regulated at the provincial level have, in addition, been a focal point as a barrier to interprovincial trade and the mobility of labour (Doern and MacDonald 1999). Later concepts of self-regulation unrelated to the professions likewise emerged, as we see further below.

Public interest regulation refers to the era beginning in the 1960s when the birth of the progressive regulatory state is said to have emerged (Ernst 1994; Harris and Milkis 1989; Stanbury 1980; Wilson 1980; Doern 1978). The larger public interest as opposed to private business interests was given political expression in regulations dealing with consumer safety and product safety (a well-known example was Ralph Nader's battle with the US auto industry). Progressive regulatory politics also centre on improving food safety, drug safety, nuclear safety, occupational health and safety, environmental assessment of projects, and assessment of environmental health and safety and particular hazards (such as acid rain). These reforms typically emerged in new laws, and in the delegated laws and enforcement mandates and actions of new independent regulatory agencies such as the Canadian Environmental Assessment Agency and, later, the Canadian Food Inspection Agency, although at times, also within ministerial departments, particularly in Health Canada.

Some areas of public interest regulation also predate the 1960s and 1970s heyday. For example, US competition and anti-trust regulation was the product of progressive politics in the 1890s and beyond aimed at eliminating and reducing the monopoly power of business in key sectors such as oil, banking, and railways (Eisner 1993; Doern and Wilks 1998). However, over the past four decades, regulation in the public interest has taken on many more diverse meanings as revealed both in studies of public opinion regarding regulation and of the public interest in twenty-first century politics (Mendelsohn 2003; Pal and Maxwell 2003).

Monopoly and *rate of return regulation* has a literature that is well established as an analytical underpinning, especially by economists in the birth phases of sectoral economic regulation. Centred on public utilities, the concepts guided the early regulation of the monopoly provision of essential services, anchored around new technologies as they emerged throughout the twentieth century (Wilks 1999; Ernst 1994: Armstrong and Nelles 1986; Doern 1978). Monopolies were said to be "natural" such as in early railway development where single networks rather than competing ones were a clear feature. Regulators were established to ensure that monopoly owners could neither extract monopoly profits from, nor discriminate among, customers and users. The system of regulation involved consumer protections yet traded off these protections against the right of private capital to a reasonable rate of return on its investment. Telephone utilities were also a key part of utility regulation, and aspects of it featured in some industries that were characterized by some as being oligopolistic rather than monopolistic. In addition to the rate of return and utility features, regulators dealt with some initial aspects of safety and quality of service, but this matured only later.

Regulatory capture theory emerged in the 1950s as a theory that critiqued public utility regulation by focusing on the underlying dynamics of power between and among regulated businesses, regulatory bodies, and consumers. Capture theory had two streams of argument. One centred on a theory by Bernstein (1955) that regulators gradually tended to be captured by the industries they were regulating. It was gradual in that the regulator went through a kind of life cycle, beginning with public interest vigour, then gradually working out a comfortable modus vivendi with the industry, and eventually morphing into a regulator captured by industry interests and enjoying the quiet life, with significant career interchange between the regulator and the industry. A second, somewhat later capture theory centred on the arguments of public choice economists that capture often occurred from the outset in the initial policy design rather than in the eventual implementation (Peltzman 1976; Baldwin, Scott, and Hood 1998). Notions of capture have continued to be a part of regulatory analysis and even of everyday non-theoretical discourse about the presumed habits of regulators even though the complexity of regulatory systems, arguably, makes capture much harder to describe and prove empirically (Etzioni 2012a; Hancher and Moran 1986; Doern, Hill, Prince, and Schultz 1999). This is an issue to which we return in regulatory regime and inter-regime analysis.

Related concepts of *policy impairment, inadequacy,* and *failure* have in various ways been a part of public policy theory and analysis for decades. We have referred in the Introduction to basic notions of impairment as suggested in the work of Lindblom (1990) and Lindblom and Woodhouse (1993). It has also been a feature of the regulatory failures and slowness in response to the 2008–12 banking crisis both regarding macro-prudential regulation and also re-regulation after the crisis (Baker 2013; Rixen 2013). This relates to our concept of unruliness in the regulatory world as do other policy theories. *Impairment* can involve human limitations, imperfect/incomplete information, ever-present constraints on time and other resources, and also – crucially – inequalities of power and authority. Notions of *policy inadequacy* and *failure* and of the limits of purely rational policy making and implementation have been a part of Lindblom's earlier theories of incrementalism, but also related theories of goal displacement, studies of policy crises and evident failure, and policy evaluation literature, where perfectly functioning policies and programs are a rarity due to mandate conflicts, resource weaknesses, and limitations and disagreements regarding causal analysis (Atkinson 2011; Pal 2011a).

The regulatory state and regulatory capitalism versus the social welfare state and the developmental state represents a further strand and set of contested views emanating from political economy centred on theories of the state (Wright 2012; Weiss 1998). Conceptions of the *regulatory state*, of course, go back to the above-mentioned night watchman state including the poor laws. The more contemporary views of the regulatory state have also been applied to the overall characterizations of the European Union, which is not, however, a social welfare state given that social welfare spending resides overwhelmingly at the EU member country nation-state level. Accordingly, the EU has relied more on the construction of a complex regulatory state (Levi-Faur 2012a; Majone 1997). Authors have also seen the European Union in more complex ways, including its function as a *developmental state*, particularly through variously defined economic development programs and rule making including competition and research and innovation (Niklasson 2012; Levi-Faur 2012b).

The notion of *regulatory capitalism* has also emerged conceptually and empirically (Braithwaite 2005, 2008; Levi-Faur 2005). It seeks to differentiate it from the 1970s and 1980s era of neo-liberalism. Regulatory capitalism seeks to capture the fact that regulation is growing markedly but is less a feature of state rule and enforcement alone and much more a system of co-regulation between the state and business interests and firms as well as other non-state interests and networks (Grabosky 2012).

In many senses, the *social welfare state* has been left out or not considered to be about regulation but rather about large distributive and redistributive tax and spending programs and entitlements built up especially in the period after the Second World War and extending to the 1980s (Rice and Prince 2013). This has always been a quite misleading view in some ways, but gradually and especially in recent years, some authors have characterized welfare state and social policy–related regulation as civic regulation (Prince 1999a), and others have argued for the ever-greater need not to see the welfare state and the regulatory state as polar opposites but rather as linked manifestations of any modern state (Levi-Faur 2012a, 2012b). We thus introduce the concept of *regulatory welfarism* both as a conceptual tool and an empirical reference to policy and practice. Indeed, in the very structure of welfare state programs and administration, complex rule-based systems were constructed in areas such as health care, housing, and education (Wincott 2012). Our analysis of the regulatory regime of social sectors in chapter 6 and of the societal framework regulatory regime in chapter 8 anchors our discussion of regulatory welfarism.

French European "regulation theory" and varieties of capitalism in Canadian political economy warrant initial treatment in the conceptual foundations. Regulation theory emerged in France and was reflected and modified in other European countries depending, in part, on particular systems of capitalism in different countries (Boyer 2001; Jessop 2002). Regulation in this theoretical tradition did not refer to the particular policy instrument notion of regulation (where regulation is just one instrument of governing) but rather something that, in today's terminology, is much more akin to broad governance structures. It concentrates on systemic features of power in systems of capitalism and at different stages of capitalism such as the Fordist and post-Fordist eras. Some features of this kind of macro-regulation as capitalist power arrangements may also be attributed to the different nature of French and European legislation where laws are written and expressed more broadly and with less delegated law compared with the Anglo–North American notions of regulation as delegated law.

Understanding regulation in this way certainly has Canadian manifestations, regulatory and otherwise, in its links to theories of the capitalist state and to Canada being subject to the power of American businesses and earlier British capital, overall and in particular industries (Clarkson 2009; Panitch 1970). The study of Canadian natural resource industries under Harold Innis' staples theory and under more recent theories of national resource-based centre-periphery relations easily resonates with these broad regulation theory notions

of power and, in comparative terms, to theories of varieties of capitalism and the regulatory regimes they impose, create, emulate, reject,
and reform (Howlett 2004; Hall and Soskice 2001). Within Canada,
particular provinces exhibit different kinds of capitalism ranging
from more state-centred varieties in Quebec and Saskatchewan to
market-based varieties in Alberta and Ontario.

Regulation and Regulatory Governance
in a Complex Networked World

The above macro-theories and historical underpinnings are foundational, while this second literature stream is somewhat more recent
and more middle level in nature. The discussion is, again, broadly
chronological but we also stress both the emergence of particular
views of regulation (empirical and normative) and the ways in which
successive approaches, reforms, and developments do not neatly
replace or succeed each other but, rather, partly lay on top of or
beside earlier theories and discourse about regulation and the kinds
of reform suggested. These theories and related forms of regulatory
advocacy reveal key features of the nature of rules and regulation,
enforcement approaches, and the presence of unruliness.

As we survey each in turn, it must be emphasized that much depends
upon the exact design of regulatory programs and the complementary
use of other policy instruments all aligned in such a way that desired
impacts (such as pollution reductions, improved safety, or positive
health effects) are achieved in ways that link up with basic incentives
for efficiency, innovation, and economic growth, as well as for political legitimacy and public support (Conference Board of Canada
2010a; Jaccard 2006; Doern 2007; Coglianese 2008)). Technologies
produced through innovation are crucial to the capacity of the regulator to regulate and to monitor various impacts and for the emergence
of new middle-level regulatory theory such as that on regulatory competition among countries/jurisdictions (Radaelli 2004).

Command-and-control regulation involves a normative approach
or claim of the existence of too many and too detailed input or pro-
cess-oriented kinds of rule making, a kind of detailed "one size fits
all" approach, even though the industries, firms, communities, and
individuals being regulated face numerous diverse situations and contexts. The charge that regulation was too command-and-control oriented has often been made regarding early environmental regulations,

and also of early forms of rate-of-return utility or economic regulation in fields such as energy and transport regulation (Stanbury 1980). There were many reasons for the subsequent effort to change the approach to regulation – business pressures and budget cutbacks – but underpinning it there was also a sense that reform had to follow the simple everyday logic of practical situations (Braithwaite and Drahos 2000; Anderson and Sprenger 2000; Stanbury 1992; Ayres and Braithwaite 1992).

Deregulation and *re-regulation* emerged as regulatory reforms in the late 1970s and early to mid-1980s in specific economic/public utility sectors such as telecommunications and transportation and also complementary acts of self-regulation such as the greater use of guidance measures and the development of industry codes (Vogel 1996). Some re-regulation in such sectors occurred to some extent mainly in aspects of social regulation and some aspects of quality of service. Focused reform efforts occurred in the mid-1980s under the Mulroney Conservative government and, in milder forms, in the late Mulroney era and early Chrétien Liberal government years of the 1990 to 1995 period (Doern, Hill, Prince, and Schultz 1999). In the United Kingdom, under Margaret Thatcher, re-regulation was an explicitly needed complementary feature because Thatcherism featured major privatization of industries that had not really had sectoral regulatory agencies but which now clearly had to have them (Vass 2007). These reform eras also sought to reform regulatory decision processes and urged a search for non-regulatory alternatives before pursuing regulation as a policy choice. Economic values and ideas were part of these reform exercises, although it is fair to say that neither was driven by a full-blown innovation policy paradigm as under some of the later developments surveyed below.

Incentive-based economic regulation recognizes explicitly the complex cost and production situations that different firms and industries (and consumers) face. The growing presence and importance of international trade rules has resulted in rule making premised on regulating outputs and *performance* rather than on prescriptive detailed command-and-control rules (Sparrow 2000, 2008; Braithwaite and Drahos 2000: Doern and Johnson 2006). In the past two decades, governments have been leading or encouraging initiatives that, by their very nature, had to rely on non-regulatory and non-statutory processes and that sought to work patiently through diverse marketplace stakeholders. Several initiatives of this type have been launched and followed through on in several areas of consumer regulation, occupational health, and environmental regulation.

Cap and trade is a particular form of incentive-based economic regulation of growing but also controversial importance in the environmental and related energy fields including climate change policy (Murray, Newell, and Pizer 2008; Stavins 2008; Jaccard 2006). In effect, the "cap" component is a form of "command" in that it sets some agreed or defined limit on emissions. The "trade" component allows firms with good environmental records to sell pollution rights or permits on the market to firms whose environmental records are less developed. This reduces the overall costs of compliance and takes into account the different economic situations of different companies. Cap and trade is, nonetheless, a controversial concept, in part, because of issues regarding exactly how stringent the cap is, the scope and coverage of industries (nationally, internationally, and regionally), and also because, in partisan political battles, it is often, usually quite incorrectly labelled rhetorically as a tax and, in particular, a tax on corporations.

Performance-based regulation is a form of rule making and compliance where the focus is on achieving and reporting on agreed stated performance outcomes/results without heavy prior prescriptive requirements as to how they are to be achieved. This approach to regulation contains many of the implicit features of flexibility and incentive-based regulation; however, it is even more outcome-focused. One Canadian national regulator that has sought to be more explicitly performance-based is the National Energy Board and also the Alberta Energy Resources Conservation Board (Doern and Gattinger 2003). Performance-based regulation is dependent on complex accountability and transparency requirements for periodic reporting about performance claims and outcomes.

Management-based regulation has similar features to performance-based regulation but it even more explicitly recognizes that regulation is increasingly a matter of de facto co-governance with private firms and related interests and organizations (Coglianese 2008; Bennear 2007). This is the case both nationally and globally (Buthe and Mattli 2013). The underlying concept of management-based regulation is "to deploy regulatory authority in a way that leverages the private sector's knowledge about its particular circumstances and engages with firms in developing their own internal procedures and monitoring practices that respond to risks" (Coglianese

2010, 160). Examples of this approach occur in several national and international regulatory realms. In the food sector, food producers, crucially, have direct responsibilities to establish and implement food safety programs and, more and more, take on the front-line responsibilities for management-based systems such as the Hazard Analysis and Critical Control Point increasingly being used in the United States, Canada, and internationally (Bennear 2007).

Governmentality is a further area of theoretical academic work germane to our analysis of the regulatory regime of social sectors and the societal framework regulatory regime. Governmentality literature (Burchell, Gordon, and Miller 1991; Rose and Miller 1992; Hunt 1999) is inspired by the writings of Michel Foucault on "the government of one's self" in particular economic and social affairs. The governmentality literature offers a set of concepts for examining changes in the role of the state and for tracing changes in state-society relationships in contemporary politics. In particular, governmentality relates to our interest in the diverse and delegated forms of governance in regulation as well as in the shape shifting of regulatory regimes, especially in the public and private relations of power in rule making and compliance.

Post-regulatory state literature is a relevant academic conceptual realm regarding the social sector and societal framework regimes that we examine. Crawford (2006, 471–2) suggests that this literature, while having differences with the governmentality perspective, shares with it "a particular conception of authority, regulation and control as primarily, and increasingly, lying 'beyond the state.'" Thus, it also posits a repositioning of rule making away from state institutions and away from command-and-control mechanisms towards multiple networks of non-state actors and less hierarchical tools of regulation. Nodal governance, networked governance, and meta-governance are among the terms depicting these changes in the sites and logics of regulation (Bradford and Andrew 2011; Crawford 2006). From research on the provision of policing and security in the United Kingdom, Crawford contends that "much of the regulatory and governance literature tends to overstate the direction and impact of recent trends and underplays its politically ambiguous, contested and volatile nature" (451). Taking note of this claim, we will discuss it further in chapters 6 and 8.

Voluntary codes and private standards constitute a further regulatory reform and approach centred on promoting the greater use of such codes and related private standards as a complementary instrument of consumer and marketplace reform in the context of multi-level global governance (Marx, Maertens, Swinnen, and Wouters 2012; Webb 2004). Voluntary codes are non-legislatively required commitments, including certification processes and reporting as well as "naming and shaming" tactics developed by both non-state and state actors. Such codes have been developed in many areas including those developed for the chemical industry, forests and fisheries, the Gap clothing stores, and in the banking and financial sector on debit and credit cards.

In some cases, firms, industry associations, and NGOs devise their own codes of behaviour standards on products and production processes and then ensure their public monitoring. In other cases, government agencies are involved in both the drafting and monitoring activities. The need for codes and standards as a preferred or complementary tool of rule making was also becoming more evident under the impetus of e-commerce and the general development of the Internet and also in the context of the above-mentioned development of complex food supply chains. This was because codes often were a faster way to respond to marketplace change that involved global cross-national commerce (Buthe 2011). Normal international law making and regulation simply took too long, and hence, some progress could be made through codes and related approaches.

The federal government also had to respond to, take part in, or monitor, other initiatives that were emerging from other stakeholders including combined environmental and consumer NGOs. These groups were increasingly launching their own standard setting, certification, and code development processes in competition with official state-sponsored processes and then using market forces to generate support for their preferred code or market outcome. This occurred in an area such as forest products where sustainable production technologies and approaches were central (Luckert, Haley, and Hoberg 2011).

In the 1990s, regulation came to be debated much more explicitly in terms of *risk assessment* and *risk management* concepts, especially in the broad realm of health, safety, and environmental rule making. *Risk assessment* refers to the determination of a quantitative or qualitative value of risk that is related to a specific situation or identifiable hazard or harm (Sparrow 2008). Analytically, it involves calculations of the size or magnitude of a potential loss (of life or other harm) and also the probability of its occurrence. It is often cast as a key step in overall risk management but *risk management* itself is also more particularly defined as the taking of steps to either eliminate or reduce such risks as much as is reasonably possible by introducing control measures ranging from outright bans right through to provisions for proscribed use and pre-market assessment and post-market as well as life cycle review and monitoring.

Such approaches involve a large set of regulators and their regulatory clientele whose activities are dependent on *science-based regulation* or on sound science but also on ideas centred on the precautionary principle (see more below). Federal science-based departments engaged in regulating health, safety, and the environment all have basic versions of a decision-making framework for identifying, assessing, and managing risks (Kinder 2010; Doern and Kinder 2007; Doern and Reed 2000).

The defence of the norm of sound science in trade regimes and other decision processes was also increased when the concepts of *the precautionary approach* and/or *the precautionary principle* were advanced in various ways through environmental regime pressures and initiatives. Precautionary concepts were often suspect in trade and business circles because they could easily amount to a relaxation of the norm of sound science or, indeed, could become the proverbial "Mack truck" clause that would drive right through international trade agreements.

Precaution implied that some decisions could be made even in the absence of such science where there were reasonable concerns that observed hazards might produce irreversible effects unless some preventative action was immediately taken (Vogel 2012). The precautionary principle gradually appeared in many international protocols and in several federal statutes such as the Oceans Act, the Canadian Environmental Protection Act, and commitments regarding biodiversity.

The *smart regulation paradigm* differs from deregulation and earlier reform agendas in that it is much more explicitly informed by innovation policy and process agendas as well as notions about the knowledge-based economy and rapid technological change (External Advisory Committee on Smart Regulation 2004). Smart regulation also swept into its conceptual arms many of the basic notions of incentive-based and flexible regulation, and risk assessment and risk management regulation. In these senses, smart regulation is not replacing earlier concepts but, rather, is complementing them and/or layering itself on top of them. Again, we have here a political geology of regulatory perspectives, that is, the accumulated stacking of distinct approaches and ideas about rule making and governance.

Regulatory cooperation and harmonization has itself been an increasing part of regulatory ideas, advocacy, and strategies. In principle and practice, it relates to both international linkages and coordination and also, within Canada, among the provinces and territories, including key aspects of reducing interprovincial barriers by opening up Canada's internal trade (Doern 2005). Regulatory cooperation refers to a wide range of institutional and procedural frameworks to build more integrated systems for rule making and implementation. Several federal departments and agencies including Environment Canada, Agriculture and Agri-Food Canada, and the Competition Bureau have developed such cooperative arrangements (Doern 2005).

Regulatory harmonization refers to processes leading to a country agreeing through negotiation to adopt common laws and rules with other countries. Such regulatory harmonization is especially present in and encouraged by various trade laws, agreements, and organizations (e.g., WTO, the Uruguay Round Agreement, the General Agreement on Trade in Services, and NAFTA) but is present in other policy fields as well. Regulatory cooperation can occur if countries and subnational jurisdictions engage in mutual recognition agreements, where each party agrees to recognize the regulations of the other party even though they are not identical or fully harmonized.

The contemporary life cycle approach is a part of the federal streamlined regulation directive but it has emerged more specifically in related health, food, and environmental realms of rule making and compliance linked to various notions of innovation (Health Canada 2006, 2007a; National Roundtable on the Environment and the Economy 2011). The life cycle concept, as we will see in chapter 4, means moving away from a single "point in time" pre-market assessment system for products to one that also follows products and processes in post-market phases, including their ultimate environmental final use phases. For example, the federal blueprint for renewal in health and drug regulation advocated moving to a product life cycle approach, implementing regulatory interventions *proportional* to risk (a process that would require the revamping of the product categorization system), in concert with a proactive and enabling regulatory system, so as to not only keep pace but to be ahead of the trend, where possible, partly through greater regulatory foresight programs and activities regarding new and changing technologies (Health Canada 2006, 7–24). Another version of life cycle analysis by Ireland, Milligan, Webb, and Xie (2012) calls for an ongoing analysis and appreciation of how any given regulatory agency faces different and changing challenges depending on whether it is in the infancy, high growth, mature, or declining stage of its existence.

Regulation as nudge has gained considerable attention and some conceptual favour in the Obama Administration in the United States and by the UK Conservative–Liberal Democrat Coalition government following the publication of the Thaler and Sunstein (2008) book entitled simply *Nudge*. Nudge in its core theory does not really refer to regulation as such. Instead, nudge favours softer approaches geared psychologically to how people think and then to design "choice environments" that make it easier for people to choose for themselves and their societies, by nudging them through the provision of appropriate information to appropriate viable and accepted better forms of behaviour (Thaler and Sunstein 2008). Nudge techniques have been advocated on issues such as supporting organ transplant donations, promoting smoking cessation, tackling obesity, and encouraging electricity and water conservation in neighbourhoods (Alemanno 2012). Sunstein (2013) has further linked choice concepts and nudge to arguments regarding the need for and practicality of simpler government. Almost inevitably, these concepts end up linking with softer forms of guidance and firmer rules already in place. These themes also easily relate to other recrafting efforts regarding complex decision making including recent work by John Kay (2011) whose theory of *obliquity* argues why many of our goals are best achieved indirectly. Nudge has also been a growing feature of those authors who focus on political and policy *issue management* in an Internet age (Pal 2013).

Networks, including *regulatory networks* have received ever greater analytical attention in the study of economic and social institutions and, thus, hold considerable importance for understanding contemporary debates on regulatory governance (Henman 2011; Svantesson 2011). In political and policy analysis, networks were initially cast by some authors as a particular inner feature of broader arrays of so-called policy communities (Coleman and Skogstad 1990). Policy communities were developed as an analytical category that went beyond traditional interest or lobby groups. Later analyses have broadened networks to some extent to encompass various kinds of expertise and the roles of universities (Howlett 2004; Howlett and Ramesh 2003; Montpetit 2004, 2009).

Meanwhile, in economics and related fields, networks are being analysed in a much broader context contrasted with markets and hierarchies as basic modes of social and economic organization (Agranoff 2007; Thompson 2004; Taylor 2001; Thompson, Frances, Levacic, and Mitchell 1991). *Hierarchies* are associated with bureaucracy, especially traditional Weberian state bureaucracy; hence, systems of top-down superior-subordinate political and administrative relations accompanied by formal rules, with related forms of civil service bureaucracies essential to representative Cabinet-parliamentary and other systems of democratic government. *Markets* are organized on the basis of "voluntary" means of exchange tied to money, commerce, and the making of profits but with key rules and protections for property rights and transactions provided by the state. *Networks* are contrasted with both of the above in that they are forms of organization characterized by non-hierarchical and voluntary relations based on trust and a commonality of shared interests and values where profit is not a defining characteristic (Agranoff 2007; Thompson 2004).

Some attributes of networks as an institutional mode are expressed in terms of constructing *partnerships*. Such partnerships can be truly voluntary in nature but more often they take on the form of policy-induced or required contractual or quasi-contractual partnerships between/among public and private sector entities and interests. In this context, partnerships acquire some of the characteristics inherent in markets or hierarchies (Kinder 2010; Hubbard and Paquet 2007).

The Internet as a defining and increasingly dominant and enabling technology has become a crucial engine of social and economic network formation and for designed systems of e-commerce and e-governance (Guadamuz 2011). For many public and private interests, the Internet has greatly reduced the costs of communication and joint action. It has also fostered new avenues for direct democracy by individual citizens, including via social networks, although the democratic promise is still more in the potential than in the practice (Rainie and Wellman 2012; Smith, Rhea, and Meinrath 2012; Borins and Brown 2008). Moreover, in commercial terms, Internet development promotes arguments that the "wealth of networks" is the new driver of technology and profit and of democratic participation (Benkler 2006). But equally, Internet-based technologies and marketing centred on Facebook, Twitter, and dynamic social networks are also producing deep concerns about privacy and its regulation including the growth of privacy merchants with data to sell that target particular consumers and citizens (Etzioni 2012a). We discuss this further in chapter 9.

Analyses of networks in public policy and in the conduct of science and research bring out the tendency for networks to be ever more complex, embedded with transaction costs and related layers of bureaucracy. This is bureaucracy not necessarily of the hierarchical kind but, rather, of a more horizontal, transactional, and vertical kind (Flinders 2008; Doern and Kinder 2007).

Conceptions of Safety, Uncertainty, Risk, and Risk-Benefit

Concepts of *safety, uncertainty, risk,* and *risk-benefit* constitute our final cluster of literature on regulation and regulatory governance. Each of these notions is surveyed in relation to its history and evolution conceptually and in regulatory practice in different sample regulatory fields. The presentation here is, again, broadly chronological; each part has persistent staying power and advocacy as a part of rules and regulation making but also regarding unruliness, not to mention notions of regulatory democracy in the various arenas explored in this book.

SAFETY AS AN ABSOLUTE MANDATE AND STANDARD

Safety as a public interest value and standard has been at the centre of regulatory governance for decades and is the lead stated purpose and value in numerous regulatory mandates of public authorities and delegated agencies. Safety implies a type of absolute quality because the origins of many regulatory mandates arise from the deaths of human beings and animals and from related notions of the sanctity of life. Some of the earliest examples concern the safety of children in the workplace and, indeed, the banning of child labour. The history of occupational health and safety in Canada, and elsewhere, has debated whether the core of worker safety conceptions centres on the nature of workers or on the nature of work. The regulation of nuclear reactors had a safety-first ethos in Canada, and globally, an ethos intensified after reported accidents or spills in some countries. In the 1950s and 1960s, the thalidomide crisis led to explicit changes that placed the safety of drugs at the heart of health product regulation, anchored by the need for objective science-based regulation and extensive pre-market testing. Still later developments fixed on core notions of safety regarding products and processes such as toys, automobiles, and medical devices.

In other regulatory fields, notions of safety took on different kinds and levels of regulatory discourse. In the broad realms of financial regulation, concepts of prudential regulation were often favoured so as to ensure the basic trust of the public in realms such as banking, investment, insurance and trusts, the so-called four pillars of the financial system that until the 1980s were kept in separate business and regulatory spheres (Davies 2010; Harris 1995, 2010). Safety in a more absolute sense was also present such as in security guarantees for personal bank deposits. In air transportation, safety mandates have been paramount, both nationally and internationally, in the early design of air traffic control systems, and in very recent times, these have been energized even more by issues of terrorism and security. For normal air safety, the assumption is that safety regimes are premised on minimizing and reducing unintended human and technical error. But in terrorist contexts, safety is security-focused and designed to deal with persons who deliberately intend to harm property, life, and limb (Ranger 2010). Similar issues and choices arise for other transport modes such as shipping and trucking, both nationally and internationally.

Safety as a regulatory discourse is less front and centre in fields such as intellectual property (patent protection and copyright), although the assuredness of such property rights has indirect notions of safety for the producer of these innovations in respect of protection from potential users and abusers of their rights (Castle 2009; Drahos and Mayne 2002). Canada's defence over several decades of regulatory systems on the "orderly marketing" of agricultural products (from wheat to potatoes) was based on protection from the uncertainties of competitive markets and excessive price fluctuations. Almost inevitably, there is slippage in the primacy and absolute nature of safety norms because of differences in the actual content of policy fields and because in other realms and activities citizens counter such safety norms with general arguments against the "nanny state" and against different kinds of risk, for example, bungee jumping, hand gliding or gambling on horse races.

UNCERTAINTY, RISK, AND ITS VARIETIES

Risks relate to potential harms and adverse impacts on individuals, families, groups, communities, subpopulations, nation states, firms, and spatial areas. As potential harms, risks immediately imply notions of uncertainty. Risks can be voluntary or involuntary and are so diverse, extensive, and ever-present that the literature often speaks of the "risk society" (Hood, Rothstein, and Baldwin 2001; Doern and Reed 2000). This pervasive world of risks includes, for example, driving one's children to school, living with an abusive spouse or parent, accidents in the workplace, crossing the street, eating fast foods and obesity, and buying and selling shares in the stock market.

In policy fields and program areas ranging from food, drugs, or nuclear reactors, to pensions, and in the broader design of government subsidies, loans, and contracts, risk is associated one way or another with a trilogy of key concepts and decision stages; specifically, risk assessment, risk management, and risk communication (Doern and Reed 2000). As we noted above, risk assessment refers to the determination of a quantitative or qualitative value of risk that is related to a specific situation or identifiable hazard. Analytically, risk assessment involves calculations of the size or magnitude of a potential loss (of life or other harm) and also the probability of its occurrence.

Risk management is defined as the taking of steps to either eliminate or reduce such risks as much as is reasonably possible by introducing control measures ranging from outright bans through to provisions for proscribed use and pre-market assessment and post-market as well as life cycle review and monitoring, for example, of a new production plant or project. In debates about food, environmental, and other product safety systems, there have always been discussions and disputes about whether risk assessments should be kept separate, institutionally independent, and at arm's-length from risk management or whether they are best kept closely housed and linked within key regulatory agencies (Alemanno 2012; Leiss 2000; Royal Society of Canada 2001).

Risk communication involves any number of processes of disseminating information about risks and uncertainty. It also entails risk avoidance, prevention, and management to citizens, communities, interests, and firms on a continuous targeted basis. Such communication can involve potential bombardment and risk overload, all the more so in a twenty-four-hour mass media and Internet world, where myriad anecdotes about risks, hazards, and harm are far more likely to be reported than systematic data about perceived, real, and relative risks. This kind of daily blizzard can easily evoke a sense of unruliness in many citizens.

Risk assessment and risk management can, obviously, be very micro in the sense that either or both can be focused on a given new product. But, the risk literature also increasingly focuses on larger clusters or groupings of risk and, hence, at variously defined risk regulation regimes for classes of products such as in biotechnology and genetics (Doern and Prince 2012) or in the functioning and nature of complex production and use characteristics in "risk domains" (Hood, Rothstein, and Baldwin 2001, 36), which in turn, may function in even larger "regulatory regimes" – nationally and internationally.

systemic
risk

These larger domain and regime groupings reflect the need to be more conscious of *systemic risk* across many product, process, and institutional lines. The 2008–12 banking crisis has focused on systemic risk and on how to do better job in the future about entire financial systems, national and international, rather than just banking (Yeh 2010). Indeed, aspects of the banking and financial product mix were cast as being closer to gambling rather than banking (Davies 2010, 79–83).

The climate change debate is overwhelmingly about systemic risk to the planet from multiple sources of greenhouse gases, as are reforms to food policy regulation, where concerns arise about macro-groupings such as foreign food imports and their extended farm gate to the dinner plate supply chains, and also about integrated sustainable food production and consumption in these supply chains (Doern 2004a).

RISK-BENEFIT AS THE GROWING REAL WORLD OF REGULATION?

There is some political and institutional slippage between the primacy and absolutist nature of safety discourse and regulatory mandates in reality (Doern and Reed 2000; Doern and Prince 2012). Safety concerns are certainly not deleted from mandate statements or from the concerns of front-line regulatory assessors or inspectors. However, larger notions of risk-benefit values are in evidence and have worked their way into the logical structure of mandates and organizational cultures in different regulatory bodies and realms. Some of this was being driven by business pressure as in the smart regulation and innovation pressures and rationales and in the need in some sectors for greater regulatory speed in obtaining regulatory product approvals. Canadian regulatory system capacities in these areas were seen as being less robust and efficient compared with other countries, especially in relation to the United States.

A particular example of this kind of mandate regime shift towards risk-benefit mandates and values came in Health Canada's *Blueprint for Renewal* and its ambitious aspirations and complex arguments for change in response to the pressures highlighted above and to other issues emphasized by Health Canada. It emerged under the Harper Conservatives in an October 2006 discussion document (Health Canada 2006). The *Blueprint* agenda was linked to changes under way in the United States, which saw the most significant pressures for legislative change to the Food and Drug Administration since the 1960s, propelled by new needs for post-market review and new forms of evidence for such assessments (Evans 2009; Fox 2008).

The Health Canada *Blueprint* report covers both health products and food, but our summary illustration here focuses on the health/ drug regime aspects of the report. Health Canada's own case for renewal is a self-critical admission that its approaches over the previous twenty years had not been up to speed for the world it now faced and had faced for some time. The *Blueprint* report points up that since 1953, the Food and Drugs Act and its regulations have "largely intended to be a consumer protection statute" (Health Canada 2006, 6). Accordingly, Health Canada's new approach to regulation identified five challenges:

1 An outdated regulatory toolkit that is increasingly limited and inflexible in responding to today's health products and food environment
2 The regulatory system's current incapacity to consider a given product through its entire life cycle, from discovery through to examining the "real world" benefits and risks of a health product or a food on the market
3 The impact of social and economic changes such as accelerating scientific and technological advances, the rise of trans-border health and environmental threats, and more informed and engaged citizenry
4 A regulatory system that currently works in isolation from the activities and policies at the stage of research and development, and those of the broader health care system

5 A regulatory system with insufficient resources for long-term efficiency and sustainability. (Health Canada 2006, 6–7)

The *Blueprint* document went on to discuss each of these challenges and self-diagnosed inadequacies, most of which, we must add, had been a part of the larger evolving processes of much more muted criticism since at least the early 1990s. Such lists of weakness and admissions of regulatory reach vastly exceeding regulatory grasp are themselves evidence of unruliness in the ways defined in this book.

Other analyses have been critical of the innovation-driven and market access–driven logic of the *Blueprint* report and of the previous smart regulation logic (Lemmens and Bouchard 2007). These critiques see that logic as being too much a business-driven way of thinking rather than a public health and safety outlook and that, by now agreeing with it, Heath Canada is weakening its core safety-focused regulatory mandate.

ANALYTICAL FRAMEWORK: UNRULINESS, REGULATORY REGIMES, AND REGIME ATTRIBUTES

The conceptual literature surveyed above informs and underpins the book's discussion of rules and unruliness, and the themes and developments regarding regulatory capitalism, regulatory welfarism, democracy, and governance in Canada. We seek to extend these foundational concepts through our own analytical framework. As previewed briefly in the book's Introduction, our analytical framework involves in particular the concept of *unruliness* seen in relation to the nature of rules and rule making, the identification and analysis of six key regulatory *regimes*, and also, within each regime, the three *attributes* that help us understand key contributing drivers of regime change and inertia.

Unruliness

Unruliness refers to inabilities to effectively develop regulatory policy and enforce rules (in parent laws, delegated laws, guidelines, and codes) because of any number of policy and mandate conflicts, democratic gaps, and governance challenges. For our purposes, we examine the three main types of unruliness as set out in the book's Introduction: (1) unruliness related to regulatory agencies, (2) unruliness related to the complexity of regulatory regimes, and (3) unruliness related to

Table 1.2 Preview Illustrations of the Three Main Types of Unruliness

1 UNRULINESS RELATED TO REGULATORY AGENCIES
- Diverse resource incapacities, where regulatory reach exceeds regulatory grasp due, in part, to budgetary inadequacies and limits/gaps in staff competences and knowledge
- Regulatory agency mandates that are rife with internal policy contradictions and conflicts and also rivalries among and between agencies
- Conflicts among and between state and societal actors and between elected and appointed officials
- Crises and emergencies that yield new or unexpected concepts of risk, uncertainty, and safety
- The growing complexity of rules, products, processes, approval volumes, and surges.

2 UNRULINESS RELATED TO THE COMPLEXITY OF REGULATORY REGIMES
- Collisions among and within larger regimes of regulation (including the six regimes examined)
- Incapacities that arise out of the growing mix of rule-making types including constitutional provisions, judicial decisions, statutes and laws, delegated law (the "regs"), guidelines, codes, and voluntary codes
- Rules becoming increasingly more numerous and deeply embedded in taxation and spending including conditional and levered spending
- Systems of regulatory representation and power relationships that may be grossly unequal and/or inadequate or if one form of preferred democracy conflicts excessively with another
- Shortfalls and complexity in dealing with the growing spatial realities of threats, risks, and hazards in dispersed regional spheres whose fluid boundaries spill over into complex ecosystems, air and water sheds, climate flows, and complicated food supply chains that cross national and international boundaries.

3 UNRULINESS RELATED TO AGENDA SETTING
- The absence of effective regulatory priority setting
- The inability to get policies and rules adopted in the first place
- Multilevel regulatory cooperation and competition internationally and within Canada's federal system of government and local government structure.

agenda setting. Table 1.2 previews examples under each type of unruliness, some aspects of which have already emerged in the literature review and others that emerge in later chapters.

Regulatory Regimes

Regulatory regimes are integrated complex realms of policy ideas, institutions, interests, and rules. The following regimes mapped and examined empirically:

1 Macro-regulatory governance regime
2 Economic sectoral regulatory regime
3 Regulatory regime of social sectors
4 Marketplace framework regulatory regime
5 Societal framework regulatory regime
6 Parliamentary democracy regulatory regime.

Regulatory Attributes

Regulatory attributes refer to basic important features that help understand some of the basic causes of both regulatory change and inertia and which also provide further insights into unruliness as set out above. The three main attributes deployed are:

1 Ideas, discourse, and agendas
2 Public and private power in regulation making and compliance
3 Science, evidence, and knowledge.

This three-part framework constitutes an analytical approach needed to understand, explain, and ultimately, tell the Canadian regulatory story over four decades set in an international and global context. The analytical framework and the empirical analysis throughout enable us to address the six central questions posed in the book: (1) What kinds of regulatory unruliness, as defined above, have been evident or addressed in the Canadian regulatory system overall? (2) How has Canadian regulatory democracy and governance changed in the past four decades? (3) How does Canada's system of public regulatory democracy and governance need to be reformed to deal democratically with rule making, compliance, and unruliness in a globalized context? (4) How and why has Canadian regulatory capitalism emerged in the past two decades in particular. and is it different from regulatory capitalism in other competitor countries? (5) Why does regulatory welfarism in social policy need a greater presence and understanding in mainstream regulatory scholarship and practice? (6) Can Canada achieve an effective adherence to regulatory agendas and to a multiple-points-in-time full life cycle system of regulatory governance as envisaged in the federal Cabinet Directive on Regulatory Management (CDRM), the main set of macro-rules about federal rule making, and in related health and environmental regulatory policy positions?

The actual or potential types of unruliness highlighted in the framework list flow, in part, from some of the issues that arise from the main literature streams surveyed above but also from features that emerge more readily when one looks empirically, as this book does, across longer periods of Canadian and related international regulatory governance and democratic history. Unruliness refers to inabilities to effectively develop regulatory policy and enforce rules because of an inability to establish policy and rules in the first place or because of any number of policy and mandate conflicts, democratic gaps, and governance challenges. But, as a concept, unruliness leaves open the issue of how one tells what regulatory effectiveness means in practice in terms of intended and unintended outcomes in rule making and compliance. Thus, the three kinds of unruliness shown above emerge from contexts and situations related to regulatory agencies, to the complexity of regulatory regimes, and to regulatory agenda setting.

Our intent is not to argue that Canada's regulatory system is unruliness incarnate. Rather, it is to show that the above kinds of actual and potential unruliness need to be better understood in regulatory scholarship and practice so that they can be recognized and addressed and so that one can appreciate why they are occurring. We need to fully appreciate the complex nature of what good or better or unsatisfactory regulatory performance might involve. This means recognition of the fact that some rules and even regimes of rules are focused on securing compliance regarding undesirable behaviour that *has already occurred* while others are focused more on *preventative missions* to insure that various kinds of undesirable behaviour do not occur in the first place. Still others set progressive standards for improved behaviour. Many regulatory agencies do all three. Some areas of regulatory performance also need to be calibrated with some kind of real or implicit "degree of difficulty" score. There are also, without doubt, different temporal dimensions to regulatory performance including concepts of regulatory life cycles and regulatory institutional learning across the medium term and longer-term periods.

As an analytical category, the notion of a *regime* is used directly as in some of the literature surveyed above or it can be and often is interchangeably used with terms such as "jurisdiction" as in the federal, provincial, or international jurisdiction, constitutionally speaking, or as a "regime" such as in analyses of risk regimes or of individual regulatory areas such as the environmental regulatory regime. As a related concept, *metagovernance* also emerges in the literature to ensure a more accurate and in-depth look at these varied middle worlds of regulatory activity, ideas, and politics and as they seek to manage the combined features of hierarchies, markets, and networks (Meuleman 2008). We define regimes as relatively complex regulatory spheres, levels, and even temporal periods with different policy, regulation making, and compliance challenges to be faced, debated, reframed, or ignored/sublimated.

Regimes, therefore, involve groupings of regulatory content and decision making that are much larger and more complex than a single regulatory department or agency of the federal government but that fall well short of an analysis of the entire federal regulatory governance system, let alone all of governance. We examine the six defined regulatory regimes, as noted above, but because of political-economic debate, academic theory and discourse, and institutional politics, there are bound to be both agreements and disagreements about the precise boundaries of regimes. Indeed, boundary issues and overlaps are also often a key feature in the analyses of regime challenges and unruliness.

Some regimes have been present and recognized analytically in academic regulatory analysis and by regulatory practitioners for a very long time (e.g., the economic sectoral and the marketplace framework regimes), and others (like the societal framework regime and the regulatory regime of social sectors), while understood among social policy scholars are somewhat more recent and/or are contending for analytical and practical recognition in academic regulatory analysis as opposed to the literature on social policy and the social welfare state. The parliamentary democracy regulatory regime is often left out altogether in core regulatory literature although, of course, it is covered extensively by scholars of representative democracy, political parties, and elections.

The *three attributes* that we map and deploy in each of the six regulatory regimes chapters are essential features for understanding regulatory regime change and inertia. Each of the three attributes in regulatory regime analysis is needed and poses different challenges regarding qualitative and quantitative evidence and regarding the time periods being covered.

The mixes of dominant and contending *ideas*, *discourses*, and *agendas* are found in historical but still relevant advocacy of paradigms such as public interest safety regulation and aspects of deregulation. These varied discourses and ideas also show up in the changing content of ministerial speeches regarding new rules or egregious regulatory compliance failures or continuous concerns about red tape. Ideas about regulation are sometimes revealed in Throne speeches; in interest group, think tank, and academic papers; and in the diverse kinds of sound-bite discourse developed by the media, Internet bloggers, and social networks, and also by political parties in partisan discourse.

Regulatory regimes contain entrenched and shifting systems of *public and private power* whether in terms of real or imagined regulatory capture or the excesses of the nanny state. Within the state, public power can involve the impacts of minority versus majority governments and also, without doubt, the extended power of prime ministers over the Cabinet compared with earlier periods or as exercised with greater focus in some regimes rather than others. Private power typically focuses on regulatory capitalism and the related power of business, Canadian and global, including its preferred regulatory departments for focused regulatory lobbying such as Finance or Industry Canada, and their arm's length regulatory agencies. Environmental, consumer, and medical interests also exercise power and influence albeit usually not on as sustained a basis as business. Governance as a concept in regulatory worlds is, of course, as we have seen earlier in this chapter, increasingly and quintessentially about interactions of public and private power and democracy, and therefore, co-governance with market stakeholders and social interests and networks.

Varied and changing kinds of *science*, *evidence*, and *knowledge* underpin the structure of different regulatory regimes both in assessing proposals for new regulations and in assessing new specific products, projects and processes, compliance strategies, and cases. On science-based governance in different regulatory regimes, there must be good analytical respect for the diverse meanings inherent in science-based government, including notions of research and development, related science activities, innovation policies, public goods, and linear and non-linear conceptions of science and technology pursued variously by front-line regulatory assessors, government labs, firms, universities, and foundations (Doern and Kinder 2007). Science-based regulatory governance also interacts with intellectual property "invention-centred" analysis and decisions regarding what is private property contrasted with a public goods realm of knowledge.

The role of science versus other forms of evidence and knowledge is an intricate feature of regulatory regime development and inertia.

Ex ante regulatory assessment involves forms of benefit-cost analysis by economists and related required forms of regulatory impact analysis (Radaelli and DeFrancesco 2007; Mihlar 1999). The science and arts of ex poste regulatory program evaluation and even more difficult life cycle analysis also loom large.

Aspects of transformational technologies are embedded in our conceptions of science-based and evidence-based regulatory governance, in that they help define what new technologies (such as biotechnology or nanotechnology) consist of and also some of their characteristics as shape-shifting new "sectors" or horizontal transformational parts of all sectors (Phillips 2007). Our discussion of networks underscores the roles of the science community as pre-eminently network-based and, thus, is also inherent in what must be empirically looked for in science-based regulation. In health and disease regulation, even broader forms of citizen knowledge and reporting from individual patients, caregivers, and diverse medical knowledge professions are increasingly important in so-called post-market regulation, that is, once products are in use in diverse markets following approval.

The pairing of science-based governance with precautionary governance is necessary in several analytical senses. The precautionary principle, as indicated above, emerged as an explicit governance norm in environmental policy, national and international, partly to counter trade-related notions of sound science (Vogel 2012; Cooney and Dickson 2005; Saner 2002; O'Riordan and Cameron 1994). As a governing norm and procedure, the precautionary principle stresses the need to respect the realities of scientific uncertainty and the need, when warranted, not to proceed with some products or processes unless one can have much higher confidence in evidenced-based standards of science and knowledge overall.

CONCLUSIONS

Drawn from three quite broad strands of literature, we have set out the conceptual foundations underpinning the analysis of rules, unruliness, and regulatory change in Canada set in an international context. Key aspects of the broad political economy of regulation, regulatory governance at more middle levels of analysis, and changing concepts of safety, uncertainty, risk, and risk-benefit inform our thinking and research.

Our central analytical framework centres on three types of unruliness, six regulatory regimes, and three key attributes within each regime. While a full empirical discussion of unruliness within and across the six regulatory regimes must wait until the regime chapters in Part II, we have highlighted the value of understanding unruliness and the six regimes as analytical features. We also noted boundary problems and disputes inherently involved in the definition and behaviour of regimes.

The roles of ideas, discourse, and agendas; the realities of public and private power in regulation making and compliance; and varied notions of science, evidence, and knowledge are crucial to the more specific assessment of change and inertia in these later empirical chapters. Our discussion here reveals the way that various regulatory reform ideas do not so much replace each other but, rather, lie beside or on top of each other resulting in political geologies of regulatory perspectives; the way in which myriad risks and risk anecdotes receive a flood of non-stop media and Internet coverage; and the way that aspirations about a better post-market monitoring of products approach seems sensible but, then again, also very difficult to visualize in terms of how it will be achieved.

Overall, an image emerges that suggests that the neo-liberalism and then regulatory capitalism phases of the past four decades or more in Canada have not meant simply a reduction in command-and-control rules and laws. Besides the recognizable neo-liberal politics of selective deregulation, we observe a multiplication in rule-making ideas, discourses, practices, and reforms in economic, political, and social and societal framework spheres. This multiplicity includes self-regula

tion, re-regulation, voluntary codes, incentive-based regulation, performance-based regulation, management-based regulation, science-based regulation, smart regulation, and regulatory cooperation and harmonization. This multiplicity becomes even more apparent in our next chapter, where we survey recent prime ministerial eras, their regulatory policies, and their regulatory legacies.

2

Canadian Regulatory Democracy and Governance in Liberal and Conservative Eras

As a necessary historical context for *Rules and Unruliness*, we take a basic look at Canadian regulatory democracy and governance in Liberal and Conservative government eras covering the past four decades. Such a historical portrait is needed to answer the overall questions we pose on Canadian regulatory democracy and its reforms. Canadian regulatory democracy and governance is an intricate set of evolving national, federal-provincial, and international policies and institutions, each influencing the other as to timing and content. Canada is a participant in international negotiations on policies about regulation overall and about policies in particular fields such as food, drugs, airline safety, biotechnology, trade, patents, and health. In most cases, Canada has agreed with and signed on to the policies adopted.

As an inquiry into the politics of regulation, this chapter surveys the major federal regulatory policy statements, strategies, and changes in the last three decades of the twentieth century and the first decade of the twenty-first century. This historical analysis shows important features of partisan political party aspects of regulation and their links to representative Cabinet-parliamentary democracy. Further key features of the regulation of parliamentary democracy, including political parties and elections are examined in more detail in chapter 9. These partisan dimensions show both continuities across Liberal and Conservative governments and prime ministerial eras as well as some key differences, as regulatory policies emerged and expanded in scope, both nationally and globally and in Canadian federalism.

Changing democratic arenas and norms are mapped in the chapter since regulatory democracy encompasses at least five arenas and criteria including the following: representative Cabinet-parliamentary democracy, federalist democracy, pluralist interest group democracy, civil society democracy, and expanding forms of direct democracy involving individual Canadians including burgeoning Internet-based social networks of diverse kinds and technologies.

Important aspects of multilevel governance and multilevel regulation appear in this historical narrative as national, international, provincial, urban, and local, and newer regional/spatial levels emerged. With them, new forms of coordination and conflict materialized as the regulatory system became more complex, embracing both direct regulatory policies and also indirect ones in particular changing regulatory fields.

Regulatory policy includes policies where regulation is referred to directly in Canadian and international policy discourse such as in the deregulation era of the early 1980s. It also emerges more indirectly through other existing Canadian and international policies, policy fields, and their related discourse on regulatory aspects. For example, the debate over, and the rule-based content of, both the Canadian Charter of Rights and Freedoms and the Canada-US Free Trade Agreement were rarely discussed under the discourse of regulation per se, but nonetheless, both were regulatory and deregulatory in profound ways.

To provide a contextual historical overview of regulatory policy, this chapter proceeds initially in terms of the time periods of the main federal prime ministerial and governing political party and partisan eras, the Trudeau Liberals from 1968 to the early 1980s, the Mulroney Conservatives in the period 1984 to 1992, the Chrétien and then Martin Liberals in the period 1993 to 2005, and finally, the Harper Conservatives from 2006 to the present. In general, direct regulatory policy in Canada has operated in the middle and lower ranked realms of politically expressed priorities in that it has received only infrequent mentions in the pinnacle federal agenda setting events of Speeches from the Throne and Budget Speeches. This is an important fact and argument in the overall story to be told in this book including our discussion in chapter 4 of the way regulatory decisions functioned overwhelmingly below the radar of macropolitics through a "one regulation at a time" approach.

PRIME MINISTERIAL AND POLITICAL PARTY ERAS:
REGULATORY IDEAS AND REFORMS

Each of the four prime ministerial eras are surveyed briefly so as to
capture the main regulatory policy ideas, changes, and trends of
both the direct and indirect kinds. Not surprisingly, they each reveal
partisan stances as well as some ideological differences regarding the
role of the state in regulatory matters, set in the different political-
economic climates of each era.

*The Trudeau Liberals: From the Just Society to Wage
and Price Controls to the Charter of Rights*

The Trudeau Liberals through their majority governments of 1968–
72, 1974–79, and 1980–84, and a minority government interregnum
from 1972 to 1974, cannot be said to have paid much systematic or
direct attention to overall regulatory policy and governance (Doern
1978; Anderson 1980; Doern and Phidd 1992 [1983]), although some
of their policy actions had significant regulatory effects. Under his
early initial "Just Society" and rational decision-making ethos, Pierre
Trudeau focused on distancing his government from the seemingly
chaotic decision making of the previous Pearson Liberal minority governments and by pushing reforms for greater public participation
including in some regulatory agency operations. But in the early and
mid-1970s, the Trudeau Liberals were forced into regulatory action
centred on wage and price controls as Canada (and the global economy) faced growing inflation that was not amenable to normal central
bank monetary policy or to fiscal policy.

During the period of price and wage controls, from 1975 to 1978,
the Liberals created a committee of ten deputy ministers to launch
initial trial studies that led to the adoption of the federal Socio-
Economic Impact Assessment (SEIA) process in 1978, a Cabinet
directive rather than a statutory provision. Building on similar pressures in the United States, the SEIA applied only to "major" proposed regulations in the health, safety, and fairness fields under
sixteen specific federal statutes. Major regulations were understood
to be those that were likely to impose private sector costs in excess
of $10 million. The SEIA process was later cancelled by the Mulroney
Conservative government under its more wide-ranging regulatory
views, which we discuss below.

The Liberal era in the latter 1970s saw increases in the development of agricultural marketing board protection, despite strong advocacy to the contrary by Liberal-era advisory bodies such as the Economic Council of Canada (Forbes, Hughes, and Varley 1982; Economic Council of Canada 1979). Nor did the SEIA process follow the Economic Council's recommendations on airline and telecommunications deregulation, although there were steps taken in this period on the latter by the Canadian Radio-television Telecommunications Commission (CRTC), which the Liberal government implicitly accepted by rejecting appeals to have them overturned. Nonetheless, the Economic Council's regulatory work, which began under Trudeau, was providing a persistent recognition that regulation was imposing significant costs both intragovernmentally and intergovernmentally; hence, it contributed to a heightened awareness of the regulatory state in Canada. Trudeau Liberals were strong supporters of regulatory intervention in foreign investment and in language policy and bilingualism, and they were caught up in the national crisis over air traffic control when Quebec-based French-speaking air traffic controllers went on strike over the issue of English as the language of international air traffic regulation.

Following their sudden and somewhat unexpected return to office in 1980, following the defeat of the short-lived Clark Progressive Conservative government, the Trudeau Liberals practised an aggressive form of regulatory and other policy interventionism. Examples were the 1980–84 National Energy Program (NEP), which included new policies and rules to deal with oil price escalation and extended federal powers over energy development (Doern and Toner 1985). These new policies and rules were highly conflictual and deeply resented in Alberta and other Western producer provinces and reverberated well beyond the period when the Mulroney Conservatives later dismantled them.

The second early 1980s policy, this time a constitutional one, was the Trudeau era's crowning achievement of the Canadian Charter of Rights and Freedoms, which also encountered strong opposition in Quebec and elsewhere, especially when it was incorporated into the repatriation of the Canadian Constitution. The Charter was important in several regulatory and rule-based senses. It meant that all regulations had to be "charter-proofed" and assessed so that they did not contravene the Charter, a need that elevated the central agency role of Justice Canada (Kelly 1999). The Charter changed some regulatory issues and political strategies into rights-based actions, rhetoric, and strategizing, since the practical meaning of rights could only be fleshed out in many instances and specific situations through court action and court decisions (Harris 2012). This included actions by Aboriginal Canadians who often thereafter used the Charter and Charter court cases as their preferred avenue of redress, largely because the courts were the least mistrusted by Aboriginal peoples compared with lobbying the deeply distrusted federal, provincial, or territorial governments (Royal Commission on Aboriginal Peoples 1996).

The Mulroney Conservatives: Rules about Rules,
Deregulation, and Free Trade

The two Mulroney Conservative majority governments from 1984 to 1988 and 1988 to 1993 can take some credit for being the first federal Canadian government to have thought seriously about the regulatory process as a whole (Schultz 1988). First, they adopted a formal regulatory reform strategy centred on rationalizing the central regulatory decision process by giving a review mandate to the regulatory affairs wing of a new Office of Privatization and Regulatory Affairs. These, in turn, grew out of the Nielsen Task Force review of government programs, which, among other things, pronounced the failure of the above-mentioned Trudeau-era SEIA process.

The Conservative reforms called for a Federal Regulatory Plan to be published annually setting out proposed departmental regulations; more open publication in the *Canada Gazette*; and a requirement that all regulations be accompanied by a regulatory impact analysis statement (Mihlar 1999). Changes also included a Citizen's Code of Regulatory Fairness and a requirement that all regulatory programs had to be evaluated on a regular periodic basis.

Although the Mulroney Conservatives did not trumpet a larger clarion call for deregulation as was occurring under the Reagan and Thatcher regimes in the United States and the United Kingdom, respectively, they did, in fact, deregulate several sectors of the economy to some extent. These included the oil and gas sector, transportation (air and rail), banking and securities, and foreign investment with links in some of these realms to the privatization of state-owned companies (Stanbury 1980; Doern, Hill, Prince, and Schultz 1999). Although they never articulated a policy favouring telecommunications deregulation and, indeed, in the mid-1980s, unlike their position on energy and the transport sectors, vigourously opposed the growth of competition, by the end of their term, the Mulroney Conservatives had endorsed major deregulatory decisions taken by the CRTC.

Overall, however, regulation increased during the Mulroney era largely because of expansion in the environmental field (under the Conservative's 1990 Green Plan) but also in other health and safety realms (Toner 2000; Doern and Conway 1995). The net impact of other particular Mulroney-era policies on regulation in sectors such as transportation, telecommunications, and banking produced mixtures of deregulation and re-regulation (Waters and Stanbury 1999; Hill 1999a; Harris 1999). These included major Mulroney policies such as the 1988 Canada-US Free Trade Agreement (Doern and Tomlin 1991).

Free trade obviously deregulates in major ways through tariff reductions to zero, and the Canada-US Free Trade Agreement entrenched key energy rules to prevent any future NEP-style interventions. However, the agreement also sought to protect some industries such as cultural industries, marketing boards, and health care, in addition to the partial protection of auto sector and textile industry trade. The free trade agreement had new rules about dispute settlement, and new rules were needed at the Canada-US border regarding the origin of goods and some services. Overall, the trade agreements (including the later 1993 NAFTA agreement that included Mexico) opened up markets, but they were bundles of rules that took up several hundred pages of text and, hence, were hardly rule-free domains. The Conservatives' successful negotiation with the provinces of the Agreement on Internal Trade was of a similarly mixed deregulatory and regulatory combination (Doern and MacDonald 1999).

The Chrétien and Martin Liberals: Smart Regulation, Innovation Agendas, Terrorism, and Climate Change Duplicity

The three Liberal majority governments of Jean Chrétien (with Paul Martin as minister of finance) and the Paul Martin minority government from 2003 to 2005 witnessed a less consistent and less traceable regulatory policy terrain, in either direct regulatory policy or in the ways regulatory change was revealed in other policy fields (Swimmer 1996; Pal 1999; Doern 2007).

With respect to regulatory policy as a whole, it was not until the later years of the Chrétien era that the Liberals provided an overall view of regulatory change. This came with the appointment of a multistakeholder External Advisory Committee on Smart Regulation (EACSR), which reported in the fall of 2004.The rationale for the initiative was initially stated by the Chrétien government as follows:

> The knowledge economy requires new approaches to how we regulate. We need new regulation to achieve the public good, and we need to regulate in a way that enhances the climate for investment and trust in the markets. The government will move forward with a smart regulation strategy to accelerate reforms in key areas to promote health and sustainability, to contribute to innovation and economic growth, and to reduce the administrative burden on business. (Canada 1999, 1)

The Throne Speech statement then went on to refer to a number of regulatory realms that would be a part of the reform initiative. These included intellectual property and new life rules, copyright rules, drug approvals, research involving humans, the Canadian Environmental Assessment Act, a single window for projects such as the northern pipeline, the Agricultural Policy Framework, Canada-US smart border needs, and capital market and securities regulation.

The EACSR report begins by defining what smart regulation is not. Smart regulation "is not deregulation" because "smart regulation does not diminish protection, as some may fear. It strengthens the system of regulation so that Canadians can continue to enjoy a high quality of life in the 21st century. The committee believes regulation should support both social and economic achievement" (2004, 9). When raising the question of what are the consequences of non-action in smart regulatory reform, the EACSR argues that "without change it will limit Canadian's access, for example, to new medications, cleaner fuels and better jobs. An outdated system is an impediment to innovation and a drag on the economy because it can inhibit competitiveness, productivity, investment and the growth of key sectors" (10).

With this smart regulation strategy at its centre, the EACSR went on to examine key features of Canada's regulatory system and five case study sectors, or realms of regulation, and then it made seventy-three recommendations. A central thrust of the recommendations was for greater regulatory cooperation with the United States, especially in situations where there are only small differences in regulations and approaches. The EACSR report is careful to stress that the public interest in regulatory matters involves *both* social/health/

environment *and* economic matters. Hence, the smart regulation concept embraces both "protecting and enabling," with enabling as the code word for commercialization, new innovative products, and "responsiveness" detailing the need to be sensitive to business firms and to the competitive situations they face. In turn, governing "cooperatively" connotes the new modus operandi to achieve public purposes through various governance arrangements (as opposed to command-and-control regulation).

Although these views of regulatory change now anchor the federal system (see more below and in chapter 4), they by no means capture all of the other regulatory changes that emerged in the Chrétien-Martin era. Most of these operated on their own track of change regarding emerging imperatives. In the first Liberal majority, all policy was dominated by deficit reduction strategies under the federal Program Review (Swimmer 1996). This included many regulatory programs, but overall, one of the main indirect regulatory impacts came with the nature and extent of cuts in federal science, the largest part of which is the research and development and related science activities deployed to support the federal regulatory system, especially in the safety, health, and environment fields. Cuts here were in the order of 20 to 30 per cent, and they certainly adversely affected regulatory capacity in a serious way (Kinder 2010; Doern and Kinder 2007).

During the second Chrétien majority government, regulation and rules of many kinds were impacted greatly by the imperatives of the post-9/11 terrorist attack on the United States. The most obvious was the impact on border regulation and procedures, where security goals were now paramount but where access to the American market for Canadian goods and services had to be preserved. Security goals were elevated in particular fields ranging from energy pipelines and nuclear facilities to air transportation and shipping.

On a very separate track, the Chrétien Liberals also created the Gun Registry. It was precipitated by the killing of nineteen women in Montreal by a lone gunman, but it gradually became a realm of regulatory unruliness when it became embroiled in controversy not only over its funding and management but also over intense objections from lawful hunters and gun users. This escalated politically into a wedge issue of rural versus urban voters, which the Harper Conservatives successfully built into its agenda both before and after its 2006 arrival in office (see more below).

Chrétien-Martin era regulatory changes and postures on climate change also revealed a difficult and often duplicitous agenda. Chrétien, in particular, lent rhetorical support to the global climate change agenda, the need to reduce greenhouse gas emissions, and to achieve the commitments of the Kyoto Protocol. But Canada's greenhouse gas emissions increased significantly during the Liberal era rather than decreased and, indeed, were among the worst among OECD countries (VanNijnatten 2002; Jaccard 2006). In other regulatory realms, the Liberal regulatory record was mixed at best. For example, in the broad area of biotechnology in food, health, and life, some legitimate areas of regulatory reform (both to encourage and regulate the industry and its diverse products) was begun by the Chrétien and Martin governments, but there was also abject regulatory failure in areas such as assisted human reproduction and genetic testing (Doern and Prince 2012).

The Harper Conservatives: The Accountability Act, a Life Cycle Approach, Law and Order Rules, and Red Tape Reduction

The Harper minority governments from 2006 to 2011 and majority government since May 2011 have both built on past approaches and reshaped the regulatory system directly and in other policy fields where regulatory ideas and challenges were central to policy success (Doern 2011a; Schultz 2011; Bradford and Andrew 2011; Stilborn 2010).

In 2007, the Harper government announced its Cabinet Directive on Streamlining Regulation (Canada 2007; Treasury Board Secretariat 2011e). This directive was replaced by the 2012 Cabinet Directive on Regulatory Management (CDRM) (Treasury Board Secretariat 2013). A key change in both these directives compared with earlier federal regulatory policy is that regulatory policy and governance is to be governed by a broader "life cycle" notion of regulation (Johnson 2006; Doern 2007). This would take the existing policy on regulation beyond its historical focus on the initial making of a regulation and on regulatory compliance to the full later cycle including eventual evaluation.

Most importantly, several commitments to Canadians underpin the CDRM, two of which are that when regulating the federal government will:

- Protect and advance the public interest in health, safety and security, the quality of the environment, and social and economic well-being of Canadians as expressed by Parliament in legislation
- Promote a fair and competitive market economy that encourages entrepreneurship, investment, and innovation. (Treasury Board Secretariat 2013, 2)

Chapter 4 examines other key goals of the CDRM including provisions whereby departments and agencies must prepare annual regulatory plans and priorities. New regulations are now required to go through an initial "triage" process to assess whether proposed regulations are likely to have major impacts or low impacts, with different levels of regulatory scrutiny then set to follow accordingly (Treasury Board Secretariat 2011f). The CDRM also encourages harmonization and mutual recognition initiatives (federal-provincial and international), and the concept of not regulating unless there is quantified evidence that regulation is necessary including through the greater use of quantitative cost-benefit analysis.

The Harper government has also introduced other regulatory initiatives such as a Paperwork Burden Reduction Initiative begun in 2008, which directed departments to reduce their administrative burden by 20 per cent, and a Red Tape Reduction Commission (RTRC) in 2010–11. The RTRC included in its membership several backbench Conservative MPs (Canada 2011a). The RTRC was driven by business concerns about regulation and about red tape reduction especially by small business (Canada 2011a; Canadian Federation of Independent Business 2010). Business concerns in the RTRC consultations centred on overall and particular compliance costs, but also on numerous particular irritants that affect businesses across Canada and in particular sectors (Martin 2011). *Red tape* as defined by the RTRC is "unnecessary and undue compliance burden." In turn, *compliance burden* is defined as "the time and resources spent by business to demonstrate compliance with federal government regulations in terms of: planning, collecting, processing and reporting of information; completing form and retaining data required by governments, inspection costs; and waiting for regulatory decisions and feedback ... and are above and beyond the daily operational costs of running a business" (Canada 2011a, 3).

The Conservatives, in a similar vein, had earlier introduced a streamlined process for the approval of major infrastructure projects, an initiative run out of Natural Resources Canada through its Major Projects Management Office. It is focused on creating a single window for approvals. When the federal economic stimulus program was underway in the 2009–11 period, steps were taken as well to waive environmental assessment requirements for projects, again, so as to speed their journey into a quick shovel-ready state of readiness and implementation (Pal 2011b).

The Harper era began with its response to the Liberals' sponsorship scandal, a response revealed in its first legislative initiative, the Accountability Act, which included some new parliamentary and other regulatory watchdog agencies including the Conflict of Interest and Ethics Commissioner, the Commissioner of Lobbying, and the Public Sector Integrity Commissioner (Stilborn 2010). In short, they initially expanded the regulatory state as a precursor to their later efforts, which were to lessen or constrain it (see further discussion in chapter 9).

The Harper government launched and spoke to a very aggressive and comprehensive law and order legislative and regulatory agenda, linked to tougher sentences and the building of more prisons, which they found difficult to get through a minority Parliament but were free to implement once they had their majority in 2011. The abolition of the above-mentioned Gun Registry had to wait for a majority government, even though police authorities supported its existence as a valuable law and order mechanism. As we see further in chapter 6, the package of these and other increased law making and policing related to morality and the protection of citizens could be cast as newer versions of the oldest form of regulation, namely, ideas about the night watchman state (Prince 2012) and of what we analyse in chapter 8 as the societal regulatory framework regime.

The Conservatives came under scrutiny for other regulation-related episodes and decisions such as Prime Minister Stephen Harper's dismissal of the head of the Nuclear Safety Regulatory Commission (Doern and Morrison 2009) on highly dubious political grounds. Major aggressive deregulatory initiatives occurred under Industry Minister Maxime Bernier in 2006 regarding telecommunications (Schultz 2008) and subsequent controversial decisions by his successor Tony Clement to reverse a CRTC decision regarding regulatory licensing, which had granted entry to Globealive as a new player in the cellular telephone market (Schultz 2011). In all three cases, fundamental issues centred on the politicization by ministers of independent regulators. So also were ministerial interventions in 2010 in the role of Statistics Canada by abolishing the long form census – largely to appeal to a small group of core Conservative voters who viewed aspects of it as an excessive regulatory intrusion by the state. This intervention resulted in the resignation of the head of that agency.

Following their majority government election victory in 2011, the Conservatives developed a highly aggressive agenda against environmental regulatory processes and environmental groups cast as "responsible regulation" but mainly intended to help insure the growth and dynamism of the western oil sands and oil and gas industries, including the need for new pipelines to generate exports (Doern and Stoney 2012). These strategies and changes extended to threats under Canada's charity tax laws in which some environmental groups as charities were said by the government to be unpatriotic because they had some funding from foreign donors.

The Harper Conservatives also took basically progressive regulatory action under its life cycle regulation policy to reform Health Canada's regulatory regime so that its historic pre-market emphasis was now to be complemented by much-needed post-market monitoring of health and food products (Health Canada 2006). It initially succeeded in having the Liberals' long-dormant legislation, the Assisted Human Reproduction Act passed, although later, aspects of it were ruled to be unconstitutional by the Supreme Court of Canada, following court action by the Province of Quebec (Doern and Prince 2012). However, in the 2012 budget, the main regulatory body under that act, Assisted Human Reproduction Canada, was abolished by the Conservatives (see further discussion in chapter 6).

REGULATORY DEMOCRACY: CONTENDING CRITERIA AND ARENAS

Whereas the previous section clearly tells a broad democratic regulatory story centred on political parties and prime ministers in power, this by no means covers the full terrain of regulatory governance as it played out in multiple arenas driven by diverse contending criteria and standards of democracy. As context for our analysis as a whole, we set out five arenas and norms of democracy (Dryzek and Dunleavy 2009; Pal 2013). They are mapped here for conceptual clarity. In practice, they interconnect in numerous ways.

The five arenas and related different criteria of democracy are as follows:

1. *Representative democracy*, which in the Canadian case is Cabinet-parliamentary democracy, where the public interest is claimed to reside in elections and majoritarian decision making but where normal majority governments are replaced by minority or possibly coalition governments and where prime ministers may centralize power, also in the name of elected democracy (Savoie 1999, 2010; Aucoin 2008; Aucoin, Jarvis, and Turnbull 2011). Representative democracy is intricately tied to political parties and their internal system of democracy and, consequently, to the role of partisan considerations in policy formation and opposition. The above discussion of prime ministerial eras certainly covers the apex of representative democracy but more aspects of Canadian Cabinet-parliamentary government need exploration, especially on the parliamentary side of the accountability and critique functions of regulatory democracy, aspects that emerge further in most of the regulatory regime chapters in Part II including chapter 9 on the regulation of parliamentary democracy itself and also in chapter 4, which examines the macro-regulatory governance regime, the regime that deals overall with rules about rules.

2. *Federalized democracy*, where regulatory politics and policy divide constitutionally between national and provincial and territorial governments yielding both conflictual and cooperative joint action and various kinds of bilateral and multilateral federalist bargains and diverse views of democratic action. Some inkling of these key arenas and criteria have been revealed already in our discussion of the Charter of Rights and Freedoms, Aboriginal governance, energy and climate change regulation, assisted human reproduction, free trade, and internal trade.

3. *Interest group pluralism*, where democracy is said to be shown through the continuous interplay of interest groups of numerous kinds involved in lobbying, engagement, and consultation with government and with each other. Democracy is said by many to be the simple resultant outcomes of this interplay. Others see deep and persistent inequalities of power, and cast pluralism not as something that achieves such benign results but rather as something that is reshaped into corporatist forms, where business interests, in particular, are more dominant. These interests include professions such as doctors and lawyers, who both provide core values about autonomy but also are rent-seekers

desirous of economic benefits in the design of regulatory regimes. These and other non-governmental organizations, as discussed in chapter 3, are also linked to an expanding realm of players within universities in diverse knowledge disciplines relevant to regulatory assessment and reporting. Interest group pluralism does not just happen. Groups lobby and strategize how to play both the long and the short game of regulatory governance; and governments, departmental and independent regulators likewise plan their engagement approaches and strategize what communications and discourse are needed when approaches go according to plan and when they do not.

4. *Civil society democracy*, where democracy is said to arise if broad social N G O s of numerous kinds are involved, including disability, environmental, human rights, Indigenous, and women's groups, principally those representing the disadvantaged and marginalized in society, many of which take up the language of equality-seekers and rights-holders, in general, and also under the Charter of Rights and Freedoms (Paehlke 2003). International regulatory governance and politics involves global and continental networks of such players who in the Internet age are able to communicate with each other in easier, less costly ways including via like-minded social networks.

5. *Direct democracy*, where democracy is said to occur when individual citizens, voters and non-voters, express their views and have influence through their own individual actions. Direct democracy functions through polling, focus groups, and increasingly social online networks, as citizens and as consumers functioning in the marketplace as environmentally and health conscious consumers. Direct democracy includes individual scientists involved as critics and even as whistle blowers within government and private firms. These forms and fora of direct democracy are all present in the regulatory regimes examined in later chapters.

Like all aspects of democracy, direct democracy is evidenced by dispute as to both its nature and presence and its legitimacy. Direct democracy has a deep historical lineage such as the direct democracy model of Switzerland, the practice of referenda in many US states and, to a lesser extent, in a few provinces in Canada. In some regulatory areas, such as biotechnology and bio-life, these kinds of direct democracy can include choices by individuals where the body is a site for reframing and defending one's self-identity in ways that are similar to those examined by social policy scholars in the politics of disability (Prince 2009; Caulfield 2003; Montpetit 2003).

While *interest groups* (business-based, N G O s, and charitable organizations) receive explicit mention in only one of the above five notions of democracy, interest group involvement is certainly pervasive and complex in Canadian regulatory governance and politics. Moreover, interest groups must also be differentiated from *interests* (Doern and Phidd 1992 [1983]). Interest groups typically have the ability to lobby and influence whereas *interests* are players who have actual power to act or not act in concrete circumstances. Thus, individual corporations can decide to invest or not invest in Canada or elsewhere. As already noted above and in chapter 1, there is considerable political economy and policy study literature that points to business interests as having disproportionate power. The notion of interests includes particular individual regulatory agencies that have statutory authority to act – and wide ranges of discretion regarding when, where, and how to create and enforce rules or dispense funds.

These conceptual and practical arenas yield many shifting public-private-personal network coalitions as the definitions of regulatory and enforcement policy problems, opportunities, crises, and agendas change across time. Each arena generates and presents certain core criteria of democracy; each also generates dispute over whether the criteria are, in fact, being met or whether other democratic arenas are inherently superior as institutional sites for advancing specific regulatory values and enforcement approaches.

MULTILEVEL REGULATORY GOVERNANCE IN A GLOBALIZED CONTEXT

Multilevel regulation involves interacting, reinforcing, and colliding rule making and governance at the international, national, subnational (provinces, states, etc.), and city/local/community levels or other connected and overlapping spatial realms (such as water pollution areas and air sheds). Multilevel *regulatory* governance is a part of the even broader study of *multilevel governance* (Wilks and Doern 2007).

At the heart of the multilevel governance concept is the dispersion of political authority across multiple centres as part of a larger reconfiguration of political authority (Grande and Pauly 2005). Multilevel governance is best defined as non-hierarchical, negotiated exchange between different actors across multiple, interdependent, and overlapping functional arenas or territorial levels (Bache and

Flinders 2004; Hooghe and Marks 2003; Pierre and Peters 2000). It explicitly recognizes the participation of non-state, private actors in public policy making, and it includes informal and formal dimensions of decision making.

Multilevel governance as a concept originated in the study of the European Union as a novel type of multilevel polity that is less than a state but more than a complex international organization (Marks, Hooghe, and Blank 1996). Indeed, the formation and expansion of the European Union as a novel multilevel architecture of governance has been the critical catalyst to think about multilevel governance on its own terms rather than as national politics, comparative politics, and international relations among states. Multilevel governance has more broadly emerged as a distinct subject largely because the above trio of conventional approaches to understanding politics simply do not adequately capture the kinds of politics and governance extant in the world of the early twenty-first century (Hooghe and Marks 2003; Bache and Flinders 2004; Doern and Johnson 2006).

Multilevel governance is part of a debate and reform movement that seeks to go beyond existing concepts of statehood and of political authority, by overcoming established distinctions built around the nation-state container: distinctions between national and international, between public and private, and between formal and informal institutions (Eberlein and Grande 2005). New forms of governance identified under the multilevel governance label transcend these established dichotomies. These governance features are now increasingly identified and discussed in the international or global governance literature, especially in patterns of transnational policy making and regulation (e.g., Braithwaite and Drahos 2000; Held, McGrew, Goldblatt, and Perraton 1999).

The North American Free Trade Agreement (NAFTA) has had some similar effects in North America but definitely not on the same scale or depth of political-institutional change (Hufbauer and Schott 2005; Hoberg 2002). This is because, in terms of depth of regional integration, the European Union clearly has strong supranational features, in particular regarding the supremacy of EU law, including effective dispute resolution. NAFTA, in this regard, remains more like an intergovernmental arrangement – notwithstanding the quasi-constitutional entrenchment of free trade principles.

As a concept, multilevel regulatory governance must contend with the notion of regulation as an expanding definitional realm ranging from rules of behaviour backed up by the sanctions of the state right through to guidelines, soft law, codes, and standards. Thus, even in the core definitions of regulation, there are numerous levels and many types of rule making. These wider elements of regulation are clearly growing in complex international agreements and regimes including growing tranches of private regulation (Buthe 2011).

Multilevel regulation includes complex systems of emissions trading where challenges arise in combining market and democratic systems of legitimization (Baldwin 2008). Multilevel regulation is increasingly a core feature of food safety regulation both in a North American and European context, where concerns about bio-food and other issues of food safety have led both to controversy and concerns about how to follow and track food supply and distribution chains (Conference Board of Canada 2011; Alemanno 2011). It has affected the rules and cost dynamics of patenting law and regulation as firms seek to patent amid different national and international systems of patent law and also to protect their patent rights through litigation (Castle 2009).

Furthermore, the analysis of multilevel regulatory governance must be cognizant of the various institutional forms it takes. Such regulatory regimes increasingly involve a series of joint actions between the public and private sectors, including various kinds of self-regulation such as in North American electricity grids and in the use of voluntary codes (Braithwaite and Drahos 2000; Jordana and Levi-Faur 2004). These are among the developments that relate to the need to understand regulatory capitalism in Canada and internationally, as previewed in chapter 1.

Multilevel regulatory governance has, in one sense, forever been an issue in any kind of liberal democratic political system operating in a capitalist market society. It has certainly always been a central feature of federalism in countries such as Canada, Germany, Australia, and the United States, where challenges regarding both regulatory competition and cooperation among national and subnational governments are well documented (Burgess 2000). Whereas it was once common to think of regulatory levels mainly in terms of federal and subnational jurisdictions, it is now important to layer in the international levels of regulation and dispute settlement in trade as well as in various sectoral and horizontal regulatory realms.

It is also important to recognize local and city-metropolitan rule making where front-line and spatial/regional competencies and jurisdictions are crucially linked to all the other senior levels of regulation and governance. The progressive take-up of alternative energy sources, for example, often begins at local levels but is also hindered in municipal planning laws, where wind power might be or might not be allowed to be installed. Furthermore, it is crucial to incorporate the allocation of authority "sideways" and "outwards" from the central state to private actors who take on public functions. To this can be added new and revitalized realms of Aboriginal governance: in Canada, Aboriginal communities are granted legal standing and constitute key constituencies that provinces and the federal government need to negotiate with, notably, in terms of northern energy development. Rule making as well as "levels" also arise from shared public and private regulation, self-regulation, and new definitions of space and territory (such as ecosystems). These often produce rules and levels that do not obey conventional national, provincial, or international, and local boundaries and jurisdictions (Abele and Prince 2006).

In Canada, a more explicit cities agenda has emerged in federal politics, in part due to the lobbying of associations of city and municipal governments but also through the growth in the past decade of infrastructure programs aimed at cities and municipalities both before and during the 2008–12 recession-era stimulus programs. But Canadian regulatory governance and regulation has had an even longer multilevel involvement with so-called one-industry towns and small cities, particularly in the natural resources sector in fields such as asbestos mining, other mineral areas, forestry, but also in a different way, with small fishing communities.

Regulatory coordination problems among departments and agencies of a single government such as the federal government are not technically an issue of "levels" of government, but to most citizens it may seem much like a levels problem simply because citizens do not always know that they may be dealing with one government. Internal fragmentation and lack of coordination can lead to turf wars and policy conflicts and inconsistencies that, in turn, shape policy processes and outcomes and often produce the three types of unruliness being examined on this book. Thus, issues, decisions, and processes vary regarding how competition, energy, environment, trade, and health regulators interact within one level of government are often problematical leading to concerns about red tape as in the Harper government's examination by its Red Tape Reduction Commission.

Often these are collisions and interactions among so-called sectoral regulators and horizontal framework regulators at national, subnational, and supra-national levels (US, NAFTA, and EU). The current sovereign debt and banking crises reveal these problems in an intensive way (Davies 2010). Multiple levels of rule making and the potential and actual coordination, and congestion challenges and problems they create, are seen by many economic interests as an inhibitor of economic growth, efficiency, and innovation both in global markets and in "internal markets." These levels, however, are also arenas and avenues to enhance democracy, to experiment with new solutions, and to pursue health, safety, environmental, and fairness-related public interest purposes (Palast, Oppenheim, and MacGregor 2003). They can potentially increase or confuse basic aspects of democratic accountability, trust, transparency, and legitimacy (Flinders 2001, 2008; Doern and Gattinger 2003).

Our analyses of each of the six regulatory regimes in Part II of this book all reveal these kinds of multilevel regulatory and governance challenges, some horizontal and trade-related and others not only sectoral but quite literally involving product "subsectors" within sectors, and still others emerging from shocks and crises such as mad cow disease (BSE), electricity blackouts, and bank failures.

CONCLUSIONS

The analysis in this chapter has set out a broad historical context and account of the emerging and ever more complex regulatory democracy and governance system in Canada. The basic history of regulatory development in the Liberal and Conservative prime ministerial eras since the late 1960s has shown both consistencies across the partisan divide but also differences that reflected either views about the preferred role of the state or simply the need to confront new problems and agendas that governments have faced in a changing world. The Conservatives have tended to take the more systematic view of the need for regulatory coordination but never in a fully consistent way. The Liberals have tended to be more sympathetic to the regulatory role of the state and picked up the innovation agenda and married it to a smart regulation discourse. For both political parties, however, over their full tenure in power, invariably, there were regulatory sidetracks and cul-de-sacs. Overall, however, neither the Liberals nor the Conservatives were inclined to use and promote the discourse of deregulation, partly because this was seen as too much of a US and UK right-wing ideological position, especially in the Reagan and Thatcher 1980s era but after it as well.

The chapter has profiled contextually the nature and evolution of five key democratic arenas and criteria for the conduct of regulatory democracy. Each has its own claim to legitimacy in political life. Each also functions in its own political world of sorts, often in a competitive way with other democratic arenas and their discourse for building legitimacy and autonomy. Each arena is in its own way increasingly public-private and networked.

Finally, building on the analysis in chapter 1, we have mapped key features of multilevel regulatory governance as crafted in both the EU and NAFTA contexts in relation to complex bottom-up pressures and ideas emerging from city and local government and from the imperatives of Canada's system of both multilateral and bilateral federalism. Newer forms of spatial/regional regulatory architecture have also been noted in an initial way.

3

The Changing Ecosystem of Canadian Regulation: Ministerial-Agency Relations and Expanding Interests

To complete our initial context-setting aspect of *Rules and Unruliness*, this chapter explores the changing ecosystem of Canadian regulation by looking more closely and historically at the nature of ministerial-agency relationships and conflicts and at the changing and expanding nature of interests in regulatory politics. We cast this set of relations and interests broadly as an ecosystem in that it is important to see these changing features as an interacting system buffeted by both internal and external change. The literature review in chapter 1 and chapter 2's account of prime ministerial eras obviously helps tell the contextual story, but ministerial-agency relationships and interests in regulatory politics need a more specific focus before proceeding to our regulatory regime chapters in Part II. These two interacting features also help us capture preliminary insights into unruliness, especially unruliness related to regulatory agencies, one of the three types of unruliness being examined in this book.

We provide an understanding of some of the central exogenous forces that can disrupt the regulatory system. In particular, we look briefly at the following three: (1) the impact of economic disruptions, specifically dramatic changes in inflation in the 1970s and early 1980s that were pivotal in regulatory agendas and degrees of state intervention and that, of course, have their more recent counterparts regarding banking and sovereign debt crises since 2008 (already emphasized and to be discussed in later chapters as well); (2) technological change of various kinds and magnitudes; and (3) international factors. Each of these brings new ideas, new demands, new crises, and new relationships to bear on existing systems of ministerial-agency relations and the structure of interests. The historical and contextual focus on ministerial-agency relations and on the expanding structure of interests is necessary to help us see their core importance regarding the basic design and evolving structure of the regulatory state with further developments to be traced in each of the Part II regime chapters when other attributes are also examined, including ideas and discourse, and science, evidence, and knowledge.

These key realities have been forged in the field of economic sectoral regulation which, as stressed earlier, lies at the heart of traditional regulatory activity and scholarship. Consequently, this overall changing ecosystem needs to be understood in that particular context. It also relates in ways that will be examined in later chapters to our initial discussion of democracy and to more recent concepts of regulatory governance. As the analysis proceeds in Part II, we show why a broader set of regimes in the twenty-first century are also part of the Canadian regulatory system and now need to be at the heart of regulatory scholarship. We show that these regimes have their own versions of even broader and more complex ministerial agency relations, expanding interests, and exogenous forces. These complex changes anchor our arguments regarding the need to examine regulatory capitalism and regulatory welfarism as revealed in a wider array of core regulatory regimes in Canada.

ECONOMIC REGULATION AS THE LABORATORY OF CORE REGULATORY SYSTEM RELATIONS, IDEAS, AND POLICIES

All governmental regulations share common characteristics, namely, they are based on state-established rules backed by sanctions; nevertheless, there are fundamental differences between different, albeit broadly defined, categories of regulation. All forms of regulation impose economic costs, but perhaps the most crucial difference between what is known as social and economic regulation is that the latter directly interferes with economic decision making by private and, in some instances in the Canadian case, public actors.

Although all forms of regulation are, in principle at least, introduced to penalize or prevent unacceptable behaviour, economic regulation is fundamentally distinct. That said, despite the commonplace nature of the term, *economic regulation* is a much contested concept. For some, economic regulation is designed to change economic conduct by private sector actors; for others, it is "public administrative policing of a private activity with respect to a rule prescribed in the public interest" (Mitnick 1980, 7). The public choice "economic theory of regulation" makes no assumption, on the other hand, of a public interest purpose but sees regulation as the product of rent seeking either by regulated firms or other economic actors (Stigler 1971; Peltzman 1976). As Schultz and Alexandroff (1985, 3) have stated, the conceptual confusion that exists in attempts to define economic regulation has produced "a confusing mix of intentions, consequences, objectives, tools, processes and targets."

For our context-setting purposes in this chapter, economic regulation involves state efforts to control the economic behaviour of individuals and firms. There need be no assumption in such a restricted definition of a public interest goal. Nor is economic regulation limited, which is particularly germane to the Canadian case, to private actors because in most Canadian regulated sectors, at least until the wave of privatizations that occurred in the 1980s, publicly owned firms, such as CN Rail, the CBC, and Air Canada, were major actors. It is equally important that the definition of economic regulation is not confined, for reasons to be developed below, to regulated firms. Under certain circumstances, the economic behaviour of customers and not just firms is regulated, and such regulation is crucial to the health of the sectoral regime.

Finally, although historically economic regulation was introduced in the rail and telephone sectors, in particular to police, or constrain, the behaviour of regulated firms, particularly the pricing of their services, it subsequently demonstrated that it was an extremely pliable governing instrument that was attractive for pursuing other wide-ranging public policy objectives. The key distinction here is that in its original manifestation, economic regulation as policing was reactive and proscriptive. Boundaries were set for the behaviour of regulated firms – rates had to be "just and reasonable" and not unduly discriminatory – and if the firms did not violate those boundaries, the regulator would not intervene any further.

Starting in the 1930s, economic regulation took on roles additional to *policing* the behaviour of firms. It could be employed, as it was in the air and broadcasting sectors, as an instrument to control entry into specific markets or submarkets. In these instances, regulation was not introduced because of some form of market failure but because the state decided that the market would not be allowed to operate. In this way, it could be a tool to *promote* certain firms over others, which was important, for instance, when the sector included a publicly owned corporation such as the CBC or Air Canada. And if it could be used as a promotional instrument for firms or public purposes, it could also be employed for the attainment of a wide set of public policy objectives as an instrument to *plan* the development of specific economic sectors through the prescription of objectives as well as the assigning to individual firms or subsets of firms within a market, roles for the attainment of those public goals. It is when economic regulation is employed as a tool for the promotion of public policy objectives, and especially for setting and pursuing such objectives, particularly through the control of entry into the sector, that it is crucial to recognize that it is not simply firms that are regulated but that markets, and hence, both producers and consumers of regulated services are regulated.

There is little evidence from the historical record that there was any appreciation that adding promotional and especially planning responsibilities to the traditional policing function would have fundamental ramifications for the politics of regulation. The basic assumption was that the governing entity, the independent regulatory agency, acting as an adjudicator, and employed since the creation of the Board of Railway Commissioners in the early 1900s, was both an appropriate entity and one that was sufficiently pliable that more positive roles could be added to the negative policing responsibility with no significant consequences for the nature of regulation or the role of the regulator.

Indeed, the comments from a recent chair of the Canadian Radio-television and Telecommunications Commission (CRTC) during a controversy (discussed further in chapter 5) suggest how well entrenched this assumption could be for at least some actors. The chair, Charles Dalfen, was responding to criticisms of the CRTC's assumption that it should be managing and supervising the development of competitive markets in telecommunications services, criticisms that would ultimately lead to a serious attack on the independent decision-making power of the CRTC:

> What do I make of this? Let's just say that regulation is as much an art as a science. Few regulatory questions invite simple "right" or "wrong" answers. The panel members had to wrestle with issues on which reasonable people might disagree ... The panel's report confirms, to my mind, that the issue is not "to regulate or not to regulate," but rather "how to regulate best." (Dalfen 2006)

A former vice-chair, Richard French, has made similar comments about a more recent conflict after the government intervened to force the CRTC to change a decision (Janisch 2012). He also complained about the dangers of politicized regulation:

> The more the government reflexively reacts to public pressure by stepping in to placate the disappointed, the more it incents future stakeholders to induce such behaviour, thus establishing a political dynamic that will feed on itself.
>
> We established independent regulators because they're supposed to have the expertise, the freedom from partisan pressures, the time and the longer-term perspectives to make the painful and complex decisions required to keep industries that are otherwise liable to market failure operating in some semblance of the public interest. Does the cabinet really want to position itself as the effective arbiter for all the campaigns of rent seeking and special pleading that an institution such as the CRTC has historically dealt with. (French 2011, 3)

The problem with both arguments, while having merit with respect to what we have labelled as policing decisions, is that regulation, since the 1960s, has been at its core politicized in many ways by delegating to regulatory agencies decision-making powers to determine the structure of industries through entry and other controls or to determine the nature of the marketplace through the power to plan sectors. To employ Redford's conceptualization, policing regulation can be characterized as being directed," that is, "overhead direction of activity setting the preconditions of administration on the basis of some measure of consensus on what will be expected of it" (1969, 199). Promoting and planning regulation, especially insofar as it is undertaken without direct and explicit political guidance on the goals and means for their attainment, an all too common feature of Canadian regulation, leads to regulators being assigned a role that entails "an extension of the political process of adjusting among interests" (ibid., 188).

Thus, economic sectoral regulators, starting in the 1960s, were politicized by being explicitly given highly political roles in allocating public values, albeit under the guise of being specialized experts. While even traditional regulators, comparable to the courts prior to the Charter of Rights and Freedoms, ineluctably on occasion made "policy" in their individual decisions, the scope and magnitude of that policy-making role was inevitably magnified, as were the opportunities to play such a role, with the assignment of promotional and planning roles to independent regulatory agencies.

Arguably, it is not normally the fact of "rogue agencies" but rather the delegation of quasi-legislative promotional and planning roles that is the essential cause of politicized regulation and the concomitant special interest pleading and public pressure that has so characterized the economic sectoral regimes since the 1960s. This politicization – and, in our terms, unruliness of the three types we are examining – has been catalyzed by two other factors. The first is the relationships between independent regulators and their political masters, elected authorities, and their political competitors from both their "home" departments and others with an interest/stake in particular policy fields. The second is political manoeuvring by affected or concerned societal/economic interests whose universe expands dramatically with the assignment of promotional and planning roles and the concomitant "adjustive" function to independent regulators. We now turn to a discussion of those factors as they relate to unruliness especially of the kind related to regulatory agencies.

UNRULINESS IN POLITICAL MINISTERIAL CABINET-REGULATORY AGENCY RELATIONSHIPS

The appropriate relationship between regulatory agencies, once described by Hodgetts (1973) as "structural heretics," has long been ambiguous. As Vandervort has noted "the political theory underlying the adoption of an independent regulatory model was never fully thought through ... [and] the political implications were either not given a uniform interpretation or not unanimously accepted" (1979, 9). For many years, when the role of economic regulation was to police, to prevent abuse of market power, there was little contention about the relationship. Regulators had, and preferred, a narrowly focused mandate, and political authorities were generally disposed not to interfere in the exercise of that mandate. For example, in the first six decades of the operations of the Board of Railway/Transport Commissioners, only six appeals (or 8%) of those filed were accepted by Cabinet. The justification for political deference was articulated by Cabinet in one of its early responses to an appeal:

A practice has grown up not to interfere with an order of the board unless it is manifest that the board has proceeded upon some wrong principle, or that it has been otherwise subject to error. Where the matters at issue are questions of fact, depending for their solution upon a mass of conflicting testimony, or are otherwise such as the board is particularly fitted to determine, it has been customary, except as aforesaid, not to interfere with the findings of the board. (Quoted in Currie 1960, 229)

If the regulatory agency–political relationship was relatively stable and non-contentious during the policing period, it ceased to be when promotional and planning responsibilities were delegated to such agencies (Janisch, 1978a, 1978b, 1999, 2012; Scott 1992). As a result, the alternative instruments available to establish political control in the event of conflicts became contestable.

As mentioned, one of those controls, and long the primary one, was the opportunity to appeal to Cabinet to overturn a regulatory decision. This mechanism had several problems that contributed to the often unruly relationship between political authorities and regulatory agencies (Schultz 1977). In broadcasting, for example, Cabinet could only send a decision back for reconsideration or ultimately set it aside; it could not change any CRTC decision to impose a new policy direction. In railway and telecommunications regulation, Cabinet possessed greater scope in that it could not only veto a regulatory decision but it could also vary it, and the courts interpreted such a power as to include substituting a completely different decision. While the latter power is rather extensive, a basic problem with it is that the regulatory agency was not required to treat any such action as a policy-making precedent and, thus, was free to continue on its preferred course of action in future decisions.

Of course, the primary method for shaping the policy preferences and behaviour of regulatory agencies was their authorizing statutes and legislative statements of policy goals and priorities. Unfortunately, this has not been used often or effectively. In some cases, the National Energy Board stands out, there was initially no statement of public policy to guide the agency. In others such as with the former Canadian Transport Commission (CTC) and the CRTC, statutory policy guidance is so multidimensional, ambiguous, contradictory, or unranked that regulatory agency policy making is largely unstructured with the result that they were given essentially a blank cheque to enunciate their own policy preferences (Schultz 1982). The inadequacy of statutory direction brings into question French's defence of regulatory independence cited earlier. It is not clear why such independence is necessary or, indeed, justified to decide, for example, whether there should be a pay television system as opposed to which applicants should be licensed or whether competitive entry should be permitted into the telecommunications sector as opposed to which applicants, once the policy governing entry has been established, should be allowed into the sector.

The third mechanism is the power for Cabinet to issue policy directives interpreting their statutes and, where multiple objectives exist, establishing a ranking of those objectives. This power has become more popular since the 1980s but before that only existed in the CRTC's original statute and, even then, was limited to three very specific matters. As conflicts ensued between regulators and elected politicians starting in the 1970s, there were numerous calls from both within government and from external bodies, such as the Law Reform Commission or the Economic Council of Canada, for greater deployment of the policy directive power, but this went unheeded at least until the mid-1980s. Even though there is today such a provision in both the transportation and telecommunications legislation, it has only been used once and that was in 2006 in the telecom sector – and it caused a great deal of controversy (Schultz 2008).

The regulatory-political unruliness of the type related to regulatory agencies, as examined in this book, has characterized all three economic sectoral regulatory agency realms. It has been compounded, however, by an additional factor. Initially, in all three sectors, the regulatory agencies were made explicitly, or became so de facto, the primary policy advisers for their sectors by the governments that created them. Subsequently, when the relevant departments were either established, for example, Energy, Mines, and Resources or Communications, or became revitalized as was the case for Transport, considerable tension and outright conflicts ensued over which should be dominant in the sectoral policy field: regulatory agency or department.

Further accentuating the conflict over regulatory agency policy making was the development of what is known as the "institutionalized cabinet" (Dupre 1987) leading to what Savoie has labelled "horizontal government" (2013). The institutionalized Cabinet eroded the primary, if not exclusive, role of individual ministers and their departments in their respective areas of competence and made consultation compulsory with other departments or governmental units that could effectively claim they had a stake in a relevant matter. The result was a highly contentious form of bureaucratic politics as competing units, previously outside the relevant circle, sought to shape regulatory policies (Doern and Phidd 1992 [1983]). Such politics became particularly significant when Cabinet was asked to rule on appeals to regulatory decisions. For our purposes, the interdepartmental dynamics reinforced both actual and potential feared unruliness in regulation that has been characteristic of the past forty years not only in economic sectoral regulation, but also in the other regulatory regimes examined in later chapters.

CHANGING STATE-SOCIETAL INTERESTS
IN THE REGULATORY PROCESS

Economic regulatory agencies were established as a deliberate act of political choice by political authorities to address complaints and concerns about the use and abuse of their economic power by firms such as railways and the telephone company (initially, it was only Bell Canada that was regulated federally; BC Telephone was added subsequently). The objective was to reduce the political contestation directed at elected politicians, the Cabinet in particular, by shippers and telephone subscribers or their advocates such as municipalities by employing a quasi-adjudicative agency and process to resolve disputes between regulated firms and their customers. The underlying idea was that a specialized, independent, impartial, non-partisan agency, employing a courtlike process and appropriate powers could defuse conflicts. While there was no assumption that this would end political controversies between firms and their customers, it was assumed that it would significantly mute them and, in the process, protect political authorities from being caught up in such conflicts.

For most of the first sixty years of the economic regulation heartland, the universe of interests involved in the regulatory process was relatively small. It included, obviously, the regulated firms and their customers, sometimes directly participating or represented by groups such as shipper organizations or municipalities. During this period, the regulator interpreted its role as being to protect customers from unacceptable rate behaviour while not preventing the firms from earning adequate rates of return or profits. One of the marks of traditional economic regulation was that it was narrowly focused primarily on the reasonableness of prices. Indeed, one indication of this was the persistent reluctance of the railway regulator to get involved in debates over rate setting for regional development and other purposes and the consequent recourse over the decades to royal commissions to address the "railway problem" (Darling 1980).

Starting in the late 1960s, the regulatory interest universe began to expand. Even under policing regulation, issues became more controversial, in part, for example, as provincial governments such as Quebec and Ontario began to intervene on the grounds that with their greater resources they could represent their citizens more effectively than previously had been possible. Perhaps more significantly, reflecting the emergence of consumer and environmental movements, new interest groups such as the Consumers' Association of Canada and Pollution Probe began to insist on their right to participate, a right that was not immediately granted as regulators did not appreciate the challenge to their legitimacy that such interventions posed (Kane 1980).

In the case of the Consumers' Association, it is not insignificant that their participation was initiated and funded by the then newly created Department of Consumer and Corporate Affairs, which sought to have a role indirectly that it otherwise could not play directly. Consumer interventions were also encouraged by the CRTC after it acquired jurisdiction over telephone regulation in 1976 as it forged what Sabatier (1988) would label an "advocacy coalition" in support of its internally generated radically expanded view of its regulatory role.

Although the trend towards an expanded universe of interests in the regulatory process was present in the 1960s and 1970s, there was an explosion of interest involvement in subsequent decades. This explosion was a consequence of what we have described as the greater politicization of the regulatory function as regulators undertook promotional and planning responsibilities. Groups and interests previously not directly affected by regulatory decisions began to appreciate the stakes involved. In broadcasting, for example, faced with opposition from private broadcasters over Canadian content quotas, numerous cultural groups representing actors, writers, directors, and independent producers began to intervene before the CRTC in support of its policy initiatives. Indeed, the CRTC was so popular with various members of the "cultural industries" that the Canadian music trade association named its annual artistic awards, the Junos, after Pierre Juneau, the first chair of the CRTC.

There were similar developments in the transportation and energy sectors. Provincial governments, for example, began to intervene before the CTC to support their chosen regional airlines. After all, if Canada could promote through regulation its chosen instrument, Air Canada, why could they not do the same? They also demanded, as discussed in chapter 5, that the CTC abandon its deregulatory policy on rail rates and order the railways to offer rates that would promote regional development.

One of the consequences of the expansion of interests was that umbrella groups such as the Consumers' Association became splintered as more concentrated groups such as those representing the elderly, the poor, or specific regions entered the regulatory process to further their unique interests. Such was the division among consumer groups in presenting a common front on issues involving competition that the Consumers' Association ceased to be an effective advocate and largely withdrew from the regulatory arena (Schultz 2000). The fact that in this case the association had also alienated one of its primary funders, the Department of Consumer and Corporate Affairs, also contributed to its demise.

Business groups faced similar problems as divisions developed, for example, between small and big businesses over the distribution of the benefits of competition in telecommunications in the 1980s and beyond, which led to competing business telecom consumer voices before the regulator (Rideout 2003). We see these business group divisions as well in the analysis in chapter 7 of the marketplace framework regime in both the competition policy realm and the banking and financial services realm.

The move to promotional and planning regulation had a profound impact on the representation of regulated firms. From the 1960s to the early 2000s, peak associations, speaking largely with one voice before both the regulatory agencies and the larger political community, represented regulated firms. As the nature of regulation changed, so did the beneficiaries, which caused conflicts among and within the associations. Former allies became competitors as, for example, telecommunications companies such as Telus and Bell Canada invaded what was once the other's exclusive territory and became adversaries before their regulator. Complicating the situation was the impact of technological forces, discussed below, that broke down barriers between sectors such as broadcasting and telecommunications such that cable companies started providing telephone service while telephone companies distributed broadcasting signals. An additional complication arose from cross-sector mergers and acquisitions.

For our illustrative purposes, one of the most significant developments in the telecommunications sector came when the CRTC became engaged in its attempt to pursue its revised statutory mandate after 1993 of ensuring "orderly development." In the process, the agency ineluctably attempted to manage the transition to competition in both broadcasting and telecommunications, which involved the agency in picking winners and losers. As a result, regulated industry voices splintered and multiplied. In fact, peak industry associations that had been dominant effective voices for their industries in the regulatory arena such as the Canadian Association of Broadcasters, the Canadian Cable Television Association, and Telecom Canada/Stentor, representing the major telephone companies, all succumbed to internecine conflict and, effectively, disappeared.

There was another major contributor to unruliness in the economic regulatory sectors caused by the vastly expanded universe of interests seeking to benefit from regulatory decisions. Although it was never the case that economic regulation was completely apolitical, the emphasis on the specialized nature of the adjudicative regulatory role, as discussed above, left the regulatory agencies free to perform their functions relatively insulated from the larger political process. In this, the agencies were supported by an organizational ethos that both discouraged political authorities from intervening as well as an incentive system that encouraged other governmental actors to respect the institutional boundaries that had been developed.

This insulation ended as the nature of regulation was transformed to embrace promotional and planning roles. In the first place, as the stakes grew, the "losers" in regulatory conflicts were no longer willing to defer to the regulatory agency but increasingly began to exploit the political appeal mechanisms to pursue their goals. Such appeals increased exponentially from the 1980s on, and in fact, the regulatory agency came to be seen as only the first stop in a multi-game process. Although not all appeals were successful, the exploitation of the political appeal process by participants routinely brought political authorities and regulators into policy and agency mandate-related conflicts (Sutherland and Doern 1985).

Complicating the situation was that regulators increasingly had governmental competitors in the form of the departments of their designated ministers. These departments aggressively sought to displace the agencies as policy makers and sought to make a convincing case that they were as institutionally competent, if not more so, than the agencies to develop the public policies appropriate for promotional and planning regulation. Consequently, they were no longer prepared to show any institutional deference to the agencies.

They supported ministerial claims that agencies had too much independent policy-making power and contended that they, rather than the agencies, were more competent, in part, because they had more resources. If this was not enough, there were other bureaucratic competitors, discussed above, which through the Cabinet appeal process, in particular, sought to put their imprint on regulatory policy.

EXOGENOUS CONTRIBUTORS TO REGULATORY SYSTEM CHANGE

We have thus far been highlighting how changes in the ecosystem of the economic sectoral regulatory system linked to delegated governance and expanded interests caused turbulence and unruliness. These core systems also confront significant exogenous shocks, some of which were of sufficient magnitude to have enduring and transformative impacts on the nature of the system, its goals, and the central relationships among its participants. In this section, we look at three such exogenous contributors and discuss, generally, the impact they have had since the 1960s.

The first major shock to all three agencies and policy fields came in the early to mid-1970s and also later in the form of a significant increase in inflation, indeed, hyper-double digit inflation. Some of this has been discussed in chapter 2 in our survey of the Trudeau era, but here our focus is more specific. Price regulation, a primary aspect of regulatory policing, being prospective and seeking to balance the interests of both the regulated and its clients/customers, has had a central assumption of economic stability and predictability. The regulated typically apply for a rate increase that will reflect recent and presumed economic conditions, including inflation rates. The normal process assumes that any requested regulatory rate increase will cover a period of several years and, especially, that the regulated firm will not be coming back too quickly or repeatedly to "the table," as it were, for another increase. In this respect, it is worth noting that, for example, in the case of the federally regulated telephone companies rate increase applications had been extremely rare in the first sixty years of regulation as they were able to finance the very significant expansion that led to one of the highest household telephone penetration rates in the world, and one certainly higher than in the United States, primarily through cost-cutting technological changes, especially after the Second World War.

The significant and immediate increase in inflation that occurred as a result of the global spike in oil prices in 1973, and again in the late 1970s and early 1980s, put pressure on the sectoral regulatory agencies and their interests. The railways had considerable freedom to raise rates without regulatory scrutiny, while the energy, air, and telephone sectors required regulatory approval. In the case of railway rates, there was an immediate demand from some shippers and especially western provincial governments that railway rate freedom should be ended. In the case of airline fares and telephone rates, their applications for increases coincided with the entrance of consumer advocates seeking to influence regulatory proceedings. Bell Canada was particularly hard hit and had more cross- the-board rate increase applications submitted to the regulator in the 1968–76 period than in the previous sixty years. Indeed, Bell on occasion filed for interim increases even while its regulator was reviewing prior applications.

The suddenness of the increases combined with recurrent applications dramatically increased the political salience of the regulatory system. It was not simply coincidental that at this time the federal Department of Consumer and Corporate Affairs was able to persuade the government not only that it should undertake a series of studies of the federal regulatory agencies but also that it be permitted to fund consumer interventions.

More importantly, the scope of the increases fostered not only a heightened public awareness of the significance of the economic sectoral regulatory agencies but a generalized suspicion that these agencies were, if not captured by the regulated firms, unduly sympathetic to them. This suspicion was undoubtedly a significant conditioning factor to the turmoil and political conflicts that the agencies would confront over the next decade.

The second, and more enduring and more frequent, exogenous shock to the regulatory regimes was technological change of various kinds. Regulated companies had always been the primary controllers of their own technologies. Railways and telephone companies had long managed the introduction of new changes in order to prevent any serious disruptions. In the case of Bell Canada, for example, with its philosophy of control over "end-to-end" service, which included complete control over both local and long distance networks as well as all equipment attached to its system, it would test any innovations in selected "model" markets, such as Peterborough, Ontario, and Victoriaville, Quebec. No service would be changed nor would any new equipment be added until extensive testing had been undertaken to ensure both system compatibility and customer acceptability.

On occasion, however, technological change was totally exogenous to the regulated system. The motor carrier industry in the 1950s and early 1960s had contributed, as a result of a number of factors including technological changes that included expanded axles, freezer cars, and containers, to the significant erosion of the market power of the railways, contrary to conventional expectations. As the federal government did not regulate this industry and, thus, could not control its expansion, its only alternative was to remove regulatory constraints on railway rate setting in 1967 (Heaver and Nelson 1977; Schultz 1980).

In other cases, however, regulators sought to manage technological change so as to protect their regulatory goals. The CRTC, in particular in the 1970s and then in the late 1980s, was very successful, first, in delaying the introduction of pay television and, then, in reducing the competitive threat from direct-to-home satellite television delivery systems so as to protect the Canadian broadcasting system from what it considered undue fragmentation which would undermine the goals that the CRTC had established and, more importantly, its chosen instruments at the time, initially the over-the-air broadcasters and then the cable television companies. Although it never came to pass, to protect the national airlines in the early 1980s, the federal minister of transport proposed that the CTC should be authorized to control airline technology by restricting regional airlines from purchasing long-distance jet aircraft.

Notwithstanding the CRTC's successful efforts to manage technology, the broadcasting and telecommunications sectors have been roiled by technological change for most of the past three decades. Even a superficial understanding of the sectors cannot avoid an appreciation of how profound the changes have been (Gilder 2000; Cairncross 1997; Owen 1999; Castells 1996). Where once the broadcasting system was centred on over-the-air broadcasting, with cable systems providing a limited number of channels (with the number and the source dictated by the CRTC), today we have hundreds of channels delivered through myriad systems from over-the-air broadcasters – now a minority – cable, satellite, and the Internet. Most recently, Canadian television made the transition from analogue to digital transmission.

The Canadian telecommunications system has experienced comparable changes that are well known. Indeed, the most important point to make for our purposes in this chapter is that such has been the impact of technological changes that today it is virtually impossible to distinguish between what were once distinct sectors. Technological changes in the communications sectors have led to changes that are structurally both deep and wide in scope (Lipsey and Bakar (1995).

We are not suggesting that what transpired was a simple case of technological determinism. What happened was that new technologies, no longer under the traditional control of either the regulated firms or their regulators, profoundly disrupted the traditional bargains and relationships central to regulated sectors. One of the first disruptions, for example, was the transformation in corporate users' attitude about their telecommunications needs and services. Starting in the late 1970s, they focused less on the costs of services, although in the pre-competitive era this was a concern, and more on the role of telecommunications in enabling them to fulfil their customer and corporate needs and, thus, establish a competitive advantage. Subsequently, residential users sought the same control with the significant decline in traditional land-line customers being a prime example of customer control. Another contributing factor was the emergence of new entrants who either through their own facilities or through bulk purchase competed with the traditional service providers to provide everything from telephone to television to Internet services.

The impact of technological change in telecommunications, which fostered, in the first instance, competition in the provision of traditional long distance telephone service, unleashed considerable regulatory conflict as regulators, telephone companies, and public interest groups fought to limit the impact on traditional regulatory bargains involving primarily local telephone rates (Schultz 1995; Rideout 2003). More recently, there have been major conflicts between the cable companies and incumbent telephone companies involving the extension of voice-over-the-Internet services that have upset both the regulatory-regulated relationships but, more profoundly, the regulatory agency–political ministerial relationship.

There have been similar conflicts over the pricing of Internet services that have been highly controversial. Perhaps even more significantly, these conflicts will only continue as a result of new technologies for the delivery of broadcasting signals that will result in fundamental challenges to the capacity of the existing regulatory system. In short, technological change, while not driving the regulatory system per se, will undoubtedly be a major force in the future for regulatory unruliness as competing interests seek to either inhibit such change or take advantage of it to further their own agendas. Indeed, the potential effect in the broadcasting sector may be transformative by mirroring the impact felt in airline and railway regulation, where customers increasingly find alternative means to exit the regulatory system completely. If this occurs on a significant scale, it is difficult to see how the regulatory system can, in fact, survive.

Still other technological impacts in other regulatory regime chapters are examined in Part II of this book. These include technologies such as biotechnology and genomics, which have had major impacts via increased volumes of products and product approvals in fields such as intellectual property and drug regulation, as discussed in chapter 7, and also in the failed effort to regulate assisted human reproduction, examined in chapter 6. They also show up in chapter 9's analysis of privacy regulation in an Internet and social network age where privacy merchants and, indeed, industries sell access to Internet data of a personal and private nature.

The third source of exogenous forces acting on regulatory regimes is international in nature and has multiple dimensions. We have already seen some of this in our discussion of multilevel governance and globalization in chapter 2. Thus, one of the central arguments is that nation states have lost varying degrees of control over their national economy and national policy making and that national regulatory regimes are particularly susceptible to external pressures especially where multinational corporations are central actors.

One case that stands out is the energy sector, where a disparate alliance of multinational and Canadian energy corporations, western provincial governments, and the US government sought to undermine the Trudeau government's national energy plan (Doern and Toner 1985). The gestation and eventual negotiation of the Canada-US Free Trade Agreement, in the period 1985 to 1988, was certainly another (Doern and Tomlin 1991). Telecommunications is somewhat of a special case with respect to the role of international forces in the transformation of that regulatory regime from a monopoly model to a competition-centred regime. Both the US government and American multinational corporations in the 1980s sought both to proselytize the rest of the world about the merits of the new American competitive model for telecommunications and specifically to influence both international and domestic regulatory regimes (Aronson and Cowhey, 1988; Cowhey 1990; Schultz 1990; Globerman, Oum Tae, and Stanbury 1993).

One of the central thrusts of the American initiative was to bring telecommunications along with other services under the discipline of international trade agreements. As a result in both the Canada-US Free Trade Agreement and the subsequent larger North American Free Trade Agreement, and finally in the General Agreement on Trade and Services there were provisions, initially largely symbolic but subsequently very substantive, covering telecommunications. It would be erroneous to conclude, however, that these developments represented Canada succumbing to US corporate and governmental pressure. In fact, they mainly reflected a shift within Canadian domestic policy-making institutions that transformed both the policy discourse and the substance of Canadian telecommunications policy (Schultz and Brawley 1996; Doern, Pal, and Tomlin 1996). Frustrated by the continuing efforts by both the CRTC and the Department of Communications (DOC) to contain competition, other governmental actors such as Industry, Trade, and the Competition Bureau, were able to overcome this opposition to transform the debate from almost exclusively a narrow domestic policy matter to a trade issue. In this context, it is worth noting, however, that no such alliance was able to dilute protectionist elements in the cultural industries sector as both the Canada-US Free Trade Agreement and NAFTA included a "cultural industries" exemption clause.

There was a final, and very significant, way in which international forces contributed to change and some unruliness in several of Canada's regulatory regimes. One aspect of this has already been noted, namely, providing Canadian interests, corporate as well as individual, new ideas and approaches to traditional regulation and arguments in support of fundamental changes. In addition to providing arguments and examples to support regulatory change, American regulatory changes, especially in the air and rail sectors, influenced Canadian markets in those sectors immediately and directly. They gave Canadian consumers of Canadian-regulated offerings such as large corporate shippers in rail or individual air passengers flying to the United States and beyond the option to "exit," in Hirshman's term, the Canadian regulatory regimes (1970), which they did in significant numbers, thereby threatening the health of Canadian railways and airlines. In the mid-1980s, for instance, air deregulation was promoted as necessary to stem the hemorrhage of Canadian passengers to nearby US airports. The CRTC, on the other hand, was more successful in preventing this happening to Canadian television viewers by imposing significant constraints on direct to home (DTH) services. Whether the CRTC will be as successful in responding to the threat posed by Internet streaming of television and radio is not immediately clear

CONCLUSIONS

This chapter has explored the changing ecosystem of Canadian regulation by looking more closely and historically at the nature of ministerial-agency relationships and conflicts and also in relation to the changing and expanding nature of interests in regulatory politics. It offers initial insights into one of the three types of unruliness we are examining, namely, unruliness related to regulatory agencies.

These realities have played out in economic sectoral regulation which, as stressed earlier, lies at the heart of traditional regulatory activity and scholarship. We have seen important differences as, first, policing and, then, more complex planning and promotional forms of regulation emerged in the Canadian system. In the context of these modes and scope of regulation, key conflicts between ministers and independent agencies emerged involving conflicting conceptions of agencies as expert adjudicative and courtlike entities; appeals to Cabinet, where the minister or Cabinet could substitute its decision for that of the regulator; and Cabinet policy directives and/or statutory mandate changes.

These ministerial-agency relationships were never just bilateral. They occurred, and were shaped by, the broadening nature of interests traced in the chapter, initially consumer and environmental interests but also major changes in the structure of business interests and growing conflicts among business interests, as well as among consumer and environmental interests. Relations changed, as well, because expanding and more diverse interests were also allied with other government departments and their ministers within the Cabinet and within the increasingly bureaucratized policy-making and decision system of executive government.

The analysis in this chapter provides an understanding of central exogenous forces that can disrupt the regulatory system. In particular, we looked illustratively and briefly at the impact of economic disruptions, specifically dramatic changes in inflation in the 1970s and early 1980s, technological change of various kinds and magnitudes, and international factors. Each of these brought new ideas, demands, crises, relationships, and complexities to bear on existing systems of ministerial-agency relations and the structure of interests.

As the analysis proceeds in Part II, we show why a broader set of regulatory regimes in the twenty-first century are also part of the Canadian regulatory system and now need to be at the heart of regulatory scholarship. These regimes have their own versions of even broader and more complex ministerial-agency relations, expanding interests, and exogenous forces. These complex changes underscore our arguments on the need to examine regulatory capitalism and regulatory welfarism as revealed in a wider array of core regulatory regimes in Canada, some of which predate the birth of modern economic regulation.

PART TWO

Six Regulatory Regimes: An Empirical Analysis

4

The Macro-Regulatory Governance Regime: Rules about Rules

Sitting at the apex of federal rules and regulatory policy making is the macro-regulatory governance regime. This regime makes the system-wide and system-defining rules about rule making by the state, with consequent implications for many features of regulatory capitalism, regulatory welfarism, democracy, and governance. We presented in chapter 2 some of the building-block stages and continuities in the construction of this regime in each of the prime ministerial eras since the late 1960s. Some features of it predate the past forty years including the constitutional reality of Canadian federalism and the division of legislative powers between the federal government and the provinces as well as the territorial governments and Indigenous governments. The *Canada Gazette* processes date back 170 years to before the country was born and extend through their modern Stage I and Stage II processes that govern material features of public information and consultation in regulation making (Canada 2011a).

We first map the current regime including its statutory and quasi-statutory guidance, oversight, and challenge functions in and around the Cabinet, individual ministerial domains, and parliamentary scrutiny (Johnson 2006; Hill 1999b; Mihlar 1999). Other aspects of parliamentary scrutiny are examined in more detail in chapter 9 on the regulation of parliamentary democracy itself, including rules and conventions regarding responsible government. We then examine the nature of regime change and inertial forces and ideas mainly by exploring the extent to which the current system can move or is moving from its strongly entrenched "one regulation at a time" approach to (1) a system based more on explicit ministerial or government-wide regulatory agendas, somewhat more analogous to long practised spending and tax agendas on the fiscal sides of governance; and (2) a more comprehensive life cycle approach to regulatory governance across the federal departments and agencies including a much greater focus on post-market product and process monitoring.

In the third section of the chapter, we take a closer analytical look at the three regulatory governance attributes in the book's analytical framework: (1) ideas, discourses, and agendas; (2) public and private power in regulation making and compliance; and (3) science, evidence, and knowledge. Each attribute is examined as a factor explaining change and inertia in the macro-regulatory governance regime. Conclusions then follow including on federal regulatory policy making and on types of unruliness.

THE MACRO-REGULATORY GOVERNANCE REGIME

To map and appreciate the macro-regulatory governance regime, we trace the nature and roles of the rules, processes, and institutions previewed in Table 4.1.

The current regulatory governance policy discussion refers throughout to a series of Treasury Board Secretariat (TBS) and other documents and guidelines (TBS 2011a, 2011b, 2011c, 2011d, 2011e, 2011f, 2011g, 2011h, 2011i, 2011j, 201k; and Canada 2007. 2011a). But, this regime is also influenced in different direct or indirect ways by developments in the macro-regulatory regimes of other countries and by the OECD, which has been exhorting and advising about such regimes over the past two decades (Jakobi 2012; Pal 2012).

The first commitments to Canadians in the Cabinet Directive on Regulatory Management (CDRM), as we noted in chapter 2, are that when regulating, the federal government will:

1 *Protect and advance the public interest* in health, safety, and security, the quality of the environment, and the social and economic well-being of Canadians, as expressed by Parliament in legislation
2 *Advance the efficiency and effectiveness* of regulation by ascertaining that the benefits of regulation justify the costs, by focusing human and financial resources where they can do the most good, and by demonstrating tangible results
3 *Make decisions based on evidence* and on the best available knowledge and science in Canada and worldwide, while recognizing that the application of precaution may be necessary

Table 4.1 Key Features of the Macro-Regulatory Governance Regime

• Cabinet Directive on Regulatory Management (CDRM)
• Statutory Instruments Act
• *Canada Gazette* consultation processes
• Constitutional and quasi-constitutional provisions
  – Federal-provincial constitutional division of powers
  – Charter of Rights and Freedoms
  – Canadian and international human rights laws
  – Major UN conventions and protocols
  – International trade agreements
  – Agreement on Internal Trade
• Oversight and challenge functions
  – Prime minister, ministers, and Cabinet committees
  – Minister of justice
  – Central agencies (especially Treasury Board Secretariat)
  – Parliament
  – The courts

when there is an absence of full scientific certainty and a risk of serious or irreversible harm

4 *Promote a fair and competitive market economy* that encourages entrepreneurship, investment, and innovation

5 *Monitor and control the administrative burden* (i.e., red tape) of regulations on business and be sensitive to the burden that regulations place on small business

6 *Create accessible, understandable, and responsive* regulation through engagement, transparency, accountability, and public scrutiny

7 *Require timeliness, policy coherence, and minimal duplication* throughout the regulatory process by consulting, coordinating, and cooperating across the federal government, with other governments and jurisdictions in Canada and abroad, and with business and Canadians. (TBS 2013, 2)

These seven expressed commitments in the current CDRM, developed and approved by the Harper government in 2012, are much more elaborate than the two commitments in the previous 2007 Cabinet Directive on Streamlining Regulation (CDSR) which were to:

• Protect and advance the public interest in health, safety, and security, the quality of the environment, and social and economic well-being of Canadians as expressed by Parliament in legislation
• Promote a fair and competitive market economy that encourages entrepreneurship, investment, and innovation. (Canada 2007, 1)

The seven CDRM commitments suggest somewhat more "managerial" content but, at their core, they still set out core policies and values about regulation and, hence, rules about rule making.

The CDRM contains provisions whereby departments and agencies must prepare annual regulatory plans and priorities and also practise a life cycle approach to regulation. This includes managerial life cycle notions and requirements that evaluations of all regulations must be conducted every five years, a policy that built on earlier spending program evaluation requirements. But broader notions of the life cycle approach involves, as we see further below, approaches that extend regulation beyond the pre-market approval stage for products to post-market monitoring. The CDRM encourages harmonization and mutual recognition initiatives (federal-provincial and international), and expresses the principle of not regulating unless there is evidence that regulation is necessary including through the greater use of quantitative cost-benefit analysis.

The CDRM elevates into macro-regulatory framework policy the Conservatives' "one for one" rule whereby departments and agencies must control the number of regulations by "repealing at least one existing regulation every time a new one imposes an administrative burden (i.e. red tape) on business is introduced" (TBS 2013, 9). There are, however, "carve outs" (exceptions) to this policy, including regulations related to tax or tax administration and in situations of emergencies and crises.

The Treasury Board Secretariat's guide to the regulatory process sets out a mandatory process that applies to "most regulations as defined by the *Statutory Instruments Act*" but also notes "that some regulations are not subject to the regulatory process ... if they are wholly or partially exempted by their enabling act or by Statutory Instruments Regulations" (TBS 2011e, 2).

The idea of establishing a forward regulatory plan also has to take into account the government's eleven-step process for developing a governor-in-council regulation that begins with planning, then analysis, and ends, after Governor-in-council approval (or rejection), with review by the Parliamentary Standing Joint Committee for the Scrutiny of Regulations (TBS 2011e). These steps in total constitute the front end of the development phase for new regulations (delegated laws).

Regulatory proposals can obviously be major or quite minor and administrative. For example, the federal *triage process* was established to differentiate medium/high impact from low impact regulatory proposals with the possible implication that the low impact ones could proceed directly to the stage II *Canada Gazette* process (TBS 2011f). Thus, the triage process, which requires departments and agencies to develop a statement that reveals a number of possible impacts, is in its own way, a system of agenda setting and, therefore, potential red tape reduction.

The Statutory Instruments Act governs the regulatory process in that it defines a *regulation* as a:

statutory instrument made in the exercise of a legislative power conferred by or under an Act of Parliament, or for the contravention of which a penalty, fine or imprisonment is prescribed by or under an Act of Parliament. This definition of regulation includes a rule, an order, or regulation governing proceedings before a judicial or quasi-judicial body established by an Act of Parliament, and any instrument described as a regulation in any other Act of Parliament. (TBS 2011e, 11)

Related instruments such as guidelines, codes, and standards may not be captured by this statutory definition, yet they are certainly a growing part of the regulatory world we are examining in this book, and in key features of regulatory capitalism and regulatory welfarism as defined in our Introduction.

The information and consultation processes of the *Canada Gazette* system are another feature of the macro-regulatory governance regime. The federal regulatory policy requires that "federal departments and agencies demonstrate that Canadians have been consulted and that they have had an opportunity to participate in developing or modifying regulations and regulatory programs" (Canada 2011a, 1). This obviously embraces a democratic ethos but it does not spell out democracy as discussed in chapter 2 in relation to federalist democracy, interest group pluralism, civil society democracy, or direct democracy. These processes create different kinds of analytical discourse about participatory strategies and styles including consultative, deliberative, and public engagement approaches (Lenihan 2012).

Part I of the *Canada Gazette* process involves a pre-publication stage where "interested parties, including stakeholders previously consulted at the beginning of the regulatory process, are given the opportunity to see how the final draft proposal is in keeping with previous consultation drafts" (Canada 2011a, 1). Stage II involves the enactment and publication stage. Although there is little doubt that consultation processes are underpinned by these requirements, there is still much more involved in actual consultation strategies by both regulators and regulated interests and also in accompanying political communication approaches to various audiences and media outlets. We see this further in more particular ways in the later regulatory regime chapters.

Constitutional and quasi-constitutional provisions, understandably, govern the substance and processes of regulation. Constitutional provisions refer to the federal-provincial constitutional division of powers and the provisions of the Charter of Rights and Freedoms (Prince 1999). The Canadian Human Rights Act is highly relevant as well. Quasi-constitutional provisions refer to rules governing rule making in free trade agreements (WTO and NAFTA) and also the federal-provincial Agreement on Internal Trade (Doern and MacDonald 1999). The latter are not constitutional in the fundamental sense of Canada's Constitution, but as embedded agreements they are, once signed, exceedingly difficult to amend or disengage from, hence, the quasi-constitutional designation. For example, the above-mentioned trade agreements contain rules about what is a subsidy and what is not, about how health and safety rules must be crafted, and they set out dispute-settlement rules and procedures. In addition to their substantive policy, rule making and rule constraining content, they also affect the nature of central agency involvement in the challenge function, including the role of the minister of justice and Justice Canada and Foreign Affairs Canada.

Numerous UN conventions and protocols are part of this quasi-constitutional array of laws and agreements. These include conventions or protocols on the rights of children, of persons with disabilities, Indigenous peoples, climate change, intellectual property, acid rain, international shipping, the ozone layer, and many others.

The oversight and challenge function system has evolved over recent decades (Johnson 2006; TBS 2011g). It is anchored foremost in core concepts of Cabinet-parliamentary government, responsible government, and democracy and, hence, in the roles and duties of the prime minister, ministers (individually and collectively), and Cabinet committees. Cabinet government is built on concepts of ministerial responsibility and accountability. These include the political imperative and convention of a minister's individual and collective support for all policies of the government, even when he or she may have, in internal Cabinet debate, been critical of, or opposed to, some policies.

Accountability to Parliament is the linked second anchor and there are processes for regulatory review by the Standing Joint Committee for the Scrutiny of Regulations. It can also recommend changes to regulations. In addition, the Standing Joint Committee reports to Parliament on problems and can propose that regulations be repealed via a disallowance motion. Individual regulatory proposals and related changed laws are also often raised in Question Period and in parliamentary committees and other processes, as we show in later chapters.

The Department of Justice's role in regulatory oversight and a challenge function centres on issues of constitutional jurisdiction regarding rule making under federal versus provincial powers, and under the need for careful legal drafting of regulations to ensure that they conform to parent statutes and, of course, to ensure adherence to the Charter of Rights and Freedoms (Kelly 1999; Sutherland 1983).

The courts are a highly authoritative oversight institution, even more so in Canada's Charter age of politics and public policy. Rules, regulations, and compliance approaches are crafted with these jurisdictional and potential court and appeal roles in mind and to ensure that compliance approaches do not involve the federal government in continuous and costly litigation and liabilities.

Foreign Affairs Canada and Industry Canada have genuine challenge roles in the above-mentioned quasi-constitutional trade agreements and related convention and protocol realms. Along with Justice Canada, trade agreements must be adhered to and/or trade dispute cases handled where Canada is initiating cases under trade dispute mechanisms or has cases brought against Canada.

Any of the above oversight mechanisms can result in change and inertia and, thus, in regulatory virtue or in red tape defined procedurally and substantively in assorted ways. The permanent regulatory oversight machinery involves both the oversight of *policy* and of compliance *implementation*. The overall regulatory policy applies to governor-in-council (Cabinet) review and approvals (the majority of regulations) but, as noted earlier, some departments or aspects of departmental regulation are under the jurisdiction of departments and their ministers only. Thus, there are some exceptions but the CDRM seeks to ensure that it applies to all departments and that any exceptions are kept to a minimum.

Regulatory proposals can form part of the basic system of memoranda to Cabinet and, thus, be examined and debated within different Cabinet committees. As a pillar of the Cabinet's regulatory oversight system, the Treasury Board's review focuses mainly through its Regulatory Affairs Sector (RAS) on the new specific individual regulatory proposals; the aim is to ensure that regulatory proposals are in conformity with the CDRM, the Statutory Instruments Act, and the *Canada Gazette* process. The TBS also ensures that required regulatory impact analysis statements (RIAS) are carried out by departments and agencies, as well as the above-mentioned even earlier stage "triage statements" intended to differentiate medium/high impact from low impact regulations (TBS 2011f).

These approval and challenge roles of the TBS are complemented by advisory, educational, and facilitating roles, mainly through its Centre for Regulatory Expertise (CORE), a small six-person unit designed to help in implementing the CDRM. CORE's annual planning process, based on discussions with departments, seeks to identify and improve analytical capacity, with attention also being paid to the different challenges faced by small versus larger departments. The RAS unit itself is a fairly small in terms of staff (just over 30 professional analysts). The relative size and capacity of the Treasury Board's regulatory review staff in a central agency with an overall expenditure and management policy and review mandate is of considerable importance. At present, RAS works on what some call a "first come, first served" basis. This is true in some senses, but the RAS is by no means a passive entity waiting for departmental regulations to arrive. The RAS is, necessarily, pro-active through the earlier triage stage and also through its knowledge of other departmental plans and what may be emerging in overall Cabinet and ministerial arenas.

The role of this central agency challenge function is not to second-guess every regulatory proposal, given that numerous regulations (new or amendments, the latter being as high as 80% of the total) proceed through the system each year. On regulatory proposals with expected high impacts, RAS's is still, nonetheless, a more limited scrutiny, early advice, watchdog, commentary, and guidance role, including on the quality of regulatory analysis. One of the related problematical issues has to do with exactly how many new regulations are approved each year. The federal government does not publish such data on an annual basis. The only occasions when it has revealed such information is when the OECD is doing a country regulatory study on Canada. The last one of these overall country reports was in 2002, when Canada's new annual regulatory approvals were near the 2000 level (OECD 2002a; Doern 2007). These data do not include rules within new legislation nor do they necessarily do a good job of differentiating major rules from minor amendments.

This more limited or constrained notion of a challenge function is the product of two realities of modern Cabinet government and bureaucratic delegated administration. The first is that regulatory departments and agencies, overwhelmingly, have the main substantive regulatory expertise and familiarity with their regulatory clientele, and therefore, Cabinet government also functions on large amounts of delegation in regulatory development and the crafting of proposals. The second, and equally important, reinforcing reality is that most regulatory proposals depend on science-based and evidence-based capacity within and across departments and also related capacities for risk assessment and risk management (Doern and Kinder 2007; Leiss 2000; Hood, Rothstein, and Baldwin 2001). Central challenge function entities have some needed expertise and perspectives of their own; however, in the total scheme of things and in the context of a large (35 to 40 members) Cabinet, and extended amounts of legal and policy delegation, there is little doubt of where the preponderance of expertise lies.

Oversight is multilevel in nature and can take many forms. In addition to the above processes and institutions, particular regulatory units within federal departments and arm's-length regulators that are a part of broader ministries (many with more than one regulatory body) are subject to oversight and challenge functions within these organizations. Departmental and ministry-level challenge functions operate so that some key issues are flagged and assessed well before they get to the central agency and Cabinet level. It is also the case that the federal government has mounted periodic or ad hoc oversight exercises and mechanisms usually cast as regulatory reform. The Red Tape Reduction Commission (RTRC) is a recent example (Canada 2011a). Others have occurred in recent times on matters such as paper burden reductions (easily similar to red tape reduction), regulatory reform, and deregulation (Hill 1999b). Special inquiries and studies on epidemics or hazards such as SARS, BSE, and listeriosis have led to regulatory change and/or new regulatory agencies being formed (Doern and Reed 2000; Doern 2010a).

REGIME CHANGE 1: MOVING AWAY FROM A "ONE REGULATION AT A TIME" APPROACH TO REGULATORY AGENDAS?

Currently, federal regulatory policy mainly operates in a "one regulation at a time" approach (Doern 2007, 2011a). Periodically, the government does review regulation in broader ways, but on an annual everyday basis, the one regulation at a time system is dominant. However, the CDRM now requires that departments and agencies are to (1) develop regulatory plans and priorities for the coming year(s) and (2) report publicly on plans, priorities, and performance, and regulatory reviews in accordance with Treasury Board guidelines (TBS 2013, 10).

With respect to regulatory plans and priorities, the following four logical definitional and practical kinds of issues/concepts are to be considered:

1 Plans considered simply as *published lists* of proposed regulations: this could include planned regulations by program.
2 Plans considered as an *explicit announced agenda*, where priorities are set and announced that mean that some proposed regulatory proposals/projects will proceed and others will not (e.g., as happens in the public spending process). Departments could also announce planned intentions to regulate because they know this well before a final form of regulatory instrument is decided upon.
3 Plans and agendas explicitly informed and disciplined by a *formal regulatory budget* (as defined below).
4 Plans for all the above types that could be *government-wide* in nature and scope and/or *department by department* (or ministry by ministry) and could be for *annual time periods or multiyear time periods*.

In addition, we need to consider the issue in any such processes for *handling emergencies that require new regulations*.

The value of publishing plans for new regulations is to provide greater, more reliable, and more predictable public notice to different interests and citizens as to how they might be impacted by new regulatory proposals. Departments and agencies and the Treasury Board Secretariat are fully aware of the CDRM requirements and are engaged in ensuring that they are implemented. In practice, however,

plan is currently a disjointed inventory

the extent of implementation is thus far varied, often limited, and inconsistent across departments.

The *published lists* option for extended regulatory forward plans appears, at a minimum, to be what is being called for in the departmental and agency duty regarding plans under the CDRM. Even lists would be an improvement compared with the system before the 2007 CDSR. This could be a useful change since business and other regulated parties would have a clearer sense of regulatory volumes and what kinds of regulatory proposals are in the queue, for the government overall and for departments that might be of greatest interest to them.

For example, Transport Canada has processed about thirty to thirty-five new regulations annually in recent years, but its newer planning and priority system indicates that as at June 2010, 147 projects were in the queue (Doern 2010b). Formation of the priority-setting aspects of the above-mentioned 147 projects is still under development. The list of 147 projects in place was prepared to give senior Transport Canada managers a better idea of how many regulatory projects were queuing up in the department. It is not clear how many of these were new regulations as such or amendments to existing regulations (see further discussion below about amendments).

The Transport Canada example illustrates that there is some progress on this front with departments saying that actual priorities among regulatory proposals are now being set, but the degree of progress varies. A sampling of federal departmental websites (a good guide as well as to how transparent are the plans) reveals that some departments are listing regulatory proposals but not priorities while other departments are not, or if they are, the plans are difficult to find or to interpret.

Plans and agendas raise still other issues regarding whether they should be expressed as, and deal with, broader programs or groupings of proposed regulations. In the latter case, this could mean new broader regulatory packages devised as delegated law (new revised "regs") or, occasionally, as new statutes. Examples here could easily be regimes such as consumer regulation; organic food regulation; regulation of biotechnology in related areas of food, health, and life; and regulation of different modes of transportation.

Plans considered as an *explicit announced agenda* would be a more significant change, whether developed and announced at the departmental level or the government-wide level (Doern 2007).

Priorities would have to be set by ministers on the advice of senior officials based upon some kind of agreed criteria or on the broader arts of political and policy values, judgment, and analysis. The implication of such an explicit agenda approach is that, compared with the status quo system, overall in the planning period a smaller set of new regulatory proposals/projects would proceed to adoption and then implementation, and by definition, others would not. As noted above, some departments say that they are now setting priorities, but it is not always clear what these are or what criteria inform these choices/rankings (for discussion on criteria, see Doern 2007). Some regulatory agenda items do make it periodically into both the Speech from the Throne and the Budget Speech. In the main, however, these key agenda-setting documents and events of governments and parliaments are not seen primarily as regulatory agendas but rather as serving larger political, policy, and fiscal purposes.

Such an agenda may divert attention and resources away from the process of improving existing regulations, hence, our earlier brief mention about the need for more expeditious processes for dealing with amendments to existing regulations. Both regulators and regulated interests and clients are often aware of changes that could be made. As with any reform, issues arise regarding the impacts on both the existing stock of regulation, as distinct from the flow, and new regulations and amendments to existing ones. Thus, both agendas and reforms regarding regulatory amendments can, in combination, help departments and stakeholder interests focus on significant new regulations.

The more one moves into such agendas, the greater are the issues of interest group politics and other forms of democracy. Public consultation and engagement processes are already complex, even more so in the Internet age. Under an agenda system of forward plans, stakeholder concerns and lobbying are likely to grow and become more publicly explicit and even contentious for a government's basic political management skills regarding interest group pluralist democracy as well as representative Cabinet-parliamentary democracy. Such interest group and stakeholder politics are accepted as a part of everyday policy and governance targeted on the development of the Speech from the Throne and regarding spending and taxation centred on the Budget Speech.

The nature of the regulatory agenda and political management concerns undoubtedly vary depending on whether there was a *government-wide regulatory agenda* or a *departmental regulatory agenda*. In the former, trade-offs would be far greater and, therefore, more controversial both for potential winners and potential losers among interests, regions, and ministers. It would also imply the need for some kind of annual or periodic "regulatory speech" analogous to the Budget Speech on the tax and spending side of governance. In other words, it would be a major further priority-setting event and debate either annually or, perhaps, every three years. Even in the latter departmental agenda domain, the trade-offs would be more complex and transparent than at present, thus creating political management concerns and capacity needs.

Plans and agendas explicitly informed and disciplined by a *formal regulatory budget* would constitute an even more significant change. A regulatory budget sets government-wide limits on the costs of new regulation on the private sector (firms and consumers) with a view to maximizing the net benefits of regulation. The core idea involved is to maximize net benefits by keeping costs under control. A regulatory agenda is seen often as a logically and democratically necessary complement because a regulatory budget implies more open and explicit priority setting of new rules, new risks, and risk-benefit opportunities.

We draw attention to it here because such a regulatory budget was on the verge of being adopted in the United Kingdom in 2009 and may well reappear as a regulatory governance change idea there or elsewhere. Our view is that it does make sense in agenda terms but that one does not necessarily need to a have a formal regulatory budget to have a viable regulatory agenda.

The idea of a regulatory budget was first advanced in the United States in the late 1970s in work by the US Office of Management and Budget (Tozzi 1979). Under a regulatory budget regime, a regulatory body would be given a ceiling on new regulation compliance costs. The idea was obviously regulation-focused, although it was always tied to the ultimate achievement of a full and complete fiscal budget. Both then and now, regulatory budgets are the missing element of a complete fiscal budget. They are, in effect, the regulatory elephant in the budgetary room.

In short, current fiscal budgets include taxing and spending but not the spending that governments mandate and require from private businesses, consumers, and citizens through regulation. This mandated spending remains "off budget." Governments, therefore, have a built-in incentive to choose regulation as a policy instrument because the costs of doing so are quite literally "hidden" and imposed on private firms and consumers. The government's own costs to carry out the state's regulatory responsibilities are, of course, captured in regular budgets but not the private sector costs.

In the view of one author, a regulatory budget would potentially provide four benefits: (1) more explicit attention to regulatory costs, (2) more cost-effective allocation because priorities would have to be set, (3) more decentralized decision making, and (4) increased legislative accountability for regulatory costs (Jacobs 1999, 155). The claimed benefit of decentralized decision making is possible in some senses because business interests and NGOs may have a greater role in lobbying for and shaping which regulations go forward and which do not. However, a real government-wide regulatory budget clearly involves centralized agenda setting and decision making as well.

A cross-government regulatory budget was never adopted in the United States: partly because of the lack of information on regulatory costs and a consistent and comprehensive set of cost estimates, partly because of stakeholder concerns that it might favour more or less regulation overall, and partly because of a lack of political will that is, arguably, even harder to secure in a US-type political system of separation of powers between the executive and Congress (Meyers 1998; Crews 1998; Thompson 1997) than in Canada. Any country, including Canada, that started a regulatory budget would face some information shortfalls but this would not, in our view, prevent it from having an announced regulatory agenda.

Elements of more specific regulatory budgets did occur in the 1990s regarding amendments to the US Clean Air Act and the US Safe Drinking Water Act, where private sector cost ceilings were used as benchmarks in the negotiations between the President and Congress (James 1998) regarding these laws and rules. Given these experiments and because of the overall logic of the case for regulatory budgets and agenda setting, advocacy efforts have occurred periodically in the United States, as have discussions in academic settings (White 1981; Thompson 1997; Kiewiet 2006).

Among OECD countries, the United Kingdom has come the closest to adopting a formal regulatory budget system. In 2008, the British government committed itself "to consult on the introduction of a new system of regulatory budgets for Departments that would set out the cost of new regulation that can be introduced within a given period" (HM Treasury and Department for Business Enterprise and Regulatory

Reform 2008, 73). The regulatory budget initiative in Britain emerged with prime ministerial backing and a decision to proceed with a consultation document published in 2008. The regulatory budget system was designed for a 2009 start-up trial run, and then made fully operational in 2010. In 2009, however, the initiative was ended largely because of the banking crisis and the related fiscal crisis, where government and business priorities shifted sharply and quickly.

The issue of *annual time periods or multiyear time periods* regarding regulatory agendas (with or without a regulatory budget) is, obviously, germane. The British system was planned to centre on a three-year regulatory budget period, in part to complement the three-year cycle of its regular expenditure budget system. It was also based on the argument that three-year systems may make more sense for regulatory agendas/budgets because of the complexity of setting up and operating new regulatory initiatives. In part, this is because new regulations take time to become fully operational, and in addition, there are normal processes to manage such as the fact that regulatory costs to the private sector and to citizens occur early on whereas regulatory benefits become more evident later – after new behaviours take hold.

The issue of *how to handle emergencies* has to be factored into the design of any more elaborate regulatory agenda-based forward planning systems. Most emergencies could undoubtedly be handled on the basis of current laws and regulations, but if an emergency required immediate *new* regulations, then the regulatory agenda/ plan, as with expenditure agenda/plans, would have to leave room for such unforeseen contingency needs and responses.

REGIME CHANGE II: TOWARDS LIFE CYCLE APPROACHES?

Current federal regulatory governance under the Cabinet Directive on Regulatory Management and other related Health Canada statements seeks to move towards a life cycle approach. Under the CDRM, life cycle means greater scrutiny and coverage beyond initial regulation making and related challenge functions into *later stages of regular evaluation*. Under Health Canada statements, life cycle means extending regulatory product and process assessment from its historic focus on pre-market assessment to a broader and more complex complementary *post-market monitoring* of product use, efficacy, and risk-benefit outcomes.

The Life Cycle as Better Regulatory Evaluation

Current policy on federal *regulatory evaluation* is anchored in both
the federal evaluation policy and in the CDRM. Sections 44 and 45
of the CDRM refer to both evaluating and reviewing linked to mea-
suring and reporting activities (TBS 2013). The CDRM, as stressed
earlier, seeks to ensure that regulatory reviews are conducted on
larger regulatory frameworks. Regulatory evaluation also flows crucially from the Treasury Board's *Policy on Evaluation* including its
Annex A (TBS 2011a) which, in turn, is linked to the Financial
Administration Act and also the Directive on the Evaluation
Function. Subject to the *Policy on Evaluation*, departments and
agencies are to "evaluate their regulatory programs according to the
time frames and cycle" in that overall evaluation policy (TBS 2013,
8). The CDRM and related management accountability policy envis-
ages required evaluation of each regulation every five years.

Subject to varied impacts and complexity issues, departments and
agencies are to assess when appropriate:

- Inputs (e.g., resources, mandate, and enabling authorities), activities, effectiveness, ultimate outcomes of the regulatory program,
  and the extent to which the program contributed to the achievement of reported results
- Value for money (e.g., relevance, efficiency, and
  cost-effectiveness)
- Governance, decision-making, and accountability processes, service standards, and service delivery mechanisms. (TBS 2013, 9)

In addition, departments and agencies are to engage in regular reviews
of "regulatory frameworks" in order to "regularly assess the results
of performance measurement and evaluation to identify regulatory
frameworks in need of renewal" (ibid.).

Although the focus of the CDRM is on requiring and encouraging
departments and agencies to evaluate regulatory programs, it is also
true that this aspect of the CDRM, despite the larger requirement in
the *Policy on Evaluation*, is still in the early stages of development
and implementation on regulation. The historic focus of regulatory
departments and agencies has been mainly on the ex ante stage of
assessing, creating, and implementing regulatory programs in the
dominant "one regulation at a time" approach highlighted above.

The larger realm of program evaluation on the *expenditure side* of government, which has a much longer history, is still not always robust, although the evaluation policy itself has been subject to an evaluation (TBS 2011j). Evaluation activity is closely linked to departmental audit activity in the overall assessment processes for deputy ministers as managers.

One way to express the place of evaluation in the regulatory governance of the federal government is to say that if a federal regulator had $1,000 more to spend on regulation, it is far more likely that the department will spend it on the development of new regulations than on the evaluation of existing ones. Ministers and regulatory heads and officials are far more likely to get into difficulty politically, legally, and publicly for failing to regulate and ensure compliance than for overt failures to evaluate regulations. Nevertheless, evaluation is, without doubt, important and necessary as a part of accountability, democracy, and effective managerial performance.

Several evaluation issues are inherent in the art, craft, and science of evaluation – and in related ex ante policy analysis activities – and there is a vast literature on the subject (KPMG International 2008; Pal 2013). In what follows, we note briefly issues regarding timing and time period coverage, scope, information, independence, and causality attributes.

Timing and time period coverage issues are contentious in regulatory and other related policy instrument–related policy and governance realms. Timing can refer to how frequently evaluation studies should occur. Inevitably, timing becomes part of the larger rational policy theory arguments, but it also raises concerns about "paralysis by analysis" – the sins of overly frequent evaluations, such as those which made the concept of zero-based budgeting inoperable in government when evaluations of all programs every year were often advocated in the 1970s and 1980s.

The *time period coverage* of any evaluation in regulatory matters garners criticism because of the overall reality that when new regulations are developed, regulatory costs emerge early on but regulatory benefits typically take longer to emerge. Environmental and health and safety regulations are often caught up in these legitimate and difficult temporal issues.

The *scope* of regulatory evaluation is clearly an issue for single versus multiple regulatory bodies, regulated interests, and officials and ministers involved in various challenge functions and reform initiatives. There are differences in the scope and degree of complexity and difficulty if evaluation is on one regulation at a time (as at the front end of regulatory planning) as opposed to evaluations of groups, programs, themes, or regimes of regulation..Indeed, there is a logical and practical reality that immediately arises in this regard. Even when a new regulation is being proposed and approved, it already tends to sit alongside or on top of other related existing regulations. Years later, when a formal evaluation of "it" as a single regulation is to occur, it is even more implausible to evaluate it on its own. For this reason, when departments do evaluate regulation, they are inclined to evaluate regulatory programs. But even these programs are likely, as *programs*, to contain other non-regulatory instruments and activities including education, information provision, and spending. Evaluating every regulation, one at a time would be incredibly expensive in both good and bad fiscal times.

The Cabinet Directive on Regulatory Management refers to "regulatory reviews" of regulatory "frameworks." Departments and agencies periodically do some of this kind of reviewing. For example, the food listeriosis crisis of 2009 led to both a specific review and a broader review of the food regulatory system including its international aspects and its underlying approaches and relationships between regulators and food companies involved in ever more intricate international and cross-border supply and distribution chains (Doern 2010a).

Information, independence, and *causal attribution* issues are ultimately closely linked. The acquisition of information for evaluation involves data that need to come from business, stakeholders, multiple government departments and agencies, and provincial, local, and foreign governments, as well as international agencies. Evaluation policies, overall, refer to the need for neutrality and independence regarding who should do the evaluation and also regarding its publication (TBS 2011a, 6). Issues of determining causality and the attribution of performance outcomes to government regulatory programs, or to regulatory frameworks, are always contentious; all the more so, when longer time periods are covered by the evaluation study or when the scope of coverage is broader. This is true, likewise, because changes in behaviour among the regulated entities and interests may be due as much or more to market realities and competitive pressures or to the role of voluntary codes and "naming and shaming" tactics and pressures (Webb 2004).

Rules about Rules

*The Life Cycle as Greater Post-market Product
and Project Monitoring*

With regard to the second notion of life cycle approaches, *from pre-market assessment to greater post-market monitoring* of products is, arguably, even more aspirational in nature than the regulatory program evaluation notion of life cycle management. Because it deals with regulatory implementation in the form of product assessment, it is much more in the hands of departmental and arm's-length regulators rather than under the control of regulatory policy and governance ministers and officials at the centre. Moreover, it is a set of monitoring activities that requires networks of co-participants in the business and NGO communities and among health professions, patients, caregivers, and users.

The life cycle concept is by no means entirely new. We have referred above to its expression in Health Canada's regulatory policy in 2006–07, but it has a longer lineage as well in environmental regulatory policy history with regard to environmental assessment of projects and of policies, and in the regulation of nuclear reactors and the long-term storage of nuclear wastes. Federal environmental assessment policy focuses on assessing proposed projects that involve federal laws or funding, but it also deals with requirements for life cycle regimes to follow the project through time, including final stages such as the closing of a mining operation or a pulp and paper plant. A report by the National Roundtable on the Environment and the Economy (2011) stresses the great value of life cycle approaches to foster sustainable economic development in Canada, while it also points to many practical obstacles along the way, including conceptual understanding, complexity, and serious gaps in science and front-line science-based regulatory and policy capacity. Concepts of sustainable development and the precautionary principle are implied in life cycle notions and aspirations, although these norms are not always realized (Bregha 2011; Canadian Environmental Assessment Agency 2010; Doern and Conway 1995).

Life cycle monitoring and regulation involves, inherently, a "degree of difficulty" and "degree of complexity" quotient, given the spatial scale (national and international) and the in-built number of regulators which might be attempting to implement such full life cycle regulatory activity. Nuclear reactor cycles can last – quite literally – hundreds of years, and diverse energy-environment regulatory systems can involve dozens of regulators in Canada and North America, with each piece of the regulatory action needing considerable capacity, coordination, and knowledge backed up by political will and focus (Doern, Dorman, and Morrison 2001).

Ireland, Milligan, Webb, and Xie (2012) explore the rise and fall of regulatory regimes in relation to the life cycles of regulatory agencies and regimes, particularly with regard to how regulatory enforcement capacities, compliance, and achievement of objectives can vary depending on whether the regulatory agency or regime is in its infancy, high growth, mature, or declining stage. More will be said later about these kinds of life cycle policy inherent in federal regulatory governance regime change overall. At present, life cycle policy is best described as desirable but also aspirational in nature and so very much a work in progress.

Still other macro-regulatory governance ideas and processes jockey for political space and policy adoption. They, too, involve notions of cycles of a different kind. For example, the British government has adopted a "one in–one out" policy whereby any time a new regulation is proposed, another existing one of equivalent impact must be ended. The Harper Conservatives, as noted above, have said that they, too, will adopt such a system in the CDRM following similar recommendations from the Red Tape Reduction Commission (Canada 2011a). Another regulatory governance measure is the adoption of processes for the regular sunsetting of regulations, the implications being that all or many new regulations would automatically lapse after a given period and, if still warranted, would then have to be explicitly renewed. The British government recently adopted such as policy.

THE THREE REGIME ATTRIBUTES

To help explain both change and inertia in the macro-regulatory governance regime, we now look at the three regime attributes of (1) ideas, discourses, and agendas; (2) public and private power in regulation making and compliance; and (3) science, evidence, and knowledge. For each attribute, we are examining change and inertia at a high macro-governance level. These attributes will also emerge in the more particular regulatory governance regimes in the rest of our Part II chapters once we take into account more substantive content issues in each of these sectoral and horizontal regulatory regimes.

colliding purposes

Ideas, Discourses, and Agendas

The role and influence of *ideas* and *discourses* is vibrant and complex, sometimes captured in prosaic legal language as in the Statutory Instruments Act but also in the far better known provisions of the Canadian Charter of Rights and Freedoms. Just as often, as in the case of the current Cabinet Directive on Regulatory Management, ideas emerge in directives and exhortative statements of intent. The CDRM's dual purposes centre on protecting health and safety and on encouraging business innovation, investment, and growth, in that order, yet without any recognition of collision points or the case-by-case ranking of these ideas and values. The notion of "streamlining" as policy discourse in the initial 2007 Cabinet Directive on Streamlining Regulation evokes efficiency and regulatory capitalism values, but the component parts of the CDSR and now the CDRM create much more complexity as well.

In the earlier phases of the building of the macro-regulatory governance regime, ideas and discourse were important in shape shifting the rules about rule making. As shown in chapter 2, the Trudeau Liberals introduced Socio-Economic Impact Analysis (SEIA), mainly to ensure that health and safety rules under eighteen named statutes were not imposing undue private sector costs at a time of economic recession and high inflation. Only later, under the Mulroney Conservatives, was SEIA cancelled and replaced with the Regulatory Impact Assessment System (RIAS) to be applied to all regulations.

The ideas and discourse in federal regulatory policy in the Chrétien-Martin era shifted to reflect purposes related to innovation and the knowledge-based economy and tied closely, as well, to globalization and regulatory cooperation. The discourse of *smart regulation* emerged in ways that combined both safety and risk-benefit ideas but also the notion that regulation had to be "enabling" and, thus, efficient and conducive to new innovative products both being produced in Canada but also coming into Canada from other innovative economies to benefit Canadian consumers who were, in the emerging Internet age, aware of and demanding access to many such products.

smart regs

The notion and language of *agendas* in macro-regulatory governance was slow to emerge and is still oblique. The Mulroney-era regulatory policy was the first to include the need for departments to develop regulatory "plans," and the Harper-era CDRM refers to requirements for "plans and priorities" and its description of the role of the Treasury Board Secretariat includes advising the government on its "regulatory agenda." Even when successive governments announced periodic regulatory reform processes and reports/statements, they tended to call them reforms rather than parts of a regular regulatory agenda. The notion of explicitly ranking new regulations and announcing such agendas may be getting closer at either a government-wide or departmental level, but as discourse it is rare and as action it is hesitant at best due to strong inertial forces, habits, and uncertainty as to how exactly it might work.

Public and Private Power in Regulation Making and Compliance

The power dimension of macro-regulatory regime evolution, change, and inertia is partly revealed in the ideas and discourse noted above and extends into the demands and relations of private interests and business power and also of NGOs and consumer interests. These institutional centres of power and influence, working through their preferred federal (and provincial) departments, ministers, and agencies, have forged the overall design and content of approaches to regulation making and compliance. Business and corporate power shaped key macro-regime features in all of the prime ministerial eras, including the Truedeau-era SEIA and RIAS requirements; the Mulroney-era free trade, deregulation, and re-regulation changes; the Chrétien-Martin provisions for smart regulation; and the Harper-era streamlining, paper burden reduction, and red tape reduction processes and initiatives.

NGOs and consumer interests exercised considerable influence, certainly in the numerous health, safety, and environmental provisions of the regulatory state which Conservative and Liberal governments alike have always mentioned first when summarizing the overall purposes of macro-regulatory governance in the CDRM and in smart regulation provisions. These interests fixed, initially, on consumer lobbies, then environmental ones, and more recently, on health and patient interests. The extended processes for regulatory engagement and participation informally and under the *Canada Gazette* process are largely the result of such NGO and consumer interest lobbying across the past four decades.

Science, Evidence, and Knowledge

The construction and extension of the macro-regulatory regime in relation to science, evidence, and knowledge are important, yet subtle. Science-based features were strong and central in early regime development and discourse and still find expression in the CDRM. Notions of "sound science" found their way into trade agreements as a form of reassurance that health and safety measures in trade agreements did not become a new form of protectionism. Science also typically meant the natural and engineering sciences.

Evidence-based regulation became more explicitly mentioned and used both in the CDRM and in the changes to macro-regulatory regime provisions in their life cycle analytical features. Evidence-based analysis included the natural sciences but also encompassed other socio-economic kinds of knowledge, especially in the evaluative arts and sciences, including cost-benefit analysis, and in the evidence that had to be assembled to extend post-market monitoring of product use. These kinds of evidence have included the social and economic sciences, law, humanities, ethical analysis, and also front-line citizen science and observation. Lawyers have, of course, always been influential actors in the regulatory world, in a number of institutional arenas. Moreover, in banking and banking regulation, Ph.D.s in mathematics were increasingly needed and also the object of regulatory concern.

This broadening of the knowledge base needed for the full scope of regulation making and compliance was easily conflated with notions of the knowledge-based economy and society. In short, smart regulation needed all sorts of smarts and, paradoxically, was making rule making more analytically based and much more complex as knowledge professions and other participants jockeyed for position or disputed the decisions made both at the regulation-making level and with respect to individual products and projects approved or not approved.

Then, again, there were also increasing concerns about policy and regulation being based on the absence of evidence and by partisan and "attack politics" charges that regulation or the absence of regulation was based on ideology and "opinions" by interests and individual ministers who, quite literally, made up their own facts (Savoie 2013). Climate change deniers are an example in this regard, but denial was also a part of debates about crime and the claimed needs for tougher sentences and longer imprisonment and, as we have seen, on the nature of the once a decade census and how its crucial information was collected.

CONCLUSIONS

Our analysis of the macro-federal regulatory governance regime – which governs and contains the macro-rules about rule making and regulation – has set out its statutory and quasi-statutory guidance and challenge processes in and around the Cabinet and the central agencies, especially the Treasury Board Secretariat. The core features of the Cabinet Directive on Regulatory Management demonstrate that, at the centre of rules about rules, two purposes and values contend for attention and adoption: one anchored in concerns about health, safety, the environment, and various notions of fairness and equity and the other on economic development, efficiency, and innovation. Although they are ranked in that order, they have been joined in the CDRM by five other policy commitments regarding regulation. The two initially listed commitments do not necessarily play out in that order or they are simply combined and, not surprisingly, become an actual and potential form of unruliness related to policy and mandate conflict or the inability to get the right policies established. In this regard, it must also be stressed that the CDRM is a Cabinet directive and not a statute itself; however, the CDRM sits beside and in close proximity to other aspects of rules about rules that are statutory and, indeed, constitutional and quasi-constitutional in nature. These complex types and mixes of rules in particular situations can easily generate inertia or water down proposed regulatory change.

Drawing on earlier historical developments, we focused here on macro-regime change pressures regarding the extent to which the current system can move, or is moving, from its largely "one regulation at a time" approach to a system based more on explicit regulatory plans, priorities, and agendas. We also examined policy moves towards a more comprehensive life cycle approach to regulatory governance across the federal departments and agencies. The regime has been shown to be caught up in unruliness tied to the absence of strong agenda setting and because it is often only aspirational as macro-regulatory governance meets obstacles and suffers from inertial interregime complexity. The life cycle aspirations, as we have seen, confront different challenges in their two different varieties, one regarding the extended evaluation of regulatory programs and regimes and the other, at the product and project level, in efforts to complement pre-market assessment with better and more diffuse post-market monitoring.

The overall challenge function, as the chapter has shown, has become more multifaceted and, thus, complex. Although the Treasury Board Secretariat anchors this process, it is by no means alone given the role of other players ranging from the prime minister, minister of justice, and the minister of foreign affairs, among others. The analysis has further shown that the expertise in the challenge process still lies overwhelmingly in the much greater capacities of the regulatory departments and agencies.

The role and influence of ideas and discourse shows that the combined purposes of the Cabinet Directive on Regulatory Management refer to public health and safety and on private investment and growth, with little official recognition of collision between these values. The discourse of smart regulation emerged in ways that combined both safety and risk-benefit ideas but also the notion that regulation had to be "enabling" and conducive to new innovative products entering the market. The notion and language of *agendas* in macro-regulatory governance has been slow to emerge and is still oblique, at best, since inertial forces remain strong and entrenched.

Regarding structures of private and public power, not surprisingly, business and corporate power has shaped critical macro-regime features in all of the prime ministerial eras, including Socio-Economic Impact Analysis and Regulatory Impact Assessment System requirements; the Mulroney-era free trade, deregulation, and re-regulation changes; the Chrétien-Martin provisions for smart regulation; and the Harper era initiatives to reduce both the paper burden and red tape. Non-governmental organizations and consumer interests have exercised considerable influence in the numerous health, safety, and environmental provisions of the regulatory state which Conservative and Liberal governments alike have always mentioned first when summarizing the overall purposes of macro-regulatory governance in the CDRM and in earlier smart regulation provisions. The extended processes for regulatory engagement and participation informally and under the *Canada Gazette* process are largely the result of such NGO and consumer interest lobbying across the past four decades. These are also among the forces and features that support the arguments about the emergence of Canadian regulatory capitalism rather than just liberalized markets.

Regarding science, evidence, and knowledge as an underlying causal attribute, science-based features were strong and central in early regime development and discourse and still find expression in the CDRM. Notions of "sound science" found their way into trade agreements. Evidence-based regulation became more explicitly mentioned and used in the changes to macro-regulatory regime provisions in their life cycle analytical features and aspirations. Evidence-based analysis included the natural sciences and other socio-economic kinds of knowledge especially in the evaluative arts and sciences, including cost-benefit analysis, and in the evidence that had to be assembled to extend post-market monitoring of product and project use. Additionally, there is increased concern and debate about whether regulation or the absence of regulation is based too often on no or little evidence and in situations where protagonists merely assert their values unsupported by evidence or conjure up their own facts.

5

The Economic Sectoral Regime: The Core Energy, Transportation, and Telecommunications Regulators

In this chapter, we examine the economic sectoral regulatory regime by examining three regulatory agencies, the National Energy Board (NEB), the Canadian Transportation Agency (CTA) and its predecessor the Canadian Transport Commission (CTC), and the Canadian Radio-television and Telecommunications Commission (CRTC). These three agencies were created to be the primary federal government institutions to influence, direct, regulate, and control the economic, but also related social, impacts of vital infrastructural, public utility, and networked industries. As we shall see, the first two of these regulators have undergone the most profound changes and today hardly deserve to be described any longer as "governments in miniature" (Schultz and Alexandroff 1985; Schultz and Doern 1998). This is because their policy mandates and their regulatory powers and mandates have been radically redefined, shared out, and reduced over the forty-year period profiled in this chapter.

Only the CRTC, at least for most of its first forty years, has been largely successful in defending its original roles and powers and keeping challengers at bay. Even the CRTC has not been immune to reform, however, particularly in the past six to eight years as mainly Conservative governments and designated ministers have rather successfully sought to impose their views on the commission and reduce substantially its traditional freedom of manoeuvre and independent decision-making capacity. Recent political initiatives suggest that the CRTC has begun the route to miniaturization that its regulatory peers followed.

In one sense, economic sectoral regulators lived, like those they regulated, a relatively quiet life prior to the 1960s. As the function of regulation radically changed from a primary emphasis on policing the behaviour or economic conduct of firms so did the political salience of regulation increase. Sectoral economic regulation, while always conflictual and, hence, political, became even more so as more and more interests, societal, economic, and intergovernmental, recognized the potential and actual impact of the decisions of economic regulators and sought to participate in the decision making, share the benefits, or attenuate the impact of those decisions (Schultz and Alexandroff 1985; Doern, Hill, Prince, and Schultz 1999).

If this were not enough to bring a constant state of potential or actual unruliness to the traditional regulatory regimes and their processes, regulatory agencies found themselves caught up in exogenous changes such as environmentalism and consumerism, not to mention inflation and fundamental technological change, that brought new actors and interests into the regulatory processes who challenged both the regulatory "stakes" and the premises and procedures employed by regulators. Chapter 3 set the context for these kinds of regulatory change agents, but we explore them in greater detail in this and later chapters. Furthermore, if these forces were not sufficiently disruptive, regulators found themselves embroiled in intense intragovernmental struggles as new bureaucratic rivals, and their ministerial advocates, entered the fray to reclaim or capture "turf" – responsibilities and roles – that had hitherto been assigned to the core sectoral economic regulatory agencies.

Some of these rivals were the "home" departments whose ministers, if not directly accountable to Parliament for regulatory decisions, were responsible for reporting to Parliament on their activities and, more importantly, because of the nature of Cabinet or political appeals against individual decisions, could use such appeals in an effort to satisfy both particular societal actors and interests as well as their own bureaucratic aspirations and to impose indirectly what they could not do directly, namely, their preferred policy choices and directions. In addition, because of the far-reaching consequences of modern economic regulation, other departments such as environment or trade or bureaus such as that responsible for competition policy or promoting regulatory reform joined the battle for influence.

This chapter focuses on three of the crucial sectoral regulators; nevertheless, it must be stressed that the notion of what economic sectors are in regulatory terms is fluid and has changed and includes other regulators in this regime that we do not examine. First, there are clearly industrial sectors within sectors, such as the oil and gas and pipeline subsectors within energy, not to mention nuclear energy that has its own separate independent regulator. Second, there are sectors that have become subject to new regulators. One example is the food industry, which is regulated by the Canadian Food Inspection Agency (Prince 1999c; Doern 2010a). Moreover, because of transformational new technologies, there are industries and regulators that can be seen as both horizontal and sectoral in nature. Thus, biotechnology and its various product realms in bio-food, bio-health, and bio-life have forms of independent regulation, not by an arm's-length commission but, rather, mainly by separate science- and product-defined branches of Health Canada as a department (Doern and Prince 2012).

The chapter proceeds mainly through a basic compact political-economic historical account of the three federal sectoral regulatory agencies looking at aspects of both change and inertia and necessar ily, but briefly, with how other regulators and governance bodies and processes moved into their institutional sphere as their industrial sectors overall changed across the decades. This is followed by a set of overall observations about the three attributes in the book's analytical framework: (1) ideas, discourse, and agendas; (2) public and private power in regulation making and compliance; and (3) science, evidence, and knowledge. Throughout the chapter, we highlight some specific examples of the types of unruliness that confronted each agency, how each coped with such forces or failed to do so, and the consequent transformations that each agency went through. Although for reasons to be discussed, the CTA regulator is no longer embroiled in major political conflicts, this is not the case for either the NEB or the CRTC. Conclusions then follow.

FROM "GOVERNMENTS IN MINIATURE" TO MERE MINIATURES

The National Energy Board

We look at the NEB's evolution in five periods: (1) the origins and initial core mandate of the NEB; (2) the relative demise of the NEB in the 1980 to 1984 National Energy Policy era, (3) the role of the NEB in the dominant Mulroney era of liberalized energy markets, and (4) the consolidation of the NEB in the 1990s to 2006 period of

shared environmental and expanded safety mandates but disconnected from the climate change and Kyoto Protocol debate and
larger regulatory failure; and (5) the place of the NEB in the oil sands
and Alberta-dominated part of the current Harper era. In each of
these periods, the NEB's core public utility regulatory function is at
the centre of what it does and how it sees itself, but much else is also
a part of its mandate reach and its changing regulatory grasp and
approaches to ever more complex – mainly market-centred – conceptions of the public interest.

ORIGINS, MANDATE, AND EARLY DOMINANCE OF
THE NEB AS CENTRE OF FEDERAL ENERGY EXPERTISE
Prior to 1959, when the NEB was established, pipeline regulation
was a minor responsibility of the transport regulator. Following recommendations from two royal commissions, the NEB was created
with its primary purpose being the development of a national energy
policy (Lucas 1977, 1978). Given this objective, what was particularly notable, initially, was the complete absence of a set of overarching ideas that could guide the development of such a policy. The
creation of the NEB was a classic case of "we have a public policy
problem; you, the NEB, deal with it." Nor was there a statement of
public policy objectives, let alone policies, to shape the primary policy goal, although as indicated below, the legislation provided a set
of provisions that the NEB was to consider in the exercise of its regulatory decision making. The only concrete component of the man-
dating National Energy Board Act was a comprehensive set of
regulatory powers including the following:

• Licensing the construction of interprovincial and international
  pipelines and electric power lines
• Licensing the export and import of electric power, oil, and natural gas
• Approving rates, tariffs, and tolls for companies it regulated.

It was presumably through the exercise of these powers that the NEB
was expected to enunciate a national energy policy (except for
nuclear energy).

   The board's core policing regulatory role was that pipeline and
international power line licences were obliged to convince the NEB
that they were "required by the present and future public convenience

and necessity" (s. 44). This role is underscored by some of the requirements the applicants were expected to establish in order to obtain a
licence including:

- The availability of oil and gas to the pipeline, or power to the
  international power line
- The existence of markets, actual or potential
- The economic feasibility of the pipeline or international power line
- The extent to which Canadians will have an opportunity of par-
  ticipating in the financing, engineering, and construction of the line
- Any public interest that in the Board's opinion may be affected
  by the granting or the refusing of the application. (s. 44)

Although the NEB was the regulatory centrepiece, provision was
made for a continuing major role for the Cabinet. The exercise of all
of the NEB's powers was made subject to Cabinet approval. In short,
the NEB did not have final decision-making power with respect to
granting pipeline certificates, export or import licences, or the
charges to be levied by regulated energy companies; those decisions
had to be approved by Cabinet before taking effect. It is worth noting, however, that Cabinet's power of approval was a "negative"
power inasmuch as Cabinet could only veto NEB decisions but not
substitute or vary those decisions, unlike its powers, as we shall see,
governing decisions made by the transport and, in some respects, the
telecommunications regulatory bodies (Schultz 1977).

In some respects, particularly those related to tariff or rate regulation, the NEB's original powers appear to be the normal powers
associated with traditional policing regulation of a public utility.
However, in addition to the licensing criteria cited above, what made
the new regime fundamentally different from traditional "policing"
regulation, was the emphasis on the implied purpose of the new
energy regulator: to plan the energy sector. That this was to be its
overarching function was made clear by the fact that before the
above powers were provided for in its governing statute, the NEB
was assigned the power to constantly review and advise its designated minister, then the minister of mines and technical surveys, on
all aspects of federal responsibilities for energy "relating to the
exploration, for production, recovery, manufacture, processing,
transmission, distribution, sale, purchase, exchange, and dispersal of
energy and sources of energy within and outside Canada ... and ...

recommend to the Minister such measures ... as it considers necessary or advisable in the public interest for the control, supervision,
conservation, use, marketing and development of energy and sources
of energy" (NEB Act, s. 22(1)).

Thus, in essence, the NEB was not designed to be simply an economic policing agency constraining the economic conduct of its
charges. It was designed to manage the energy sector through the
development of an integrated, overarching plan for that sector.
Despite its dominant expertise, however, no national energy plan
was developed or proposed by the NEB during its first decade of
operations. This is not to argue that it did not play a more positive
role as opposed to simply policing the behaviour of those subject to
its jurisdiction. Like other federal regulators, the NEB settled into a
close, some would subsequently argue too cozy, relationship with
those it regulated. In modern political science parlance, energy regulation in the 1960s was an extremely closed network comprised of
the regulator and the immediately regulated. Others seldom were
tempted, nor were they encouraged, to enter the "sacred garden" in
this first decade.

In lieu of developing an integrated national energy policy, the NEB
chose to concentrate on one role, that of promotion, specifically promoting the export of natural gas and oil to the United States. As
McDougall (1982) has noted, the NEB embraced "export orientation" as its primary concern in this period:

> the board revealed that it was more concerned with expanding
> the volume of export sales than with realizing the full value of
> those sales ... In the area of pipeline construction, the board
> made several decisions to approve new or expanded pipeline
> facilities that were explicitly justified, at least in part, with refer-
> ence to the favourable impact they would have on the future
> marketability of Canadian oil and gas in the United States. (99)

During most of this decade, there was little opposition to this promotional role of the NEB because there was little conflict among those
concerned with NEB regulation, especially because there appeared to
be enough oil and gas to satisfy Canadian consumers at reasonable
prices. For most of this decade, as well, there was little demand, inside
or outside of government, for a national energy policy.

The 1970s, however, exhibited several changes regarding how others were viewing the NEB. First, traditional participants before the NEB began to challenge the board's "export orientation." Large industrial users such as BC Hydro as well as representatives from the consuming provinces joined them in their advocacy that their residents and industrial consumers would suffer from a too liberal policy of exports (McDougall 1982). Second, the NEB's ability to manage the emerging conflicts was made even more complicated with the emergence of consumer and environmental groups with different ideas that challenged the promotional emphasis the board had adopted. These new actors brought new ideas and an insistence that they had both a right to participate in NEB hearings and have their views taken into account.

A third change came from within the federal government, particularly other departments with overlapping responsibilities. One of the first was the Department of Energy, Mines, and Natural Resources (EMR), created in 1966 with one of its prime responsibilities being to advise its minister on energy issues. For the first five years of its existence, EMR was prepared to defer to the NEB with a similar mandate; after that, the department became much more aggressive and went so far as to lobby the government to restrict funds for the NEB for policy advisory personnel on the grounds that the board was simply duplicating what the department was mandated to do (Doern and Toner 1985; Doern 1999a).

Other departments, such as Transport, Fisheries, and Forestry also became active in advising on energy issues as did External Affairs with respect to Canadian-American concerns. Another department, Consumer and Corporate Affairs, while not intervening directly in NEB proceedings, had an indirect impact through its funding of consumer group interventions before regulatory agencies including the NEB (Schultz 2000). One of the reasons for the growing success of this departmental invasion of the NEB's policy space was the increasing concern that that the board was too close to the energy industry, which made the government overly reliant on industry information.

THE NEB IN THE 1980 TO 1984 NATIONAL
ENERGY PLAN ERA
The mid- and late 1970s was characterized by oil and energy turbulence globally, which resulted in a doubling and then a tripling of

world oil prices. These energy price and supply shocks changed national energy policy and the NEB's role in it out of all recognition. The issues ranged from conflicts between energy-producing and energy-consuming provinces and citizens, foreign ownership of energy companies, Canadian energy self-sufficiency and the question of exports to the United States, the distribution of revenues as a result of the sudden and drastic rise in oil prices between the federal government and energy-producing provinces, the urgency of northern energy development, and the appropriate mix of environmental standards. Against this background of mega-conflict, it was obvious that the idea of expert-based, non-political regulatory agency such as the NEB designing a national energy plan was dead.

That this was the case was made clear in 1980, when the newly elected Liberal government unveiled its National Energy Plan (Doern and Toner 1985). This was an economic regulatory regime based on a set of ideas that constituted a fundamental break with those that had been central to the previous regime, a radical change in institutions as well as public policies to give effect to the ideas. The primary ideas were, first, promoting security of energy supply which went beyond sufficiency; second, Canadianizing the energy sector to reduce to 50 per cent the extent of foreign control; and finally, redistributing the benefits of the greatly increased world price in oil through revenue sharing among all Canadians to meet the claimed objective of fairness, rather than permitting all the benefits to accrue to the energy-producing companies and provinces.

The primary policies to give effect to those ideas included petroleum incentive grants to encourage Canadian corporate exploration and development, a reservation of a 25 per cent interest for the federal government in any oil or gas found in the newly designated Canada Lands in the Arctic, a special place for the federal Crown corporation, Petro Canada, and finally, not relying on market mechanisms to set and distribute the pricing of energy, especially oil.

A combination of existing and new institutions was established to pursue and implement the new set of public policies. Among the new institutions were the Canada Oil and Gas Lands Administration, the Office of Industrial and Regional Benefits, the Petroleum Incentives Administration, the Petroleum Monitoring Agency to monitor the extent of foreign ownership, and a strengthened Northern Pipeline Agency, created in 1978 to supervise pipeline development. One key characteristic of some of these agencies is that while they played an indirect regulatory role, they were created, in large part, to play developmental planning roles.

The NEB played no role whatsoever in the formulation of the National Energy Policy. The NEB was completely shut out of the policy development process, and its regulatory roles were further reduced by the creation of new regulatory and energy policy implementation institutions. Henceforth, the primary role of the NEB was to be limited to the traditional policing regulatory role with respect to interprovincial pipeline tolls and the prevention of market power abuse.

THE NEB IN THE MULRONEY ERA OF LIBERALIZED ENERGY MARKETS

The election of the Mulroney Conservative government, in 1984, brought fundamental changes to the energy regulatory regime. As we have seen in chapter 2, the Conservatives embraced market-based ideas and concomitant policies on the assumption that as much as possible, markets, not government regulation, should determine energy prices, output, and allocation. The first step, taken in 1985, was to deregulate crude oil marketing and pricing as well as the licensing of exports. This was followed by gas pricing deregulation and the substitution of direct buy-sell relationships and negotiations between gas producers and users (Toner 1986; Doern 1999a). The only role in these areas for the NEB was to resolve disputes through arbitration rather than rule making. This was extended by ending the NEB's surplus reserve rules governing exports and substituting a much lighter monitoring and challenge process. The Mulroney era's later signature Canada-US Free Trade Agreement, in 1988, also consolidated liberalized energy markets, in large part because of a desire led by Alberta to prevent any future National Energy Policy–like policy interventions and adventures (Doern and Tomlin 1991).

The Mulroney government kept the NEB's core pipeline utility regulatory functions but gave it strengthened environmental and safety regulation mandates. As a result of both the economic deregulatory initiatives and the newer regulatory focus on environmental assessments and safety monitoring, the NEB in the Mulroney era returned to a changed version of the "quiet life" that marked its first decade. The NEB was also moved out of Ottawa and relocated to Calgary, where it functions in the heart of the Canadian energy industry, and it was increasingly funded by industry fees rather than by taxpayers (Doern 1999a; Doern and Gattinger 2003). The NEB also sought to be more business-like under the then-growing ethos of reinvented government and aspects of the new public management with its greater customer and client service focus while continuing to view energy as an essential service networked industry.

The Mulroney period saw the development of joint federal and provincial offshore regulators to deal with the developing offshore oil and gas industry. Thus, new sectoral regulators such as the Canada-Newfoundland Offshore Petroleum Board and the Canada-Nova Scotia Offshore Petroleum Board were established (Clancy 2011; Sinclair 2011). But offshore energy regulation had to be quintessentially energy-environmental regulation virtually from the outset, in part because of different kinds and complexities of risk, centred on the oceans and the fisheries and, hence, on a different array of global energy exploration and production companies but also shipping and common resource players and communities.

THE 1990S TO 2006: THE NEB'S SHARED
ENVIRONMENTAL AND EXPANDED SAFETY MANDATES
DISCONNECTED FROM THE CLIMATE CHANGE
AND KYOTO PROTOCOL REGULATORY FAILURE

While the NEB had been under pressure to adopt an expanded environmental regulatory role, the mandate requirement was fundamentally triggered by the passage of the federal Canadian Environmental Assessment Act in 1995. The NEB was a "responsible authority" under the act and, thus, had to coordinate its assessments on a joint basis with Environment Canada's Canadian Environmental Assessment Agency (Doern 2007, chapter 4).

The NEB was also required to find its own way of practising *sustainable development*, a policy commitment of Natural Resources Canada, its parent department and of the Chrétien-Martin Liberal governments. Sustainable development policy refers to policies whose intent is to ensure in any number of areas of governance that the environment and its ecosystems are left in at least as good a state for the next generation as they were for the current generation (Toner 2006; Jaccard 2006). Cast somewhat more loosely, such policies are often seen by governments as those that take into consideration the economic, social, and environmental effects of policies, the so-called triple bottom line. The NEB finessed this sustainable development pressure in that it was very reluctant to see its statutory mandate contain sustainable development obligations, but it did argue in its annual reports that it did, in fact, practice sustainable development in the triple bottom line sense of the concept (NEB 2001, 24). In later reports in both the Liberal and Harper eras, the NEB has also argued that its goal was *sustainable energy development* which may or may not have meant sustainable development but which does harken back, especially in an Alberta historical context, to early oil and gas conservation measures.

It is fair to say that the NEB was largely disconnected from the climate change debate and Canada's abject failures to meet its international commitments under the Kyoto Protocol regarding reductions in greenhouse gas emissions. Canada, as a Kyoto Protocol signatory country, undertook to reduce its greenhouse gas emissions by 6 per cent below its 1990 levels averaged over the period 2008–12. But, instead, Canada's emissions increased markedly (Rivers and Jaccard 2009). The core problem is how to achieve the reductions, which in Canada's case were set without reference to the cost of meeting them or any clear sense of the mixture to be used of regulation and technology.

As Canadian analysts have shown, the Canadian underperformance was largely the result of policy and regulatory failures. But it was also due to Canada's higher population growth and also better overall economic growth compared with many other countries during the last decade. However, they were to do so under a guiding policy principle (not a rule) that no region should bear an unreasonable burden from implementing the Kyoto Protocol. Thus was implanted, at the political level, the central importance of a policy regarding equity considerations among Canada's regions (Eberlein and Doern 2009).

Such a policy was undoubtedly needed in an overall national unity sense, but it was especially imperative for accommodating Alberta, which was already often rhetorically casting federal policy on Kyoto as "another NEP," a reference to the 1980 Liberal National Energy Policy that was detested in Alberta. Of course, Alberta knew that it was the province at the heart of the carbon-producing part of Canada, albeit not the core carbon-using part (Brownsey 2005, 2006). Central Canadian industries were also major carbon emitters, and of course, Canadians as consumers are energy polluters in a fundamental sense as well. In the end, the Harper Conservatives in 2011 withdrew Canada from the Kyoto Protocol and did not suffer much politically for having done so (Doern and Stoney 2012, chapter 1).

Much like the above-mentioned National Energy Policy era, the NEB was essentially not directly engaged in the climate change process. It was undoubtedly hearing from Alberta and other national oil and gas interests and contributing some analysis of Canadian and global energy markets, but otherwise the NEB could, again, basically hunker down into its core pipeline public utility and now augmented but narrowly interpreted environmental roles.

THE NEB IN THE CURRENT OIL SANDS AND ALBERTA-
DOMINATED HARPER ENERGY POLICY
In the decade from 2002 to 2012, the NEB's changing view of itself is partly captured in sample annual reports that both chronicle and respond to new pressures and market dynamics during the latter Chrétien years and then in the Harper minority and majority government contexts. For example, the 2004 annual report states that the NEB's overall purpose is to "promote safety, environmental protection and economic efficiency in the Canadian public interest within the mandate set by Parliament in the regulation of pipelines, energy development and trade" (NEB 2005, 1). This same statement also leads off the first Harper NEB annual report for 2007 (NEB 2008, 1).

By the time of the 2011 Harper era report, however, the NEB's stated purpose is reordered to "regulate pipelines, energy development and trade in the Canadian public interest" (NEB 2012a, ii). The safety and environmental aspects of the NEB's mandate are mentioned in the next "goals" section. This expressed reordering may be the NEB's reading of the federal political tea leaves where, as we have already seen in chapter 2, the Harper era has been featured by a strong pro-energy development and resource export ethos and set of policies cast increasingly under the discourse of Canada as an energy superpower. It was reiterated as well in a 2012 Senate report whose title is *Now or Never* and which argues for why Canada must act urgently "to seize its place in the new energy world order" (Standing Senate Committee on Energy, the Environment and Natural Resources 2012, 1).

But these are not the only ways in which successive reports capture and reflect the NEB's more recent approaches and the ways they have been expressed. Regarding the NEB's core role, the 2004 report refers to how it both needs "to *protect* and *enable* in order to achieve outcomes that are in the public interest" (NEB 2005, 1). The enable function "implies a responsibility to *make possible*" (ibid., 1–2) and, hence, is a somewhat gentler substitute for the NEB's developmental role for the energy industry. The report also cites the NEB's Liberal-era smart regulation approaches that include the greater deployment of goal-oriented performance-based regulation and service standards. But in more particular substantive ways, the report draws attention to key issues and engagement challenges such as high and volatile energy prices, strained infrastructure given new oil sands production, and issues regarding Aboriginal legal rights.

The 2007 NEB summary of itself leads off with a focus on its high capacity workload in the face of having to deal with issues that "grew in complexity" (NEB 2008, 1). That year the NEB had a staff of about 300 but in the mid-1990s its staff had been cut to 260 or about a 50 per cent reduction from the late 1980s (Doern and Gattinger 2003, 102). Staff capacity has grown in the Harper years to about 400 in 2011.

While such staff changes and data can only be taken so far in ana-lytical terms, they do relate to the issue of how many front-line and middle-level analytical resources can a regulatory agency have and still get the job done given that the job was growing quite markedly and in complex ways. This kind of issue is, ultimately, tied as well to the need for other kinds of partnered market and NGO-based eyes and ears in management-based approaches to regulation and compliance, as discussed initially in chapter 1.

Thus, the 2007 NEB annual report highlights early on the Board's risk-based life cycle approach that "relates to a company's performance as well as the scope of regulatory oversight required through the life cycle of a project" (NEB 2008, 1). But the Board also refers to its establishment of a Land Matters Consultation Initiative, a general growing problem but one triggered especially by angry and aggressive landowners in Alberta, in particular, defending their property rights against energy company development encroachments. Such property rights and related land and resource management and boundary issues had often been important in Alberta politics and, as will be seen in chapter 7, property rights arise in the overall marketplace framework regulatory regime in issues related to intellectual property and common public property resources.

By the time of the 2011 annual report, the NEB was stressing its needed broadening approaches in public engagement (NEB 2012, 1–2). This included pre-eminently consultations regarding Canadian Arctic offshore drilling. A report late in 2011 set out the information that the Board would need to assess in any future applications for Artic offshore drilling (NEB 2011). The previously mentioned Land Matters Initiative had by 2011 resulted in the Board forming a Land Matters Group, which was drafting approaches to company involvement programs. More broadly, the Board drew attention to how it has taken steps in getting companies to develop "a strong safety culture through a management systems approach" (NEB 2012, 2, 14). The dynamics of the oil sands era was also revealed through the fact that the applications to the Board for various approvals and licences had doubled over the previous year.

At the centre of current Harper-era NEB-related strategy is the Harper government's determination to drive and promote energy exports, in part because of the potential of growing Chinese and East Asian demands for oil and gas and in part because of the need for some kind of counterweight to oil sands supply opposition in the United States (Doern and Stoney 2012). The Joint Review Panel mandated by the NEB's statute and the Canadian Environmental Assessment Act is currently embroiled in a lengthy and controversial hearing process on the proposed Enbridge Northern Gateway pipeline involving more than 4,000 intervenors.

This hearing is taking place in the context of a larger set of conflicts involving the Harper government. One is that it has already indicated that it supports the construction of the pipeline. It has imposed a strict deadline on the review panel to complete its report. The streamlining order also specifies that the federal Cabinet will have the final say, not the NEB (Environment Canada; NEB 2012a, 2012b).

This follows the Harper government's frustration with, and verbal attacks on, environmental groups, which allege that some are using "foreign money" and/or exceeding their budgets for policy advocacy and intervention and thus abusing their tax free charitable status. Consequently, the Harper government has legislated major changes that affect the NEB/environmental hearing and decision-making process. In the first place, it has imposed conditions on who may henceforth obtain standing to appear before the NEB. They must now be "directly affected" by any proposed pipeline, which suggests that people who wish to intervene must be on or near a pipeline's proposed route. This would, for example, exclude large numbers of those who are currently participating in the Northern Gateway project. Many of these changes also reflect Alberta energy regulatory regime practices including newly proposed extensions of them (Alberta 2010, 2011).

The NEB is presently at the centre of up to five multiple pipeline proposals for new or extended pipelines.

Overall, the NEB's five-decade evolution is necessarily a two-part story. At its core, the NEB still retains its basic policing public utility sectoral regulatory role albeit in a more complex oil and gas market, now dominated by high volume, globally significant oil sands development. This it has carried out despite significant periods when it was basically shut out of broader energy policy and regulatory developments in both the National Energy Policy and climate change periods and, to some significant extent, in the current Harper export-driven agenda. But the NEB has also been subject to, and a player in, other regulatory mandate tasks centred on an environmental assessment mandate but also on broadened notions of pipeline safety, security, and risk management. And, of course, as we have seen, the NEB has seen other regulators, departmental and arm's-length in nature, move into what is now increasingly a more complex regulatory terrain, whether cast as sectoral regulators per se or as a mix of interacting sectoral and framework regulators. This is even truer if one includes other provincial regulators whose roles we have referred to but not examined. These include regulators where the dominant energy concerns, depending on provincial resource endowments, are centred more on electricity.

The Canadian Transportation Agency and Canadian Transport Commission

Although its institutional roots can be traced to Canada's first independent regulatory agency, the Board of Railway Commissioners established in 1903, the CTA, known from 1967 to 1987 as the Canadian Transport Commission (CTC), was Canada's second modern regulatory agency. Created in 1967, the CTC was, like the NEB, to be the primary planning agency for the sector with an overarching responsibility "to coordinate and harmonize" all modes of transportation under federal jurisdiction. As the then minister of transport, and soon to be first president of the CTC, stated during the parliamentary debates on its creation: "one of the most important things of all is to have one unified organ of government divorced from any of these different modes of transport which will look at all of them, compare one with another, and, when considering the regulation of one, would take account of what is happening in the other fields" (quoted in Janisch 1978a, 168).

ORIGINS AND MANDATE OF THE TRANSPORT REGULATOR
Prior to 1967, the federal transport regulator, then the Board of
Transport Commissioners, had a comprehensive mandate in name
only as it was in effect primarily a railway regulator. As such, the
central idea behind the regulatory regime was that railways had
quasi-monopolistic market power and consequently there was need
to police railway rates to protect shippers by ensuring that rates
were "just and reasonable" and "not unduly discriminatory." From
its origins, in 1903, the railway regulator resolutely and consistently
rejected the idea that it should use its rate regulatory power to promote economic or social goals (Darling 1980). As it stated in another
context but drawing on its six decades of railway regulation, its role
was "to regulate not initiate." Subsequently, it stated that it "had no
duty ... to mould [a tariff] suitable to various conditions and areas
of traffic, dependent upon a multitude of conditions" (quoted in
Schultz and Alexandroff 1985, 77). One of the consequences of this
restricted definition of its regulatory role was the recurrent need for
the federal government to resort to royal commissions to address
"the railway problem" and to provide subsidies to respond to the
demands of both unions and regional interests that could not find
accommodations from the regulator.

The decision to adopt a profoundly different economic regulatory
regime was the result of the MacPherson Royal Commission (Janisch
1978a, 1978b; Heaver and Nelson 1977, 1978; McManus 1978).
The new regime was premised on a single overarching idea, namely,
that the railways had lost, for the most part, their market power as
a result of the growth of competition, especially from the trucking
industry and, consequently, should be released from most of the constraints of rate regulation. The emphasis on competition, and the
concomitant decreased reliance on regulation to police railway rate
behaviour, was demonstrated in the objectives of new national transportation policy which stated:

> it is hereby declared than an economic, efficient and adequate
> transportation system making the best use of all available modes
> of transport at the lowest total cost is essential to protect the
> interests of all users of transportation ... and these objectives are
> most likely to be achieved when all modes of transport are able
> to compete. (National Transportation Act 1966–67, c. 69, s. 3)

The statute went on to assert that "regulation of all modes of transport will not be such as to restrict the ability of any mode of transport to compete freely with other modes of transport" (ibid.). The policy instrument chosen to achieve this objective insofar as the railways were concerned was to end rate regulation, as it had existed since the early 1900s, and to grant them considerable, albeit not complete, freedom to set their rates without regulatory approval. The policy of rate deregulation was not absolute, however, as shippers were granted the right to appeal rates once filed by the railways with the CTC, but the long-standing onus on the railways to justify them was shifted to shippers to establish that there was a prima facie case that any challenged rates were contrary to the public interest, a requirement that would prove to be a very high threshold of proof for shippers. Despite this threshold, the appeal mechanism was couched, as McManus (1978) has noted in very vague criteria such as "the public interest," "undue obstacle," "unfair disadvantage," and "unreasonable discouragement." The vagueness of these criteria would become a source of much conflict that would threaten to undermine the new regulatory regime within a few years of its creation.

Before turning to a discussion of other aspects of the new regime and its immediate development, several comments are necessary. The first is that it should be acknowledged that the National Transportation Act (NTA) of 1966–67 was clearly the first major deregulatory initiative not only in Canada but also in North America. Second, although it is commonplace to link deregulation with conservative governments as reflected in the subsequent cliché linking Thatcher-Reagan-Mulroney as the arch deregulationists, this was an initiative of the Pearson Liberal government, one widely regarded as among the most progressive in Canada's history. The embrace of deregulation in 1967 was not motivated by so-called neo-liberal or neo-conservative principles but was seen as a progressive initiative that would advance both consumer interests and the national economy. Similar arguments would be made in the coming decade in the United States, by public interest advocates such as Ralph Nader and liberal politicians such as Senator Ted Kennedy and President Jimmy Carter. The Canadian railway precedent and its apparent success in improving railway productivity profoundly shaped American liberal reconsideration of regulation and its alternatives.

As mentioned, the primary institutional feature of the new transport regulatory regime was the Canadian Transport Commission.

One aspect of this new entity was that the agency, like the NEB before it, was also expected to be the primary policy adviser to the minister of transport and the Cabinet. As a consequence, the Ministry of Transport publicly announced that it would reorient its mission and limit itself to operational matters so as not to conflict with the CTC on policy matters. The CTC mandate, however, was not as straightforward as the preceding description may suggest. Although it was to monitor and enforce the substantial deregulation of railway pricing, it was, as noted, also mandated to "coordinate and harmonize" all modes of transportation under federal jurisdiction, which would appear to be an invitation to plan the transport sector, something that was in conflict with its deregulatory thrust.

The new legislation assigned licensing and price-setting responsibilities for the Canadian airline sector to the CTC, thus ending the approximately thirty years of Cabinet licensing of airline entry. Licensing of airline entry, particularly the allocation of routes, was subject to applicants' meeting a "public convenience and necessity test," one that had been employed since 1937 primarily to promote the interests of the publicly owned national carrier, Air Canada, as it was renamed in 1965. Related to this test was the fact that at least for the first decade of the CTC's existence, Air Canada continued to have special status before the regulator that allowed it, if it had ministerial approval, to pre-empt regulatory consideration of competitive applications for routes it wanted.

As a consequence, the CTC's mandate was a rather complicated and somewhat inconsistent mixture of light-handed regulation of railway rates, planning the entire transport sector, and controlling the extent and nature of competition in the airline sector. This was unquestionably a mandate that would lead ineluctably to considerable political conflicts, and thus, it is perhaps not surprising that appointments to the CTC of all the three major economic regulators were the most political and partisan in nature, especially the position of president. The first four presidents of the CTC were former Cabinet ministers, three Liberal and one Conservative, who went directly from Cabinet to the regulatory agency. In no other federal regulatory arena has this practice been matched. As we shall see, although the CTC was on occasion far more deferential to its political "masters" than other economic regulators, most notably the CRTC, there was still ample opportunity for political conflicts and regulatory turmoil and concerns that the CTC had too much independent policy-making power.

UNRULINESS IN TRANSPORT REGULATION, 1967–87

Unlike the NEB, there was no golden age for the CTC, as it quickly became embroiled in three major conflicts that would roil the economic regulatory regime and, in part, contribute in 1987 to its transformation. Each conflict involved fundamental questions about the nature of the regime and the role of the regulator and involved a complex set of actors, societal and governmental. The first brought into question the CTC's commitment to its planning role of "coordinating and harmonizing" all modes of transport subject to its jurisdiction. The second was a fundamental challenge to the central idea of deregulating railway rate setting that was the cornerstone of the 1967 legislation. The third centred on the airline industry and would reflect the emergence of new players in the regulatory system and the impact of international, largely American, influences on regulatory ideas

One of the central principles of the 1967 regulatory regime was that its basic philosophy was that any mode of transport could compete freely with any other mode. The justification for the relaxed regulation of the railways was the intense competition they faced from interprovincial and international trucking. It was this competition that the MacPherson Commission emphasized as its justification for reducing significantly the regulatory controls on railway tariffs. Furthermore, as the trucking industry, as a result of the 1954 delegation of federal authority to regulate the extra-provincial segment of the industry to the provinces, was regulated by a mosaic of conflicting and competing provincial controls, the new regime was premised on the termination of that delegation and the imposition of unified federal control. The trucking industry had long been an opponent of federal regulation, fearing that it would be employed to favour its competitors, the railways, but was persuaded by the departmental architects of the new regime that it would receive equal regulatory, that is, relaxed, treatment by the CTC (Schultz 1980, 1995).

Termination of the federal delegation could not be done unilaterally, however, but would involve complex negotiations with the provinces, which had employed their individual regulatory systems – not surprisingly – to pursue provincial goals and interests, including those of provincial trucking companies. These negotiations began in earnest in the early 1970s and soon were dominated by two factors. One was the fact that, notwithstanding its legislative mandate, the CTC indicated that it had no desire to exercise its planning function to coordinate and harmonize all modes of transport.

Despite the fact that as minister of transport the first CTC president had invoked the centrality of bringing trucking regulation under federal jurisdiction, under his direction the CTC made it clear it did not want jurisdiction over the extra-provincial trucking industry and, consequently, did everything possible to undermine federal attempts to recapture its jurisdictional responsibilities. This led it into direct conflict with the newly reorganized Ministry of Transport (MOT).

The previous ministry early on realized that it had ceded far too much of its policy role to the CTC in the 1966–67 legislation and sought, through its reorganization, to assert its policy primacy over the CTC (Langford 1976). While the MOT was technically responsible for managing the intergovernmental negotiations over recovering its jurisdiction over the trucking industry, the CTC, which had to be consulted on the federal bargaining positions, in effect created such an effective roadblock (pun intended) that the negotiations failed and with the failure derailed one of the primary functions of the CTC, much to its satisfaction.

The second major challenge to the 1966–67 regulatory regime came as a result of two factors. While the railways quickly embraced their newfound rate-setting freedom, the western provinces, encouraged by some regional shippers, increasingly became hostile to the new regime. In particular, starting in 1973, they argued that the current policy and CTC's light-handed approach to railway rate regulation was hindering western economic development (Heaver and Nelson 1977, 8). The Liberal government, then a minority government with little representation from the West, was receptive to the demands. The argument was that the CTC was focusing exclusively on the "economic and efficient" component of its mandate and, as such, was insufficiently concerned about the disadvantages that railway rates might impose. They insisted that regional economic development should be included as a goal of transportation and, hence, of regulatory policy. This issue came to a head in 1974–75 and pitted western provinces and producers against Ontario and Quebec and their producers. When the CTC tried to resolve the conflict by postponing a 25 per cent rate increase, the railways successfully appealed to the Supreme Court for a ruling that the CTC did not have the legislative authority to impose such a suspension (ibid., 250–2).

The Liberal government, although now with a majority but still suffering from limited western representation in its caucus, responded with a two-pronged legislative proposal. The first was to add as a fundamental objective to guide the CTC that the transportation system was to be an instrument of support for the achievement of national and regional social and economic objectives. If implemented, this would have transformed railway regulation, in particular, into a promotional tool. In addition to such a profound change in the basic ideas of the regulatory regime, the government also proposed that it be given the power to issue policy directions to the CTC regarding the interpretation of the statutory policy objectives.

This proposal reflected, in part, the government's concern that emerged shortly after the creation of the CTC that it had, in fact, delegated too much policy-making power to the regulator and that Cabinet appeals, which were becoming more frequent, and not only, as we shall see in railway decisions, were inadequate as a means of transmitting policy guidance. It is worth noting, however, that in part because of staunch opposition from both the railways and most shipper organizations, these proposals were not transformed into legislation.

The third challenge to the 1966–67 regulatory regime came in the airline sector and it came in two forms. The first was the challenge to the national carriers from regional airlines while the second came from consumer discontent with airfares and offerings. From the beginning of airline economic regulation in 1937 until well into the early 1970s, the overarching goal of the regulation of entry was to promote and protect the national publicly owned carrier, Air Canada. Only in the 1960s was competition from Canadian Pacific Airways gradually permitted and, even then, under very strenuous conditions (Corbett 1965; Stevenson 1987).

In the pre-CTC era, the regulator had used its licensing power to require applicants to demonstrate that any application to serve a route met the legislated test of "public convenience and necessity." This test was employed to protect, first, Air Canada, and then the other national carrier, Canadian Pacific Airlines, from competition that might threaten their profitability and ability to serve. Prior to 1967, the regulator had only an advisory role to the Cabinet in licensing entry, and this relationship explains why it was deferential to its political masters when in 1966 the minister of transport outlined the conditions under which regional airlines would be licensed, including notably, the condition they would not be able to compete directly with the two national carriers (Stevenson 1987). This deference carried over to the CTC when in 1969 the minister of transport announced more detailed regional spheres of operation for the five regional carriers who were "to supplement the domestic mainline operations of Air Canada and CPA ... They will not be directly competitive on any substantial scale" (quoted in Schultz and Alexandroff 1985, 44). The CTC adopted this policy statement as binding on it even though neither the minister nor the Cabinet was legally authorized to direct the CTC on policy issues.

The development of the regional air policy was an indication that federal air regulation had been transformed from a promotional into a planning tool with the government even going so far as to suggest that the regulator might have to regulate its licensees' aircraft purchases so as to give effect to its policy. The problem, as Stevenson noted, was that the five operating regions to which the regionals were to be confined were "arbitrary, artificial, and, most significantly, for the future health of the industry, unequal" (1987, 75). Notwithstanding these qualities, there might not have been a problem with the overall objective of using licensing to plan the air sector but for one major development.

Provincial governments, which had largely ignored the air transportation field prior to the 1970s, began to mirror the federal government's nation-building air objectives by promoting their own regional champions for provincial policy and political purposes (Schultz and Alexandroff 1985; Stevenson 1987). Disputes developed involving all five regional airlines with the regulatory agency caught in the middle of a wide-ranging series of intergovernmental conflicts. On one occasion involving Alberta's purchase of Pacific Western Airlines, that province successfully challenged before the Supreme Court of Canada the authority of the CTC to review the purchase. On other decisions where the CTC used the government's policy statement to deny provincially supported route applications, the provinces successfully appealed to Cabinet to overrule its regulator, thus undermining its own policy statement.

Nothing better demonstrates the turmoil in federal air regulation than the policy flip-flops that occurred in the first half decade of the 1980s. In 1981, the federal minister of transport who could not persuade his Cabinet colleagues to endorse his preferred policy released a policy paper that sought to re-establish a version of the now-discredited regional air policy. Canada was to be divided into two regions with controls on length of flights regional carriers would be permitted supplemented by CTC regulation on the types of aircraft that carriers could purchase. Almost every concerned interest criticized the new policy including the federal Department of Consumer and Corporate

Affairs and the Economic Council of Canada and, in fact, a parliamentary committee which concluded that "the prospect of competition is the principal inducement to efficient performance in the airline industry" (quoted in Schultz and Alexandroff 1985, 58). Although the then-minister rejected the call for deregulation, his immediate successor in 1984 released his own policy statement that called for the effective end of the use of regulation to control airlines and to substitute competition, at least for southern Canada. It is worth noting that the president of the CTC indicated to the minister that he would give effect to the new policy, again notwithstanding the fact that the minister lacked legislative authority to compel the CTC to do so (Stevenson 1987, 191).

The second major cause of turmoil in the air sector came as a result of growing consumer discontent with airline prices and offerings in the 1970s. With the growth of disposable income in the 1960s, more and more Canadians wanted to travel but found it far too expensive. A partial substitute was found in international charters but strict conditions were placed on such offerings so as not to undermine the profitability of the two national airlines that operated internationally. Consumer groups began to appear before the CTC to demand lower prices and varied ticket options for domestic flights but, as happened when they appeared before the NEB, the CTC was reluctant to grant them either any legitimacy or accede to their demands (Kane 1980). Recognizing the consumer pressures, the national airlines sought to deflect them by offering special fares but at such restrictive numbers and conditions that they could not meet the demand (Reschenthaler 1978). Consumer groups subsequently appealed to Cabinet to overturn the CTC's approval of the restricted fares which Cabinet supported and ordered the CTC to compel the airlines to offer such fares on a much less restrictive basis. Again, it is worth noting that Cabinet had no authority to issue the second part of the appeal decision (Reschenthaler and Roberts 1978).

One of the factors fuelling consumer discontent in the latter half of the 1970s was the American deregulation of airlines introduced in 1976, which was accompanied by a significant decline in prices as well as the growth of new airlines seeking to cater to consumer demand. Furthermore, increasingly, Canadians living near American cities close to the Canada-US border such as Burlington, Vermont, Buffalo, New York, and Bellingham, Washington, to name just three, were opting to drive to those cities to take advantage of the much cheaper fares to fly to American destinations, especially in the south, than were available from Canadian airlines. This resulted in a significant loss to the Canadian market and was one of the primary reasons behind the 1984 deregulation proposals.

THE DEMISE OF TRANSPORT REGULATION, 1985–2012
By the mid-1980s, the transportation regulatory regime was in disarray. Indeed, a subsequent regulator described it as "obsolete" (CTA 2012). Planning was no longer possible for the airline sector as mergers and acquisitions had eroded the national/regional airline distinction, and passengers continued to leave the Canadian system to take advantage of low American fares at the nearest border airports. There was a similar development in the rail sector as a result of the American deregulation in the late 1970s. Large Canadian shippers requiring long-haul service found that they could exploit the opportunity to negotiate confidential contracts at the nearest Canada-US border crossing to use American railroads for the largest portion of their travel before returning to the Canadian system. The loss of this traffic was a major blow to Canadian railway companies (Schultz 1988, 1995; Hill, 1998, 1999a; Heaver and Waters II 2005).

In 1985, the new Conservative government announced its proposals for the regulation of the transport sector, which it enacted in 1987 (Canada 1985b). While it appeared that little would change as the primary policy objective was the existing somewhat contradictory goal of an "economic, efficient and adequate system" to which the goals of "safe and viable" had been added, this was misleading. Notwithstanding these goals, the new economic regime emphasized new goals, new regulatory roles and instruments, and a fundamentally reduced role for regulation and the regulatory agency.

The new regime, incorporating the pro-market approach adapted by the government for the energy sector as well as the previous Liberal government's proposed air policy, was the first truly comprehensive and integrated regulatory policy regime for Canadian transportation. Its core idea was that the rail and air sectors no longer needed even policing regulation, for the most part, let alone planning regulation. Regulation would no longer be available for either exogenous objectives such as regional development in the setting of rail sectors or the promotion/protection of individual companies in the air sector. Markets would be allowed, indeed encouraged, as the primary control mechanism and regulators, when called upon, would be strictly confined in the role they could play.

Moreover, the CTA's parent department, Transport Canada overall has, since the 1980s and 1990s shed or devolved many aspects of direct management and regulation which is mainly why its portfolio of agencies as a ministry is so large (Hill 1999a; Ranger 2010). These include airports, ports, and other regulatory agencies that are now highly decentralized or made independent. These changes were made under the rubric of both privatization and liberalization (in the 1980s) and the mid-1990s program review budget cutting and efficiency rationales (Doern 2010b).

More specifically, in the air sector, Canada would be divided into two geographical zones, north and south, with the south completely deregulated. Rather than employing the anti-competitive "public convenience and necessity" test, would-be entrants need only establish that they were "fit, willing and able," which granted very limited discretion to the regulator. There would be no route, schedule, or fare regulation in the south, and airlines could discontinue routes subject to minimal, formal advance notification. There would be residual regulation for airlines serving the north as it was presumed that competition at the time was not possible.

Similar changes were imposed on the railroads. The previously liberalized system of minimum and maximum rates would be replaced by rate deregulation and the use of railway-shipper negotiation of confidential rates. To further one of the central premises of the new rail regime, the system would be tilted in favour of shippers (Hill 1988) in that if individual shippers and a railway could not successfully negotiate a contract, both could submit a final offer to the regulator for approval, but what was crucial to the new system was that the regulator was restricted to choosing one or the other offer. Similarly captive shippers were guaranteed liberalized interswitching and "competitive line rates" to get them to the nearest point where they could transfer to another railroad (Heaver and Waters II 2005). The one major concession to the railways in the new regime was they were given greater, but not complete, freedom to abandon non-economic branch lines.

In addition to confining the regulator within very narrow constraints to act as an instrument for dispute resolution, the new regime radically reformed it as an organization. Renamed the Canadian

Transportation Agency, the membership and the staff of the new body was significantly reduced and the terms of the former were cut in half to five years. Just as importantly, two major changes were imposed to emphasize that the CTA would no longer have a policy role. One was to subject its rules and regulations to prior Cabinet approval before taking effect. The other was to grant Cabinet the authority to issue binding policy directives on any matter within its jurisdiction.

As discussed above, one of the major provisions of the 1966–67 regime called for the resumption of federal jurisdiction over the extra-provincial trucking industry, a provision that was never implemented. The 1987 legislation adopted a different approach to this issue. Although recognizing that the existing system of multiple provincial jurisdictions inhibited the competitive nature of the trucking industry, the new legislation, reflecting in part the new government's approach to federal-provincial relations did not opt to reclaim its jurisdiction. Instead, it passed legislation to encourage the provinces to deregulate the industry and allow it to harmonize the regulatory system to remove barriers to competition. The incentive for the provinces to cooperate was that, given railway deregulation, maintenance of heavy-handed provincial regulation of trucking would undermine its competitive potential. Provinces quickly indicated that they understood.

The 1987 legislation also contained a novel provision that required independent reviews every five years "to assess the impact of the Act ..., evaluate the state of competition in the transport sector, examine implementation issues, and determine whether the 1987 legislation was equipped to deal with present and future challenges in Canada's transport sector" (Hill 1999a, 73). As a result of these reviews, over the past twenty years, several changes have been legislated that reinforced the pro-market, deregulatory regime as well as the reduced role of the regulator. One was to extend the deregulation of the air sector to the area designated the "north" of Canada. Another was to further liberalize railway branch line abandonment. A third was to remove the review of mergers and acquisitions from the purview of the CTA and subject them to the Competition Act (Heaver and Waters II 2005).

In conclusion, it is hard to understate the profound shift that occurred following the 1987 and also later reforms. Where transportation issues had been centre stage in Canadian politics from

Confederation on, and consequently, the regulatory agency and its actions or non-actions a major player in the political debates, the post-1987 substitution of a regulatory regime – which placed overwhelming reliance on the operation of markets and a concomitant narrowly prescribed, largely technical, and reactive role for the CTA as an adjunct to, not director of, market forces – was a revolution. The success of that revolution is clearly shown by the acceptance of Liberal governments in the 1993–2006 period of the new paradigm and the almost complete disappearance of transportation issues from political debates in Canada.

The regulator is now mainly the market, and the CTA as a regulatory agency is largely a consumer complaint agency including on issues regarding the treatment of passengers/users with disabilities (CTA 2011, 2012) and on railway service performance (Minister of Transport 2013). Its role could not be more confined, and in fact, one can only ask if there is any continuing justification for a separate agency rather than a departmental unit responsible for its remaining tasks. Indeed, if anything, Transport Canada as the CTA's parent department has become the larger but still very market-focused regulatory body (Doern 2010b).

Transportation *safety* has, of course, been a focus historically in transport regulation, again across all modes. For example, in 1990, the Transportation Safety Board of Canada (TSB) was established. The TSB investigates transportation occurrences and accidents in the marine, pipeline, rail, and air modes of transportation. It works with other federal departments and regulators, but when the TSB investigates an accident (such as the 2013 Lac-Mégantic rail accident referred to in this book's Introduction) no other federal department except National Defence and the RCMP "may investigate for the purpose of making findings as to the causes and contributing factors of the accident" (TSB 2013, 2).

In addition, for the past decade, in particular, safety issues have been joined by concurrent needs to secure transportation *security*. Indeed, in Canada these security concerns began not just with post-9/11 terrorism prevention concerns but even earlier, with the 1985 Air India crash due to terrorism, as well. Indeed, the combined safety and security issues and regulatory and management needs helped produce Transport Canada's policy document, *Moving Forward* (2007), whose subtitle stressed the imperatives of "changing the safety and security culture."

The differences in the regulatory nature of safety versus security needed emphasis in the department as a multimodal and intermodal regulator. As former Transport Canada Deputy Minister Louis Ranger stressed, "transport safety and security programs are fundamentally different in that they focus on very different types of risks. 'Safety risks' originate from unintended failures, errors or misfortunes whereas 'security risks' originate from deliberate or malicious attempts to disrupt, disable or destroy" (2010, 12).

Thus, while the CTA aspects of the story represent a genuine lessening of regulatory presence compared with earlier periods, one can never, as was the case for the National Energy Board, leave out what was happening in the larger departmental setting in response to new regulatory pressures, especially after 9/11.

The Canadian Radio-television and Telecommunications Commission

The CRTC is the third modern economic regulatory agency examined here. Created in 1968, in part to resolve the internecine conflicts between the existing broadcasting regulator, the Board of Broadcast Governors, and the public broadcaster, the Canadian Broadcasting Corporation (CBC), and just as crucially to impose public control on an emerging technology, cable distribution of broadcast signals, the CRTC quickly established its institutional dominance, first, in the broadcasting sector and, a decade later, in telecommunications. While its policy decisions as well as their implementation have often been criticized (Hardin 1985; Caplan and Sauvageau 1986), the CRTC, until very recently, has exercised unquestioned dominance over the sectors through its role as the primary architect of Canadian broadcasting and telecommunications policies. This dominance is all the more impressive given the unruliness the CRTC regularly faced as a result not only of fundamental economic and technological developments but of the constancy of the intragovernmental competitive battles to supplant it as the primary policy maker for the communications sector (Schultz 1999a; Doern 1998b).

Only in the past six years has the CRTC's pre-eminence been successfully challenged, and while it has to date not suffered miniaturization as extensive as that of its sister agencies in the transportation and energy sectors, recent developments suggest that the CRTC's dominant position is being eroded and may be at an end. In this section of the chapter, we first outline the original broadcasting mandate of the CRTC and provide evidence both of its successful imposition of its policy preferences as well as its ability to maintain its institutional pre-eminence in the face of serious challenges over the course of its first four decades. The next section addresses the telecommunications component of the CRTC's mandate and its record since it acquired jurisdiction over telecommunications in 1976. The concluding section analyses the contemporary challenges to both its institutional prerogatives and its hitherto unassailable dominance.

BROADCASTING REGULATION: ORIGINS
AND MANDATE OF THE CRTC

The CRTC was established in 1968 as the first independent regulator with a wide-ranging decision-making capacity for the broadcasting sector. Its predecessor, the Board of Broadcast Governors, created only a decade before, had only an advisory role on broadcasting licences – Cabinet made the final decisions, which increasingly, became politically controversial – and from the outset had been in almost constant conflict with the other primary public sector actor, the CBC, over their respective roles (Peers 1979; Stewart and Hull 1994).

The central and most enduring idea behind the regulatory regime dated from the introduction of broadcasting regulation, best articulated in Prime Minister Bennett's justification for the creation of the predecessor of the CBC in 1932:

> this country must be assured of complete Canadian control of broadcasting from Canadian sources, free from foreign interference or influence. Without such control radio broadcasting can never become a great agency for the communication of matters of national concern and for the diffusion of national thought and ideals, and without such control it can never be the agency by which national consciousness may be fostered and sustained and national unity still further strengthened. (Quoted in Bird 1988, 21)

This statement amply demonstrates that Canadian broadcasting regulation was not introduced because the market could not work but that it must not be permitted to work. Consequently, broadcasting regulation was necessary not simply or even primarily to police broadcasters but to control the sector for non-economic, exogenous objectives.

In the thirty-five years before the creation of the CRTC, the primary instruments for the pursuit of the objective of Canadian control of broadcasting had been initially the public broadcaster, the CBC, as both producer and regulator of the private stations and subsequently the CBC as producer and the Board of Broadcast Governors as regulator subject to the licensing authority of the Cabinet. The CRTC constituted an institutional but not an ideational break with the past regime. The CRTC was granted an almost open-ended mandate as expressed in the first two clauses of the statement of broadcasting policy in its authorizing statute:

> broadcasting undertakings in Canada make use of radio frequencies that are public property and such undertakings constitute a single system, herein referred to as the Canadian broadcasting system, comprising public and private elements; the Canadian broadcasting system should be effectively owned and controlled by Canadians so as to safeguard, enrich and strengthen the cultural, political, social and economic fabric of Canada. (Broadcasting Act 1968, s. 3)

The final clause of its legislation was equally crucial for it stated, "The objectives of the broadcasting policy for Canada ... can best be achieved by providing for the regulation and supervision of the Canadian broadcasting system by a single independent public authority." The statement of public goals for broadcasting combined with the authority granted to the CRTC to supervise the system were central to the CRTC's conception of its primary role: the public planner, through regulation, of the entire broadcasting system.

An important characteristic of the CRTC's role as regulator was its relationship with political authorities, both its designated minister and Cabinet as a whole. Unlike the situation in the case of energy and transportation regulation, the CRTC was given far more decision-making control, free of political direction. In the broadcasting sector – telecommunications would be different, as discussed below – its decisions did not require prior political approval before taking effect nor could they be changed by political authorities. Cabinet could only refer a challenged decision back to the CRTC for reconsideration or veto it; it could not alter it. This granted the CRTC more discretion than either the NEB or the CTC/CTA. The agency also was free from political control in its regulation-making powers.

The CRTC was, however, the first regulatory agency that was subject to Cabinet directions on policy matters. Its original legislation gave Cabinet the authority to issue such directions to the CRTC, but it is worth noting, only on three very narrow matters. The most important subject matter for a direction pertained to setting limits on foreign ownership of broadcasters and cable companies. A direction that set this limit at 20 per cent was issued six months after the CRTC was established, thus setting the policy on the matter. Cabinet could also issue a direction to the CRTC if persuaded by the CBC that a condition imposed on its licence by the CRTC was unreasonable.

A potential major problem that the CRTC would face as a policy maker was that unlike the situation in transportation and energy, almost coincidental with the creation of the CRTC, the Department of Communications was established as the primary policy adviser to the minister and the government; however, this proved not to be a serious problem for the regulator in its efforts to establish itself as the primary policy maker for broadcasting and, subsequently, telecommunications.

In sharp contrast to both the NEB and the CTC, the CRTC enthusiastically embraced its planning responsibilities under the guise of "supervising" the single broadcasting system. Within a few years of its creation, for example, the CRTC issued regulations that restricted cable companies from carrying more than three commercial and one public American broadcasting stations in order to prevent the spread of American broadcasting influence which could undermine the "single system" (CRTC 1970). Similarly, building on a prior attempt by its predecessor, the CRTC imposed Canadian content requirements on both public and private television and radio broadcasters. One of the notable features of the CRTC's approach to its mandate that distinguished it from the CTC (Janisch 1978b) was that it was prepared to articulate its policy preferences in the form of guidelines and regulations (Bird 1988; Grant, Keenleyside, and Racicot 1993). In doing so, the CRTC unabashedly and publicly acknowledged that it, indeed, made "policy" and, in fact, was the policy maker for broadcasting.

These initiatives, which were often imposed over the strong objections of the regulated, had a symbolic as well as practical purpose. They were designed to demonstrate the resolve of the CRTC to establish itself in the face of industry opposition as the primary policy maker that took its mandate very seriously. Over the next three decades, as it sought to control and shape the fundamental economic and technological changes that confronted the broadcasting sector, the CRTC would encounter opposition from its regulated firms, from provincial governments, from foreign broadcasters and American politicians, and notably, from its own minister and the Cabinet. In almost every battle until quite recently, the CRTC largely emerged the winner – with both its authority undiminished and its preferred policies intact.

UNRULINESS CONTAINED IN THE BROADCASTING SECTOR
Although the first three decades of the CRTC's record are replete with examples of how effectively the CRTC dealt with mandate-related unruliness in the broadcasting sector and successfully rebuffed threats to its dominance, two examples, in particular, are very illustrative. The first occurred in the 1970s as the cable industry matured and encountered limitations on the growth in its primary business of distributing television signals and sought alternative business opportunities. One of these, drawing on American experience with HBO, was to seek permission to introduce pay television to Canadians (Woodrow, Woodside, Wiseman, and Black 1980; Woodrow and Woodside 1982; Henderson 1989; Hall 1990). At this time, the CRTC's chosen instruments for the attainment of the Canadian broadcasting policy were the traditional broadcasters, public and private. They were opposed to such services on the grounds they would lead to a further fragmentation of the single system and undermine their financial ability to meet their Canadian content objectives. After an aggressive lobbying effort by the cable industry, the CRTC agreed to hold a public hearing, after which it ruled against the introduction of pay services.

Denied by the CRTC, the industry turned its attention to the Department of Communications and sought to persuade it to employ its statutory policy role to order the CRTC to license pay television. Six months after the CRTC's decision, the new minister of communications, in a speech crafted by her officials and the principal lobbyist for the cable industry and delivered at its annual meeting, announced that the department intended to develop a policy on the introduction of pay television, which she declared to be "inevitable." She promised that Cabinet would be issuing a policy statement and indicated that she expected CRTC compliance. Notwithstanding this ministerial intervention, the CRTC quickly showed that it and it alone had the authority to determine when pay television would be introduced. The CRTC was prepared only to hold another public hearing, and after this was held announced that it was "premature and impossible to endorse the introduction of a national pay-television service at this time" (CRTC 1978, 4). It would be another five years before such a service was licensed by the CRTC, and notably on its terms, not those preferred by either the department or the cable industry (CRTC 1983).

The second case demonstrating the CRTC's dominance and concomitant ability to confront both technological and political mandate-related unruliness came in the latter half of the 1980s. The issue this time involved a far more serious technological threat than pay television, namely, the licensing of direct-to-home (DTH) "pizza-dish" satellite television services. Resolution of this conflict would culminate not only in a major public conflict between the Commission and Cabinet but a threat by the chair of the CRTC to take the government to court over its attempt to interfere not only with the commission's independence but with its preferred policy outcome (Fraser 1999).

This conflict had its roots in the development of second generation high-powered satellites, combined with digital video compression, that had enabled American consumers to by-pass both over-the-air broadcasters and cable systems (Schultz 1999b). It is worth noting that in the early 1980s the CRTC, disappointed with the performance of the traditional broadcasters, especially the private networks, had designated the cable industry to be the primary chosen instrument for the attainment of Canadian broadcasting policy objectives. If DTH services were permitted, particularly through American service providers who at the time were the only alternatives available, Canadians would have direct and comprehensive access to American signals, thus allowing them to "exit" the Canadian regulated system just as rail shippers and airline passengers had. Not surprisingly, those opposed to such services being made available to Canadian consumers labelled them "death stars" for, if permitted, they would threaten the very rationale for the Canadian regulatory regime and, of course, its current beneficiaries, the cable industry and the broadcasters. If permitted, it was predicted that "the Canadian television industry as we have come to know it, the whole symbolic ecosystem of politicians, regulators, broadcasters, specialty services, cable carriers, producers and various hangers-on ha[d] two years to live" (Ellis 1992, 23).

Such predictions underestimated the CRTC's resilience, determination, and ingenuity in the face of threats to both its position and its policy preferences. A first move was an unofficial approach by a senior CRTC official to Bell Canada and the cable industry suggesting that they form a consortium to offer DTH services (Fraser 1999). When the Competition Bureau intervened to caution the companies that this was probably anti-competitive, this option was dropped. The next move was for the CRTC to announce that it was naturally in favour of "customer-driven tv" and to acknowledge that "any attempt to impose protectionist measures as a means to safeguard the Canadian broadcasting system would only prove to be counterproductive and impracticable" (CRTC 1993).

The CRTC then proceeded to create measures to establish such protection. Following what it called a structural hearing to discuss "the evolving communications environment," the CRTC announced requirements designed to encourage the development of "a strong Canadian DTH industry," one that would discourage non-Canadian service providers seeking to enter the Canadian market. It proposed to exempt Canadian DTH firms from regulation if such firms met a series of conditions among which was exclusive reliance on the use of Canadian satellite facilities, no original programming, only foreign programming approved by the CRTC, and finally, more channels devoted to Canadian programming than non-Canadian programming (CRTC 1994a).

Such conditions effectively precluded the applicant for a licence then before the CRTC that was a partnership between the American owner of DirecTV, the only American DTH provider at the time, and the Canadian firm, Power Corporation. There was only one applicant that did meet those conditions which was owned by Bell Canada, and became known as Bell ExpressVu and, consequently, it would be the only company to be exempt from regulation. It is important to note that the CRTC was not proposing to prohibit other entrants but only to submit those who did not meet the exemption conditions to a rigorous and time-consuming regulatory review, one which, if undertaken, would clearly give the exempted firms a competitive advantage.

The uproar that followed the CRTC's announced course of action was unprecedented since its creation. Cabinet was forced to intervene to create a Policy Review Panel of three distinguished federal public servants that ultimately concluded that the CRTC's actions were anti-competitive and that Cabinet should issue a policy directive to the Commission ordering it to license all qualified applicants under the same terms and conditions. In addition, such a directive would compel the CRTC to eliminate the requirement for the exclusive use of Canadian satellite facilities.

Cabinet's decision to issue such a directive caused an unprecedented major public conflict between the CRTC and the government. The chair of the CRTC described the directive before a parliamentary committee as "retroactive regulation [that was] intrinsically unfair and destabilizing" (*Globe and Mail*, 1995). He argued that such a directive threatened the Commission's independence and integrity" and, furthermore, that he thought that it was illegal and the commission might challenge it in court. His argument emphasized the stakes the CRTC considered to be at risk: "the Government's power of direction was never meant to usurp the commission's exclusive role in implementing broadcasting policy for Canada. It was plainly and unmistakably meant only as an instrument to guide broadcasting policy as a general orientation" (ibid.). This was a statement that every chair since 1967 could have made for it articulated the view that the CRTC alone and no one else was responsible for making broadcasting policy other than through legislative means.

In the end, the government issued a directive to the CRTC that it appeared to comply with and, just as significantly, did not follow up on its threat to legally challenge the government. The suggestion of a vanquished, chastened regulatory agency, however, is illusory. The CRTC, notwithstanding the Cabinet directive, was ultimately the clear winner in this battle. In the first place, the Canadian-American partnership assumed to be the most serious threat to the CRTC's policies opted not to pursue a licence, and Canada ended up with two service providers, one owned by Bell Canada, the other by the second largest cable company, that met the policy objectives and conditions imposed by the CRTC. Moreover, the long-term threat that DTH services were feared to make to the Canadian broadcasting system and its policies was contained. The CRTC effectively transformed the much feared "death stars" into cable in the sky. The "whole symbiotic ecosystem," which had been presumed to be so threatened, survived intact with the CRTC entrenched unchallenged in its role as primary policy maker.

TELECOMMUNICATIONS REGULATION IN TURMOIL,
1976–2006

In 1976, jurisdiction for the regulation of telecommunications was transferred from the Canadian Transport Commission to the CRTC,

which was renamed the Canadian Radio-television and Telecommunications Commission. For most of the preceding seventy years,
telecom regulation was not particularly politically salient, in part
because the federally regulated firms, namely, Bell Canada and British
Columbia Telephone Company, seldom applied to their regulator for
rate increases as they were able, for the most part, to finance their
expansion internally, especially after the Second World War. Another
reason for the low salience was the fact that, unlike the air and rail
sectors where it had significant financial stakes in the industry with
Crown corporations, the federal government had a minimal role in
the telephone sector.

In the first half of the 1970s, federal telecommunications regulation
became much more controversial when, in large part as a result of the
high rate of inflation that occurred, Bell Canada in particular almost
annually sought significant rate increases, which the CTC largely
granted. This gave rise to charges that the regulator had been captured by its wards and such was the political controversy that, after
one increase, Cabinet had to intervene to reduce it in order to prevent
an NDP vote of non-confidence which would have brought down the
minority Liberal government. Adding to the dissatisfaction with the
CTC regulation of the telephone industry were controversial decisions on the attachment of terminal equipment such as telephones
and faxes to the network and support for consumer participation.
For many observers, the disenchantment over railway and airline
regulation now extended to the telephone sector with the widespread
perception that the regulator was hopelessly stuck in the past.

The federal minister of communications described the transfer of
telephone regulation from the CTC to the CRTC to the House of
Commons as mere "housekeeping" to tidy up the federal regulatory
system. At the time, no attempt was made to introduce new telecommunications legislation so the CRTC would continue to be responsible to regulate Bell and BC Tel's rates to ensure that they were "just
and reasonable" and not "unduly discriminatory," which was the
1906 regulatory mandate. All the CRTC had, in effect, were CTC
precedents to guide it. The CRTC, however, quickly made it clear
that as far as it was concerned, telephone regulation was no longer
business as usual and precedents were of limited relevance. Within a
few months of the jurisdictional transfer, the CRTC, under the guise
of an anodyne statement on "procedures and practices" proclaimed
that telephone regulation was entering a fundamentally new era.

The agency declared that the public interest required that telephone services "should be responsive to public demand over as wide a range as possible, and equally responsive to social and technological change" (CRTC 1976; Schultz and Alexandroff 1985). Furthermore the CRTC announced that notwithstanding CTC precedents, it would not be following its predecessor's narrow, traditional interpretation of its regulatory mandate:

The principle of "just and reasonable rates" is neither a narrow nor a static concept. As our society has evolved, the idea of what is just and reasonable has also changed, and now takes into account many considerations that would have been thought irrelevant 70 years ago, when regulatory review was first instituted. Indeed, the Commission views this principle in the widest possible terms and considers itself obliged to continually review the level and structure of carrier rates to ensure that telecommunications services are fully responsive to the public interest. (CRTC 1976)

The implications of the CRTC's proposed approach were profound: the previous era of policing regulation, with its focus on a negative, reactive, proscriptive role was over and was to be replaced by regulation not simply of individual companies but, as it was in broadcasting, of a "single system" and, thus, amenable to positive, prescriptive regulatory initiatives and supervision.

The CRTC's behaviour matched its rhetoric because, through a series of decisions over the next five years that reflected regulatory preferences and not simply, or even primarily, reactions to external demands, the telecom sector experienced a degree of unruliness unmatched in its history. It reversed a CTC decision, using the same legislative provision, to award costs, payable by the regulated firms, to consumer groups participating in telecom regulation. This decision not only infuriated Bell Canada, which fought it, unsuccessfully, all the way to the Supreme Court but gave the Consumers' Association of Canada both the legitimacy and the resources to become an effective participant in the regulatory process (Trebilcock 1978; Schultz 2000).

This action was somewhat ironic because only a few years previously the CRTC had shown in broadcasting regulation the same scepticism about consumer representation that the NEB and CTC had demonstrated (Kane 1980). In another major initiative, the CRTC ordered Bell and BC Tel to submit their interprovincial telephone rates negotiated through the TransCanada Telephone System for regulatory approval, something that had not been done previously. It also imposed quality of service standards on the regulated, something that the CTC had denied it had jurisdiction over.

In another major decision, the CRTC reversed, again, a CTC decision taken only a few years earlier to order Bell Canada, under extremely stringent conditions, to permit the attachment of equipment to its system from a competitive supplier, a decision that was towards a form of consumer bill of rights. Subsequently, the CRTC liberalized the equipment market completely by ordering Bell and BC Tel to permit customers, business and residential, to attach their own equipment, such as telephones, answering machines, and private branch exchanges, to the telephone company networks.

What was once a monopoly controlled by the telephone companies became a widely competitive market. Adopting the CRTC's independent attitude in broadcasting, the regulator even rejected a Cabinet-approved application from Telesat Canada, the joint public-private satellite company, to join the TransCanada Telephone System on the grounds that it would be anti-competitive and, therefore, not in the public interest. Cabinet had to intervene through an appeal to reverse this decision. Finally, in one of its most important decisions, the CRTC approved the application to connect Bell and BC Tel's only competitor to their local networks to provide a competing private line long distance service. Although affecting a relatively small corporate market, it was a fundamental assault on the traditional incumbents' monopoly provision of long distance service.

It is important to note that although these CRTC decisions had a significant competitive impact, particularly in the terminal equipment market, they were not motivated by the embrace of pro-market ideas similar to those described above that were imposed on the CTC and the NEB. To the contrary, the regulatory-induced turbulence between 1976 and 1981 was motivated by a desire to improve telecommunications regulation by lessening the information load on the CRTC, increasing the capacity of intervenors to help carry the regulatory, burden and giving it benchmarks by which to assess the behaviour of the regulated firms (Dalfen 1989). That this was the case was clearly demonstrated in 1985 when the commission, after conceding that many benefits, societal and economic, would flow from greater competition, rejected an application for public long distance competition (Stanbury 1986). It was also shown by the determination of the commission to prevent such competition coming in through the back door, as it were, through the resale and sharing of telephone services (CRTC 1985).

Conflict over the latter form of competition in the second half of the 1980s clearly demonstrated the increasing mandate-related unruliness faced by the CRTC. After the 1985 decision to impose strict limits on resale and sharing, an aggressive new entrant began offering such services. In 1987, however, Bell Canada convinced the CRTC that the new entrant was offering, in effect, a form of public long distance service contrary to the commission's rules. The CRTC agreed and ordered Bell to terminate service to the company. When the new entrant appealed the decision to Cabinet, the CRTC was confronted with a very effective coalition of governmental actors including the Competition Bureau, the Office of Privatization and Regulatory Reform, International Trade, and Finance that lobbied Cabinet members on the side of the new entrant. After a series of delays, further appeals, and further delays, the CRTC recognized that it had suffered its first major defeat and conceded. The company was allowed to continue and the resale market, the first real inroad into the public long distance market, was liberalized (Hancock 1992).

In 1992, the CRTC finally endorsed long distance competition but in a manner that caused considerable turbulence including the bankruptcy of the long-time primary advocate for such competition, Unitel, formerly CNCP Communications. In addressing the application from Unitel for national competition, and another from a regional competitor, the CRTC opted for unlimited competition, both on territorial grounds, that is, national, regional, or provincial, and from both facilities-based and resale (CRTC 1992; Globerman, Oum Tae, and Stanbury 1993; Surtees 1994). But, again, it must be stressed that this decision did not entail a new set of ideas that were market-based substituting for more traditional, pro-regulatory ideas. Indeed, the then-chair indicated that notwithstanding the embrace of competition, it would be "regulation as usual."

As if to reinforce this position, 1992–93 witnessed new telecommunications legislation (Janisch 1999; Senate of Canada 1992). It is worth stating that, although there were three unsuccessful attempts to pass new legislation in 1977 and 1978, from then until 1993, the CRTC was able to effect the major restructuring of telecommunications regulation and public policy for the sector through its novel

reinterpretation of the 1906 provisions of the Railway Act. Aside
from one major component of the new legislation, which involved
an attempt by the Department of Communications to supplant the
CRTC as the primary policy maker, a subject to be discussed in the
next subsection of this chapter, the new legislation stands out for
two reasons. One was that it enabled the CRTC, if it presumed that
markets were working effectively to control corporate behaviour, to
forbear or refrain from regulation. This forbearance was not strictly
deregulation because the CRTC could at any point reintroduce regulatory controls, but would be employed over the next decade to further liberalize a number of telecommunications markets, including
perhaps the most important, namely, the local telephone service
market (Schultz 1999a, 1999b; Doern 1998a, 1998b).

The second major aspect was the surprising part of the legislation,
namely, the policy objectives that presumably were to guide the CRTC
in its future decision making. Again, unlike the policies the Mulroney
Conservative government had imposed on the energy and transport
sectors, and their regulators, that reflected a fundamentally different
pro-market set of ideas and a rejection of traditional approaches, in
telecom, the same government opted for an approach similar to what
it legislated for broadcasting in 1991. The first objective was still "to
facilitate the orderly development in Canada of a telecommunications system that serves to safeguard, enrich and strengthen the cultural, social, political and economic fabric of Canada" (quoted in
Telecommunications Policy Review Panel 2006, 3–4).

Notwithstanding the controversies over the CRTC's embrace of
competition as a supplementary tool and the debates over the introduction and spread of competition over the previous decade and a
half, the best "policy guidance" on this issue that the new statute
said that the CRTC should seek as its sixth objective, "to foster
increased reliance on market forces for the provision of telecommunications services" (Telecommunications Act, s. 7(f)). In other words,
competition if necessary, but not necessarily competition!

The CRTC, however, chose to follow its own interpretation of
its new mandate (CRTC 1994b; Globerman, Janisch, and Stanbury
1996a; Schultz 1999, 1999b). Significantly, it opted for a radical
reorientation of the respective roles of regulation and competition,
with the latter not simply one of the objectives but, in fact, henceforth
it would be the primary lens through which the commission would
fulfil its responsibilities. The CRTC justified its new approach on the

grounds that the telecom environment was changing "in ways that outpace the ability of regulators to recognize and define; let alone control" (CRTC 1994a). As a result the commission concluded that regulation should concentrate on those services where monopoly still prevailed but should strive to open all telecommunications to competition, including the local telephone market – which was the last remnant of monopoly (CRTC 1994b).

POLITICAL TURMOIL AND THE CRTC

In all the economic and technological turbulence that has confronted the CRTC in both its broadcasting and telecommunications responsibilities, there have been two constants. The first is, as the preceding discussion illustrates, the CRTC has clearly been the dominant policy maker, a role that it relished and aggressively defended. The second is that political authorities and departmental officials, from the first decade of CRTC regulation, have insisted that they – and not an independent regulator – should have that role. In the latter half of the 1970s, legislation was introduced three times that included a comprehensive provision for Cabinet to issue policy directives to the CRTC. In the 1980s, both Liberal and Conservative ministers of communications introduced legislation to that end. In all five instances, the proposed legislation did not proceed beyond first reading.

It was only in 1991 with a new Broadcasting Act and in 1993 with the Telecommunications Act that the Cabinet gained the authority to issue broad policy directions to the CRTC on both broadcasting and telecommunications matters. It was only in 2006, however, that such a direction was issued, a subject we shall turn to below. Before doing so, it is instructive to discuss a major provision in the original proposal for telecommunications legislation in 1992 because of what it tells us about departmental and regulatory agency competition. When the government introduced its proposed legislation, it included not only the directive power but also a provision that would have created a licensing power.

The significance of this power is that the minister of communications, on the advice of departmental officials, would have exercised it. The CRTC would have been reduced to the role of adviser to the minister. This power was clearly designed to accomplish what had taken place in the energy and transport sectors, that is, make the department the primary policy decision maker. Those who participated in the Senate review of the proposed legislation were almost universally critical of this provision and ultimately the Senate Committee, even with a Conservative majority, strongly recommended that it be dropped. Recognizing that he had not sufficiently appreciated the significance of the proposed departmental power grab, the minister of communications, conceding the point, removed the ministerial licensing provision from what became the Telecommunications Act (Janisch 2012).

Notwithstanding the existence of a policy directive power, the CRTC continued for more than a decade to be the dominant policy maker for the communications sector. Most importantly, its initial embrace of competition over regulation weakened. Where it had in 1994 seen a loss of control, only a year later it spoke of challenges "to articulate and define" regulatory responses. In addition, the CRTC now defined its role in telecommunications as being to "supervise and regulate" the telecommunications sector even though its statutory mandate gave it no such role (CRTC 1997).

Emphasizing its responsibility to promote the "orderly development" of the telecommunications sector, the CRTC started to practise what economists had long warned about when a regulator had to address competitive questions, namely, attempting to manage competition and the competitive process. One way the commission did this was to embrace the goal of "sustainable competition," which meant that it had to be "fair" to new competitors. The primary instrument to attain fairness was asymmetric regulation. New entrants would not be subject to regulation, while incumbent firms would be subject to detailed regulatory scrutiny and controls. The tensions that resulted coalesced around the introduction of a new technology for offering local telephone service, namely, VOIP or voice over Internet protocol (CRTC 2005).

The conflict over VOIP produced the most significant assault on the CRTC's policy-making role, an assault that, arguably, portends a much-reduced role for the commission. The assault began when the Liberal government of Paul Martin was persuaded by Bell Canada to undertake a public review of telecommunications policy, a review that the CRTC had previously rejected. The resulting report by the Telecommunications Policy Review Panel (TPR Panel 2006) was sharply critical of the CRTC's "balancing approach," which was interpreted as pursuing the goal of promoting interests of new entrants over the incumbent firms. The Panel concluded:

Application of the doctrine has resulted in a new, high level of regulatory intervention aimed at shaping the structure of markets, rather than allowing market forces to determine the success or failure of different service providers. The relative degree of intervention by the CRTC on behalf of the new entrants has been very substantial and has led to the imposition of extensive constraints by the CRTC on the activities of the major suppliers of many telecommunications services (the incumbent firms). (Ibid., 3–8)

The TPR Panel not only recommended that this approach be terminated but that "market forces should be relied upon to the maximum extent feasible as the means of achieving Canada's telecommunications policy objectives" (ibid., 3–6) and that, consequently, the rate regulation should be significantly reduced.

The new Conservative Minister of Industry Maxime Bernier seized upon the report for both personal and philosophical reasons and, as a result of a combination of adroit political manoeuvres on his part and miscalculations by the CRTC, was able not only to reverse the commission's decisions but to fundamentally recast telecommunications policy (Schultz 2008). The government issued the first policy directive to the CRTC that did not simply reorder the existing statutory objectives but recast them profoundly. Drawing on the review panel's recommendations, the CRTC was ordered in its decision making to "to rely on market forces to the maximum extent possible as the means of achieving the telecommunications policy objectives" and concomitantly to reduce regulation as much as possible so as not to interfere with the operation of market forces (quoted in ibid., 159).

Although the directive and its employment to justify overturning a specific CRTC decision was criticized as unprecedented on the grounds of political decision-making taking precedence over quasi-judicial decision-making the minister and the government were unwilling to back down. The government had established, for the first time since the creation of the CRTC, after a number of unsuccessful attempts to do so by governments of different political stripes, that political authorities would henceforth control telecommunications policy making – and that the CRTC's role would be circumscribed. That the CRTC understood what had happened to it was evident in the following statement from the new chair of the CRTC after the Cabinet had ordered a major decision to be varied to comply with the policy directive: "the message is clear: the government wants to move quickly towards more reliance on market forces in telecom services, less regulation and smarter regulation. I welcome the clarity and I welcome the variation order" (von Finckenstein 2007, 2).

Although the consequences for the CRTC flowing from this imposition of political control were not as great as what had befallen the NEB and CTC, it was clear that its policy-making discretion was to be substantially reduced. Two subsequent developments support this conclusion. In one, the CRTC ruled that a company, already granted a licence to provide cellular telephone service by Industry Canada under its spectrum licensing powers, was not eligible to operate as a common carrier because it was not Canadian-controlled (Schultz 2011). Cabinet, however, intervened on its own initiative and not in response to an appeal, to overturn the decision. After one of the competitors launched a court challenge on the grounds that Cabinet had exceeded its authority by not acting within the Telecommunications Act, the Federal Court ruled against the government on the grounds that it "inserted a previously unknown policy objective" into the statute (quoted in ibid., 213). Although the Federal Court of Appeal overturned this decision, before the Supreme Court could hear an appeal, the government announced that the foreign ownership restrictions governing telecommunications would be amended to increase the amount of foreign control for a company with less than 10 per cent of the market. This made the Supreme Court appeal moot. This case illustrates how far the current Harper Conservative government is prepared to go to impose its preferred policy outcomes on both the telecom sector and the CRTC.

The second case is far more disturbing as it illustrates how unclear the relationship between Cabinet and the CRTC on policy matters has become (Janisch 2012). Furthermore, unlike in particular the conflict discussed above that led to both the issuance of a policy directive and overturning a regulatory decision where the government and the minister, while disagreeing with the CRTC, at no time showed disrespect for the agency, the most recent case of political involvement was characterized by an obvious high degree of disdain on the part of political authorities.

This case involves the CRTC's decision in 2011 to impose a usage-based pricing scheme for Internet access (CRTC 2011a). What occurred following the decision has been described by Janisch as "a complete disregard for the legal regime" (2012: 51) governing the respective roles for both Cabinet and the CRTC. The decision produced tweets from both the prime minister and his industry minister criticizing the decision. Subsequently, following an online petition organized by a consumer group, the chair of the CRTC was summoned to appear before a parliamentary committee to defend the commission's decision. Rather than doing so, he simply and totally capitulated to the public – and especially political – pressure and announced that there would be no need for a formal appeal to Cabinet as the commission would review the decision on its own motion. The commission was put on notice by the industry minister that nothing short of a major reversal would be acceptable. In essence regardless of the outcome of the CRTC review, under a Conservative government, this ruling would not be implemented. In any event, the minister and the government need not have worried as the commission adjusted its decision sufficiently that the controversy largely disappeared (CRTC 2011b).

To conclude this section, while the CRTC has not been miniaturized to the same extent as its regulatory sisters, it is clear that over the past six years both its policy-making authority and its stature as an independent agency, at least in terms of its role as telecommunications regulator, has significantly diminished. The CRTC, clearly, no longer dominates other actors nor can it ignore at will elected political authorities. In the broadcasting sector, thus far, its authority has not yet been subject to the challenges it faced in telecommunications. That said, the CRTC faces major broadcasting challenges and unruliness. Among these are media mergers and concentration issues and the highly exceptional simultaneous public relations and regulatory campaigns being waged by opponents. Given the political controversy, this is an issue that undoubtedly will involve political intervention. Even more threatening are anticipated technological developments posed by services such as Netflix, AppleTV, and Google which allow media consumers the opportunity to exit the regulated sector with consequences similar to that experienced in the air and rail sector. The future is definitely not friendly for the CRTC.

THE THREE ATTRIBUTES

Ideas, Discourses, and Agendas

Looking across the three core sectors of the economic regulatory regime, as revealed over several decades, it is not hard to see both the ideas that remain in some form at the heart of the regime as well as their varied forms of discourse both in terms of policy ideas and the shifting discourses that may or may not be statutory. The CTC/CTA

story shows the early centrality of the idea of planning and coordinating all transport "modes under federal jurisdiction." The CRTC's
purposes regarding broadcasting were, in fact, non-economic in that
they sought to produce a "single system" that would "enrich and
strengthen the cultural, political and social fabric of Canada." The
telecom mandate ideas of the CRTC also centred on the "orderly
development" of the telecommunications system. The early NEB
mandate was to develop a national energy policy but, as we have
seen, with no overarching ideas stated; any guidance norms were
bound up more in listed powers including decisions based on ensuring the "present and future public convenience and necessity."

Underlying these ideas were certainly core features of the need to
regulate public utilities as complex kinds of national and regional
infrastructure with monopoly or quasi-monopoly power that had to
be restrained. Thus, overall, the three regulators had initial purposes
such as the NEB's regulating pipeline tolls so as to "prevent market
abuse," and both the CRTC and CTC had duties to ensure that "just
and reasonable rates" were charged by supplier firms.

Clearly, however, the later pattern of ideas and discourse both in
official policy and in criticism and opposition by Cabinet ministers,
key interests, and agenda-setting events such as royal commissions
and regulatory reform, morphed in many ways. These included ideas
and interpretive discourse that helped produce and reflect the miniaturization dynamics stressed throughout the chapter. Thus, the NEB
has had both explicit liberalization and deregulatory ideas captured
in notions such as export promotion and the NEB's role as an economic "enabler" as it practised various kinds of "responsible regulation." The NEB also acquired – nominally, at least – some sustainable
development mandate discourse as it took on shared environmental
assessment tasks.

For the CTC/CTA, the bursting of the ideational gates inherent in
its demise was both extensive and partly cyclical. Thus, regionalism
as a stated mandate idea was initially absent, and was later to be
fostered and then disappeared. Explicit deregulation was anchored
under Mulroney-era liberalization ideas but even earlier under the
Pearson Liberals, the latter explicitly focusing on the "consumer
interest." The Mulroney agenda and ideas also proceeded under the
discourse of "freedom to move" (Canada 1985b; Hill 1988).

As we have seen, the CRTC has held on longest to its initial core
mandate ideas, although these were often cast in terms of the

regulator's "fear of fragmentation" as new technological imperatives took hold from early telecom technologies such as satellites and extending to the now pervasive Internet. Orderly development was not a form of discourse that could be credible any longer.

Public and Private Power in Regulation Making and Compliance

The interplay of public state-centred versus private corporate, industrial, and broader consumer/user and environmental interest group power in regulation making and compliance conveys a similar overall set of shape-shifting changes. Indeed, this is inherent in the argument advanced about the change from the three agencies as "governments in miniature" to "mere miniatures." Public power federally has been shown, first, to be centred in regulatory agency versus ministerial Cabinet and departmental structures of governance and democracy. The NEB was born when there was no energy policy ministry, and hence, initially, federal actions gave it the lead role as a virtual single source of energy policy and regulatory expertise. But later, under the auspices of both Energy, Mines, and Resources and then Natural Resources Canada, the parent departments became competitors for institutional turf and policy territory. Environment Canada, Consumer and Corporate Affairs, and Foreign Affairs shared space and pushed in as environmental, consumer, and free trade agendas took hold. Prime ministerial power was also evident in both the National Energy Policy and climate change and Kyoto Protocol eras as the NEB was basically shunted aside.

The CTC/CTA and Transport Canada and Ministry of Transport nexus shifted markedly as outright regulatory policy conflicts led to frequent bouts of unruliness of the regulatory agency–related type suggested in our analytical framework. Thus, agency mandates faced partially uncontrollable challenges because of changes, technological and otherwise, in key transport modes including trucking, rail, and air.

The CRTC was born in and around the time of the establishment of a new Department of Communications, which was itself new technology–centred in terms of its mandate but, as we have seen, the CRTC was able to defend and maintain its own power and turf much longer than the other two agencies. But, as shown above, this power equation changed rapidly in the Harper era.

The structure of private power was clearly a part of the above agency miniaturization journey. Often corporate power was exercised through alignment with provincial governments such as in trucking and airlines, and oil and gas and, hence, with federal-provincial and, indeed, international regulatory politics and policy. On the corporate side, the NEB faced challenges and criticism from hydroelectric interests, most provincially owned, and in varied ways in oil and gas from producer versus consumer provinces/regions. New challenges emerged from small versus large energy firms and from Canadian versus foreign-owned firms. The CTC/CTA had to manage corporate power exercised by Air Canada and, later, regional champions such as West Jet but also market pressure when US deregulation created cheaper options, via US suppliers, for Canadians as shippers, air travellers, and holiday planners. For the CRTC, corporate power came from the CBC initially, but then from a new array of both telecoms and broadcasters (and, indeed, changed meanings of what both these business activities now were) seeking entry to an industry with changing competitive, product, and social boundaries.

Science, Evidence, and Knowledge

Our third attribute reveals a somewhat more subtle and often subdued regulatory regime story whose trend line is not is not as sharp and clear as in the first two attributes above. For the most part, science-based regulation is not the first·form of evidence and knowledge one thinks of in the economic sectoral regulatory regime. Technical and engineering-related capacities are obviously central in different ways in all three regulatory agencies, certainly regarding pipelines and key aspects of transport safety. Science-based regulation emerged more centrally in the NEB as it took on a shared environmental assessment role. Offshore oil and gas issues in relation to the fisheries and oceans and to shipping emerged where even more complex ecosystem and habitat-based science and knowledge loomed large in concert with more complex notions of risk, risk-benefit, and spatial reach and impacts.

While the NEB was cast initially as the place where Canada's main federal energy expertise was created and lodged, this was not a claim that could be made for very long. In the CTC/CTA and CRTC agency realms, some core expertise was clearly assembled and needed for both regulatory effectiveness and capacity, but there were always issues of playing catch-up with new technologies. For the CTC/CTA this occurred at a periodic but steady pace, whereas for the CRTC, especially in the current Internet and related cell phone and social media era, the technologies were fast changing.

Evidence and knowledge of other key kinds also underpin the birth and evolution of these three agencies. Certainly, micro-economics and, therefore, economists (in Canada and internationally) played key roles in the advocacy and design of public utility regulation, in identifying the nature of regulatory capture, and in the advocacy of later deregulation and liberalization strategies. Royal commissions such as the McPherson Royal Commission, but also exercises such as the freedom to move policy reviews and papers are also relevant here (Canada 1985b; Hill 1988). Moreover, consumer and environmental advocacy and knowledge centres also contributed to reform and to ongoing scrutiny.

CONCLUSIONS

This chapter has provided an analysis of change and inertia in the economic sectoral regulatory regime through a comparative examination of the origins and historical evolution of three regulatory agencies, the National Energy Board, the Canadian Transport Commission/Canadian Transportation Agency, and the Canadian Radio-television and Telecommunications Commission. As we have seen, these three agencies were created, initially, to be the primary federal institutions to influence, direct, regulate, and control the economic and related social impacts of vital infrastructural, public utility, and networked industries. Underlying these ideas were, certainly, core features of the need to regulate public utilities as complex kinds of national and regional infrastructure with monopoly or quasi-monopoly power that had to be restrained. Thus, overall, the three regulators had initial purposes such as the NEB's regulating of pipeline tolls so as to prevent market abuse, and both the CTC and subsequently the CRTC had duties to ensure that telephone rates were just and reasonable.

Our overall conclusion is that each of these regulatory agencies have been transformed historically from "governments in miniature" to mere miniatures, with the NEB and CTA/CTC propelled by a fast continuous track to miniaturization and with the CRTC holding out longer, but now also succumbing. Some essential inertia is, certainly, observable especially because the three regulators still retain some important utility and infrastructure regulatory powers and tasks, but these vary across the three policy realms and are reduced considerably overall. The miniaturization-related change process has also exhibited almost continuously, in each decade, frequent and concerted unruliness, particularly regarding policy conflicts built into agency mandates or in efforts to challenge them or for regulators to simply ignore some mandate features that seemed and often were unworkable. Individual regulatory chairpersons are also a factor here, especially in the case of the CRTC, where individual agendas and a willingness to take on ministers to protect and assert the agency's mandate slowed down the miniaturization process for many years. In terms of the three types of unruliness being explored in the book as whole, unruliness is mainly of the regulatory agency–related type centred on these frequent policy and mandate conflicts, some of which, as shown above, were linked to major kinds of technological change.

The chapter has shown that each of the three regulatory agencies examined here had to give up regulatory space, powers, and capacity in part because both public and private centres of power took from them or required them to share turf. These transformational shifts were also propelled by technological changes of different magnitudes and by firms and business interests that sought market access and deregulation, as well as by co-regulation when needed or acceptable.

Changes were caused by an array of consumer and environmental interests that sought broader public interest goals and outcomes, collectively often initially cast as social regulation. Indeed, in the case of the CRTC, in particular, we have seen that social and cultural purposes and ideas were central from the outset. In later chapters, we make the case for different, broader notions of the "social" in regulation and regulatory scholarship as analysed in our account of the regulatory regime of social sectors in chapter 6 and of the societal framework regulatory regime in chapter 8.

Nevertheless, it must be stressed that the overall economic sectoral regulatory regime remains at the heart of basic regulatory scholarship and practice because it was – and remains – the home base of analytical debate and discourse about when, why, and how governments should intervene or withdraw from regulating markets in capitalist political economies such as Canada. The chapter has shown in this regard that the scope and boundaries of markets have changed, and these, in turn, exert political and economic disputes regarding property rights in all three of the core regulatory areas examined in this chapter, namely, energy, transportation, and communications.

6

The Regulatory Regime of Social Sectors: Registered Charities, Citizenship and Immigration, and Assisted Human Reproduction Technologies

The regulatory regime of social sectors, while not a customary analytical category in the orthodox literature on regulation, is a central domain of rules and rule making in modern governance. This regime of rule making by the state, and other societal institutions, deals with laws and rules that relate primarily to protecting and fostering the well-being and the life of individuals, families, and specific groups in Canadian society. The regime of rule making is a key part of regulatory welfarism as both a concept and a central argument that we develop in this book.

In this introduction to the chapter, we examine conceptual foundations including the nature of "the social" in this regulatory regime. In the next section, we map the current regime including its different kinds of regulatory forms and methods. Then we examine three relatively diverse social sectors selected for closer analysis, namely, the charitable sector, citizenship and immigration, and the policy area of assisted human reproduction technologies (AHRTs). The first two have long-established historical roots while the third is of more recent construction. Of interest in this chapter is that each has exhibited its own patterns of historical inertia, but in the current Harper era, each has evidenced considerable change, although in quite different ways. We then look at the regulatory governance attributes of (1) ideas, discourses, and agendas; (2) public and private power in regulation making and compliance; and (3) science, evidence, and knowledge. Each attribute is examined as a factor explaining change and inertia in the regulatory regime of social sectors. Conclusions then follow including observations on unruliness and on the overall direction of recent trends in regulatory governance in this regime.

As a prominent object of regulatory actions, with assorted values, institutions, decision processes, interests, temporal periods, and compliance challenges, what is the social? Typically, the social refers to a general population or to various communities of people at different levels of governance, including the concepts of citizen and citizenship, and to human interactions, community roles, and shared activities. At times, the social refers to such normative values as sharing, cohesion, obligation, reciprocity, and solidarity, as well as to structures and interests that are wholly or largely non-market in aims and operations. At other times, the social refers to actors and relationships beyond the state basically in a civil sphere. In all cases, the social is a space of potential and actual political intervention, a site of relations of power in which the regulatory state is highly likely to be present (Rice and Prince 2013; Rose 1996; Squires 1990).

Even as social programs bear directly on individual Canadians through income transfer payments, tax measures, or the delivery of health, education, and other personal services, these programs bundle up into areas of practices, clientele groups, networks of constituencies, and policy communities. We refer to these aggregations as social sectors. Even national social programs like Employment Insurance (EI) or Old Age Security (OAS) may contain a set of national standards and cover the national community, but this does not make them *framework* realms as we use that concept in chapter 8; rather, national social programs represent vertical or constituency-based policies and related set of rules; each is a form of collective provision against a particular set of risks of life and work.

Social sectors relate to vertical dimensions of government structures in that policy processes extend outward to particular constituencies of the population with a relatively select number of identifiable issues and actions. In this chapter, the three diverse social sectors we examine are the charitable sector, citizenship and immigration, and the emergent bio-realm of assisted human reproduction technologies and their attempted regulation.

Much of what we discuss in this chapter (and in chapter 8) is on the margins of the mainstream regulatory literature in economics, law, and political science. Strands of scholarly literature discussing the charitable sector, specifically registered charities, can be found in public administration, social work, and tax law, within a larger literature on the voluntary sector and social economy. On citizenship and immigration, there is a larger set of works in Canada in ethnic studies, history, law, policy studies, and sociology. On assisted human reproduction, there is a modest yet growing literature in ethics, feminist studies, health policy, legal studies, and governance. As noted in chapter 2, we also draw on literature previewed there dealing with governmentality and the post-regulatory state, inspired by the writings of Michel Foucault on "the government of one's self" in particular economic and social affairs.

THE REGULATORY REGIME OF SOCIAL SECTORS IN HISTORICAL CONTEXT

Historically, at the federal level of the Canadian state, immigrants and refugees and their sponsors, Indians and other Aboriginal peoples and their communities, and, armed forces members and veterans and their families are the selected categories of people with distinctive relationships to the Canadian government in terms of services, expenditure programs, laws, and rules (Hodgetts 1973, 107–29). Similar constituency-based sectors today include ethnoracial communities, people with mental or physical disabilities, senior citizens, tenants and others with housing issues, women and children, and workers, labour relations, and occupational settings.

In the early 1970s, the main social sector regulators federally were located in six government departments: Indian Affairs and Northern Development, Labour, Manpower and Immigration, National Health and Welfare, Secretary of State, and Veterans Affairs. Of the three sectors we examine in detail later in this chapter, only one, citizenship and immigration, was within the traditional core of this regulatory regime. Today, in the 2010s, federal organizations engaged in social sector regulation are primarily in seven portfolios: Canada Revenue Agency (CRA), Canadian Heritage, Citizenship and Immigration, Aboriginal Affairs and Northern Development Canada (AANDC), Health, Employment and Social Development (until mid-2013 called Human Resources and Skills Development Canada or HRSDC), and Veterans Affairs. This observation illustrates a theme of this chapter, which is that "the social" is not an unwavering space of governmental structures and activities; more accurately, the social is a dynamic entity with fluid elements and porous boundaries with other regimes of state intervention.

On this shifting quality and scope of the social sector regulatory regime, consider the following developments over the past four decades:

• Increasing number of categories protected from discrimination in
  human rights legislation, the introduction of the Canadian
  Charter of Rights and Freedoms, and a court challenges program
  for strategic litigation by community groups (a program subse-
  quently terminated, then reintroduced, then terminated again)
• Employment equity legislation and the federal contractors
  program
• Indian self-government through negotiation and legislation, such
  as the Cree/Naskapi Act 1984 and establishment in the early
  1990s of the BC Treaty Commission process
• Non-Smokers' Health Act 1989 and regulations
• Creation of Office of the Veterans Ombudsman and a Veterans
  Bill of Rights
• The Indian Residential Schools Settlement Agreement and the
  Indian Residential Schools Truth and Reconciliation Commission
• Political and regulatory targeting by the Harper government
  of charitable groups in the environmental sector
• Shifts in organizational forms and locations, such as the merger
  of Labour into HRSDC, moving the Patented Medicine Prices
  Review Board from the then ministry of Consumer and
  Corporate Affairs to Health Canada, the creation of the Public
  Health Agency of Canada, consolidation of the review and
  appeal structures in Veterans Affairs, or the fairly recent forma-
  tion and then closure of the Assisted Human Reproduction
  Canada agency with its remaining federal activities absorbed
  into Health Canada.

In the present day, the federal social sector regulatory regime operates mainly through seven departments and about thirty-five agencies,
boards, commissions, Crown corporations, and tribunals housed in
these portfolios; about half of these agencies are attached to Canadian
Heritage dealing with various aspects of cultural activities and facilities, followed by five each in Aboriginal Affairs and Northern
Development, and in Health Canada. Notable agencies include the
CBC, the Immigration and Refugee Board, and the Public Health
Agency, all which have sizable annual budgets for program spending;
most others, like the Canada Industrial Relations Board, the Registry
of Specific Claims Tribunal, and the Veterans Review and Appeal
Board have relatively modest budgets in funding and staffing. For
2011–12, the CBC budget was just over $1 billion, the PHAC budget

was about $622 million, and for the Immigration and Refugee Board the program budget was around $153 million. By contrast, most federal agencies, boards, and commissions in this regime tend to have annual budgets of under $10 million.

Why and how have these changes and continuities taken place in this regulatory regime? Hodgetts offers the insight that such developments in governmental responsibilities are "a response to the peculiar need and expectations of one particular community" as well as reflecting "the significant shift" in Canadian society "from an individualist to a collectivist philosophy" (1973, 90 and 98). Cairns and Williams concur that there has been a growing belief, as expressed in the views and agendas of many groups "that identities can be chosen, social arrangements reconstructed, and society transformed by human action" (1985, 9).

The number, the nature, and even the name of social sectors have evolved considerably since the 1970s, driven in part by the major increase in the participation of women in the labour market as well as the ongoing pluralization of Canada in ethnic, racial, and other terms socially (Rice and Prince 2013); by the constitutional recognition of many groups in the Charter of Rights and Freedoms altering self-conceptions of numerous social groups; and by the growing consciousness of, and discourse on, rights, whether expressed as the rights of adoptive parents, civil rights, disability rights, equality rights, gay or lesbian rights, human rights, treaty rights, or the inherent rights of self-government. From a political perspective, each sector is a distinct arena of group conflicts and struggles and a mix of setbacks and accomplishments.

Most social sectors tend to comprise groups facing some significant disadvantage or experiencing an important vulnerability: "Because of the continuing experience of inequality in terms of particularistic features (such as age, gender and race), social groups organize themselves to redress and change existing patterns of inequality" (Turner 1988: 43). Groups interact with public authorities at all levels seeking legal rights and policy remedies along with any symbolic recognition or service provision (McCreath 2011; Miki 2005; Prince 2009). Social movements seek the removal of attitudinal and systemic barriers, the reduction and prevention of discrimination, and the sustained advancement of accessibility and equality of opportunity firmly grounded in legislation and regulations. Thus, leading regulatory ideas in the social sector regime include positive state intervention in workplaces and other domains of life (articulated, e.g., as affirmative action, employment equity, and reasonable accommodation); protection of human health and safety against the risks of disease, injury, or insecurity; equality of opportunities, rights, and access to the benefits of society and fair treatment as citizens or as clients; integrity and honesty in the processing and payment of benefits to clientele; and in principles pertaining to administrative and public law, the accountability, review, and independent adjudication of decisions by regulators on claims.

Given the mix of departments and agencies and of social groups and regulatory ideas, the political profile of this regime varies among regulators and fluctuates over time. It can be argued that, at any given time, some of the regulators in this regime have an elevated profile on the agendas of the federal government, Parliament, constituency groups, and other stakeholder interests. Aboriginal affairs, matters of immigration, health care, and medical surveillance are perennial issues of high priority in political and policy systems. For much of the past forty-year period, the charitable sector had a relatively low profile, although its prominence has risen in the past decade or so; the same observation can be made of the assisted human reproduction sector along with veterans' affairs. The political profile of these sectors links to the social intentions and economic impacts (and also power effects) of rules and laws in this regulatory regime.

Among the functions regulation serve are those that (1) symbolically reassure a public that authorities are taking legal action on a given issue or problem, (2) socially recognize a group in a specific context as deserving of a regulatory policy response, (3) structurally modify the status order of a community by altering the terms of conditions of citizenship regimes, and (4) strategically seek to obtain the support and compliance of a population group. The economic effects of this regime are very important, widely recognized, and frequently debated. Immigration levels and classes of applicants have direct consequences for investments and business networks and for labour market functioning (Harrison 1996). Rules on the access to employment-related benefits such as Employment Insurance can have work incentive or disincentive consequences. The Hazardous Materials Information Review Commission registers claims for exemption from suppliers and employers who want to withhold confidential business information. This commission decides on the validity of the claim, adjudicates and issues decisions on compliance of material safety data, and administers appeals to these decisions. The work of the Patented Medicine Review Board illustrates the economic effects of compliance and enforcement. This board is responsible for regulating the prices that patentees can charge for patented drug products sold in Canada. The Canadian Artists and Producers Professional Relations Tribunal determines the rights of self-employed artists and producers, and the Canada Industrial Relations Board has powers of granting, modifying, and terminating bargaining rights as well as offer mediation and other dispute resolution services. Public interest intentions involve protecting and promoting the health, safety, and security, as well as the social and economic well-being of Canadians as expressed in legislation and other regulatory forms.

Regulating in the social sector regime involves a large variety of regulatory methods and forms utilized by public authorities, which we can summarize into the following seven different kinds of rules: constitutional powers, statutory authorities, judicial decisions and opinions, negotiated agreements, programmatic rules, softer techniques of governing conduct, and self-governance.

At root are constitutional forms of public powers based in the Constitution Act of 1867 and the Constitution Act of 1982, with implications for the allocation of legislative powers to the federal and or provincial orders of government in addition to the Canadian Charter of Rights and Freedoms conferring on citizens and residents such rights and freedoms as Aboriginal rights, security of life, equality, and multicultural heritage. Key aspects of health, labour, immigration, and social programs are shared jurisdictions between the federal and provincial governments, shaping the scope of activity, often requiring intergovernmental collaboration, and invariably prompting political disputes over respecting jurisdiction.

The criminal law is a source of authority of great magnitude for the federal government in this regulatory regime (and also in others) in assisted human reproduction, food and drug programs, public health, and immigration policies (Jackman 2000). The mandate of each federal portfolio in the regime is anchored in a departmental statute plus further acts of Parliament for which they are wholly or partly responsible to administer. Veterans Affairs Canada, for example, has an elaborate mandate consisting of a department statute together with twenty-one other pieces of legislation, twenty-five distinct sets of regulations, and six orders-in-council or Cabinet decisions.

Judicial decisions and opinions are often taken for granted as part of the legal context in policy and governance, but such decisions and opinions deserve specific mention as a source of rules and conventions, and as a response to (or cause of) perceived unruliness in a social sector or in other realms of public administration. In the areas of administrative, constitutional, common, or criminal law, both courts and tribunals render decisions on questions of jurisdiction, the scope of delegate authority and exercise of discretion, the reasonableness of procedures, and the exercise of duties, and the stipulation of remedies.

Negotiated agreements are another prominent regulatory form in the social sector regime. This may be statutory or administrative in nature and may be an accord that is international, such as social security agreements with other welfare states; intergovernmental, such as federal-provincial arrangements on immigration or federal-provincial-First Nation agreements such as on claim settlements and self-governance; intersectoral, such as a mediated settlement in industrial relations between employees and employers; and, interdepartmental, such as a memorandum of understanding between two federal departments on shared roles and responsibilities.

Programmatic rules refer to the myriad policy and practice procedures, contract terms and conditions, program standards, and activity guidelines. This is the stuff of administration, monitoring, enforcement, and compliance measures all interpreted and enacted by officials at the middle ranks and front lines of government agencies. Programmatic rules are intrinsic to the spending policy instrument in the appearance of regulations regarding eligibility, amount, and duration of direct transfers to individuals to families or seniors or veterans; payments to the provinces or territories; transfers to Aboriginal organizations; and grants and contributions to community organizations (Phillips and Levasseur 2004). Regulatory mechanisms like these also pervade health and social services delivered to assorted client groups (Prince, Mopfu, Hawkins, and Devlieger 2010).

Next are so-called softer techniques of governing the conduct of individuals or groups within a social sector. This category of regulating includes voluntary codes of practice, advice and recommendations to publics, educational materials, and multimedia campaigns that may well entail the social marketing of preferred practices across a range of activities. These softer forms of state power may lack the obvious bite of hard rules and stiff penalties, but they do resemble more formal regulatory tools in that they are legally sanctioned efforts by public agencies to influence the actions of others in the pursuit of certain policy objectives. Softer in sanctions, however, does not necessarily mean these techniques are any less prescriptive in standards or any less explicit in governance networks (Prince 2010a). What is being attempted often involves the de-normalization of certain social behaviours, for instance, smoking or drinking and driving, making them less acceptable and also stigmatizing – or even illegal – for the person engaging in such conduct.

Lastly, in the sense of distance from the core of the state, are regulatory forms and methods called self-governance or the government of one's self. The governmentality literature, which we discussed earlier, emphasizes the role of citizens in playing an active and central role in their own regulation in reference to governmental aims and policy objectives. In this context, regulatory authorities include public authorities, of course, but also non-state agencies through the norms and actions of churches and other faith organizations, neighbourhood groups, ethnic communities and agencies, families, nonprofit organizations, and professionals.

THREE SELECTED SECTORS: REGISTERED CHARITIES, CITIZENSHIP AND IMMIGRATION, AND ASSISTED HUMAN REPRODUCTION TECHNOLOGIES

We turn now to three diverse sectors of policy and governance arrangements selected for a closer examination of the social sector regulatory regime. Our examples are the Charitable Program of the CRA; the broad mandate of the Citizenship and Immigration portfolio with primary focus on matters of immigration and refugees, and to a lesser extent, on citizenship and multiculturalism; and the relatively short and politically turbulent history of the Assisted Human Reproduction Agency of Canada (AHRC).

Registered Charities

On the role of welfare states and social politics in contemporary societies, Turner has observed that "almost every attempt to expand social rights brings with it the potential for wider, more effective state regulation. The only alternative would appear to be voluntary, charitable agencies which seek to institutionalize altruism in non-profit organizations" (1988: 63). An escape from state regulation or other social controls, however, is not to be found in the voluntary sector and charitable organizations. Systems of rules operate on and in charities through contracts, grants, and contributions from governmental organizations (Laforest 2009a; Phillips and Levasseur 2004), through the regulatory regime for registered charities and other "qualified donees" under the Income Tax Act of 1985 (CRA 2011; Friesen, Alasia, and Bollam 2010), and through the careful surveillance and meticulous regulation by some non-profit organizations on prospective clients and current recipients of aid (Elson 2011; Rice and Prince 2013). Even those on the margins of society have a rendezvous with regulation.

The policy paradigm of the Canada Revenue Agency, as conveyed in agency documents and working practices, maintains that paying taxes is a legal obligation as well as a civic responsibility and that, in matters of tax administration, the agency's role is to protect Canada's revenue base and the integrity of the tax system. The CRA does so by promoting compliance by individuals, business, and charities and by addressing non-compliance in a series of steps with varying and progressive degrees of legitimate coercion. A fundamental element of the tax system in Canada is the primacy of self-assessment and self-filing by individuals, families, firms, foundations, and other community organizations.

Self-governance and, thus, self-compliance are core elements of tax administration and the regulatory regime associated with the tax system as a whole. Prime operational priorities of the CRA are to build and sustain trust and confidence in the tax system, to promote compliance with tax laws and regulations, and to make non-compliance with applicable legislation and rules more difficult. Compliance is understood to encompass full observance of tax laws with respect to filing, registering, remittance, and the reporting of taxes and benefits in a voluntary, accurate, and timely manner – in other terms, paying all of the income taxes one owes and receiving all of the tax credits or deductions one is due, no more or no less.

With respect to the Charitable Donations Tax Credit and Deduction, issues and trade-offs concern the determination of legitimate charities that operate exclusively for "charitable purposes." Charitable organizations registered under the Income Tax Act are given *the privilege* of issuing official donation receipts; the language of the CRA does not refer to absolute rights or assumed entitlements to be registered and thus receive tax-assisted donations; instead, it is a benefit and opportunity subject to authorization. The main client groups under the Charitable Program are the approximately 85,000 registered charities and a number of registered Canadian amateur athletic associations. Other "qualified donees" include Canadian municipalities and other public bodies performing a function of government, housing corporations that exclusively provide low-cost housing, and, outside of Canada, certain universities and certain other charitable organizations.

Core values include fairness and consistency in the treatment of client organizations in terms of regulatory burdens and sanctions, transparency and accountability by such means as public access to organization documents, and the "good governance of charities," which entails financial probity, the principle of "no undue benefits" to any persons associated with the charity, and a commitment to full compliance with applicable laws and regulations.

The major federal statutes pertaining to the charitable sector are the Income Tax Act and regulations, the Canada Revenue Agency Act of 1999, the Tax Court of Canada Act of 1985, and the Charities Registration (Security Information) Act of 2001. Other relevant legislation includes the Excise Tax Act of 1985, the Federal Courts Act of 1985, and the Canada Not-for-Profit Corporations Act of 2009. Of course, the core law is the Income Tax Act, a massive statute that sets out the fundamental rules on the computation of income (and the inclusions, subdivisions, and deductions) to determine the liability for tax on taxable income of every person resident in Canada in a given year. The statute also deals with the processes of tax returns, assessments, payments, refunds, appeals, and penalties.

Enacted in the immediate aftermath of 9/11, the Charities Registration (Security Information) Act concerns the registration of charities while having regard to considerations of national security, criminal intelligence information, and the safety of persons. The stated objective of the act captures well both the specific issue and the more general aims of the CRA on this sector. The act's purpose is "to demonstrate Canada's commitment to participating in concerted international efforts to deny support to those who engage in terrorist activities, to protect the integrity of the registration system for registered charities under the *Income Tax Act*, and to maintain the confidence of Canadian taxpayers that the benefits of charitable registration are made available only to organizations that operate exclusively for charitable purposes." (Income Tax Act, s. 2). In 2000, Canada signed the UN International Convention on the Suppression of Financing of Terrorism; the Charities Registration

(Security Information) Act is thus seen by federal authorities as supporting Canada's international obligations to counter terrorism as well as supporting Canada's domestic security agenda (CRA 2011).

The core state institutions and governmental roles in the Canadian charitable policy sector administer the relevant legislation and make this regulatory regime operational. These institutions and roles are the following: the CRA and its minister, the Charities Directorate of the CRA, Finance Canada and its minister, the Tax Court of Canada, the Federal Court of Canada, and the minister of public safety. Through its Charities Directorate, the CRA is the federal regulator responsible for registering and monitoring charities in Canada. In Finance Canada, a section within the Tax Policy Branch has responsibilities for the tax treatment of charitable donations and for reporting and compliance activities of charitable organizations. The Tax Court and Federal Court are the judicial arenas for formal appeals of notices of assessment to a registered charity from the minister of the CRA. The minister of public safety has certain responsibilities under the Charities Registration (Security Information) Act to support the minster of the CRA in the administration of that legislation.

Other institutions and actors, both state and non-state, in the charitable policy and regulatory sector include the Taxpayers' Ombudsman, who reports to the CRA minister; umbrella NGOs that represent foundations or health charities; professional organizations such as gift planners, law societies, and bar associations; tax specialists, financial advisers, and trust administrators; and other organizations that offer education and training to registered charities, for instance, university-based institutes for voluntary sector studies. These other actors and institutions are beyond the state, and basically offer advice and information as services rather than deal in regulatory powers delegated or otherwise. Further afield in the international realm, the CRA regulates gifts by Canadian taxpayers to foreign charitable organizations and donations to "prescribed universities" outside Canada, and also has a "guidance document" that describes recent case law and basic principles for Canadian registered charities carrying out activities outside of Canada.

Additional to legislation and regulations, the mix of regulatory forms in the charitable sector include common law. That is, judgments by courts over a long period that deal with the meaning of charity (the advancement of education, the relief of poverty, the advancement of religion, and other purposes beneficial to the community), with the operations of charities, and with whether they qualify for registration or continued registered status. Charity law, therefore, contains important precedents and principles that govern policy and the actions of regulators and charities.

In an effort to improve voluntary compliance, the CRA deploys an array of softer techniques of information materials and outreach activities to specific target groups within the charitable sector, such as rural and small charitable organizations. Along with numerous tax guides and pamphlets, "guidance products" provide information on applying for registration as a charity, operating as a charity, and the revoking of registered status. There are information circulars on practice issues such as record keeping, as well as information letters and interpretation bulletins, and the CRA regularly publishes a registered charities newsletter, which is available online.

Moreover, the CRA sponsors compliance-based educational programs and varied information sessions that deploy the tools of webinars, webcasts, and electronic mailing lists to organizations in the sector. In a related fashion, the Charities Partnership and Outreach Program has the twin objectives of increasing compliance and building *a responsive charitable sector* – a term that effectively summarizes the notion of the government of one's own conduct. The Charities Partnership and Outreach Program seeks to encourage self-governance by raising awareness of the regulatory obligations of registered charitable organizations and registered amateur athletic associations under the Income Tax Act and by assisting organizations in enhancing their capacity to meet those obligations. These obligations include satisfying an annual disbursement quota requirement, filing a registered charity information return and financial statements, and operating within the bounds of applicable legislation and regulations.

The CRA's policy on graduated sanctions in tax administration is clearly evident in compliance and enforcement activities in the charitable sector. If a registered charity is found to be in non-compliance, as a result of monitoring and auditing of charities, the CRA may, first, send out what is called an "education letter" to the charity; second, the CRA may then enter into a "compliance agreement" with the charity, setting out the steps that must be followed in order to comply with the Income Tax Act and outlining the consequences of any continued infractions; third, sanctions may be applied by the CRA, a financial penalty or perhaps suspension of tax receipting privileges, although the waiver of penalties may also occur in certain situations; and, fourth, the CRA may recommend the revocation of registered status as provided for under the legislation (s. 168).

During the Harper Conservative years, three trends with respect to the charitable sector are noteworthy for our analysis. One trend concerns charitable donation incentives. A series of tax assistance measures introduced in the 2006, 2007, and 2011 federal budgets aim to encourage the donation of publicly listed securities to public charities, and then extended to all registered charities, by allowing the exemption from capital gains tax on donations of certain shares. In addition to offering an incentive for donations of this kind, these measures add another layer of activity for administration and monitoring for the CRA and the charities sector.

A second trend involves strengthening the regulatory system of the charitable sector. This policy development is about extending certain regulatory requirements that previously applied only to registered charities to now bring in registered Canadian amateur athletic associations, municipalities, other public bodies, low-cost housing corporations, and certain universities and other charities internationally. New powers, rules, and penalties are also happening for the greater public transparency and accountability of qualified donees, for official donation receipts, for record-keeping practices, and governance practices of charitable organizations and athletic associations. In conjunction, recent initiatives by the CRA focus on the detection and deterrence of non-compliance by registered charities. These activities include auditing charities participating in tax shelter arrangements, auditing charities suspected to be engaged in "false receipting," and publicizing serious cases of non-compliance through agency newsletters and other information vehicles (CRA 2011).

The third trend concerns the political activities and transparency of registered charities. The Harper government has contended that some registered charities are not respecting the rules on political activities (a 10% limit of their resources on political advocacy and action) and are not transparent enough in disclosing the foreign sources of their financial support. Conservative politicians have claimed that some environmental groups had received funding from foreign interest groups and socialist millionaires. The federal 2012 budget allocated $8 million to the CRA for education and compliance programs with respect to political activities by registered charities and for requiring charities to provide greater information on

their funding sources. Most commentators view this move as a targeted reaction by the Harper Conservatives to the opposition of conservation organizations and environmental foundations to the
Alberta tar sands and proposed pipeline projects.

It is tempting to suggest that a paradox is at work in the charitable
sector: the prominence of both self-governance and command and
control, of encouraging altruism by regulating charity. However, in
our liberal market society, the giving of donations, even tax-assisted
ones, is shaped by perceptions of self-interests, worthy causes, and
good governance.

Citizenship and Immigration

Citizenship and Immigration is a prominent and long-standing federal
portfolio, a major social policy sector in Canada with conspicuous
international dimensions. It is a portfolio highly regulatory in nature
with a strong reliance on direct rules, hierarchy, and central steering as
a governance style; a style that predates the Harper Conservative era,
although almost certainly accentuated in recent years. Our depiction
of governance in citizenship and immigration differs from that of
Bradford and Andrew (2011), but complements their recognition of a
diversity of governance modes within the portfolio.

Citizenship and Immigration regulatory policy consists of the following: immigration intelligence, risk assessment, medical surveillance, fraud prevention and detection on migration, and enforcement,
while admitting about 250,000 newcomers to Canada every year;
the determination of thousands of refugee claims, the detention and
review of claims and possible deportation; processing over 160,000
citizenship applications annually, conducting tests and oaths or affir-
mations of citizenship, implementing fraud detection and revocation
of citizenship activities, and resumption of citizenship; managing the
Temporary Foreign Workers Program and assessing the foreign
qualifications of particular professions and occupations; and in the
area of multiculturalism, addressing issues of racism, anti-Semitism,
unjust discrimination, and community resilience.

The citizenship and immigration sector operates a gatekeeper function for the Canadian state and society. It sets the terms and conditions of admission into the country and into the formal status of
citizenship, of becoming a resident and then a citizen of Canada
(Bloemraad 2006) and a member of a provincial community, raising

important and at times challenging issues of difference, accommodation, and social inclusion or integration (Leroux 2010; Omidvar and Richmond 2003; Ryan 2010). A dominant policy idea in this sector relates to protection: protecting the health, safety, and security of Canadians; protecting selected refugees; protecting Canada's borders against criminals or terrorists; protecting the integrity of citizenship as an identity; and protecting ethnic, racial, and religious communities against prejudice and hate crimes. Other major rhetorical ideas include human diversity, social opportunity, economic prosperity, humanitarianism, and international justice. The international dimension is explicitly contained in the department's mission and the objectives of this sector, underlined by Canada's international legal obligations appearing in various UN conventions, covenants, and protocols.

Key pieces of legislation are the Department of Citizenship and Immigration Act of 1994, the Immigration and Refugee Protection Act of 2001, the Balanced Refugee Reform Act of 2010, an Act to Amend the Immigration and Refugee Protection Act of 2011, and the Protecting Canada's Immigration System Act of 2012. Other relevant laws are the Canadian Multiculturalism Act of 1985, the Canadian Race Relations Foundation Act of 1991, and the Citizenship Act of 1985. The Immigration and Refugee Protection Act is the centrepiece law in this social sector as it deals with immigration to Canada and the granting of refugee protection to persons who are displaced or in danger. On immigration policy, statutory objectives include maintaining the security of Canadians, protecting the health and safety of Canadians, and promoting international justice and security by fostering respect for human rights and by denying access to Canadian territory to persons who are criminals or security risks. With respect to refugee protection, statutory objectives include saving lives and offering protection to the displaced; offering safe haven to persons with a well-founded fear of persecution based on race, religion, nationality, political opinion, or membership in a particular social group; establishing fair and efficient procedures to maintain the integrity of the Canadian refugee protection system; and, at the same time, fulfilling Canada's international legal obligations on this issue. International dimensions also feature in the multicultural area, in that Canada is a party to the International Convention on the Elimination of All Forms of Racial Discrimination, one of its objectives being to ensure that all individuals receive equal treatment and equal protection under the law, while diversity is valued and respected.

The specific mix of regulatory tools and mechanisms in the citizenship and immigration sector is diverse and extensive. Notable in various laws and policies is a command-and-control form of regulation. In immigration services, core program activities involve investigation, detection of fraudulent documentation, inland control, and the removal, detention, and release of individuals. Official roles include investigators, secondary examination officers, case presentation officers, adjudicators, and expulsion officers who work with removal units to deal with persons ordered to leave the country. Under citizenship legislation, fines and imprisonment are authorized for such offences as making false representations, trafficking in certificates, and counterfeiting a certificate of citizenship, of naturalization or of renunciation.

Through the device of Ministerial Instructions (MIs), the minister of citizenship and immigration is a regulatory authority. MIs are allowed under the Immigration and Refugee Protection Act and enable the minister to issue special instructions to immigration officers when processing applications. MIs are usually targeted at a particular group or program (e.g., immigrant investors or federal skilled workers) and are time limited in effect. MIs are a means to limit the number of applications by introducing an annual cap or to introduce a temporary pause or create a specific eligibility stream. To illustrate, an MI from July 2012 directed immigration officers "not to process any work permit applications from foreign nationals seeking employment in businesses that are in sectors where there are reasonable grounds to suspect a risk of sexual exploitation – namely strip clubs, escort services and massage parlours" (Department of Citizenship and Immigration 2012). The minister described this move as protecting vulnerable foreign workers from the risk of abuse.

International agreements form a significant element of the policy and regulatory context in citizenship and immigration. Canada is a signatory to approximately thirty conventions and protocols concerning human rights in the areas of refugees; women and children; torture, slavery, and forced labour; economic, social, and political rights; humanitarian law; and transnational crime. Canada is a signatory to the 1951 Convention Relating to the Status of Refugees; the 1967 Protocol; and the Convention against Torture, Cruel, Inhuman or Degrading Treatment or Punishment. On immigration policy more generally, the Department of Citizenship and Immigration is a member of the International Organization for Migration and works with other international migration policy institutes like the Organization for Security and Cooperation in Europe. Within the Canadian federation, intergovernmental agreements are now a significant form of regulatory policy on immigration, which is a shared jurisdiction between the provinces and federal parliament (Bradford and Andrew 2011). Over the period 1991 to 2005, the Canadian government signed agreements with all provinces on immigration, and the first meeting of ministers responsible for immigration was held in 2002 to discuss matters of policy coordination, program funding, and delivery of services.

In the realm of programmatic rules, operational manuals on policy or enforcement or on processing applicants, among other topics of practice, impart guidance to staff at both Citizenship and Immigration and the Canada Border Services Agency. In the course of a year, dozens of more specific operational bulletins are issued providing instructions to staff on particular rules or specialized administrative procedures. The terms and conditions in grants and contributions to newcomer settlement agencies and ethnic associations exercise a form of control in terms of what is and is not funded, and for how long; the result being that agency sustainability is a chronic issue as is the lack of support for planning and networking among agencies (Bradford and Andrew 2011; Omidvar and Richmond 2003).

Finally, as a provocative form of self-governance, in 2011, the Harper government introduced a new government immigration fraud tip line, inviting the public to call in tips on people they suspect are defrauding the immigration system or are involved in knowingly concealing material circumstances in the citizenship process. The immigration minister defended the move arguing that the fraud tip line will help crack down on those who seek to devalue Canadian citizenship. Opposition immigration critics described the move as about form rather than substance, focusing on a minor issue rather than on other more serious problems of application wait lists or foreign credentials (Hiltz 2011). From a governance perspective, the fraud tip line invites a particular type of neighbourhood watch and local exercise of power by individuals over other people. This stands in contrast to other public actions as local groups that sponsor refugees or local employers that offer work opportunities.

In the citizenship and immigration sector, the present set of federal rule makers and regulators is centred in the Department of Citizenship and Immigration and its minister; and the two administrative bodies attached to that portfolio, the Immigration and Refugee Board of Canada (IRBD) and the Citizenship Commission. The IRBD is an independent administrative tribunal that adjudicates cases on immigration inadmissibility, detention reviews, appeals, and refugee protection claims made within Canada (IRBD 2011). The Citizenship Commission is chaired by the senior citizenship judge and comprises citizenship judges located throughout the country. While it reports directly to the minister, the commission is separate from the department and operates along the lines of an administrative tribunal. The commission reviews citizenship applications, and the citizenship judges, acting as quasi-decision makers, assess applicants to ensure they meet the requirements of the Citizenship Act and regulations, and administer the swearing-in oath (or affirmation) for Canadian citizenship.

Other core federal government organizations in the sector deal with matters of health, security, and justice. Health Canada and the Public Health Agency of Canada play roles, as do provincial and territorial public health authorities. In the case of Health Canada, decisions on entry to the country are based on medical assessments of immigrants, refugees, and seasonal workers among other groups, as to whether a person is admissible, admissible with surveillance, temporarily inadmissible, or inadmissible altogether. On matters of justice, the Department of Justice and its minister are involved, as can be the Federal Court of Canada, the Federal Court of Appeal, and the Supreme Court of Canada on questions of law dealing with citizenship applications, for example. On matters of safety and security, the Department of Public Safety and its minister play important statutory roles in this sector, as do the Canada Border Services Agency, the RCMP and other law enforcement agencies, and the Canadian Security Intelligence Service (CSIS). These agencies are involved with issues of enforcement, fraud, confidential information, and risk assessments in the immigration system. Under the Immigration and Refugee Protection Act, the minister of citizenship and immigration is responsible for the administration of the legislation. The minister of public safety is responsible for examinations at ports of entry; the enforcement of the act, including arrests, detentions, and removals; and for establishing policies on inadmissibility to Canada on the grounds of security, organized criminality, or violation of human or international rights. Overall, it is the Cabinet (governor-in-council) that may make regulations on matters referred to in the act. Still other federal government organizations related to this sector are Foreign Affairs and International Trade, Human Resources and Skills Development, and the Canadian International Development Agency. Citizenship and Immigration has departmental services in over seventy countries co-located with Foreign Affairs.

In the international domain, relevant organizations in this sector include the UN Commissioner for Refugees and the UN Working Group on Resettlement; inter-governmental consultations on asylums, refugees and migration policies; the International Organization for Migration; the OECD and NAFTA; and the G-8 Migration Experts Subgroup. The domestic policy community on citizenship and immigration includes Amnesty International, the Canadian Bar Association, the Canadian Chamber of Commerce, the Canadian Police Association, and many other national and local associations, including settlement service agencies.

Under the Harper Conservatives, and especially under the leadership of Jason Kenny as minister of citizenship and immigration since 2008, quite a few measures have been taken to strengthen government control and exercise regulatory powers over the sector. In 2010, the Balanced Refugee Reform Act was passed with the purpose of providing for what the government called a faster and fairer refugee determination system in Canada. Politically, the balance being addressed is to expedite the processing of claims by reducing certain rights of process and appeal available until then under the system. Important elements in this legislation are that legitimate or genuine refugees will get protection in two or three months rather than the two years under the previous system (achieved partly by the faster removal of those who do not qualify for refugee protection); authority is granted to the government to establish a biometric visa system for Canada's immigration screening system, aligning the country with several others worldwide; and authority for adopting stronger measures and penalties to deter human smugglers.

In 2011, an Act to Amend the Immigration and Refugee Protection Act passed; an earlier version in the previous Parliament was called the Cracking Down on Crooked Consultants Act. Immigration consultants not properly licensed or registered were the prime target of this legislation. The specific amendment establishes a new offence of anyone other than an authorized representative to conduct business for a fee of an immigration application or proceeding. It also provides the minister with the regulatory power to designate or revoke the designation of a body responsible for governing immigration consultants, and to provide for transitional measures with respect to such a designation, or revocation of a designation. Outcomes of this amendment are that the Canadian Society of Immigration Consultants has been replaced by a new body, the Immigration Consultants of Canada Regulatory Council; and the federal government has explicit authority to oversee the activities of the immigration consultant industry and its regulatory body. From the Harper government's perspective, a more professional and transparent regulatory body is in place that is working more closely with the Department of Citizenship and Immigration and law enforcement and agencies in tackling unethical immigration consultants.

Also in 2011, the Conservative government introduced stronger rules in the Temporary Foreign Workers Program including a more thorough appraisal of the authenticity and substance of jobs offered by employers and a two-year suspension from the program for employers who do not meet their declared commitment to their workers (Citizenship and Immigration Canada 2011). In 2012 came the Protecting Canada's Immigration System Act that, in the rhetoric of the government, is designed to support law-abiding immigrants and target bogus asylum claimants, human smugglers, and those who pose a risk to Canadian security and safety. This legislation was admitted to be a response to the growth in recent years in fake asylum claims from particular countries within the European Union.

Other regulatory measures in this sector by the Harper government display the same theme of cracking down or getting tough, whether on dubious citizenship applications or unscrupulous immigration consultants. The latest at time of writing is the Faster Removal of Foreign Criminals Act (Bill C-43) in June 2012, with the purpose of safeguarding the integrity of the immigration system against high-risk individuals such as drug traffickers, child abusers, and murderers. In the bill are provisions to remove a right of appeal for all those with a sentence of six months or more and for those persons who have committed a serious crime outside Canada to be barred from accessing the Immigration Appeal Division of the Department of Citizenship and Immigration. This is a highly contestable reform because deportation can result from minor crimes, for example, possession of six marijuana plants, and back to countries from which the deported have long departed.

Assisted Human Reproduction Technologies

Of the three social sectors of regulatory policy and governance we are exploring in this chapter, assisted human reproduction technologies (AHRT) is the newest, dating from the late 1970s. It occupies a dynamic environment with rapid developments in research and breakthroughs in science, along with shifting practices in clinical care. It may also be the most sensitive ethically and has been politically controversial in Canadian federalism with a fundamental challenge to the constitutionality of the centre-piece federal legislation on the subject. It deals with the role of the state on the subject of human life itself; of people as prospective parents, children, family members, donors, recipients, patients, and clients. The following discussion draws from our earlier work, especially Doern and Prince (2012).

The field of AHRT embraces issues of egg, sperm, and embryo transplantation, therapeutic and human cloning, genetic research, sex selection, genetic manipulations and applications, xeno-transplants, and embryonic stem-cell research, genomics, and personalized medicine. More specifically, this sector includes the application of genetic technologies to human procreation, such as pre-implantation genetic diagnosis, prenatal genetic diagnosis, in vitro fertilization, and other reproductive technologies. Genetic testing and screening raise a host of actual and potential controversial issues including the following: genetic testing as a basis for prenatal detection of inherited diseases, determination of fetal sex for non-medical reasons, assessment of a person's eligibility or lack of it for health and life insurance coverage or for employment, the privacy and uses of genetic information, and genetic intervention and what it might mean for the inclusion or exclusion of persons with disabilities and, thus, the diversity of human conditions in society.

The foremost federal legislation in the sector is the Assisted Human Reproduction Act of 2004, which authorized establishing a federal regulatory agency, the Assisted Human Reproduction Agency of Canada (AHRC), which effectively became operational in 2007–08. The declared purposes of the legislation are to protect and promote the health, safety, dignity, and rights of Canadians who use or are born of assisted human reproductive technologies; to promote scientific advances that benefit Canadians; and to foster an environment in which ethical principles are applied in all aspects (AHRC 2011). The agency's two areas of program activity were (1) licensing and enforcement of a regulatory framework for AHRT and (2) health information and knowledge management for AHRT.

In comparison with the other social sectors under review, the language of ethics and of rights figure more in the assisted human reproductive sector in both statutory and general policy discourse. The policy ideas of protecting health and safety apply in this context to donors, parents, and offspring born of AHRT. Other policy ideas and discourse relate to building families, making informed choices, protecting people against the risks associated with AHRT, respecting human dignity, using these technologies in ways that reflect the ethical standards and values of Canadians, and thus prohibiting "unacceptable activities, such as human cloning" (AHRC 2011).

The main federal government organizations involved in the assisted human reproduction sector are the the following: the Assisted Human Reproduction Agency of Canada (terminated in 2013 and its activities merged with Health Canada) and a science advisory panel to the agency; Health Canada and its minister; the Canadian Institutes of Health Research; and the RCMP, which has jurisdiction to enforce the Assisted Human Reproduction Act in regard to penal investigations and penal proceedings. The AHRC established memoranda of understanding (MOUs) with Health Canada and the Canadian Institutes of Health Research. The MOUs with Health Canada were on compliance and enforcement activities and the personal health information registry. Under the arrangement, Health Canada was responsible for developing policy and regulations on assisted human reproduction while the AHRC was responsible for implementing the regulations. The Supreme Court of Canada also has played a critical role in the sector in a reference about the Assisted Human Reproduction Act (Mitchell 2011; Whyte 2011).

Other state organizations in this sector include provincial and territorial governments, in particular their ministries of health and perhaps their ministries of family and social services. Internationally, the AHRC participated in the Collaborative Discussion on Cross-Border Reproductive Care. This relates to the situation that "growing numbers of AHR users are travelling to foreign destinations to access AHR services, which presents both health risks for patients and their offspring and health costs for Canadian society" (AHRC 2011, 16).

Of the institutions involved in making rules and decisions on AHRT, several lie outside the formal structures of the Canadian state, such as families, religious organizations, and disability groups. In fact, these social structures can be thought of as both self-regulating institutions and institutions regulated by formal and informal rules generated by other structures. Other non-governmental bodies, in particular health professional associations and related licensing and accreditation bodies contribute to the formulation and implementation of rules governing assisted human reproduction. Examples include the Society of Obstetricians and Gynaecologists of Canada, the College of Physicians and Surgeons, the Canadian Paediatric Society, and the Canadian College of Medical Geneticists. Additionally, the AHRC had links with equivalent agencies in other countries.

Beyond such forms of professional self-regulation, an even wider view of regulation in the bio-life realm, in terms of rule making, enforcement, and compliance, involves the personal self-regulation of individuals within families, religious communities, ethnic or racial groups, and other relevant social categories. At play here are rules of behaviour backed not by the sanctions of the state but rather by social structures, cultural mores, belief systems rooted in religious faith, and public morals, as well as personal dreams and fears of health risks in having a child created as a result of fertility drugs, donated semen, eggs, or embryos, and/or because of inherited genetic disorders. The effect of these norms and values on the considerations and choices of individuals or couples can be quite influential. On the actual decisions and actions of people, a cultural responsibility or a personal sense of obligation, for instance, reinforced by experts, elders, or confidants may well outweigh the impact of a statutory right or public service.

Techniques of socially based self-regulation in the AHR sector embrace a multitude of activities including the following: gathering specialized information from experts and increasingly from the Web and social media; consulting with individuals and organizations, including self-help or support groups; calculating the risks and benefits of particular technologies or tests; reflecting on core norms and internalized principles of one's sense of identity; and acting upon oneself.

Following on a 2008 Quebec court challenge of the Assisted Human Reproduction Act, in December 2010 the Supreme Court of Canada gave a reference opinion on the legislation, the result of which the legislative authority of Parliament to act in this area has been severely constrained and partially confirmed (*Reference re Assisted Human Reproduction Act*, 2010 SCC 61). Several key parts of AHRC's mandate and the legislation itself were constitutionally overturned. Among other issues, this judicial ruling suggests a limited federal role in the direct regulation of controlled activities by health practitioners and in medical facilities, areas that a majority of Supreme Court justices said were ultra vires or beyond the legal capacity of the federal government. This means that the accreditation, licensing, and review of fertility clinics and other health and research facilities concerned with assisted human reproduction are under the jurisdiction of provincial governments.

Federal regulatory powers the Supreme Court upheld constitutionally include the prohibitions on commercialization of an individual's reproductive capabilities (i.e., paying for donor eggs or for a surrogate mother), human cloning, and sex selection, as well as the requirement for a donor's consent to use their gametes or in vitro embryos. However, as a leading health policy analyst in Canada observes: "The reality is that many surrogates and egg donors are paid, but it is done in a nudge-nudge-wink-wink fashion. It's time to get the exercise above board. Similarly, because paying for sperm is illegal in Canada, virtually all sperm used for *in vitro* fertilization is imported from the United States (where it is paid for). How exactly does that protect the Canadian public? It gives the whole assisted human reproduction field a black-market feel, unnecessarily frightening and stigmatizing would-be parents" (Picard 2012).

Further unruliness results from the ambiguity over what authority the federal government retains for collecting information on controlled activities under the act as part of a larger health surveillance system. Less contentious have been the knowledge transfer activities of the AHRC (which Health Canada may continue to do in some manner) of monitoring research and clinical trends, and providing information to health professionals, parents and family groups, and the general public on topics of infertility and assisted human reproduction. Overall, the federal government's main role in this sector will involve, probably, informational and international activities: "Most of the issues surrounding fertility are health issues, not legal issues. This is an area to be dealt with by provincial health regulators, not federal criminal law" (Picard 2012).

REGIME ATTRIBUTES

Having provided a profile of the three social sectors, we now consider the regime attributes in our analytical framework: (1) ideas, discourses and agendas; (2) public and private power in regulation making and compliance; and (3) science, evidence, and knowledge (interpreted here as uncertainty, risks and knowledge). These attributes allow us both to examine and compare the sectors in relation to both regulatory change and inertia, and types of unruliness in the context of concepts of regulatory welfarism, governance, and democracy.

Ideas, Discourses, and Agendas

Each of the social sectors in federal regulatory policy contains a relatively distinct group of ideas and discourse in a context of evolving conceptions of issues and identities and roles of the state and society. Some of the oldest policy ideas are to be found in the charities sector in the meaning of charitable purposes inherited from seventeenth- through nineteenth-century British common law and still influential in the present age of charity law and regulatory policy making. The ideas of citizenship and immigration have shifted and expanded in recent times with an enhanced awareness of threats to security and to state-run systems of admissibility. While the policy language of assisted human reproduction exhibits the modernity of science and genetic research, this sector is stirred by long-standing ethical beliefs and individual hopes of having children.

The "rights revolution" has not affected equally all social sectors. A rights discourse is most evident in the citizenship and immigration sector, expressed institutionally as the network of Canada's international legal obligations, as the rule of law and procedural rights of reviews and appeals, and as the rights and responsibilities of Canadian citizenship. The charities sector emphasizes a discourse of civic duties in paying taxes and of privileges in being and receiving registered status as a charitable organization. The discourse of the Assisted Human Reproduction Agency of Canada evoked human rights in its statutory mandate but with little specificity as to their meaning or application in the sector, in part because so few regulations were developed by Health Canada for the AHRC to implement and enforce.

In terms of scope and profile, undoubtedly, citizenship and immigration has the most elaborate political vocabulary and pervasive symbolism. As Bradford and Andrew (2011, 226) remark: "From a high-level symbolic perspective, immigration is central to narratives of nation-building and identity formation." Indeed, at least five discourses circulate in the citizenship and immigration sector. (1) There is an economic discourse related to labour market considerations, foreign credential recognition, and the relative prosperity of immigrants over time. (2) There is a humanitarian discourse that highlights refugee protection, family reunification, and Canada as a safe haven. (3) There is a cultural discourse that celebrates Canada as a nation of immigrants, of multiculturalism, and accommodation of diversity. While this is true at the federal level, in Quebec there is the discourse that rejects multiculturalism for "interculturalism," of "reasonable accommodation" and more recently the proposal from the Parti Québécois in 2013 for a Charter of secularism. (4) There is a civic discourse that talks of participation, citizenship, and social cohesion. And (5) there is a discourse of system integrity or risk management, a political language to justify new and stronger laws and tougher sanctions for addressing fraud, terrorism, and other threats to the safety and security of Canadians.

The *agendas* in the regulatory regime of social sectors are about encouraging certain positive decisions and activities: legitimate donations to registered charities and good governance by charities and associations; law-abiding immigrants, bona fide refugees, and professional immigrant consultants; ethical scientific research, public awareness, and assisting Canadians to build families with assisted human reproduction technologies. At the same time, social sector regulatory agendas are about various controls and discouragements: false receipting for charitable donations, medical surveillance of immigrants and visitors to the country, and prohibiting sex selection in a fertility clinic. Upholding Canadian values while making rules is implicit in these social sectors. Recent Liberal and Conservative federal governments both have had policy agendas on the charities sector, although not on the voluntary sector as a whole (Elson 2011; Phillips 2009); a well-defined agenda expressly on citizenship and immigration (Alieweiwi and Laforest 2009; Bradford and Andrew 2011); but a tentative and low priority agenda for assisted human reproduction (Doern and Prince 2012; Jones and Salter 2009).

In an era of continuing retrenchment in many public services, emerging new social risks and persisting old needs, and people searching for ways of making contributions and building connections, the role of charitable organizations is increasingly important. The events of 9/11 in the United States triggered a national security agenda in Canada that touched the charity sector with the passage of the

Charities Registration (Security Information) Act to support the Chrétien Liberal government's measures to counter terrorism. A more obvious and expected link to the law and order agenda of recent federal governments is the focus in immigration on border management and national security.

A change of government is an occasion for changing public policy agendas. This is evident with the Harper Conservatives' approach to many areas of social policy, including citizenship and multiculturalism, where a greater emphasis is being given to the responsibilities of citizenship and notions of integration and shared values over rights and diversity (Bradford and Andrew 2011, 273–4). Agenda events in the assisted human reproduction sector include a royal commission in the 1990s, parliamentary committee hearings over a number of governments in the 1990s and early 2000s, then legislative and consultation processes which finally yielded the Assisted Human Reproduction Act in 2004. The capacity of the AHRC, however, was substantially constrained by the absence of policies and regulations developed by Health Canada that were essential for the agency to perform much of its mandate. Court challenges ultimately led to the demise of the AHRC, which the Harper government confirmed in its 2012 budget. Social sectors are shaped partly by the agendas of governments, no doubt, but also by the advocacy efforts of non-governmental groups and by shifts in relations of power between governments and between public and private interests.

Public and Private Power in Regulation Making and Compliance

Our analysis establishes that the federal state remains active in exercising powers of regulatory policy and enforcement. In recent years, the Harper government has strengthened rules and extended the overall regulatory regime over the charitable sector in Canada and for related organizations operating abroad. Priorities of the CRA in the charities program emphasize promoting compliance with tax laws combined with making non-compliance more difficult by fortifying detection and deterrence measures.

Citizenship and immigration has been an especially dynamic social sector with both new and amended legislation in the areas of citizenship, immigration, and refugee protection, invariably with augmented authorities and penalties. This is a sector with multilevel governance that comprises several federal policy institutions; joint jurisdiction between the federal and provincial governments in the field of immigration; societal bodies of community groups, churches, and ethnic associations; and international bodies. While in some program areas of citizenship and immigration policy the Harper government is "steering at a distance" (Bradford and Andrew 2011), in areas we have examined in this chapter the Conservatives are steering from the centre.

The case of the immigrant consultant industry shows that the market is not always seen as the ideal mechanism for providing services. The Harper government stepped in with new powers for overseeing and regulating this professional service, resulting from direct intervention by the minister of immigration and his officials. This is some distance from laissez-faire and deregulation. This federal action, by creating a more transparent and, thus, governable space, may be said to reflect aspects of new public management such as the accountability of the industry body and the institution of performance expectations.

In the assisted human reproduction sector, the fate of the Assisted Human Reproduction Act indicates how all power is relational. In this specific case, the critical relation is the constitutional division of powers and the role of the courts in adjudicating disputes over the scope of authority exercised by one order or the other. The AHRC and overall federal policy in this sector is partly a failed effort, then, by both Liberal and Conservative governments in rule making and compliance (Doern and Prince 2012). Nonetheless, the assisted human reproduction sector offers another instance in recent times of the federal assertion of general regulatory powers.

Science, Evidence, and Knowledge

In the regulatory regime of social sectors, we have identified a number of policy themes – protecting Canada's revenue base and managing the compliance of registered charities; maintaining the security of Canada's borders, ensuring the integrity of the immigration and refugee system, and upholding the value of Canadian citizenship; and, promoting and protecting the health and safety of patients, donors, and children born of assisted human reproduction technologies – all are responses to uncertainties and insecurities, and all point to core functions of modern national governments.

Evidence regarding risks in the charitable sector includes wilful non-compliance by some taxpayers "fabricating expenses like charitable deductions to purposefully understate their tax liabilities" (CRA 2011, 14). In response, the CRA undertakes a regular cycle of audits along with providing numerous information products intended to raise clients' awareness of the benefits of compliance and the costs of non-compliance. In the immigration and refugee systems, certain applicants may pose risks to health and safety in Canada because of identity fraud, organized crime, or violations of international human rights. Knowledge-based strategies to address such risks include intelligence from CSIS and the RCMP as well as fingerprint and photo technology, and biometrics data in issuing visas (Citizenship and Immigration Canada 2011). Particular risks of the sponsorship of immediate family members for immigration to Canada is mitigated by federal policy requiring that a permanent resident or Canadian citizen assume responsibility to provide for basic needs of their sponsored relative for a number of years. The rationale for this form of self-governance (and governing at a distance by Ottawa) is to determine the genuineness of the sponsorship and to protect the public purse at all levels of government from unwarranted expenses in income assistance or social services. The Citizenship and Immigration Canada website states:

> If you sponsor a relative to come to Canada as a permanent resident, you are responsible for supporting your relative financially when he or she arrives. As a sponsor, you must make sure your spouse or relative does not need to seek financial assistance from the government ... If payments from a federal, provincial or municipal assistance program are made during the validity period of the undertaking to the person you are sponsoring or his or her family members, you will be considered to be in default of your obligations, may have to repay to the government concerned any benefits they received, and will not be allowed to sponsor other members of the family class until you have reimbursed the amount of these payments to the government concerned.

In the assisted human reproduction sector, science, evidence, and knowledge regarding medical risk factors concern mistaken beliefs about infertility, about AHRT, and travelling abroad for treatments. Other risks are political, whereby private practices and public rules both may challenge ethical standards and basic values of Canadians. Lastly, the downfall of the AHRC and key sections of the federal legislation throws up uncertainty, and also unruliness, as to the future regulation of the fertility industry in Canada (Blackwell 2012). The soft instruments of knowledge transfer and information sharing with individuals, lawyers, researchers, fertility clinics, and professional health associations emerge as strategic activities in such a muddled policy environment.

CONCLUSIONS

This chapter has examined the regulatory regime of social sectors by looking at three such sectors – registered charities, citizenship and immigration, and assisted human reproduction. Overall, the regime is an interacting assemblage of policy ideas and rules, government departments and agencies, as well as societal institutions and relations of power. The concept of a sector relates to vertical dimensions of rule making and public policy applied to particular groups and activities. The meaning of "the social" varies somewhat in each sector, but all deal with individual and family well-being, with human development, and social existence. The charitable sector implies a politics of a better life; citizenship and immigration a politics of a new life, refugee protection, the politics of life or death; and assisted human reproduction is a politics of life itself. The magnitude and capacity of each sector has implications for the public profile of a given category of citizens, the type of policies developed, and the extent of coercion that may be applied.

Within each social sector is a general constituency along with one or more particular groups deemed problematic from the perspective of the state in terms of unruliness. For instance, in the charitable sector, issues of non-compliance whether by individuals, businesses, or charitable organizations are explicitly part of the legislative powers, operational priorities, and administrative practices of the Canada Revenue Agency. Elements that contribute to the complexity of this regime include the limited capacity of small and rural-based charities, as well as tax shelter arrangements, offshore organizations, and groups involved in political activities. In this sector, the flip-side of unruliness is the recognized legitimacy and full compliance of a nonprofit entity to qualify as a registered charity and to receive tax-assisted donations. In recent times, there has been a concerted purposefulness to agenda setting in the charitable sector including the goal of ensuring that charities are not involved in financing terrorist or criminal activities.

In citizenship and immigration, unruliness is apparent with regard to the problems of fraudulent immigration consultants, bogus asylum claimants, and human traffickers, along with possible medical risks associated with refugees, seasonal workers, and immigrants. Ministerial instructions and operational bulletins are two devices that target specific instances of unruliness in this sector, for a particular issue, group, and period of time with respect to immigration, refugees, and border services. Policy changes in recent years have sought to alleviate these kinds of unruliness in the regime by strengthening oversight of the immigration consultant industry and by increasing penalties and removing or reducing rights of review and appeal by foreign criminals and refugee claimants.

In assisted human reproduction, unruliness is expressed, in part, by constant worries of unethical practices by individuals or by health specialists, by an underground economy for surrogates and egg donors, and by Canadians travelling abroad to access services. Unruliness in this sector also relates to regulatory agency complexity, whereby Health Canada was responsible for developing policy and regulations, the Assisted Human Reproduction Agency of Canada was responsible for implementing the policies and rules, and the RCMP was responsible for enforcing key sections of the legislation. Health Canada's inertia in developing rules in a timely manner greatly limited the effectiveness of the AHRC to build credibility and implement the legislation. Moreover, the agenda setting here was quickly and critically judicialized – with the Quebec court challenge in 2008 and the Supreme Court of Canada's reference opinion in 2010 – which essentially rendered the AHRC a shell, overturning much of federal statutory policy on the issue of assisted human reproduction technologies.

Overall, from the standpoint of the regulated, unruliness in this regime relates to the growing number and the widening reach of rules; the severe resource constraints of many non-governmental organizations to have the capacity to manage the burdens of accountability requirements; tensions in the charitable and immigration sectors over the place of advocacy in program funding contracts; and ambiguities in the legal meaning in the federal legislation governing fertility clinics.

With respect to the scholarly literature on regulation, contrary to what some assert is an age of the post-regulatory state, we see considerable examples of where the Canadian federal state is far from hesitant in bolstering the machinery of government, exercising legal powers, and using regulatory tools in particular social policy fields. More in keeping with the governmentality literature, our analysis suggests that even in neo-liberal times with general restraint on government spending or taxing, it does not necessarily mean an overall reduction in actual state intervention and governing. A more likely picture, according to this literature, is a reconfiguration of the objects and mechanisms of regulation playing out across an array of sectors in contingent and shifting ways.

We identified seven types of regulatory methods operating in and around the regulatory regime of social sectors: constitutional powers, statutory authorities, judicial decisions and opinions, negotiated agreements, programmatic rules, softer techniques of governing conduct, and self-governance. On general trends in rule making, there have been developments in all types of rule making and governance; the complete regulatory tool-kit is fully deployed in the social sector regime. Constitutional powers have deeply shaped both the citizenship and immigration and the AHR sectors, although in quite different ways of legitimating or curtailing federal powers. All three sectors saw new legislative initiatives in the past decade or so, most actively in the immigration and refugee protection system. Decisions by courts and tribunals on matters of jurisdiction, statutory interpretation, and administrative procedure are influential on a frequent basis in all the social sectors. Negotiated agreements are a significant feature of this regime, particularly for citizenship and immigration, as a device for structuring roles and relationships on a number of scales of governance. On developing and applying programmatic rules, the charitable sector has moved ahead selectively yet explicitly; citizenship and immigration has moved strongly and continually, it seems; and the assisted human reproduction sector has gone slowly and softly. Softer techniques of governing conduct by government agencies as well as self-governance by individuals and client groups are essential to social policy implementation and compliance, with growing emphasis on educational and persuasive tools.

Finally, various forms of democratic governance are apparent in the regulatory regime of social sectors. In terms of representative democracy, Parliament has been an active lawmaker in these areas, authorizing government initiatives, and the federal Cabinet is the central executive body for approving regulations under most statutes. Political parties clash regularly over the details of laws or the techniques employed and occasionally divide over the basic merits of a law, as in the case with the Assisted Human Reproduction Act of 2004. The significance of federalized democracy is unmistakable throughout this regime in the issues of shared jurisdiction in immigration, the role of intergovernmental agreements, and challenges to the exercise of federal criminal power in matters of reproductive health. In actuality, many social sectors in Canada primarily are under provincial jurisdictions.

Interest group pluralism and civil society democracy are nearly synonymous with the idea of social sectors. In practice, NGOs define the nature and gamut of the charitable sector; the citizenship and immigration sector is populated with community groups, ethnic associations, newcomer agencies, and networks of settlement services; and the assisted human reproduction sector consists of health enterprises, medical associations and other health professionals, research institutes, clinics, women's groups, and family support groups. Direct democracy in the social sector regulatory regime relates to self-governance by individuals and families and by client organizations, and the government of one's own conduct is inevitably linked to public rules.

7

The Marketplace Framework Regulatory Regime: Competition, Banking and Financial Services, and Intellectual Property

The marketplace is a complex arena of myriad exchanges between producers and sellers of products and processes and with consumers and users of such products and processes. The broad intent of the marketplace framework regulatory regime is to govern horizontally across the economy with rules and guidance approaches and, indeed, to ensure that sectoral industry preferences are not encouraged; otherwise, one is essentially fostering industrial policy rather than marketplace framework policy. The politics of this regime do not succeed entirely in avoiding or downplaying sectoral interests, in part, because sectoral regulation has been proceeding through other channels and also because industrial and producer interest groups tend to be organized sectorally, and there are many more of them than broader dispersed horizontal multi-industry lobby groups. Our analysis deals with federal marketplace framework policy and regulation in the past two decades but set in a longer forty- to fifty-year historical context and in the context of international ideas, pressures, and crises, especially in the banking and financial services sector but also in different ways in the competition policy and intellectual property realms.

The chapter first looks at the general nature and scope of the regime, focusing mainly on its economic marketplace framework goals and values but with some mention, as well, of its social impacts, including aspects of fair markets, product quality, and consumer choice. We then look more closely at the evolution over the past four decades of three selected marketplace framework regulatory realms: competition policy, banking and financial markets, and intellectual property with a focus on patents. The analysis includes an appreciation of their diverse delegated governance modes of regulation,

about fifteen agencies in total anchored in and around Industry
Canada and the Department of Finance and the Bank of Canada. It
also includes a broad account of the political economy of regulatory
reform stages and episodes, the mixes of statutory and regulatory
rule making versus guidance approaches, and a sense of caseloads
and volumes and, hence, of the rhythms of front-line regulation. This
is followed by an exploration of our three regime attributes as elements in explaining both change and inertia across the three framework regime examples. Conclusions then follow regarding types of
unruliness, but also the complex nature of regulatory democracy
and the growing presence of regulatory capitalism.

THE MARKETPLACE FRAMEWORK REGULATORY REGIME

There are more marketplace framework regulators now than there
were four decades ago, in part because the ideas and discourse about
that marketplace and how it ought to function in a more globalized
economy have broadened. In the Trudeau era, the main marketplace
regulators were housed in a then relatively new Department of
Consumer and Corporate Affairs, a title that came as close to using
an implied marketplace as Canada has ever had (Doern 1988; Doern
and Phidd 1983, 1992). The consumer half of the marketplace
received the lead billing and corporate affairs covered an array of
arm's-length regulatory bodies aligned to the department that dealt
with, for example, corporate law and the formation of companies,
intellectual property, bankruptcy, and weights and measures.

By the mid-1990s, under the impetus of a federal program review,
these same areas of marketplace rules were lodged in Industry Canada
along with regulators such as the Competition Bureau, and Investment
Canada, formerly the Foreign Investment Review Agency (Doern
1996b). Although neither consumer affairs nor corporate affairs were
in the two-word Industry Canada title, they took on a different and
also somewhat more important role because Industry Canada was
beginning under the influence of liberal economics and free trade
agreements to downplay somewhat its historic focus on industrial
policy via its fifteen or so industrial sector branches previously supported through tariffs and then subsidies (Blais 1986). By the mid-
1990s, one could easily add both international trade and also
procurement rules to the inventory of this regime overall. Marketplace

competition and fair markets were strong mandate motivations but so, too, were policies about competitiveness across the economy and then, later, innovation and systems of innovation. These core marketplace framework regulators were seen both by successive ministers and often by the media and consumers and citizen/voters alike as very technical realms of regulation and not the kinds of areas where politicians could easily build noticeable careers. Amid considerable ministerial turnover at Industry Canada, the particular marketplace framework regulators beavered away typically several steps removed from the political spotlight even when, periodically – perhaps on average every decade or so – their regulatory parent legislation was being reviewed and possibly changed but also often just delayed or ignored under inertial realities of the larger federal agenda.

The framework regulatory regime has stretched further, particularly under the horizontal impetus of environmental and sustainable development paradigms, laws, and regulations and, hence, to the notion of sustainable marketplaces (Toner 2006). These additional features and horizontal aspirations have affected how consumers and consumerism are defined and how consumers see themselves in more ways as consumer-citizens and environmentally conscious consumers (Locke 1998; Princen, Maniates, and Comca 2002; Doern 2006). Consumer movements came to include more explicitly the views of key business sectors and firms as consumers themselves. Moreover, corporations are under much greater regulatory and other kinds of pressure to practise corporate social responsibility especially vis-à-vis their sustainable development obligations and pressures from environmental NGOs.

By far the largest normative thrust of this regime is a marketplace characterized by competition and efficiency across the Canadian economy. Nonetheless, in each of the three selected regulatory realms examined here, there are issues regarding fair markets and related social impacts. Hence, there is unruliness of both the agency mandate and policy conflict kind and, as we see below, of the inter-regime complexity kind and the agenda-setting kind, as well. The agency mandate conflict types of unruliness include issues related to truth in advertising in competition policy, prudential regulation and consumer education in banking and financial regulation, and patenting controversies regarding property rights versus knowledge dissemination in the public domain.

THREE SELECTED REALMS: COMPETITION POLICY,
BANKING AND FINANCIAL SERVICES,
AND INTELLECTUAL PROPERTY

Competition Policy

Competition policy and regulation are designed to promote rivalry
among firms, buyers, and sellers through actions to restrict anti-
competitive activities such as certain mergers, cartels, conspiracies in
restraint of trade, misleading advertising, and related criminal and
economic offences (Competition Bureau 2011a; Conklin 2001;
Trebilcock, Winter, Collins, and Iacobucci 2002; Doern 1995a). Most
areas of competition law deal with offences or behaviour that has
already occurred or is alleged to have occurred. The merger aspects
of competition policy, however, deal with *prospective* or hypothe-
sized future behaviour that may arise when firms have merged.

Canadian competition law, regulation, and policy overall centres
on the federal Competition Act and the Competition Tribunal Act
but it also includes the Consumer Packaging and Labelling Act, the
Textile Labelling Act, and the Precious Metals Marking Act. The
purpose of the Competition Act as the overarching framework law
is to:

- Promote the efficiency and adaptability of the Canadian economy
- Expand opportunities for Canadian participation in world mar-
  kets while at the same time recognizing the role of foreign com-
  petition in Canada
- Ensure that small and medium-sized enterprises (SMEs) have an
  equitable opportunity to participate in the Canadian economy
- Provide consumers with competitive prices and product choices.
  (Competition Bureau 2011a)

Other laws and regulations that govern particular regulated sectors
such as telecommunications, energy, and transportation also help
define limits for horizontal competition policy as a framework regulatory field and the extent to which "regulated conduct" can be used
as an exemption from competition law (Janisch 1999).

Important in competition regulation is the role of guidelines and
related interpretative documents such as pamphlets and bulletins
rather than delegated law expressed as regulations. For example, since

2000 the Competition Bureau has engaged in thirty-nine consultations, most regarding enforcement guidelines on a range of regulatory issues such as merger enforcement, a leniency program, predatory pricing, and environmental claims (Competition Bureau 2011b). There are four main competition policy and regulatory institutions:

1 Industry Canada and its minister have a role in any changes in competition law. They also have indirect influence arising from Industry Canada's custody of other marketplace framework laws and regulators and because the minister is the lead federal minister for consumer affairs.

2 The Commissioner of Competition is a statutory person, rather than the head of a multimember commission structure, that is directly responsible for the administration and enforcement of the Competition Act and the three labelling statutes. The Commissioner can launch enquiries, challenge civil and merger matters before the Competition Tribunal, make recommendations for prosecution on criminal matters to the Director of Public Prosecutions (DPP) in the Department of Justice, and intervene as a competition advocate before federal and provincial bodies.

3 The Competition Tribunal is a specialized independent adjudicative body; with economics, business, and legal expertise, it hears cases on civil matters such as mergers, misleading advertising, and restrictive trade practices.

4 The Competition Bureau is Canada's main independent law enforcement body, headed by the Commissioner of Competition. The Competition Bureau says that its "basic operating assumption … is that competition is good for both business and consumers" (2011c). The structure of the Bureau reflects the different mandate realms and types of civil and criminal offences it must enforce and secure compliance with. Thus, there are deputy commissioners and related units/branches for the following: mergers, criminal matters, fair business practices, civil matters, compliance and operations, economic policy and enforcement, public affairs, and legislative and international affairs. The case volumes vary enormously across these units, with the merger branch being by far the best known and dealing with the highest volume of decision cases.

In the period being examined, competition policy came to be seen and linked to broader ideas and discourse about *competitiveness and innovation policy.* But these levels of discourse may or may not have direct legal or regulatory impacts or mandate expression. The most recent example of this emerged under the Harper Conservative government with the release of the report of the Competition Review Panel entitled, *Compete to Win* (Canada 2008). The report recommended a sweeping national Competitiveness Agenda, only one part of which related to the Competition Act. It also focused on changes to the Investment Canada Act and on liberalizing investment restrictions in sectors such as air transport, uranium mining, telecommunications, and the merger aspects of the financial service sector. Overall, competitiveness and innovation policy paradigms refer, as we have seen, to a much broader array of policies and actions by federal and provincial governments that impact on the ability of industries to attract capital investment in a global market and to continuously innovate both in the adoption of the best global production technologies and in the development and production of new products, goods, and services; Doern and Stoney 2009). Such policies include the ability to attract, keep, and train and educate the best human capital possible. Increasingly, such policies also include adherence to, and support for, sustainable development. A further key reason why these policies extend well beyond competition policy per se is that, ultimately, they involve the full array of policy instruments. Competition policy is largely law- and rule-based, whereas innovation and competitiveness policies encompass the use of instruments such as taxation and numerous current or potential spending programs in areas such as R & D, education and skills, and regional grants and incentives.

In principle, there should be no sectoral preferences in competition policy; nevertheless, it is apparent (see more below) that some sectors have both formal and informal recognition and power than others. In most jurisdictions, competition policy reform has increasingly sought to reduce and eliminate any such preferences (Wilks 1999; Trebilcock, Winter, Collins, and Iacobucci 2002; Doern and Wilks 1996a). As in most areas of law and policy, however, there are exceptions that are sectoral and that arise out of political pressures or realities and also out of arguments about the nature of competition as an operational concept in different sectors.

For instance, regulated industries with previous or partial natural monopoly features (e.g., telecommunications, energy, transportation) have hitherto been exempt by law and by norms such as a "regulated industries" defence against possible charges of anti-competitive behaviour. Sectors such as sports and labour unions have also been exempt. The banking sector has received special treatment, in part because of the powerful role of the Department of Finance in banking and finance law and policy and because of the inherent power of the banking lobby. Air Canada and its dominant position in the airline industry also seems to be the product of some sectoral political preference expressed on a case-by-case basis or because of different sectoral statutes such as banking and transportation legislation.

Another trend in comparative competition policy and law is to move away from the application of any generalized "public interest" criteria for mergers or other aspects of competition policy. The availability of these criteria reached their zenith in countries such as the United Kingdom, but the clear tendency has been to come closer to stricter per se offences and definitions of anti-competitive behaviour (Wilks 1999; Doern and Wilks 1996a). The above reference to the banking sector, however, does illustrate the residual presence of broad public interest criteria (see more below). Different boundary issues also emerge in our discussion below regarding patents as one form of intellectual property.

The nature and frequency of regulatory change and aspects of inertia are revealed by regulatory reform occasions and the contexts in which they have occurred or, indeed, were postponed. Four periods are highlighted briefly, both to reveal regulatory content and also the politics of competition regulatory change. These periods include (1) the lethargy of the 1970s to the mid-1980s, (2) significant Mulroney-era changes in 1986, (3) discussions in the Chrétien-Martin era; and (4) recent changes during the Harper Conservative era.

In the first period, from 1970 to the early 1980s, five initiatives were launched by successive ministers of consumer and corporate affairs (ministers stayed in the portfolio for an average of two years) to reform completion policy, each ultimately failing (Doern 1996a). These included (1) a draft bill in 1971, (2) a major 1977 study, (3) a 1977 draft bill, (4) a 1981 framework paper, and (5) a 1983 bill. Part of the political problem was that competition policy was seen or presented as being technical in nature rather than political, especially by some interests that were not keen to foster more competition. Nonetheless, relative to other priorities and problems during this period as a whole, competition policy did not attract much attention either among relevant ministers or at the prime ministerial level.

There were problems in how to mobilize any viable consensus among key business interest groups, whose composition was changing. In the 1970s, the main national business lobby groups were the Canadian Manufacturing Association (CMA) and the Canadian Chamber of Commerce (CCC). But, in the early 1980s, the then Business Council on National Issues (BCNI) (now the Council of Chief Executives) and the Canadian Federation of Independent Business (CFIB) had emerged, thus creating a more complete although by no means harmonious set of cross-sectoral interest groups. In the competition and other fields, the CFIB's small business members were often highly suspicious of big business in Canada (Coleman 1988). Some of the latter suspicions were exasperated when competition consultation initiatives focused on the so-called gang of three": the BCNI, the CMA, and the CCC.

The log jam was broken in the early Mulroney-era partly because business interests saw the Mulroney Conservatives as more pro-business overall and also because the earlier gang of three was expanded by a new minister, who himself had small business experience, to include the Grocery Products Manufacturing Association and the Canadian Bar Association. A Minister's Advisory Committee on the Competition Bill was established, and the eventual new bill was sold politically and publicly as a bill that would be fair to small business. The essence of the current system was crafted and passed in the 1986 Competition Act.

It was not until June 2003, that the then Chrétien Liberal government put out a discussion paper entitled, *Options for Amending the Competition Act: Fostering a Competitive Marketplace*, with a number of options under consideration to amend the Competition Act (Canada 2003). The discussion paper was a direct response to the proposed changes to the act recommended in a report of the House of Commons Standing Committee on Industry, Science and Technology (2002). The government's discussion paper represented a commitment to "modernizing the Competition Act in the face of a rapidly changing economy" (Canada 2003, 1).

The basic thrust of the proposed changes was to provide the Competition Bureau and the Commissioner of Competition with a broader and more varied toolkit of instruments to ensure compliance and enforcement of the legislation as a whole. It is important to stress that the reform discussions in Parliament and elsewhere, although couched in a concern to modernize the law, were not particularly informed by the larger innovation agenda. In other words, the nature of innovation per se and theories or theorizing about competition, in a knowledge-based economy were not examined in the kind of focused way suggested by some authors as being increasingly necessary (Porter 2001; Hemphill 2003; Kay 2003).

The Harper-era 2009 amendments to the Competition Act were passed not as a separate legislative package but rather as part of the omnibus Budget Implementation Act. The changes allowed for more effective criminal enforcement against the most serious types of cartel agreements, while providing businesses with more freedom and flexibility to benefit from legitimate alliances with their competitors (Competition Bureau 2011d). Other changes, including those regarding merger enforcement, were achieved via a guidelines approach.

These latest changes do not address what some sectoral interests were arguing about the needs of competition policy in small open economies (Doern 2004a). For example, in 2003, the pulp and paper or forest products industry argued that Canada, as a small open economy requires a "uniquely tailored competition policy" and, in particular, one that for mergers is "comprised of a flexible structure more sympathetic to efficiency-enhancing mergers and higher industrial concentrations" (FPAC 2003c, 2). Drawing on the work of authors such as Michal Gal (2001) but also on the industry's own knowledge of its core production structure and economics, the industry argument was centred on the view that the key problem is that domestic firms in small economies face major difficulties in achieving "minimum efficient scale" (MES). This dilemma is accentuated when entire industries (such as pulp and paper) face this problem. The Forest Products Association of Canada (FPAC) argued that the Competition Bureau "has seemed unwilling to allow many Canadian firms to achieve MES through mergers because of the basic dilemma created by the smallness of the Canadian economy: striving for productive efficiency requires that firms achieve MES, but allowing domestic firms to expand to such a scale inevitably results in high industrial concentration and potentially anti-competitive effects" (FPAC 2003c, 3).

FPAC also argued that if there are any doubts by the Competition Bureau about FPAC's preferred more flexible policy on mergers, these doubts should be dispelled by a key feature of the Canadian economy which is that it is subject to "extensive exposure to international competition" (FPAC 2003c, 4). FPAC then went on to argue

that "merger policy should, in general, apply to areas of the economy where free market forces do not produce natural competition.
Where there is already a source of competition whether domestically
or from abroad, there is little need for intervention" (5–6). Similar
views were expressed by FPAC to the above-mentioned Harper-era
review in 2008 (FPAC 2008).

Unlike areas such as trade policy or patent policy regulation, there
is no global competition regulator, in part, because of different national
views about the nature and extent of competition. The closest pan-
national but not global body is the EU's Competition Directorate.
There are, however, undoubted growing cross-national pressures for
better integration. Merger cases can often involve decisions by several
national regulators simultaneously. The above FPAC positions often
referred to other forestry nations such as Finland, which were major
global competitors for Canada's forestry industry, but the Finnish
competition regime was much more supportive of allowing mergers
and allowing the development of big forestry firms. Competition policy reviews of Canada by international agencies such as the OECD
argued that Canada's system needed to be more like that in the United
States, Canada's largest export market (OECD 2002a, 2004).

However, for Canada, the US competition regime presented very
real challenges both to governments and to Canadian business if it
was openly or even gradually emulated in Canada. The US system
was characterized by both clearer and what were more actual
offences, by multiple avenues for competition cases to be launched
(by two federal agencies, state attorneys general, and direct private
action by individuals) and by a huge and aggressive legal profession
that could win triple damages in successful legal cases. Underpinning
the US system was a history of populist democracy in the origins and
evolution of the anti-trust or competition field (Peters 1996).

The Canadian system was different in all these respects – indeed,
virtually the polar opposite. Some changes have since been made to
allow more direct private litigation in Canada but not with the US
highly contentious triple damages system. The great majority of
cases are still launched by federal regulators that obtain their information in a variety of ways both internally and from competitor
companies and consumer complaints.

Nonetheless, all of the recent Canadian competition reform discussion papers contained strong declarations that Canada should
adopt more international and US competition best practices, but

successive federal governments have been cautious in their replies in terms of later reform actions and inactions (Crane 2008; Canada 2008; Commissioner of Competition 2008; VanAudenrode, Royer, Pinheiro, and Faye 2008).

Our survey above of the structure and evolution of the Canadian competition regime touches on key issues about changing ideas, discourse, and business and public power relations; the discussion of science, evidence, and knowledge, however, has so far been more oblique. The competition realm is not characterized as one involving science-based regulation, but it certainly has complex features regarding evidence and knowledge. This, in turn, requires brief illustrative comments regarding the different types of competition policy offences and their inherent nature and volumes and, therefore, the different mixes – in particular of law and economics – as varied judgments about matters such as regulated conduct, abuse of power, and efficiency exemptions are argued in specific case situations.

Merger assessments and decisions involve the microeconomics of defining and determining what the relevant market is. Moreover, these decisions, as mentioned earlier, are about prospective possible future behaviour if a merger is allowed. Decisions are of a high volume nature and must be made according to defined short-term decision cycles and amid a Competition Bureau policy and cultural view that most mergers are good for competition and for competitiveness. Moreover, merger cases involve civil matters rather than criminal offences.

Other areas of competition offences are quite different. For example, the task of ensuring truth in advertising includes both criminal and civil provisions (hence, greater mixtures of law and economics as the core evidence and knowledge base). Ensuring truth in advertising involves greater deployment of compliance strategies (including information and education) rather than only hard enforcement, mainly because the case volume is quite high and diverse and typically involves a wide range of business and consumer sectors and smaller and larger firms. So, there are different arts of judgment involved by front-line assessors or case handlers. Overall, as noted, lawyers are also involved when criminal matters are central and where court or tribunal actions are involved, including of course, Justice Canada lawyers. There are also budgetary limits on the Competition Bureau and the Commissioner of Competition regarding how often it wants, or can afford to, launch major expensive legal cases not only to catch offenders but also, possibly, to have successful case decisions serve as a deterrent regarding the prevention of similar offences in the future.

The above examples tend to refer to evidence and knowledge bases within the competition agencies in the handling of case implementation. But, of course, there are both related and other kinds of knowledge in the larger political, consumer, and business interests as they battle over reforms to competition law, resistance to such reforms, and also over communications and discourse about competition advocacy, what competition means or ought to mean in a global economy, and in terms of the evolution of the Canadian economy as well as its current structure, threats, and opportunities.

Banking and Financial Services

Regulation of banking and financial services is the second realm of the marketplace framework regulatory regime to be examined. Its pan-economy reach is obvious in that access to short-term and long-term financing is a common essential everyday need for businesses, consumers, governments, and social entities across the country. In Canada, and globally, its framework values include prudential supervision and risk management (including recent concerns with systemic risk and the prevention of contagion in both banking and sovereign debt) efficiency, stability, and national and global competition. Regulation of banking and financial services involves the balancing of conflicts among such ideas in the face of new financial needs, financial complexity, and newer invented instruments/products such as derivatives, and new kinds of hubris and risk-taking by lenders and borrowers (Davies 2010; Brunnermeier, Goodhart, Hellwig, Persaud, and Shin 2009; Calmes 2004; Harris 1999).

At the heart of the banking system is the issue of confidence because it essentially makes its core money by taking a deposit (say, $100) from an individual saver and lending it out several times to other borrowers. This kind of ultimate "con" required "confidence" that the depositor would get his or her funds back with interest – at any time. The crucial fear in any bank crisis is a run on the banks as individuals lose confidence and demand the return of these funds. There are, of course, many types of lender-borrower arrangements and transactions; but at the heart of all of them, confidence must be maintained both by the financial institutions through their own policies and by regulators.

At the same time, this realm has been bound up in sectoral politics and economics both among the banking and financial subsectors such as the chartered banks, insurance, trust and mortgage loan companies, investment dealers, co-operatives, and financial intermediaries such as mutual funds, and hedge funds. Sectoral pressures emerge from particular industries (from agriculture to energy and their views of gaps or costs regarding their particular financial needs) and also in newer industries such as biotechnology where firms search for higher risk so-called angel investors – affluent individuals who provide capital for start-up firms.

The framework nature of Canadian banking and financial services regulation operates at the apex of political and bureaucratic power. Nationally, its regulators are anchored in and around the Department of Finance and the Bank of Canada and, internationally, increasingly around networks of similar power structures in an age of global banking and frequent financial crises. At the same time, these powerful regulators are, paradoxically, quite weak in that they play a constant game of regulatory catch-up with never-ending changes in the nature of banking and finance, and often they do not have enough up-to-date expertise (Harris 1999). In the current crisis period, for example, some authors are explicitly raising the need for both *micro-prudential regulation* (regarding individual institutions) and *macro-prudential regulation* (regarding factors that affect the stability of the financial system as a whole) (Brunnermeier, Goodhart, Hellwig, Persaud, and Shin 2009).

The regulatory system includes the national and international role of the private bond rating agencies, which were blamed for failures to gauge the subprime mortgage crisis but which were also a powerful source of information to lenders about the sovereign debt strengths and weaknesses of different countries (Applebaum and Dash 2011). The role of the rating agencies was linked to what Nobel economist Paul Krugman called the "bond vigilantes," investors who would, could, or did, "pull the plug on spendthrift governments, driving up their borrowing costs and precipitating a crisis" (2010, 1).

Canada's approach to trying to keep up has included a history of regular ten-year Bank Act reform processes and related consultations including quite major parliamentary committee review processes. More recently, this regular review process has been shortened to five-year sunset review processes for legislation on banking and financial services. This is sensible and seemingly orderly and, thus, contrasts with the less regular and less predictable rhythms of competition law changes discussed in the previous section. Thus, legislative and regulatory change, overall, is more incremental and gradual but in the 2008–12 period of global crisis, Canada has changed some of its practices more quickly and urgently without going through these periodic reform exercises.

The current set of federal rule makers and regulators is complex and includes the following: (1) the Department of Finance, which has both the lead role in any legislative change but also an overall political-economic responsibility for the soundness and stewardship of the financial system in concert with its lead role in overall fiscal policy; (2) the Bank of Canada, which has overall arm's-length responsibility for monetary policy and interest rates with a primary mandate on ensuring low inflation, crucially provides liquidity to the financial system, advises the federal government on the structural design of the financial system, oversees clearing and settlement systems for day-to-day financial transactions, and also conducts extensive research that is published on a regular basis; (3) the Office of the Superintendent of Financial Institutions (OSFI), which supervises federally regulated financial institutions; (4) the Canada Deposit Insurance Corporation, which administers and monitors the federal system of deposit insurance to maintain confidence in the financial system by depositors, particularly in banking; (5) the Financial Consumer Agency of Canada, which has a mandate to protect consumers and also to inform consumers of financial issues; and (6) all of the above entities participate in the Financial Institutions Supervisory Committee (FISC), which meets regularly to share information, coordinate actions, and advise the federal government on financial sector issues (Bank of Canada 2011).

Without doubt, it is the Department of Finance and the Bank of Canada that dominate this governance structure. But there are key provincial regulators to take note of as well, including securities commissions that regulate and administer the issuance of, and trade in, securities such as stocks and bonds, and regulators that govern credit unions and *caisses populaires*. Changes in provincial securities industry law and regulation in the 1980s and 1990s contributed to considerable overall financial deregulation and the overall situation of Canada having multiple provincial securities regulators has led, in the current crisis, to the federal government proposing the creation of a national securities regulator in the face of fast moving global realities. However, the Supreme Court of Canada ruled in December 2011 that the federal government could not proceed as planned because the federal legislation was beyond federal jurisdiction and intruded into provincial jurisdiction. Most provinces argued against the federal plans before the Supreme Court. As a result, the Harper government had to begin work on a new as yet undefined model (McFarland 2012).

International regulatory systems and coordination and conflicts among them are, increasingly, central to the overall regulatory story. The Canadian regulatory system as a whole has been given considerable applause nationally and internationally for its role in sparing Canada the worst effects of the 2008–12 financial crises (Ratnovski and Huang 2009; Nivola and Courtney 2011). We explore this recent experience but first stress that the picture overall is intricate and varied as this realm of framework regulation was incrementally constructed. In Canadian history, financial breakdowns (and linked fiscal crises) can be traced back to the 1930s when responses involved the conjoined issues of strong opposition to the banks, the formation of Social Credit political parties in the Canadian prairies, and a fear that some provinces would go bankrupt (Ascah 1999).

In the Harper Conservative era since 2006, it has been the global fiscal and banking crisis that has occupied centre stage, mainly with the Conservatives supporting and taking credit for the banking system and its regulatory structure as it had congealed before the start of the 2008–12 period of crisis (Harris 2010). The attributed causes of the crisis began much earlier and with inevitable differences in what institutions and countries should be blamed and what macroeconomic and regulatory policies – or failures to act – were most blameworthy (DeLong 2011; Stigler 2011). These centred on both banking and subprime mortgage crises but extended quickly to sovereign debt crises especially for several Euro zone countries.

The United States and the United Kingdom and, more particularly, New York's Wall Street and London's financial heartland, The City, were the initial core locales of the global banking crisis origins. As the duelling/competing leaders in financial markets, they were where the new banking hubris was born and encouraged, either ignored or undetected by financial regulators (Krugman 2008; LaBrosse, Olivares-Caminal, and Singh 2011). Whether cast benignly as innovative banking or, more accurately, as casino capitalism, the banking parts of the global crisis were forged by a combination of factors and primal urges ranging from excessive profit and greed to new, highly complex mathematically modelled and computer-designed technologies for assessing and taking risks and for the packaging and repackaging of varied financial assets that many bank executives themselves scarcely understood (Davies 2010). Regulators functioning under publicly avowed "light touch" regulation in the United Kingdom and the cumulative effects of earlier financial deregulation in the United States took a deserved top-ranked place in the regulatory institutional failure and blame game league rankings.

Added to this core story was the US subprime mortgage part of the crisis. Guided partly by longer-term George Bush–era policies to foster home ownership, the complex US mortgage lending market had gradually produced lending and buying practices that went well beyond the normal market and risk calculus (Krugman 2008). Mortgages were given to large numbers of Americans without any or significant down payment requirements, and mortgage financing was also caught up in the risks absorbed by US government-run mortgage bodies such as Fanny Mae and Freddy Mac. It was precisely many of the new already lax mortgage instruments that then became repackaged into the bank asset nether world referred to above. When the crash came in 2008 and beyond, the effects were felt everywhere in the United States as individual citizens had their mortgages foreclosed when they could not pay or others were able to easily walk away from their homes, leaving empty homes blotting otherwise pleasant-looking urban neighbourhoods or, worse yet, hollowing out entire areas of American cities.

The first policy response to the banking crisis was in the United Kingdom and United States when bank bailouts became necessary, largely on the grounds that banks or at least some banks were, indeed, too big to be allowed to fail. In the United Kingdom, this came first with a smaller UK bank, Northern Rock, followed by partial state ownership and forced mergers of large mainstream banks such as Lloyds TSB and the Royal Bank of Scotland (Haseler 2010; Lodge and Hood 2011).

In the United States, bailouts of its much more decentralized banking system focused on the need to deal with the varied overreaches and dubious risk practices of particular large, well-known, and powerful financial institutions such as Lehman Brothers. When Lehman Brothers was allowed to go bankrupt in 2008, the shock to the financial system was such that it caused a run on even ultraconservative money market funds. This kind of panic caused the Bush Administration's Treasury Department to seek permission from Congress to use taxpayer money to support the system (Carmel 2009).

Even though there were some grounds to believe that both the UK and US governments would get their bailout money back eventually, the immediate effect was that a smallish UK fiscal deficit became quickly a big and noticeable one, and the already large US deficit became even bigger. Moreover, as the overall effects of the crisis kicked in in the form of negative growth and growing unemployment, both central banks lowered interest rates to unprecedented levels. They also began the practice of *quantitative easing*, the modern-day electronic equivalent of printing money when a central bank buys its own government-issued bonds, such as gilts, or bonds issued by companies, and this results in giving money to sellers (mainly banks) which, in turn, will hopefully be inclined to lend more.

The core banking crisis and its impacts on deficits and on a recession – now seen as the worst overall since the 1930s – quickly spread to other countries (Eatwell and Milgate 2011). Indeed, some scholars were moved to say that this was not a banking crisis or a recession but rather was fast becoming a "great contraction," much deeper, longer lasting, and more difficult to recover from than a mere recession (Rogoff 2011; *Economist* 2010). The other countries included, most visibly, those often small countries whose own banking systems had national brands of financial hubris but tied as well to what was happening to the United States and the United Kingdom. The latter included countries such as Iceland and Ireland and then quickly became a kind of second-phase crisis concern for sovereign debt of EU and Eurozone countries such as Greece, Portugal, Italy, and Spain, which was, in turn, tied to bank lending excesses.

The US and UK epicentre was also taken special note of by the fast-growing Chinese, Indian, and overall Asian and East Asian economies whose banking systems had not imploded and whose economies then fared better in the aftermath of the recession. They still had concerns about the world economy and their own prosperity and, as we note further below, they were also gearing up to increase their influence and power in the coming negotiations over what kinds of global fiscal and financial regulatory regime would emerge in the wake of the crisis.

The essence of the Canadian story in the 2008–12 period of global financial crisis is the avoidance of a banking crisis as a result of more conservative and cautious lending practices by Canada's banks and also some sensible regulatory policy regarding both banks and the mortgage market in Canada. Nonetheless, the biggest fiscal deficits in Canadian history were incurred because of the deep recession in Canada caused mainly by the bank crisis and economic recession in the United States, still by far Canada's biggest global market. Various assessments show that in Canada the impact of the global banking meltdown was less severe than it was in virtually every other industrial democracy. This appears to be due more to the more conservative management practices in the country's largest banks and, to a lesser extent, to the character of aggregate prudential oversight by regulators (Harris 2010; Kravis 2009).

However, there were a number of episodes that did threaten financial instability in Canada. The collapse of the asset-backed commercial paper market represents the most serious one, and it was accompanied by the Office of the Superintendent of Financial Institutions denying any culpability for the market's collapse despite OSFI's overarching mission (Harris 2010). Other accounts during the crisis argued that Canada's banking system was among the soundest in the world and that no bank bailouts were needed as a result; Finance Minister Jim Flaherty, for example, trumpeted the virtues of the Canadian banking and financial system in virtually every speech he made in Canada and internationally (Canada 2011a).

Similarly, analyses of why the American sub-prime mortgage boom and bust did not take place in Canada centred on Canada's different and better consumer protection laws and practices nationally and provincially (Ireland and Webb 2010). Such analyses and inherent Canadian pride in the "superiority" of its regulatory regime were immediately accompanied by a cautionary warning. The lending practices and subprime mortgage agents, lenders, and insurers that were major causes of the American crisis were starting to creep into Canada just before and then during the period when the American subprime boom turned into the subprime bust (Ireland and Webb 2010). The net result of these more prudent Canadian banking and mortgage regimes was that Canada's recession was almost immediately deemed to be a fiscal deficit crisis problem in the main, and it was also deemed to be serious but less severe than for other countries on both the deficit and sovereign debt fronts.

In the Harper years, changes to Canada's financial regulatory system were bound up in the crisis atmosphere overall and revealed mainly in the Conservative government's Economic Action Plan reports and statements (Department of Finance 2010a). In basic regulatory terms, the Harper government, as already discussed, announced its intention to establish a Canadian Securities Regulator but the Supreme Court of Canada declared key elements of federal proposals as being unconstitutional. In addition, measures were announced to improve federally regulated private pension plans and a Code of Conduct was proposed for the credit and debit card industry in Canada. While these regulatory matters received some emphasis in the Economic Action Plan, even greater emphasis was given to various measures in the crisis period to improve access to financing through the temporary Extraordinary Financing Framework.

In September 2010, Finance Minister Jim Flaherty announced the scheduled five year sunset review of legislation governing financial institutions following the last review completed in 2007 (Department of Finance 2010b). He pointed out that, since 2007, extensive changes to the regulatory framework had been made, and so "the current exercise is not likely to lead to major reforms" (ibid.). Again, Flaherty stressed and cited international comments that Canada was the global leader in regulating its banks and financial institutions.

The longer-term regulatory evolution of banking and financial services as part of the marketplace framework regime is, however, much more mixed. The long-term history since 1960 is one of gradual liberalization, although the story of institutional learning and memory loss is also present in the Mulroney and Chrétien and Martin eras as globalization increased and challenged and changed the balances and conflicts between prudential virtue and stability, competition and efficiency, and trade liberalization in a greater services-centred economy (Calmes 2004; Harris 1999).

A useful reference point for the federal banking regulatory system is the work and the 1964 final report of the Royal Commission on Banking and Finance (the Porter Commission) (Canada 1964). The work of the Porter Commission occurred in an era when the banking and financial system was heavily regulated, including a separation of powers between financial and market intermediaries, closely managed exchange rates, and interest rate ceilings. Therefore, controls went well beyond the needs of prudential regulation and seriously constrained competition and efficiency. The Porter Commission set out a pro-competition and efficiency agenda that began to be acted upon, but only very gradually and incrementally in the coming decades, beginning with the ending of lending and deposit rate ceilings in the 1967 Bank Act reforms.

In the 1980 Trudeau-era Bank Act and related reforms, competitive and efficiency ideas were in the ascendency, partly because of international developments and pressures including those from the United States regarding access to the Canadian financial market (Calmes 2004). Entry was eased, as were the required reserves so that Canada's banks could compete better with the growing near-banks in Canada. The reforms also introduced new schedules of banks with the "big five" anchored in Schedule A.

In the Mulroney era, a set of 1984, 1985, and 1986 discussion papers on the regulation of financial institutions triggered reform but, again, in a slow-moving way. Choices and debate here centred on models such as the existing four pillars (banks, insurance, trusts, and investment dealers) and the emerging universal bank model. The four pillars were less viable as firms within each pillar gradually got into some aspects of the other pillars' financial products. The universal bank model in Canadian discussion centred on a holding company option rather than a true universal bank. This was partly to ensure that the early 1980s bank schedule structure could be maintained. The 1992 Mulroney legislation opted for some greater competition among the pillar firms but still with rules that were several steps removed from the universal bank system (Harris 1999; Daniel, Freedman, and Goodlet 1992).

In the above processes, the federal regulators and power centres were always concerned about how to manage and control the system in terms of bank and financial system power. The big five banks had always had a privileged place based on their history as an oligopoly and as a set of fairly conservative financial entities. It was easier for the government to deal with a known power structure rather than an open and uncertain one. Financial services regulatory reforms also became subject to automatic reviews every five years, and the 1996 review under the Chrétien Liberals continued the process, as did a Task Force on Financial Institutions. In both the Mulroney and Chrétien periods, banking and financial services came under more scrutiny by trade authorities, internationally and nationally, as free trade negotiations and discussions entered more into trade in services as opposed to a historical focus on trade in goods.

Thus, overall in the current Harper era but earlier as well, it is possible to argue that Canada's banking and financial services regulatory regime moved in the direction of greater competition and efficiency in its underlying goals and ideas, but with concerns about prudential supervision and the norms of confidence and trust in financial markets never far behind in the consciousness of regulators. There had also been pressures to allow mergers among Canada's big five banks so that they could play larger international market roles, but these were never acted upon or allowed.

When the 2008–12 banking and then closely related sovereign debt crises hit, prudential norms re-emerged, aided and abetted by the discourse regarding banks that were *too big to fail* or the establishment of systems of ring-fencing core banks that would, indeed, still be bailed out in future crises and leaving others as "failable" when the state would ostensibly not help out and thus would, in theory, let them fail. However, there were mandate conflicts and complexities and much room for unruliness if national banks became overexposed in other countries' sovereign debt financing and had to be dealt with differently or not at all.

From here on, banking and financial services regulation would undoubtedly be directly impacted by international regulation and changing power structures. There was little question early on that a new and changed global power structure was being created, partly through an energized G-20, the relative demise of the G-7 and G-8, and also through changes in the funding and governance of international economic agencies such as the World Bank and International Monetary Fund, and the international Basel Committee on Banking Supervision (Stigler 2011).

The G-20 was established in 1999, following the 1997 East Asian financial crisis. As Canada's finance minister, Paul Martin had been a leading advocate of the G-20, arguing that there was a growing global need for better representation of developing countries and East Asian economies in global economic governance. Initially, G-20 meetings involved annual meetings of finance ministers and also central bank governors. Following its first eight years, the G-20 was given only passing marks largely because it was assessed to be mainly an entity that supported the agendas of the smaller Western-dominated G-7.

The G-20 status and power structure changed markedly, however, during the 2008 to 2012 crisis period. Political leaders attended the early crisis period 2008 summit in Washington, the 2009 summits in London and Pittsburgh, and also the 2010 Toronto summit. The

G-20 became the focal point for the drafting of consensus joint approaches on stimulus programs, when to end such programs, and also banking regulation reforms aimed at dealing with systemic risk and preventing a repetition of the current crisis.

There was considerable momentum in these meetings and discussions; however, it was also the case that member nations that had done well or better in the crisis did not necessarily want to be dictated to as to how they should deal with their particular manifestations of crisis, not to mention their politics. Hence, there would have to be flexibility allowed given the different situations member countries faced. Increasingly, Canada and other countries had to calculate and strategize new timing realities as to (1) their negotiating positions in Basel banking and finance rule discussions and (2) the sequence of adopting Basel and other financial rule and institutional changes versus national ones and, indeed, federal-provincial ones. Another G-20 initiative in 2009 was the establishment of Financial Stability Board (FSB) with a broader membership of countries and also a stronger regulatory and monitoring mandate and capacity to help prevent future crises in an ever more complex global financial system. The first head of the FSB was Mark Carney, governor of the Bank of Canada who, at the time of this writing has ended his tenure at the Bank of Canada and has been appointed governor of the Bank of England.

Intellectual Property

Intellectual property, our third marketplace framework regime example, has grown in importance in the context of federal and international innovation and trade policy after many decades of functioning out of sight and out of mind in national politics and economic agendas. Historically, intellectual property has been divided into two fields, "industrial property" and "copyright." Protection of industrial property includes protection by means of patents, trademarks, and industrial designs. Copyright gives authors and other creators of works of the mind such as literature, music, and art, rights to authorize or prohibit, for a certain period of time, certain uses made of their works. So-called neighbouring rights also supply rights to performers such as singers and musicians. In this section, we look at patents and the Canadian Intellectual Property Office (CIPO).

The central framework policy trade-off in IP, as a whole, is between that of protecting creations and inventions of the mind and disseminating such creations for the broader good of society (Castle 2009; de Beer, Gold, and Guaranga 2011; Doern 1999b). Especially regarding patents, the IP area we focus on, the rules both protect the patent holder (provided that a patent is renewed through the periodic payment of fees) and also provide for detailed information about the invention to be made public so that others might further invent as well. When looked at within a nation state, economists express the need for the state to determine such trade-offs because of the presence of a public good. In the first instance, the new intellectual creation is a public good because one person's consuming of it does not diminish anyone else's capacity to consume it. Private markets could not easily prevent such consumption. Moreover, because such private actors could not appropriate the gains to themselves, they would have only limited incentives to innovate or create. Society would be worse off because secrecy would be encouraged, and there would be an undersupply of such ideas, creations, and innovations. This creates the case for state intervention, but it does not in itself make the case for *how far* to intervene or *what instruments* to use to intervene (Doern and Sharaput 2000; Trebilcock and Howse 1995).

If, at the other extreme, the state intervenes and gives IP creators and owners full control, then it is creating monopoly economic power over the patented invention, with resultant higher prices, economic inefficiencies in general, and a lessened exchange and use of the innovations themselves. Consequently, there emerges the search for a regulatory or interventionist balance, in short, a set of trade-offs between two principles or policy rationales that are both seen to be, in this sense, "in the public interest" across the economy.

As a framework-oriented policy, the pressure overwhelmingly is to define one overall trade-off to foster intellectual creativity rather than create special ones for different industrial sectors such as computers or pharmaceuticals. But, in theory and in practice, such varied sectoral trade-offs are also possible, and they have certainly driven key aspects of the politics of patents given that key sectors internationally and in Canada have driven patent and related agendas.

In policy and regulatory terms, the core IP regulatory institutions (and related interests) include the following: the Canadian Intellectual Property Office, an advisory Patent Appeal Board, the Copyright Board, the Trade-marks Opposition Board, Industry Canada, Canadian Heritage, Foreign Affairs Canada and International Trade Canada, big business such as the pharmaceutical industry, and the IP professions such as patent agents but also the patent examiners which function within CIPO. As suggested above, these core players centre on the protection and rights function but by no means exclusively.

The secondary set of institutions and interests include these: other federal departments and agencies such as the Patented Medicines Prices Review Board, and Health Canada and Agriculture and Agri-Food Canada (and their regulatory units) whose clientele may have major or periodic concerns about patents; provincial governments; small and medium-sized enterprises (SMEs); university, educational, library, and research institutions; and small individual inventors or creators.

CIPO is the agency responsible for the greater part of IP administration in Canada (CIPO 2007, 2011a; Doern and Sharaput 2000). CIPO is a special operating agency, financed mainly by IP fees rather than by taxpayers and, hence, has special management powers and financial flexibility designed to make it a better and more service conscious organization. Patent examiners in CIPO examine patent applications against three criteria for granting a patent: first, the invention must be new or novel; second, it must be useful, functional, and operative; and third, it must show inventive ingenuity and not be obvious to someone skilled in that area – the non-obviousness criteria.

Patents tended early on to be more of an engineering nature, but today large volumes of patents deal with other science products and processes including genetic and genomic applications (Doern and Prince 2012). Thus, CIPO patent examiners have to come from a variety of technical and science backgrounds including biology. CIPO functions increasingly in an era of high volumes of patent applications with national governments, including Canada, seeing rates of patenting as being itself international criteria of innovation in global rankings with Canada still struggling in the patent race (Conference Board of Canada 2010b).

CIPO itself must be differentiated from the role of the Commissioner of Patents and Registrar of Trade-Marks. The chief executive officer (CEO) of CIPO is also the Commissioner and the Registrar. In the latter capacities, CIPO's head official is a statutory person. The role as a statutory person is important because all of the regulatory powers reside in this legally defined role. This is to ensure that decisions on patents and trademarks and other IP rights are based on independent objective judgments and not on political considerations. In other respects, however, as CEO, the head of CIPO, functions within the jurisdiction of Industry Canada. For example, if legislative policy changes were being considered to the Patent Act they, would ultimately, be the responsibility of the minister, although it is possible for the commissioner to comment on amendments to the legislation for the minister's consideration and approval. All of the other previously noted aspects of Industry Canada's mandate mentioned in the competition realm analysis apply in the IP patent realm as well. Of particular importance is the fact that Industry Canada's Intellectual Property Policy Directorate and its Patent Policy Directorate are also engaged in international IP and trade negotiations and monitoring (Industry Canada 2011).

CIPO's statutory base flows from six acts, one for each type of IP, under which there are also separate regulations (CIPO 2011b) The Patent Act is underpinned by a set of Patent Rules. The patent regulatory system also has the above-mentioned Patent Appeal Board. Crucially, the courts are heavily involved, largely because there is no patent police force to protect patent rights. The enforcement occurs mainly through private litigation, a process that increasingly, in some areas of invention, thrives on the entrails of complex patent thickets patrolled by patent trolls, especially in the aggressive, litigious US political culture (Canadian International Council 2011; Bessen and Meurer 2008; Boyle 2008).

CIPO has also been involved in numerous consultations, but most of these are very technical and administrative in nature (CIPO 2011c). In the current Harper era, the political sensitivity of these consultations has centred mainly on new copyright legislation issues rather than patents (Geist 2011). As we see, however, from the brief policy-regulatory history that follows, other pressures are building on the patent side regarding where the protection versus dissemination trade-off should occur in the interests of both creativity and innovation, and regarding what an invention is and the limits to property rights, where the boundaries of property in patents are increasingly blurred (Dutfield 2003).

Canada's patent laws congealed in the 1980s Mulroney era with some important carryover in the Chrétien era following the completion of the negotiations on the General Agreement on Tariffs and Trade (GATT) that led to the formation of the World Trade Organization (WTO) and its Trade-Related Intellectual Property Rights (TRIPS) system (Doern and Sharaput 2000). The essence of

Canada's new patent policy and law, influenced overwhelmingly by US pressures and by key sectoral business interests within the US economy, was that it extended the length of patent protection to twenty years. Patents are intended to produce a temporary monopoly to reward intellectual effort and ingenuity. Basic economic logic suggests that these periods of protection ought to vary greatly by field or sector depending on varying cost structures, investments, and payback periods. This also suggests that countries would have different views about what kinds of protection across sectors would make the most sense given their national state of development, comparative advantage, and strategies for development. Thus, the market economics underlying patent protection suggests the suitability of many periods of protection – and that these periods could also change over time.

The political and institutional logic of patent policy as framework law differs, however, somewhat from the market logic. For major economic actors, the basic logic is simply the longer the protection period the better. This view was driven in the United States and in Canada by firms such as those in the national and global pharmaceutical and biotechnology industries, which sought out and achieved maximum effective protection. Their desire for maximum periods was driven by factors such as high upfront costs in R&D and in obtaining ever-lengthening drug approval processes by other government regulators in several countries. In the 1980s, they saw their *effective* protection being reduced and sought change in national laws and trade regimes.

Canadian and US changes also went lockstep with perceived weaknesses by the United States and also the European Union regarding the international enforcement regime for IP and patents. Under the earlier pre-WTO GATT, the international regime for intellectual property fell well short of a harmonized regime (Sell 1998, 2010; Doern 1999b). Indeed, IP issues were largely outside the GATT purview. Moreover, international IP organizations such as the World Intellectual Property Organization (WIPO) did not contain a formal courtlike process for dispute resolution. It regularly reported on disputes but had no GATT-like panel process for dispute resolution (Doern 1999b; Trebilcock and Howse 1995).

The Uruguay Final Round Act included, for the first time, a comprehensive agreement on TRIPS that seeks to balance the conflicting values inherent in IP and between developed and developing countries (Sell 1998, 2010). It greatly strengthened the role of the WTO but it also established a new body, the Council on TRIPS and mechanisms to help developing countries get ready for the new stricter regime.

During the Uruguay Round, the issue of mandates in IP between the WIPO and the proposed World Trade Organization generated considerable dispute. The developing countries preferred the WIPO as the lead institution because it had facilitated diverse IP policies and institutions in developing countries. The United States and Europe, but especially the former, preferred a stronger WTO mandate because they wanted better dispute settlement and enforcement of harmonized IP rights, especially regarding key developing countries whose IP regimes were either weak in law or weak in their implementation. As a result, the Uruguay Final Round Act included, for the first time, not only the WTO itself but also a comprehensive agreement on TRIPS that, in principle, seeks to balance the conflicting values inherent in IP and between developed and developing countries (Sell 2010; Marcellin 2010).

During these negotiations, the US pressure on Canada pinpointed Canada's preferences given to generic drug manufacturers and was brought to bear both before and during successive FTA, NAFTA, and GATT negotiations (Doern and Sharaput 2000).

In the late 1980s and early 1990s, in particular, there were few if any effective counter-pressures from those interests/countries making the counter-arguments. Developing countries mounted some counter-pressure but were eventually worn down by more powerful forces. Consumers, in some overall sense, had a vested interest in less monopolistic practices, but at both the national and certainly at international levels, they were a weak, diffused, and virtually voiceless interest on patent issues. Perhaps the only exception to this was in the health sector where health ministries and NGOs were often a surrogate representative of consumer, patient, and disease-specific interests (Doern and Prince 2012).

In the later part of the Chrétien era and the Martin years, a further area of patent policy emerged, namely, the patenting of higher life forms (as opposed to microbial life forms which are patentable in many countries) and the broader economic and ethical issues inherent in regulating this aspect of biotechnology. American law allows such patenting, whereas EU and Canadian law does not and is only considering the need for special procedures. Debate here turns on what constitutes an *invention*, and the degree to which the manufacture or the composition of matter was under the control of the inventor as opposed to control by the laws of nature. These concerns raise serious ethical issues about patenting life forms, and similar issues attend other genetic testing products and bio-life processes (Castle 2009; Boyle 2008).

Meanwhile, emerging counter-pressures and arguments about the limits of patents and property rights began to occur because of the need for public science in the larger innovation process and because of the dangers of excessive patenting. All patents are issued by nation states, and national patent systems basically focus on the protection side of the core protection-versus-dissemination trade-off. As the Doha trade negotiations began in 2001, and as criticisms emerged since then, the focus has turned more to the dissemination side of this policy equation; that is, to the dissemination, public goods, and related public science and public knowledge side of the trade-off (Dutfield 2003; Castle 2009).

At the level of the WTO, this shift in focus to dissemination transpired through changes to the TRIPS agreement that were intended to create greater *access to medicines* including especially bio-health products by WTO member countries with insufficient or no manufacturing capacity in the pharmaceutical sector that would allow them to make effective use the compulsory licensing allowed under TRIPS. In Canada, this change took the form of federal legislation to create Canada's Access to Medicines Regime achieved through amendments to the Patent Act (Canada 2006; Mills and Weber 2006).

Under the provisions of the TRIPS agreement (Art. 31), compulsory licensing or government use of patents is allowed without the authorization of the patent owner. One of the conditions under which this can be done is when such use is predominantly for the supply of the domestic market. TRIPS also prevents WTO members with manufacturing capacity from issuing compulsory licences "authorizing the manufacture of lower-cost, generic versions of patented medicines for export to countries with little or no such capacity" (Canada 2006, 1).

In 2003, WTO members agreed to a waive stipulation regarding this provision whose purpose was to "facilitate developing and least-developed countries' access to less expensive medicines needed to treat HIV/AIDS, tuberculosis, malaria and other epidemics" (Canada 2006, 2). Canada was the first country to announce that it would implement this waiver, and in May 2004, Canada's legislative framework was given parliamentary approval and a year later its regulatory provisions came into force. Alas, due to industry opposition and other Canadian and international bureaucratic inertia, the policy has not had much actual effect (Mills and Weber 2006), and thus, the rules and policy are being reviewed by the Harper government.

Both the WTO's waiver and later permanent amendment on this matter, and the Canadian regime to implement it, were motivated by wholly desirable broader foreign and international development and health policies. However, the policy of access backed by legislative and regulatory change additionally had to ensure that Canada was still complying with its overall international obligations under TRIPS and also the North American Free Trade Agreement, was respecting the integrity of its own patent law, and was responding to the competing industry and NGO interests involved in this issue.

Access to medicines is one issue in the much larger debate over the patent regime. Other analyses are often biotechnology-specific and draw attention to the actual unwieldy natural bio-world (which would not be patentable) in contrast to practices and pressures in patent law to create "discrete immutable biological 'objects'" (Carolan 2010). Similar biotechnology-focused criticism centres on the need to reign in the scope of patents in the interests of garnering public trust and contributions to public benefits and knowledge (Caulfield 2009).

Criticism relates even more broadly to concerns about excessive patenting, the ease of getting patents for questionable inventions, and the rise in some fields of patent thickets that are harmful rather than conducive to innovation (Canadian International Council 2011; Castle 2009; Conference Board of Canada 2010b). These concerns are crucial, although they have not yet led to major legislative and regulatory change in Canada or internationally.

The role played in the past by requirements for *compulsory licensing* is another feature of this trade-off. These requirements, which now are seriously restricted, once were based on the belief that inventions made and patents granted should actually benefit consumers and society, and thus, if the inventor was not going to turn the invention into a product or process actually available in the market, then others should be able to do so, through the payment of a licence fee to the patent holder. Licensing certainly exists in the current system, but persons or firms that want to be able to use the patented item or process then have to negotiate with the patent holder and, in the end, the patent holder may decline to license. Licensing issues are at the centre of patented genetic diagnostic tests.

With respect to innovation, patents do not themselves produce innovation in the form of actual products and processes available in the marketplace (Canadian International Council 2011). Patents, rather, are about registering and legitimating claims to possible innovation opportunities. Innovation of this more complete kind only occurs when firms or other inventors that hold patents can acquire investment capital to fund not only the needed steps to get through the rest of the subsequent regulatory approval system for products but also the manufacture, marketing, and sales stages of the full innovation and commercialization process (Conference Board of Canada 2010b).

In this overall *innovation strategy* context of the past twenty years, federal policy is generally supportive of the growing importance of IP and, especially, patents as a crucial feature of commercial originality and advance by ensuring that Canadian companies are patenting and are aware of their patent rights and of the need to patent in the innovation age. But, again, patents constitute invention and not yet innovation in markets. As a part of IP framework policy, law, and regulation, the horizontal cross-industry nature of patents is strongly defended by core interests in Canada, and internationally, but there are clearly growing arguments made and interests being marshalled about where the core protection versus dissemination trade-off should and can be made – both sectorally and overall – in the public goods versus private property debate.

THE THREE REGIME ATTRIBUTES

We now look across the three sample marketplace framework realms in relation to the three regime attributes. We take note of the story they help tell about both change and inertia.

Ideas, Discourses, and Agendas

It is certainly possible to see across the four decades a gradually greater presence of regulatory ideas regarding competition and efficiency as stated framework cross-economy purposes. This is quite apparent in competition and in banking and financial services. It is less apparent in intellectual property where the protection-dissemination trade-off is involved and where goals are expressed in terms of creativity and invention. At a different layer of discourse with only indirect actual rule-based content, one sees ideas regarding innovation and competitiveness especially in competition regulation and, to some extent, in intellectual property regarding the great encouragement of more patenting. The prudential supervision norms are, of course, central to banking but, in the wake of the 2008–12 banking crisis globally, goals related to systemic risk in the entire financial system have loomed large but not necessarily with clearly agreed ideas as to how to achieve them and avoid future international crises.

While economy-wide framework aspirations and features are in evidence, it is also clear that sectoral interests and exceptions or special provisions are part of the four-decade history in the interplay among interests and due to diverse kinds of regulatory content and inertia. Regulated sectors, and regulated conduct exceptions are still very much present in the competition regulatory system. In banking and financial services, there are clearly different regulatory features regarding the big banks compared with insurance, trusts, and investment firms. In the patent aspects of IP regulation, there is no doubt that the changes that led to twenty-year patent protection were spearheaded by sectors such as drugs and biotechnology, but the twenty-year protection then became available to inventors in all sectors.

With respect to agendas and agenda events, both competition and IP regulatory reform were relegated to periodic and rarely central agenda events and occasions. This meant that both these realms exhibited unruliness of the agenda-related kind, where it was simply difficult, and for long periods impossible, to get new rules established in the first place. The banking and financial regulatory system, however, had very regular and planned – initially ten-year and then five-year – formal sunset review processes that were reasonably high profile but which also took considerable time. This realm has also experienced bank crises periods, such as the present one, where the regulatory system climbs rapidly to the apex of political and regulatory agendas anchored around the minister of finance and the governor of the Bank of Canada.

Public and Private Power in Regulation Making and Compliance

On the public side of the power equation, the analysis has shown that all three realms have multiple federal regulatory bodies and some

provincial ones, as well. Two of the realms have regulators that cluster around and within Industry Canada, a senior ministry without
doubt, but not in the same league power-wise as the Department of
Finance and the Bank of Canada regarding banking and financial
services both in normal periods and in crises. The structure of power
regarding business interests and consumers varies considerably across
the three realms.

In competition regulation, the coalitions of major business interest
groups and also small and medium-sized enterprises were unstable
across the four decades as they and successive ministers sought to
find the right climate and occasions for change in a field that was
several steps removed from top-of-mind politics and policy in federal agendas overall. This was also true for patent changes until key
powerful sectors such as drugs and biotechnology used both national
and international trade-related arenas and negotiations to garner
their preferred long periods of patent protection.

In banking and financial services in Canada, the power of the "big
five" banks and their oligopolistic range has been a constant feature,
although in the past decade or so, the various financial service subsectors gradually achieved some of their pro-competition objectives.
In the total structure of power in the three realms, consumers are
largely players with less direct lobbying power than business interests. But consumers are otherwise present in marketplace situations
of diverse kinds, being one of the key ultimate beneficiaries of marketplace framework regulatory rules. This includes prudential supervision of the banks where the ultimate nightmare scenario is a
contagion run on the banks by ordinary deposit holders who have
lost confidence.

Science, Evidence, and Knowledge

The three framework realms we explored reveal a genuine and great
diversity with most under the combined evidence and knowledge
categories rather than science-based regulation. The strongest science (and engineering) need and capacity is found in the patent
aspects of intellectual property. But in this realm, it has to be focused
uniquely on the assessment of "inventiveness" in the combined decision trio of novelty, workability, and non-obviousness. Legal expertise is crucial, as well, especially because it is mainly private legal

actions that insure the rights of patent holders rather than any CIPO patent police force.

In the competition realm, microeconomics and law are prominent in relation to the particular nature of criminal law offences versus civil matters and in the different kinds of particular offences or possible offences such as truth in advertising and mergers. In the banking and financial services realm, banking and finance-specific technical data and product knowledge are intricately woven into the regulatory system as are changing notions of how to assess risk to individual financial institutions and to the system as whole.

CONCLUSIONS

Canada's marketplace framework regulatory regime is an essential element of both economic policy and regulatory governance. We have traced its overall characteristics as a regime and through a closer look at the competition, banking and financial services, and intellectual property regulatory realms. But there are still other realms that we have not been able to cover, ranging from foreign investment and trade rules to bankruptcy and corporations law but also including key aspects of environmental regulation. The growing extent of the regime's horizontal reach across the economy – and across all industries – has been evident, as have been the underpinning ideas and norms regarding economic competition and efficiency. The ideas and discourse of the regime have been driven by views of economics and the growing need for regulatory capitalism centred on public-private regulatory and guidance arrangements nationally and, compellingly, at the international and global level.

The regime is also, without doubt, an evolving political and democratic construct that has been built incrementally and also episodically by successive Liberal and Conservative governments and prime ministerial eras. But the systems of power and the types of democracy have varied considerably across the three realms. Banking and financial services have been anchored closely to the apex of political power in an around the Department of Finance and the Bank of Canada, whereas the competition and intellectual property realms operate at a second-tier level of power centred in and around Industry Canada. In agenda-setting terms, banking and financial services regulation has operated in regular planned review periods and/

or in crisis periods, whereas the other two realms have had to fight and compete for political agenda space and attention in crowded national agendas.

The democratic politics of the regime's evolution has been centred on interest group pluralism and, of course, Cabinet-parliamentary democracy. But the pluralism has been business-focused with consumer and broader social interests, although variously acknowledged and mentioned in mandate statements and laws, operating at a secondary level as a much more dispersed player. Interestingly, despite the nominal pluralism, the regime tends not to be composed of multimember representative regulatory commissions. Instead, key regulators have been fashioned as statutory persons in the competition and IP patent realms so as to reinforce their independence both from ministerial politics and from interest group politics and their role as evidence- and knowledge-based regulators dealing with varied but often high volumes of cases regarding both offences and approvals.

The relative reliance in regulation making on rules, regulations, and guidelines has changed both over the four decades and across the three realms examined. Guidelines and soft law are more present and needed by the politics and nature of competition law and regulation and its varied criminal and civil offences compared with either patents or banking, although the latter have some guidelines in their regulatory toolkit as well. Thus, regulatory capitalism is much more present but in varied ways across the three realms examined.

Unruliness of the regulatory regime–complexity kind emerges in our closer look at even just three realms of the marketplace framework regulatory regime. In part, the greater the presence of guidelines in and across each realm the greater the potential for different forms of unruliness and inherent regulatory density. But also it arises from the fact that, while the aspirational policy intent of the regime is for framework rules to prevail and not industrial policy-style preferences and protections for industrial sectors, we have seen that policy and case enforcement conflicts on sectoral issues and political interests are still very much present, although less so than four decades ago. These sectoral concerns involve issues that show up in periods of regulatory change, such as the role of small business in competition law and the drug industry in patent law change but also between the banks and other financial service sectors such as insurance, trusts, and investment. But sectoral and, indeed, individual company sectoral issues can occur in the compliance and assessment processes regarding cases and approvals such as in mergers and patent assessments.

Other types of regulatory agency–related unruliness emerge when one simply looks across the three realms at the range of ideas and purposes that receive expression in statutory and regulatory mandates. While competition and efficiency and also fair markets receive expected and necessary attention, so also do strong ideas of prudential supervision, confidence, and trust and systemic risk in the banking and financial services realm, and the conferring of property rights and product monopolies in patents along with greater access to patented medicines. Layered on top of these ideas, sometimes in specific ways, but more often as rhetorical policy discourse are ideas such as innovation and competitiveness. There are, undoubtedly, many boundary grey zones or black holes and collision points when these ideas meet across the fifteen or more federal regulators as well some at the provincial level and, even more compellingly, at the international level. These are bound to be uncertain and even bewildering for the regulators and the regulated firms and consumers with the latter firms and consumers being "frameworked" over by several regulators and several sets of rules, regulations, and guidelines.

8

The Societal Framework Regulatory Regime: Law and Order, Morality and Sexuality, and the Welfare State

The societal framework regulatory regime has a macro-level scale and form of governance for coordinating relations in populations. Along with our examination of the regulatory regime of social sectors in chapter 6, it completes empirically our development of regulatory welfarism as a central concept and argument in this book. The broad purpose of this regime is to regulate horizontally across Canadian society with criminal law powers and other legislation, ethical rules and moral declarations, and social welfare program rules and disciplinary effects, many embedded in expenditure- and tax-related conditions and requirements. In this chapter, we first look at the general nature of the regime focusing on its historical context, the idea of social management or managing society, the goals and values of the societal framework regulatory regime, and social and economic impacts for private sector firms, group identities, and family well-being. Although the analysis covers a long historical period that predates the welfare state and extends back to the historic night watchman state, the current Harper Conservative era looms large in the chapter because of its key policy and regulatory changes since 2006.

We then look more closely at the three diverse societal framework regulatory realms: law and order, morality and sexuality, and the welfare state. The analysis includes an appreciation of their detailed legislative and rule-embedded complexity, and their centralized and delegated governance modes of regulation. It also includes a broad account of the mixes of statutory, regulatory rule making, and guidance approaches. This is followed by an exploration of our three regime attributes as elements in explaining both change and inertia

across the three framework regime examples. We then offer concluding observations on unruliness, regulatory democracy, and regulatory welfarism.

To preview the discussion, our basic propositions about developments in the three framework regulatory realms include the following: Notable changes are taking place in the law and order realm
with greater emphasis given by recent federal Liberal and Conservative
governments to issues of anti-terrorism and national security. Under
the Harper Conservatives, there has been a striking intensification of
rule making in crime control and community safety. Earlier federal
governments, in the 1970s and 1980s, exercised a relatively active
role in articulating notions of equality and human rights, but more
recent governments have disengaged from an agenda of social justice.
Regulating morality and sexuality is not a passé area of state intervention from some bygone age; nor is it solely about enforcing prud-
ish community standards or making paternalistic rules of conduct for
other people. There is also an expansive side to moral and sexual
regulation in the issues under debate, the forms of discourse in circulation, and the possibilities of actions under consideration.

The welfare state is a mode of societal regulation and compliance
governance. Even its core of income redistribution benefits and the
provision of services to people in need are vehicles of regulation.
More generally, as Mishra notes, "The government or the state sector is not merely a supplier of welfare. It is also the legitimate regulatory agency of societal values and activities" (1990, 112). Social
policies and social rules are intertwined through notions of minimum standards and eligibility criteria.

Just like the marketplace framework regulatory regime examined
in chapter 7, the politics of the societal framework regulatory regime
do not succeed entirely in avoiding sectoral interests, in part because
social groups tend to be organized sectorally, and there are many
more of them than broader horizontal coalitions or social movements. While chapter 6 examined regulatory interventions *in* society
in regards to particular groups, in chapter 8 we are examining regulatory interventions *of* and *on* society; system-wide rules and enforcements of what Squires calls "political interventions into the ordering
of the population" (1990, 12).

Realms of the societal framework regulatory regime incite public
debates and provoke close scrutiny by the media, political parties,
countless stakeholders, and other governments in Canada and

internationally. Law and order, morality and sexuality, the welfare state: these are quintessential issues of democratic politics. All three realms deal with basic values of society and core functions of the state in governing the conduct of citizens and strangers.

THE SOCIETAL FRAMEWORK REGULATORY REGIME IN HISTORICAL CONTEXT

To put into historical perspective the horizontal regulatory reach across Canadian society, consider the observation that "there is very little organizational evidence of the national government's interest in assuming responsibility for the well-being of the whole Canadian population until the end of the First World War" (Hodgetts 1973, 107). Although this is true with respect to social programs – federal departments of Health and Immigration and Colonization were established around that time and what would eventually be called the welfare state came mostly after the end of the Second World War – there were public departments and agencies of national concern with public security of the Canadian population since Confederation. Examples are the Department of Justice, the Solicitor General, the Supreme Court of Canada, the Northwest Mounted Police, a superintendent of General Indian Affairs, and federal penitentiaries.

Of course, since then there have been major shifts in governance and policy developments in the social management of the Canadian population. A royal commission describes this governmental task of managing society as the need "continuously to foster a moral coherence and a social solidarity out of the diversities which we bring to the national and provincial communities" (Canada 1985a: 10). This statement expresses the principle that there is such a thing as society, a collective entity, a moral order that is more than the sum of the current individuals in a given place. Furthermore, this task of social management involves developing and administering national policy frameworks, governing relations among disparate social groups, and fashioning a collective self-image of people.

Social management goes beyond spending instruments or symbolic measures for the recognition of multiple identities. Regulatory frameworks serve a significant function in governing the moral and social cohesion of individuals as members of a national political community. Types of rules in the societal framework regulatory regime encompass a broad array of legislation and delegated regulations, agreements, program conditions, education, suasion, and information campaigns. Criminal law powers stand out as a prominent form of rule making in this regime. Policy practices and processes concerned with regulating society include normalizing and abnormalizing behaviours, mainstreaming and marginalizing individuals for certain deeds or misdeeds, legislating on the permitted and the prohibited, the decent and the deviant, and the worthy poor and the unworthy. Regulatory actions target relations within the state, between the state and society, and within society.

Political aims of the societal framework regulatory regime incorporate values of social integration and cohesion. Additional values and public goals entail developing a regime of common citizenship in which all people can participate; human dignity and tolerance and the rule of law; and equality, equity, and notions of sharing, fair treatment, and social justice. In managing society along these lines, federal and provincial governments have significant effects on the performance of the economy. The regulatory realm of law and order, for example, offers the markets and business firms a framework of rules and a good degree of public stability in which entrepreneurial activities can be pursued and private property rights are respected in the economic sphere. Numerous rules in the welfare state are designed to address issues of the mix of work incentives and work disincentives, of active labour market policies and workforce participation generally, of counter-cyclical budgeting and economic stabilization, and of savings, consumption, and equity investment decisions by Canadians.

Rules in the societal framework regulatory regime also have social effects, intended and otherwise. Moral and sexual regulations, for instance, can legitimize certain forms of conduct or stigmatize others and, thus, marginalize a group that may well already be marginal and disadvantaged. In the area of disability income assistance, in which both orders of government in Canada have programs, screening rules that restrict access to individuals and families struggling to meet basic needs have the effect of manufacturing poverty and perpetuating dependence on charity (Prince 2009).

Different yet somewhat overlapping strands of literature address the issues of law and order, morality and sexuality, and the welfare state in contemporary regulatory governance. On law and order as a societal framework regulatory regime, analytical work comes from several academic fields including criminology, justice studies, political science, sociolegal scholarship, and critical social policy. Studies variously conceptualize the regime as the regulatory state (Prince 1999b), the new regulatory state (Braithwaite 2000), the post-regulatory state (Crawford 2006), the security state (Hallsworth and Lea 2011), and the night watchman state (Prince 2012). Related concepts to the night watchman state model in political science and sociology are the law and order state or the minimal state; in political economy, the coercive and legitimation functions of welfare under capitalism; in public administration, the regulatory state; and in critical social policy studies, the disciplinary welfare state.

Hallsworth and Lea (2011) describe the emergence of what they call the *security state* as a successor to the welfare state, a novel state form that combines crime control, social policy, and national security. In their words, "we witness three fundamental transformations in the nature of the State: first, crime control becomes the pre-eminent paradigm for social control; second, social policy and welfare become progressively criminalized; while, third, the functions of the State are increasingly distributed through an assemblage of state and non-state actors" (144).

On the societal framework regulatory regime that deals with matters of morality and sexuality, important conceptual and empirical foundations are found in criminology, history, feminist work, gay and lesbian studies, political science, sociology, and critical social theory. From works on social deviance and control has emerged a distinct moral regulation literature with inquiry into three topics: the role of regulation in the historical formation of modern states; the phenomenon of moral panics and the activities of moral entrepreneurs and social reform movements; and, in order to regulate conduct, the construction of people with specific subjectivities to be placed in certain ethical categories (Corrigan 2006; Glasbeek 2006). This body of work examines various areas of law, certain areas of behaviour, and social relations, along with particular mechanisms of governing. Influenced by the governmentality approach discussed in earlier chapters, some of the moral regulation literature focuses on non-state forms of regulation and projects of ethical self-governance (Dean 1994; Hunt 1999), while some concentrates more on state control and coercion (Chunn and Gavigan 2004; Davidson and Davis 2012).

Regarding the welfare state as a societal framework regulatory regime, three strands of writings are worth noting. One strand is a large body of work on the shrinking government and the "hollowing out" of the state (Shields and Evans 1998); the shifting form of citizenship away from rights to obligations (Roche 1992); and related claims of the death or at least decline of "the social" state towards government of the community (Rose 1996). We touched on these ideas in chapter 6 and will revisit them in this chapter.

A second related strand examines the changing functions and modes of governance of the modern state; a conversion away from the Keynesian velfare state to a formation called the regulatory state (Mabbett 2011; Majone 1997), the Schumpeterian workfare post-national regime (Jessop 1999), or the workfare state (Peck 2001). To illustrate, Majone (1997) contends that in many European countries since the late 1970s the positive role of the state has been reduced and the role of the regulatory state has correspondingly increased; in short, "rule making is replacing taxing and spending" (139).

The decline in income redistribution and service provision by the state has been due to the constraints of stagflation and economic globalization as well as policies adopted on privatization and welfare reforms (Mishra 1990). Majone (1997) makes a sharp distinction between the positive, interventionist state and the regulatory state in terms of their main functions, policy instruments, arenas of political conflict, characteristic institutions and key actors, policy style and policy culture, and political accountability. Majone describes the main function of the positive or welfare state as redistribution and economic stabilization, whereas for the regulatory state it is correcting for market failures. This is a narrow concept of regulation, as our discussion in chapter 3 made clear, as well as of the welfare state.

A third strand of more recent writing on the welfare state as a framework regulatory regime challenges this hard distinction between the regulatory state and the welfare state. It questions the depiction of regulation as a separate government function and a policy type distinct from the redistributive characteristics of the modern welfare state. It also questions the claim that the Keynesian welfare state has been replaced by a shift to increasing regulation of service provision and networked governance arrangements. Wincott (2012) points out that this line of analysis of a fundamental change in state forms rests on an "epochal generalization" of policy regime transformation and commits "anachronistic fallacies in welfare state history" by exaggerating the actual nature of social interventions in both the so-called golden decades of the welfare state and the subsequent years of decline (see also Rice and Prince 2013). Wincott usefully remarks upon the need to bridge the relative isolation between

welfare state analysis of social policy specialists and law and society
scholarship by criminologists. Rodger echoes this observation: "The
world of welfare and the world of criminal justice, while never very
far apart, are now moving increasingly together in terms of establishing modes of social discipline considered appropriate for living
and working in a complex, postmodern society" (2008, 2).

THREE SELECTED REALMS: LAW AND ORDER, MORALITY
AND SEXUALITY, AND THE WELFARE STATE

Law and Order

Our discussion of the law and order realm in Canada focuses on the
Justice and the Public Safety portfolios of the federal government.
The minister of justice ultimately is obliged to represent the basic
integrity of the state (not just the government) in the performance of
perhaps its most sensitive function, the execution of the laws of the
state and the administration of "justice" in the carrying out of the
state's right to use legitimate coercion in accordance with law (Doern
and Phidd 1983, 1992). As the official legal adviser to the federal
cabinet, the justice minister is responsible, in whole or in part, for
more than fifty statutes in numerous areas of federal law: Aboriginal,
access to justice (legal aid and public legal education), criminal justice, family law, and youth in conflict with the law, and youth justice.
The Department of Justice drafts legislation and regulations, provides legal services to other federal departments and agencies, and
examines bills and regulations to ensure their consistency with the
Canadian Charter of Rights and Freedoms.

These responsibilities and activities structurally position Justice as
a central agency within the federal executive and legislative arenas
(Kelly 1999; Sutherland 1983). The Justice portfolio comprises the
department plus seven other organizations with mandates for a fair,
relevant, and accessible Canadian justice system; equality and respect
for human rights and the prevention of discrimination; judicial independence; protection of privacy rights of individuals; transparency
and accountability of the federal government; and, independent,
impartial, and fair public prosecutions (Justice Canada 2011).

Public Safety Canada (or the Department of Public Safety and
Emergency Preparedness) is the successor federal organization to the
Solicitor General of Canada. Established in 2005 by the Martin Liberal

government, signalling the growing importance of this policy realm
after the terrorist attacks in the United States in 2001, Public Safety
consists of policy and program activities in border management, crime
prevention and corrections, community safety and partnerships, emergency management response to major disasters, law enforcement and
policing (including Aboriginal policing), and national security and
international cooperation. Understandably, the core values of Public
Safety are broadly expressed as secure and safe communities, the country, and the world. More specifically, these values translate practically
into various trade-offs among program goals of protecting Canada
from threats to national security, ensuring oversight and accountability
in compliance with laws, respecting civil liberties and human rights,
and ensuring economic trade and stability in the movement of goods
and people across the border (Whitaker 2003, 2005).

Multiple pieces of significant federal legislation characterize the
law and order regulatory realm. On the judicial side are the Supreme
Court Act of 1985, the Federal Courts Act of 1985, and the Judges
Act of 1985. In terms of rights, legislation includes the Canadian
Charter of Rights and Freedoms of 1982, the Canadian Bill of Rights
of 1960, the Family Orders and Agreements Enhancement Assistance
Act of 1985, the Canadian Human Rights Act of 1985, and the
Employment Equity Act of 1995. With respect to international affairs,
laws include the Extradition Act of 1999, International Transfer of
Offenders Act of 2004, Mutual Legal Assistance in Criminal Matters
Act of 1988, Proceeds of Crime (Money Laundering) and Terrorist
Financing Act of 2000, Crimes against Humanity and War Crimes
Act of 2000, and the State Immunity Act of 1985. On the administra-
tion of justice are such laws as the Canada Evidence Act of 1985, the
Witness Protection Program Act of 1995, and the Director of Public
Prosecutions Act of 2006, all under the gaze of the massive Criminal
Code. Regarding law enforcement and corrections are the Royal
Canadian Mounted Police Act of 1985, the Canadian Security and
Intelligence Act of 1985, and the Youth Criminal Justice Act of 2002.
In the field of combatting terrorism, major pieces of federal legisla-
tion are the Anti-terrorism Act of 2001, the Public Safety Act of 2002,
the Public Safety and Emergency Preparedness Act of 2005, and the
Justice for Victims of Terrorism Act of 2012.

Apparent from the analysis is that legislation with supporting
regulations constitutes a major type of regulatory form in the law
and order realm. This realm contains a dense thicket of statutes and

delegated statutory instruments for the main departments and also the agencies, boards, commissions, courts, and investigative offices in the Justice and Public Safety portfolios. For example, the minister of public safety has sole responsibility to Parliament for sixteen acts and that department is affected by other federal statutes, while close to a hundred federal laws pertain to the operations of the Canada Border Services Agency (CBSA), which is an outlier, but other agencies such as the Correctional Service of Canada administer and function within the immediate context of sixteen federal laws (Public Safety Canada 2008, 71–3). Another prominent form of regulatory policy making in the law and order realm is the negotiated agreement, both international and intergovernmental agreements. Examples are the Canada-US Agreement on Emergency Management Cooperation, the Biology Casework Analysis Agreements with provinces and territories, the First Nations Policing Program Agreements that serve about four hundred communities across the country, and the RCMP Police Service Agreements with most provinces.

Information and education activities are softer forms of regulating in the realm, in emergency management outreach, for instance. Social media and social marketing campaigns have been undertaken in recent years on the issue of family preparedness for a disaster and on the issue of cyber threats via the Internet with the intent of informing Canadians of genuine risks and providing information to mitigate threats and enhance personal preparedness; in other terms, facilitating the government of one's self in times of emergencies; self-governance in prevention, response, and recovery.

In the Canadian government, besides the departments of Justice and Public Safety, the main policy and regulatory institutions include the Federal Court, the Federal Court of Appeal, and the Supreme Court of Canada, the CBSA, the Parole Board of Canada, the RCMP, the Correctional Service of Canada, and the Canadian Security Intelligence Service (CSIS). Other smaller agencies with ombudsman-like roles have emerged in recent decades, including the Office of the Correctional Investigator, the Office of the Federal Ombudsman for Victims of Crime, and the Commission for Public Complaints against the RCMP. Still other recently established organizations reflect the national security agenda of gathering and analysing intelligence and assessing risks of terrorism. On matters of border security and management, Public Safety works with the CBSA, RCMP, CSIS, Transport Canada, and the Department of Foreign Affairs;

and, on the American side, with the US Department of Homeland Security and the US Department of Justice.

Non-governmental organizations have long served an assortment of roles in the law and order realm. In the areas of corrections and reintegration, Aboriginal community groups provide healing supports while national voluntary organizations offer community services to offenders. With respect to hate-motivated crimes, federal government organizations work with places of worship and community centres along with other non-profit agencies; and in child welfare and youth justice, to cite one more example, the Canadian Centre for Child Protection and the Canadian Crime Stoppers Association are important non-state organizations in this policy community.

Morality and Sexuality

Corrigan (2006, 68) observes, "We live in worlds which are as much moral as material: indeed there is no way of operating and handling the material which does not involve forms of expression some of which carry a higher evaluation than others." As a societal framework regulatory realm, morality and sexuality concern the use of criminal powers, other areas of law, and still other regulatory instruments that make authoritative evaluations of what beliefs and behaviours are socially proper and acceptable by a political community and which are not, and among the latter which warrant state prohibitions and punishments. The legal enforcement of morality, according to Hart (1963: 25) is intended "to suppress practices condemned as immoral by positive morality," that is, by "the morality actually accepted and shared by a given social group."

Brooks suggests that issues of social morality, whether based on religious beliefs like Judeo-Christian creeds or secular values like political ideologies, "involve a conception of the social good and a particular vision of society" (1994, 72). He further suggests that "morality issues continue to be prominent in contemporary politics" (ibid.), a claim to which we and other commentators find considerable supportive evidence (Hunt 1999). Bird and Stoney (2006) have written on Canadian public policies governing sin; in this case, the dubious indulgences of alcohol consumption, gambling, and tobacco use. State rules on these activities involve their availability in terms of packaging and warnings, price and taxation (sin taxes), place of marketing and distribution, and allowable age of access or use. Regulating sin, claim Bird and Stoney, is "one of the most difficult and controversial areas of regulation that governments and societies confront" because of the complex interplay of public attitudes, health and social costs, and economic and trade considerations. As a result, the rules governing these so-called sinful activities "reflect pragmatic choices rather than moral absolutes" (247–8). This politics of pragmatism is evident in tobacco control policy making in recent decades in such federal legislation as the Non-smokers' Health Act of 1988, the Tobacco Products Control Act of 1988, the Tobacco Sales to Young Persons Act of 1993, and the Tobacco Act of 1997 (Pross and Stewart 1994; Bird and Stoney 2006). Besides pragmatism, the politics of the tobacco policy field involves the politics of federalism; in 1995, the Supreme Court of Canada ruled that major parts of the Tobacco Products Control Act of 1988 were ultra vires or outside the legal capacity of the federal government – this led to a new law, the Tobacco Act of 1997.

Dominant ideas in this realm of societal framework rule making include distinctions between public actions and private conduct, civil and religious beliefs, the public and private spaces of the state and the bedroom (McLaren and McLaren 1986), morality and immorality, consensual relations between people, and the age of consent (Dauda 2010). Terms appearing in Canada's Criminal Code include *indecent* and *indecency, obscene, immoral, scurrilous, disgusting, disorderly conduct,* and *vice.* Part V of the Criminal Code is entitled "Sexual Offences, Public Morals and Disorderly Conduct." In more than thirty sections, there are offences pertaining to sexual interference of persons under the age of 16 years, sexual touching and sexual exploitation, sexual exploitation of a person with a disability, incest, anal intercourse, bestiality, rape and the attempt to commit rape, indecent assault, voyeurism, gross indecency, child pornography on the Internet and other medium, corrupting children, immoral theatrical performance, adultery, sexual immorality, indecent exposure and exhibition, and habitual drunkenness.

Sexual governance is about the evaluation and regulation of human desires and pleasures within normative and legal contexts (Gotell 1996). As a field of public issues and state activities, sexual governance includes the following: abortion; homosexuality and law reform; family planning and contraception; censorship in broadcasting, film, and literature; prostitution and soliciting; sex education in schools; legislated access to marriage and divorce; and public health measures on sexuality and sexually transmitted diseases (Davidson and Davis 2012). Illustrating that regulatory fields invariably overlap, sexual governance includes fertility controls and services, rape and attempted rape, and transgressive or pathological sexual acts such as bestiality and necrophilia. This assortment of issues connects to the constitutional responsibilities of the provinces as well as the federal government.

In addition to the Criminal Code, other notable federal laws are the Marriage (Prohibited Degrees) Act of 1990 that forbids marriage between specified related persons; the Modernization of Benefits and Obligations Act of 2000 that updated numerous federal statutes in relation to common law developments on the rights of same-sex couples to various benefits and obligations; the Sex Offender Information Registration Act of 2004, the purpose of which is to assist police services to prevent and investigate crimes of a sexual nature and the Civil Marriage Act of 2005, which deals with legal capacity to get married for civil purposes. The significance of the Civil Marriage Act is that it gives public recognition to particular forms of sexual diversity in Canada (Rayside 2008). Couples of the same sex and couples of the opposite sex have equal access to marriage for civil purposes. At the same time, the act affirms that officials of religious groups are free to refuse to perform marriages that are not in accordance with their spiritual beliefs. The act, therefore, espouses and seeks to balance values of equality before and under the law, equal benefit of the law without discrimination, human dignity and respect, and freedom of conscience and religion.

What state institutions are directly involved in regulating morality and sexuality? A statement by Valverde and Weir (2006, 77) on such regulatory activities in nineteenth-century Canada applies to our governance arrangements in the twenty-first century as well: "The sexual in particular was not an autonomous regulatory site subject to the jurisdiction of distinct institutions: there never have been ministries of sexuality. Rather, sexual and moral regulation have frequently been constructed and inscribed within other institutional locations: ministries of revenue and finance, and of citizenship and culture, have exercised moral regulation. All departments of the state, including the military, have at times been, and potentially always are, sites of moral regulation." This interpretation certainly argues for how the policy and governance of this realm operates horizontally across government and across levels of government within the Canadian federation. For example, government departments of children and family services, health, and justice; law enforcement agencies at all levels; national courts (Federal Court and the Supreme Court of Canada), provincial and territorial courts, and superior courts. At local levels of public governance are municipal councils, school boards, health authorities and hospital boards, library boards, parks commissions, and police boards. In addition are the human service occupations and professions of lawyers, teachers, social workers, nurses, doctors, child and youth care workers, juvenile workers, court officials, family therapists, psychologists, and psychiatrists. All are potential sites of regulating morality and sexuality.

Along with legal compulsion by state institutions, self-regulation in social relations is a second modality of moral and sexual regulation. Both the legal and social modes of regulating sexuality and morality coexist in public policy and practice (Chunn and Gavigan 2004). In civil society are interest groups and social movements; churches, synagogues, and other faith-based organizations; child protection agencies, family services, and child welfare societies; each involved in challenging certain moralizing practices and producing and enforcing preferred norms of conduct. All of these non-state institutions can be agencies of moral and sexual regulation in Canadian public affairs.

Rather than concentrate on the motives of regulators or on specific institutional sites, Hunt (1999, 279) defines *moral regulation* as "a process in which moral discourses, techniques and practices make up the primary field of contestation." In a similar vein, Valverde and Weir restrict the meaning of moral regulation to "the production of moral subjects" and deviant subjects, "the formation of ethical subjectivity" (2006, 77 and 83); of making good citizens and deserving clients (Strange and Loo 1997). Modern projects of regulating or governing one's self aim "to stimulate the self-monitoring and self-governance of citizens" (Hunt 1999, 216). Hunt contends that "self-governance is not new, but rather that the forms of self-governance have shifted significantly" from self-control of character to self-formation of a personality and lifestyle (4). In this regulatory realm, active undertakings of self-governance in contemporary times include practising safe sex, not drinking and driving, saying no to drugs, and being responsible with alcohol consumption while pregnant. Regulatory tools involved in working on one's own morality and sexual being can involve information, education, advice, and warnings along with practices of self-examination, confession, intervention and support by peers, and an altered presentation of everyday selves (Hart 1963; Hunt 1999; Prince 2010a).

Running through the Harper government's law and order agenda are important aspects of regulating morality and sexuality. Various pieces of the tough on crime reform package since 2006 address protecting women and children from sex offenders; raising the age of sexual consent from 14 to 16 years; ending the "legal defence loopholes" for child pornography (Lee 2007). The Safe Streets and Communities Act of 2012 is a current example of this intermingling of the realms of law and order and morality and sexuality. Core elements of this law deal with protecting children and youth from sexual predators by toughening penalties (setting mandatory minimums and increasing maximums) in the Criminal Code for offences luring a child, procuring a child for illegal sexual activity, and sexually assaulting a child; and by creating two new offences: providing sexually explicit material to a child for the aim of facilitating the commission of a sexual offence against that child, and communicating via Internet or any other means of telecommunications to make arrangements to commit a sexual offence against a child.

The Welfare State

At a broad level of expression, welfare state ideas include community and diversity, citizenship rights and responsibilities, health and human well-being, equality and equity, justice, security, and stability (Prince 2005). Traditional arguments to justify social services and transfers relate to meeting needs, providing compensation for certain losses, and offering insurance against specific risks. In recent years, the principal reasons advanced to justify social spending and interventions refer to investments in human resources, economic growth, and competitiveness. While traditional concerns such as assistance to the disadvantaged are still important, they have been overshadowed in the past twenty years by initiatives more acceptable to the requirements of a globalizing economy. The policy environment and social objectives are described increasingly in terms of ability to respond to labour market trends, human capital development, and the imperatives of international trade. This has altered the composition of many social programs as well as changed somewhat the meaning of human well-being and social development.

Universality is a major value in public health care and education policy, while the contributory principle of social insurance and the selectivity principle are also significant precepts in pensions, disability benefits, unemployment benefits, social housing, and welfare benefits. Income support programs such as social assistance, tax expenditures, or social insurance with defined contributors and recipients, reflect and reproduce societal divisions (Rice and Prince 2013).

Different time frames operate within the realm of the welfare state. The historical age of several federal social programs is lengthy, some stretching back to the 1920s, and many from the heyday of the welfare system, spanning the 1940s into the1970s. This historical feature has implications for the initial pattern and goals of a program, along with the subsequent pathway of policy development that create a legacy of social expectations and learning for a clientele, and also feedback – both negative and positive – for politicians and officials. Temporal considerations are readily apparent in the regulatory elements of social programs; in determining eligibility with respect to the individual's age, length of residency in the country or province, a person's work history, financial contributions made over a given period, the duration of benefits, and timelines for filing, preparing, and presenting an appeal on a tax or expenditure decision.

At the centre of the federal welfare state are Employment and Social Development (until the July 2013 cabinet shuffle, Human Resources and Skills Development Canada or HRSDC) and Health Canada. Employment and Social Development has strategic outcomes in relation to an inclusive labour force; safe, fair, and productive workplaces and cooperative workplace relations; and income security for Canadians. Thus, in income security, important legislation includes the Canada Pension Plan Act of 1985, the Canada Pension Plan Investment Board Act of 1997, the Employment Insurance Act of 1996, the Canada Employment Insurance Financing Board Act of 2008, the Old Age Security Act of 1985, the Universal Child Care Benefit Act of 2006, and the Canada Disability Savings Act of 2007. On labour and industrial relations, legislation includes the Canada Labour Code of 1985, the Fair Wages and Hours of Labour Act of 1985, the Employment Equity Act of 1995, the Canadian Centre for Occupational Health and Safety Act of 1985, and the Wage Earner Protection Program Act of 2005. In the area of education and learning, key legislation includes the Canada Student Loans Act of 1985, the Canada Student Financial Assistance Act of 1994, and the Canada Education Savings Act of 2004.

The integrity of program delivery processes is an important regulatory idea that informs most of these areas both regarding equity and
fairness. For Employment and Social Development, this means ensuring that services and benefits are delivered securely to clients, that is,
that no personal information is at risk of loss of privacy; that over-
payments are recovered from such programs as the Canada Pension
Plan (CPP) and Employment Insurance (EI); and that social insurance numbers are legitimate and accurate via the Social Insurance
Registry (HRSDC 2011).

Health Canada is a key social framework regulator in relation to all
its mandate areas, which include preserving Canada's health care system; health protection via its extensive regulatory roles in food, drugs,
and biotechnology; and health promotion. Health Canada also has
crucial roles in international and global health organizations and networks. For Health Canada, major legislation includes the Canada
Health Act of 1985, the Controlled Drugs and Substances Act of 1996,
and the Food and Drugs Act of 1985. Regulatory purposes emphasize
protecting and promoting the health and safety of Canadians.

Finance Canada is also a strategic participant in the welfare state
regulatory realm. First, because of its near monopoly role in tax policy, including personal and corporate income and GST/HST tax and
tax expenditures on matters pertaining to education and other social
welfare activities. Second, because of its dominant role regarding the
federal transfer payments to the provinces, especially the Canada
Health Transfer (CHT) and Canada Social Transfer (CST), alongside
the other transfers like equalization payments to "have-not" provinces, labour market agreements, and territorial formula financing
agreements with the Northwest Territories, Nunavut, and Yukon.

Finance Canada's role regarding federal transfer payments to the
provinces is a primary function in regulating federalism and overarching social policy in Canada. In recent years, a considerable
debate has re-emerged over the question of a vertical fiscal imbal-
ance in the federation, variously understood as the inadequacy of
federal grants to provinces, the mismatch of expenditure and revenue powers under the Constitution, and the actual use or underuse
of governing authorities by one or the other order of government.
Third, the Office of the Superintendent of Financial Institutions
(OSFI) and the Office of the Chief Actuary, both housed in Finance,
perform duties vital to the Canadian pension and retirement income
system. The OSFI supervises financial institutions and federally regulated private pension plans.

In respect of financial institutions, the OFSI determines whether they are in sound financial condition and are complying with their governing statute law and supervisory requirements under that law. In respect of pensions, the OFSI is mandated to (1) determine whether federally regulated pension plans meet the minimum funding requirements and are complying with the other requirements of the Pension Benefits Standards Act of 1985 and its regulations and supervisory requirements under that legislation; (2) to promptly advise the administrator of a pension plan in the event that the plan is not meeting the minimum funding requirements or is not complying with other requirements of the Pension Benefits Standards Act and, in such a case, to take, or require the administrator to take, the necessary corrective measures to deal with the situation in a timely manner; and (3) to promote the adoption by administrators of pension plans, policies, and procedures designed to control and manage risk. These responsibilities appear in the Office of the Superintendent of Financial Institutions Act of 1985, the purpose of which is to contribute to public confidence in the Canadian financial system by federal regulating financial institutions and pension plans. With the global economic downturn in 2008 and related banking crisis and a recession in Canada, as well, concerns arose over the solvency of a number of pension plans in the Canadian economy, attracting greater attention to the role of the OFSI in managing the unruliness of market events.

Relationships between the Canadian state and civil society are a significant feature of this realm, in particular the voluntary sector in the expression of desired norms, the provision of necessary services, and the development and operation of social programs. Governments have identified the voluntary sector as one of the prime sources in the community for providing additional social care and volunteers as untapped sources of community support. Wider institutional definitions include informal helping, families, and kinship networks.

Indeed, more than 175,000 non-profit organizations, many more than the 85,000 registered charities we referred to in chapter 6, make up the formal voluntary sector in Canada, including Aboriginal organizations, social advocacy groups, local service clubs, and social economy enterprises. The lead federal social department has also called for new social partnerships with "innovative charities and forward-looking private sector companies" in addressing social needs and issues, such as homelessness training and skills development (HRSDC 2011, 42).

The current mix of regulatory instruments in the welfare state realm, thus, includes the following: old and new pieces of legislation as illustrated earlier; multiple intergovernmental agreements (bilateral, multilateral, and omnilateral with all provinces and territories); treaty or final agreements with First Nations; ongoing initiatives and amendments to rules and standards in the Canada student loans programs, EI, and labour programs; guidelines and recognized "best practices" in, for example, employment standards and workplace health and safety; and tools of persuasion, information, and social marketing. In terms of the international aspects of the welfare state realm, Canada has entered into social security agreements with over thirty countries in recent decades. An example of the internationalization of public policy programs under the federal government's jurisdiction is explicitly linked to like policies in other welfare states. The purpose of these agreements, from the perspective of Canada, is to coordinate the operation of old age benefits and the Canada Pension Plan with comparable programs in other nations that provide pensions for retirement, old age, disability, and survivorship. The intent is that Canadians working abroad would have the same rights under the social security laws of another country as the citizens of that country, and that citizens from another country now living in Canada would not face restrictions here upon receiving payment of the other country's pension.

In recent decades, the redistributive function of the welfare state in Canada and elsewhere has been weakening – as evidenced by public service retrenchments, social policy drift and inaction, the reduction of tax brackets and tax levels, and rising levels of inequality in the market incomes of families. During this period of what some have prematurely or inaccurately called the death of the Keynesian welfare state, the regulatory role of the state has grown in many areas of human and social development. In fact, the decline and redesign of redistributive policy has important regulatory effects with social and economic consequences. Examples here include allowing employers to pay foreign temporary workers less than minimum wage rates; EI rules that obligate recipients to accept a wider span of substitute employment at lower wages; greater use of the tax system to deliver targeted social benefits with all the accouterments of control associated with revenue administration.

Major policy decisions by the Harper Conservatives have contributed to these trends, such as abandoning a federal role in promoting the development of regulated child care and early learning facilities across the country and in not attaching any explicit conditions to federal transfer payments to the provinces and territories for public health care. At the same time, Liberal and Conservative federal governments over the past forty years have introduced new rights and responsibilities in parental leave and family-friendly workplace policies, often with implications for labour relations and employment standards. Family-friendly workplace policies are designed to aid workers in balancing the demands of paid employment and the needs of their family life. Parental leave policy includes benefits and interventions related to maternity, paternity, adoptive parents, job-protected leave, special leave (such as for grandparents or child care), the right to work while on leave, and the right to workplace accommodations because of caregiving or home care responsibilities.

THE THREE REGIME ATTRIBUTES

The societal regulatory framework seems obvious in the traditional law and order functions of justice and public safety. The primary institutions concerned with law and order are the courts, police, law offices, prisons, and parole boards. Here government acts as lawmaker, umpire, and enforcer. Regulating morality represents one of the ways in which the government seeks to create an environment of control over the way people think about certain issues and the way community members construct their relationships with each other. We have also drawn attention to the regulatory practices operating in and through federal social welfare programs. Community groups are particularly concerned with the way welfare regulations control the behaviour of individuals and families. All social programs are rule-infused, having regulations that control entitlement, regulate the flow of benefits, create conditions for withdrawal of support, and establish power and dependency relationships.

Ideas, Discourse, and Agendas

Perhaps the fundamental idea of this regulatory framework regime is the concept of *the political society*: a population in a given territory, with a system of jurisdictions, citizenship practices, and a moral order, all of which involves a level of cohesion and integration. The primary focus of rules and laws is "broadly directed to the citizen body as a whole" (Hodgetts 1973, 129).

Neutral rule making by public authorities: there is no such thing. This reality is clearly evident in these three regulatory framework realms examined. With respect to ideas and discourse, moral and sexual regulation may, on the surface, seem more judgmental than rule making that deals with law and order or welfare or, for that matter, economic sectors or parliamentary affairs. However, in all regulatory regimes, making and enforcing rules involves evaluating circumstances, identifying risks and benefits, judging behaviours, ranking goals, and then choosing particular actions or non-decisions. Moreover, in all regulatory regimes there are disagreements about what to do, how and when.

Such disagreements reflect competing convictions and rival beliefs about the public interest, the conditions of social order, and the quality of human well-being. The modern state in liberal democratic and capitalist societies is not economically indifferent and is not politically disinterested, so why is it thought by some that the state should be ethically "neutral on the meaning of the good life?" (Sandel 2009, 215). Through legislation and other regulatory tools, the state is promoting and encouraging certain behaviours and relationships, while rebuking and discouraging other kinds of conduct. As Pinker explains, "in the context of social welfare the principle of justice seeks to ensure not only an acceptable allocation of rewards but also of punishments in the interest of the common good" (1971, 112; also see Rodger 2008).

The law and order realm contains the basic legal, policing, and judicial concepts and values of the state and society. Since 2006, when the Harper Conservatives took office, a significant shift has been taking place in the ideas and discourse that dominate federal social policy making in Canada. The Harper record on social policy is a distinctive intermingling of policy cancellations, new interventions, program reductions, and non-decisions on many issues. The pecking order of purposes in social policy has been rearranged, with an expanded emphasis on regulatory functions by the federal government. This regulatory governance is selective in focus, emphasizing judicial, correctional, and policing more than occupational health and safety, pay equity, or human rights (Prince 2012, 54).

With respect to agendas and agenda events, the societal framework regulatory regime addresses systemic issues as well as individual cases of crime and restorative justice, morality and sin, poverty and social security. At a macro-level, attention is directed at societal

trends and community patterns in human affairs. The public visibil-
ity and emotive impact of specific rules and overall regulation-
making processes are shaped by public philosophies and everyday
practices of what is taken for granted by the population and policy
makers. These philosophies, practices, and assumptions can alter
through time, as do the framing of issues, the actors participating in
regulatory policy debates, and the concrete solutions being put forward. Prime Minister Stephen Harper approaches the law and order
realm in a manner both politically and philosophically different from
his recent predecessors. For Paul Martin, Jean Chrétien, and Brian
Mulroney, issues of law and order were obviously important, but
certainly not a defining issue for their governments or persistently
dominant items on their public policy agendas to the extent they
have become under Harper's leadership. Policing numerous forms of
social unruliness is a central motif of the Harper Conservatives.

Public and Private Power in Regulation Making and Compliance

On the public side of the power equation, the analysis shows that the
societal framework regulatory regime exercises sovereign authority
to intervene in a considerable number of policy issues and program
areas and in the domains of public and private lives. Wacquant
(2009, 175–6) writes, "The police, courts, and prisons are not mere
technical implements whereby the authorities respond to crime – as
in the commonsensical view enshrined by law and criminology – but
core political capacities through which the Leviathan both produces
and manages marginality, and inequality."
    Such rule making takes place at the summit of the state, at the top
of the public institutions of justice, the courts, national security agencies, and the welfare state. This relates to what Foucault called the
"macrophysics of sovereignty" – a distinct type of power concerned
with the overall social order, founded in constitutional and criminal
law, and functioning in state-society relations: "If the concept of
'social' has any meaning then it must embrace those relations of
power and authority by which societies are formed, transformed and
sustained" (Squires 1990, 16). In managing society, the state is no
mere spectator of social affairs, no "relativistic bystander" (Crawford
2006, 454). The modern state is active in ordering social relations
and directing social standards of conduct. Public power contains "a
deeply moral dimension, embodying virtues and values, as well as a

performative idea of citizenship" (ibid.). "Welfare states," as Taylor-Gooby (1991) has noted, "are not simply about doing good to individuals by meeting their needs, they are about sanctioning, controlling and directing people's behaviour as well" (208). He adds that legitimate authority is "the state's central gift to the community" (212).

The Harper law and order agenda involves a policing of the state as well as a policing of society (Prince 2012). Conservative social policy is producing shifts in intergovernmental relations and in the nature of social citizenship. Following Prime Minister Harper's agenda of "open federalism," leadership on key social policy areas as demonstrated by the later Chrétien and Martin Liberal governments has all but gone, effectively decentralizing social citizenship to the provinces. With the increased attention by the Harper governments to matters of security and law and order, relations between citizens and the federal state have become more legalistic and procedural in nature; from social entitlements to public enforcements. On the current emergence of what they call the "security state," Hallsworth and Lea's remark that "the State is back, and it is beginning to look rather unpleasant" (2011, 142).

A standard view of moral and sexual regulation is that it involves state-authorized assessments of "goodness and badness" backed by penalties and other mechanisms for compliance (Bird and Stoney 2006; Davidson and Davis 2012). Some commentators describe legal moral and sexual regulation, at least in historical terms, as "imposing upon aboriginals, the poor, immigrants, children, and women standards of conduct idealized (but often flouted) by the principal power holders in early-national Canada: wealthy Anglo-Celtic Protestants and, to a lesser extent, bourgeois French Catholics. Examining the history of the legal enforcement of moral regulation inevitably exposes the broader patterns of unequal power relations in Canadian history" (Strange and Loo 1997, 9). Another Canadian scholar of moral regulation indicates that "the term "regulation" is preferred to "control" in large part because it can better allow for issues of agency and resistance" (Glasbeek 2006, 5).

This is a useful reminder that an important difference exists between announcing a regulatory policy agenda and making rules, on the one hand, and regulatory enforcement and actual compliance, on the other. Issues of human agency and a political capacity for resistance are potentially crucial factors in understanding all three types of unruliness in our times. Regulating morals and sex involve not only external impositions but also internal inclinations. This literature also draws attention to the role of non-state forms of regulation and, thus, the private side of power relations (Hunt 1999).

Conservative and Liberal federal governments over the past thirty years have been ambivalent with regard to the legitimacy of voluntary organizations in undertaking policy critiques and public protests, and in making demands for economic betterment and social justice. Canadian tax laws, as discussed in chapter 6, continue to place strict limits in the advocacy and public education work of registered charities. In addition, governments have cut funding for policy research to groups representing literacy issues and women's interests. Such limits restrict the democratic potential of the voluntary sector and depoliticize social life. Instead, governments and public service bureaucracies tend to view voluntary organizations as service providers and as noble sites of giving and helping, rather than also as important partners in policy making and governance – and as essential sites of political advocacy and social citizenship.

Further to the private side of power in societal regulation, trends in the last generation entail a greater emphasis by governments on people's duties and obligations as compared with their rights along with a greater regulation and surveillance of those on welfare and others in civil society (Roche 1992; Little and Hillyard 1998; Chunn and Gavigan 2004; Crawford 2006; Peck 2001). Concurrently, civil society groups are pressing for new or enhanced human rights and more adequately enforced rights. These may be Aboriginal and treaty rights of Indigenous peoples; public health care entitlements; equality rights for the gay, lesbian, bisexual, transgender, and queer communities; or full citizenship rights for people with physical and mental disabilities (Redden 2002; Ralston Saul 2008; Prince 2010b). The time of social citizenship is never really past, at least not for long in contemporary societies.

Science, Evidence, and Knowledge

Integral to the interplay of science, evidence, and knowledge in regulatory policy and governance are notions of risk. In the societal framework regulatory regime, risks tend to be viewed as major threats or harms to the general population. Following the terrorist attacks of 9/11, Canadian policy has developed "a more comprehensive and inclusive definition of threats to security" (Whitaker 2005: 80). The scope of threats is multifaceted, encompassing public health threats from communicable diseases and pandemics, border security, transportation safety and security, emergencies related to natural disasters, immigration and refugee enforcement, terrorist threats and organized crime. What the Department of Public Safety calls "a rapidly evolving threat environment" includes new risks to digital infrastructure and information technologies, violent extremism, critical physical infrastructure across the country, and sexual exploitation of children on the Internet (Public Safety Canada 2011, 12).

In identifying such threats, there is an important element of social construction and political manipulation on whether harms are legal issues or matters of morality and sexuality, material and/or symbolic, immediate or longer term, specific to an individual, or consequential for society at large (Hunt 1999; Rodger 2008). Media-facilitated moral panics and public perceptions of lawlessness and personal vulnerabilities contribute to the politics of the societal framework regulatory regime, where government reassurances are as crucial, it seems, as research studies or risk assessment tools in the justice or correctional systems (Barron 2011; Brooks 1994; Mallea 2011).

With the focus of this regime on society and the general population, it is essential to policy makers, interest groups, and regulators alike to have aggregate levels of data on trends of crime, demographics, and epidemiology. This has been true for past Liberal and Conservative governments across the four prime ministerial eras covered in this book. A feature of the Harper Conservative government's policy style in law and order, however, is their greater reliance on a strict moralism and limited or selective empiricism in understanding issues and framing responses. Statistical data and policy research seem to have little privilege and weight in the contemporary night watchman state. Wacquant (2009) offers insight into how the Conservatives have managed this marginalization of knowledge in law and order policy making: "The more the question of crime is posed in dichotomous terms geared to electoral games in the public sphere, the less relevant the empirical knowledge produced by experts and the technical constraints faced by correctional administrators become to the conduct of penal policy" (155). Thus, as expertise and evidence is discounted, "moral entrepreneurs in ... politics can shape the mission of the police, courts and prisons to suit their own agendas" (ibid.).

One effect of the numerous law and order legislative initiatives by the Harper government is that new kinds of evidence, knowledge, or information will be generated by these interventions. In turn, these forms of penal and corrective knowledge will have implications for political discourse in framing subsequent policy in the realm, perhaps deepening in public opinion the acceptability to punish and incarcerate as a government response to many issues. At the same time, the Harper Conservatives are investing in the gathering and better sharing of intelligence information and in forensic services including DNA analysis by the RCMP (Public Safety Canada 2011).

Similarly, in the realm of regulating morality and sexuality are mixes of informal or social ways of knowing and expert knowledge (Hunt 1999). This means, as Valverde and Weir (2006, 78) suggest, that "any full analysis of social regulation requires that regulatory discourses be analyzed from the perspective of their production and circulation. The ways in which facts were constituted, collected and publicized (the text-as-process) is as important as the content (the text-as-product)." This applies equally to the welfare state realm where Employment and Social Development and other federal departments sponsor research and public opinion research on policies and attitudes.

Nevertheless, both federal government and non-governmental advisory councils and research institutes have been recently dismantled including the National Council of Welfare, the Canadian Council on Social Development, and the Canadian Policy Research Network. In addition, the Harper Conservatives have retrenched the activities of Statistics Canada, resulting in changes to the census long form and the cancellation of several social surveys. These trends in the devaluation of public policy analysis and evidence to inform decision making are not unique to the Harper government, but in recent years, seem to have intensified in Ottawa. They make it more difficult to adequately understand and effectively respond to perennial social problems and emerging new risks in Canadian society (Jenson and Saint-Martin 2003).

CONCLUSIONS

The societal framework regulatory regime has a horizontal policy reach across society as a whole for the population of the political community. The regime is concerned with societal goals and regulatory means for governing the general public and for steering society with the purpose of maintaining and/or changing important community values, as well as social roles, behaviours, and arrangements. As is the case with regulatory policies and politics more generally, the societal framework regulatory regime involves the authoritative allocation and expression of values. What may be more particular to this regime is its central function of the political construction of community standards and legal enforcement of these beliefs, morals, and norms. This relates to our theme of inertia versus change in regulatory regimes. On the surface, much of the societal framework regulatory regime concentrates on inertia or enforcing stability rather than on enacting change; that is, the attention of societal rule making and administration concerns issues of maintaining moral order and social cohesion, upholding public security, and sustaining community integration and solidarity of the population. However, as the analysis in this chapter shows, state agencies and non-state actors are not indifferent to reforming legislation or to developing and implementing new rules to do with law and order and morality and sexuality. In fact, governments have exhibited a willingness to respond to perceived threats to national security and to new risks such as cyber bullying or Internet pornography. The Harper government has introduced a multitude of alterations and modifications to the Criminal Code and related laws evoking images of the night watchman or security state. Accompanying these changes in rule making are shifts in relations among ideas and interests as well as in balances between rights and duties.

The sovereignty of the nation state, and of federal public power, is clearly on display in this regulatory framework regime. This power, of course, is not monolithic or omnipotent within Canadian politics and society. Regulatory actions and proposed measures in the societal framework regime customarily arouse stakeholder interest, prompt civic debate if not dissent, and provoke concerns by Aboriginal, provincial, and local governments including, at times, constitutional challenges. There are also checks and balances on our system of prime ministerial and Cabinet government such as the rule of law, fundamental rights and freedoms, and the independence of the judiciary.

With respect to analysts who have predicted the death or demise of the social state, our conclusion, by contrast, is that rule making has not necessarily replaced taxing and spending by the state. We have stressed that rule making in the societal framework regime occurs through taxing and public spending rules and requirements as well as in relation to non-state actors and organizations. This is what regulatory welfarism is about in contemporary times. And while a solid argument can be made that trends have intensified of late, the welfare state has always drawn in surveillance activities with supports, sanctions with services, rules and rights, coercion and care. Not merely entitlements, social programs also should be thought of as compilations of administrative and professional expectations, eligibility rules for inclusions and exclusions, and complex mechanisms of surveillance and enforcement.

A core of federal government departments and portfolios are centrally involved in developing and administering laws and rules in this regime. Some rule-making activity is incremental with selective amendments to program standards and regulations; yet there are also episodes of comprehensive and high-profile changes in this framework regime, notably, in tobacco control, specific treaty arrangements, equality rights to civil marriage, and more recently, by the Harper Conservatives, terminating major intergovernmental agreements in social policy and omnibus bills dealing with law and order reforms across several parts of the Criminal Code. As forms of purposeful agenda shaping and active policy drive, making rules on law and order, morality and sexuality, and the welfare state are noisily contested political events. Emotions and stakes are high because "questions are not only about how individuals should treat one another. They are also about what the law should be, and about how society should be organized" (Sandel 2009, 6). Regulatory welfarism involves debates on which behaviours are socially acceptable or tolerated and which are not; on which are regarded as private activities and which are public affairs, warranting policy responses of permissions or prohibitions. From processes of social evaluations and state judgments enacted through rules and sanctions, regulatory welfarism has the effect of formulating ethical and unethical conduct, consequently, producing categories of deserving and undeserving clients, responsible and irresponsible parents, good and bad citizens.

With respect to our analysis of unruliness of all three types, it must be recognized that even under the contemporary night watchman state, there are agency and policy conflicts within laws and programs, and also in pure enforcement terms, there are limits to ensuring public safety and security. In the law and order realm, there is mixed evidence to support certain measures in recent crime reform agendas (Lee 2007; Prince 2012), and always present are unintended consequences of punishment and incarceration such as wrongful convictions. In the realm of morality and sexuality, there is the unruliness of the inter-regime complexity kind, such as that regarding cyber technologies apparent in communicating pornographic images or stealing personal identities; there is the unease of certain individuals, groups, or generations as to the perceived decline in community standards or in personal responsibilities; for others, there is the sense of real challenges to establishing and enforcing societal framework rules in an increasingly multicultural and multifaith country. In the welfare state realm, the signs of unruliness are multiple and seemingly growing: they appear in the growing economic and social inequalities; the sense of vulnerability in a divided economy of good jobs and poor jobs; the declining social protection against any number of risks, old and new, and the affiliated turbulence experienced in financial, housing, and labour markets; resource limits in regulatory capacity to enforce labour standards or occupational health and safety rules; the activism and resistance of many social communities to cutbacks and to new regulations; the patchwork of standards and entitlements across jurisdictions; the tone in much of our contemporary political discourse that citizens are the risky subjects to be controlled and sanctioned.

Unruliness further appears in the multiple trade-offs involved in making rules in this framework regime. There is a trade-off in civil marriage legislation between same-sex couples having equal access to marriage for civil purposes and religious officials having the freedom to refuse to perform marriages; in criminal law reform, the trade-off between a government setting mandatory minimum sentences for certain offences and respecting the independence of the judiciary; in the welfare state realm, a trade-off between principles of universality and selectivity in social program rules; and in state-civil society relations, a trade-off between government praising voluntary sector organizations as valuable partners in meeting community needs while restricting the ability of these organizations to engage in public advocacy and education work on tough social issues. Such trade-offs and ensuing tensions yield a mixed if not contradictory pattern of regulatory policy developments. We have identified a number in this chapter: the extension of social security rights of Canadian workers abroad through international agreement while domestic social programs have declined in value; the retreat of federal leadership on child care and early learning while parental leave and other family-friendly workplace policies are promoted by Ottawa; the growing surveillance of welfare clients while privacy commissioners seek to defend the identity of citizens more generally; initiatives in the security community to better share intelligence for reasons of border control at the same time the capacity in civil society of policy analysis and research is weakening.

Of the types of democracy at work in the societal framework regulatory regime, representative democracy figures prominently in terms of policy leadership by prime ministers and their Cabinets with the support of their caucuses. The Harper Conservatives' actions on crime and punishment are a recent illustration of this exercise of executive authority within parliamentary government. At other times with other governments, academic criminologists, lawyers and law societies, and other groups in the justice policy community have enjoyed more input and influence on federal policy on law and order (Lee 2007; Prince 2012). Federalized democracy is notable in this regime in terms of assigning extensive legislative powers to the federal government in criminal law and in the areas of morality and sexuality and less so in the broad realm of the welfare state. For example, regulatory powers with respect to most workplaces and to pensions in Canada fall under the jurisdiction of the provinces. In the area of tobacco control, the Supreme Court ruled that major sections of the Tobacco Products Control Act were outside the legal capacity of the federal government, which led to a new Tobacco Act. Overall, though, the policy field of tobacco control has mainly exhibited characteristics of interest group pluralism and aspects of civil society democracy (Bird and Stoney 2006). This is a case where power relationships were roughly equal between industry and health interests (Pross and Stewart 1994), but many other areas of this regime involve seriously unequal relations of power among interests and groups. Opportunities for pluralistic or deliberative forms of democracy marked by reasoned communication and rational argumentation seem slight for many issues of societal regulation. A main finding of our analysis of moral and sexual regulation is the important dual roles of state-based forms of governance and of self-governance. Governing one's ethical self can be a form of direct democratic action as well as choice of lifestyle and even a form of personal resistance to societal rule making and enforcement.

9

The Regulatory Regime for Parliamentary Democracy: Parties, Elections, Responsible Government, and Parliament's Watchdog Agencies

In conventional mappings by mainstream regulatory scholars, there is a curious omission: the regulatory regime for parliamentary democracy. By this regime we mean, first, the rules, laws, regulations, and conventions governing political parties, elections, and responsible government, as both a constitutional principle and a partisan political matter regarding the relations between elected members of Parliament (MPs), the Cabinet, and the prime minister. The regime also includes the unelected Senate of Canada; however, our focus in this chapter is on Canada's elected House of Commons. Second, this regulatory regime involves the growing number of parliamentary watchdog regulatory agencies that act as agents of Parliament's House of Commons, the elected representatives of the people. These include watchdog agencies, often referred to euphemistically as "gotcha agencies," regarding elections, privacy, lobbying, access to information, conflict of interest and ethics, and public sector integrity. These are the two related realms in the regime for parliamentary democracy that we examine in this chapter.

In the analysis of each realm, we trace longer-term historical features across the past forty to fifty years and then focus on more recent debates and reform pressures, particularly in the current Harper Conservative era, where core criticisms of democratic decline, initially raised in the Chrétien era, have loomed large. In both realms, however, the story of both regime change and inertia emerges.

We remind the reader that in previous chapters we discussed key features of regulatory democracy, including the concepts and arenas of Cabinet-parliamentary, federalist, interest group pluralist, civil society, and direct democracy. In chapter 4, the macro-regulatory regime and its pivotal Cabinet Directive on Regulatory Management (CDRM) contains several norms and ideas about democracy, including consultation, accountability, transparency, secrecy, and even the notion of regulatory streamlining itself. The previous chapters dealing with sectoral and framework economic and societal regulatory regimes are replete with concerns about the nature of lobbying and the nature and inequalities of access and power by different kinds of interest groups. We have also already discussed key features of the growing and controlling power of the prime minister in both the Harper and earlier Chrétien-Martin prime ministerial eras. Moreover, all of the chapters in Part II of the book show the interweaving presence of, and contradictions among freedom of information, privacy, and secrecy as values.

After considering changes and inertia in these realms of the parliamentary democracy regime, we then look across the overall regime with regard to the attributes of (1) ideas, discourse, and agendas; (2) public and private power in regulation making and compliance; and (3) science, evidence, and knowledge. In the concluding section, we offer a final look at what this ultimate regulatory regime, this fundamental constitutional and political regime, reveals about the nature of unruliness and, of course, about democracy, regulatory and otherwise.

THE REGULATORY REGIME FOR PARLIAMENTARY DEMOCRACY

Two realms constitute the regulatory regime for parliamentary democracy. The first realm, which includes political parties and elections, and responsible Cabinet-parliamentary government, sits at the historic pinnacle of this regime with the power of the prime minister assuming ever-greater governing control. We, therefore, look at key historical developments in the regulation of parties and elections and in the rules and conventions regarding how Parliament functions vis-à-vis the Cabinet and the prime minister in crucial areas such as the convening, prorogation, and dissolution of Parliament and what the modern meanings of responsible government are or ought to be (Aucoin, Jarvis, and Turnbull 2011; Bakvis and Jarvis 2012; Blidook 2012; White 2006).

The second realm of the regime centres on parliamentary watch-dog agencies. With one or two exceptions, this realm has been shaped more recently, in the past four decades, although it is tied to some historic long-standing secrecy aspects of Cabinet government and ministerial responsibility, as well as to strategic aspects of secrecy in property rights and protection inherent in capitalism. We are interested in the evolution of these agencies as a group of watchdog entities and also, illustratively, in the broad trajectories of development regarding a sample of these as individual agencies. Paradoxically, many of these are debated more in the context of accountability, with the discourse of "regulation" as such often scarcely even mentioned (Shepherd and Stoney 2010). For example, the three new or changed agencies created by the Harper government in 2006 were a part of its Accountability Act, the first of the laws it introduced as a then new minority government. The Harper government, certainly, did not sell it as an act of increased regulation and potentially increased red tape, although in fact, it partly was and is. The group of watchdog agencies are, in effect, Parliament's own "civil service," and thus, the agencies' mandates raise issues regarding the role of expertise and experts linked to traditional practices of elected MPs as watchdogs themselves on both sides of the parliamentary partisan divide.

There is increased potential for mandate clashes among agencies overall or in particular case situations, such as cases involving access to information versus privacy and in other grey boundary spaces as well within lobbying regulation and rules regarding whistle blowing. Indeed, one recent book has accurately characterized the process as "brokering access" to freedom of information in Canada (Larsen and Walby 2012). In addition, there are high levels of potential unruliness when government departments face what may look and feel like regulatory overload as they seek to implement and change both their core departmental statutory, regulatory, and policy mandates and also, concurrently, comply with the varied and often conflicting parliamentary watchdog mandates and expectations. As the object of regulation, government departments often feel that the watchdog red flag values and processes seem a lot more like red tape, a view often expressed to them when they themselves are, in turn, regulating the private sector and civil society.

REGIME CHANGE AND INERTIA I: PARTIES, ELECTIONS,
AND RESPONSIBLE GOVERNMENT HISTORICALLY AND
IN THE AGE OF PERMANENT CAMPAIGNING AND PRIME
MINISTERIAL DOMINANCE

The first set of linked regime features and changes concentrate on
the regulation of political parties, laws, and rules regarding the conduct of federal elections and the rules and conventions regarding
responsible government as a central feature of Canadian parliamentary democracy. We trace these regulatory regime features from their
diverse historical origins through to the current period, which many
think of as an age of permanent partisan campaigning and prime
ministerial dominance (Aucoin, Jarvis, and Turnbull 2011; Fletcher
and Blais 2012; Aucoin 2008; Malloy 2004). Some reference to provincial and international comparative developments is also necessary, although our focus is clearly federal.

Political Parties

On the regulation of political parties, the basic story is essentially one
where for long periods political parties were thought of as private
unregulated entities of like-minded persons seeking the right to form
a government. Indeed, the very capacity to build political parties
often relied on rampant forms of employment patronage and contracting (in a pre-welfare state context) to gather further adherents,
not to mention front-line electoral troops for campaigns. Histories of
nation builders such as Prime Minister Sir John A. Macdonald but
also earlier pre-Confederation accounts show the underpinnings of
these key developments, including how they would now be seen as
forms of favouritism, bribery, and corruption (Ralston Saul 2010;
Gwyn 2011, chapters 14 and 15; Gwyn 2008).

When political parties later were regulated (see more below), analysts
partly referred to these rule-making systems in the language of a familiar regulatory term, namely, as *public utilities* of a quasi-oligopolistic
kind (Carty and Young 2012). In the current period, the regulatory discourse could just as easily characterize them as a *networked regulatory*
realm, particularly since permanent Internet-based campaigning
involves multimedia third-party NGO advocacy and direct democracy
of kinds that are intricate and difficult to regulate (Fletcher and Blais
2012; Doern and Kernaghan 2012; Brooks 2011).

Carty and Young (2012, 106) characterize the pre-regulation era as "one hundred years of waiting" for public rules despite many episodes of scandal. Not until 1963 did the House of Commons define a political party in Parliament as any group that contained twelve or more elected MPs. Furthermore, it was only with the 1966 Barbeau Report by the Commons Committee on Election Expenses that major recommendations for change emerged (Carty and Young 2012, 108–9). In particular, the change most needed was that "political parties should be legally recognized and, through the doctrine of agency, legally responsible for their actions in raising and spending funds" (Barbeau Report 1966, 37). But this was still a narrowly based view of political parties, and only in 1970 and 1974 did Parliament legislate, first, on party registration and ballot labelling and, then, on election expenses.

A second key development was the work and report of the Lortie Commission (1991), which saw parties as a much broader and central part of Canadian parliamentary government and democracy than hitherto recognized. The work of the Lortie Commission also reflected Canada's then recent passage through a period of broadened and intensified debate by political parties, social movements, and interest groups both as the Charter of Rights and Freedoms was entrenched in the repatriated Canadian Constitution in 1982 and as the great 1988 "free trade" election mobilized various groups aligned with or opposed to mainstream political parties (Dobrowolsky and Jenson 1993; Doern and Tomlin 1991).

The Lortie report dealt with core issues of political parties as "primary political organizations" and with the growing democratic practice of third-party advertising as in the free trade debate. As Carty and Young (2012) stress, "the Lortie Commission expressed its view that elections ought to be essentially understood and conducted as discussions among disciplined political parties and candidates rather than as a free-for-all with a range of unregulated intermediary organizations competing with parties for the attention of the public" (114). The commission also dealt with other perceived weaknesses of political parties at that time, including their flaws regarding internal democracy and continuing habits of unethical behaviour. In essence, political parties were seen as ineffective at self-regulation, despite or perhaps because of their oligopolistic privileged position at the apex of political power and democracy.

The response to the Lortie logic and critique was left to the post-1993 governing Liberal Party in the context of the 1993 election, which had seen the electoral collapse of the Progressive Conservative Party, the rise of the Reform Party, and the growth of the Bloc Québécois following the failure of the Meech Lake constitutional accord. Although strongly opposed by the Reform Party, the Chrétien Liberals' eventual response to Lortie late in the Chrétien era emphasized public subsidies for political parties and strong limits on private donations to parties (see more below), but it was also underpinned by a much narrower conception of political parties, much closer once more to seeing them as private organizations rather than as primary political entities.

The Harper Conservatives, reflecting their Reform Party roots, eventually ended the public party subsidy features of party financing following its achievement of a majority government in 2011. This rule change went ahead even though the Conservatives had become the main beneficiary of the previous system. But the earlier system had also served to sustain the funding of the separatist Bloc Québécois.

Thus, the paradox of the political party aspects of the regulatory regime story is that despite their central place in Canadian democracy and in Parliament, political parties were neither a feature of Canada's written Constitution nor were they regulated in a way that reflected their actual place as primary democratic political organizations. The political party story extends explicitly to the regulation of elections and election campaigns.

*Political Parties and the Regulation of Elections
and Election Campaigns*

On the regulation of elections and election campaigns, three phases and aspects of rule making are noteworthy: changes to the Election Expenses Act in 1974; amendments to the Canada Elections Act in 2004 and 2007; and more recent examples of actual or potential unruliness as Elections Canada tries to regulate in the context of Internet technology, the new arts and practices of permanent campaigning, and particular border-line electoral tactics such as robocalls during the 2011 federal election attributed to various rogue or real supporters of the Conservative Party or, perhaps, to the party itself due to its extensive stock of private data on Canadian voters. We also discuss the Chief Electoral Officer and Elections Canada as a Parliamentary watchdog agency in this section (rather than in the broader analysis of watchdog agencies later in the chapter).

The 1974 changes to the Election Expenses Act included spending limits for parties and candidates, disclosure of spending, partial public reimbursement of election expenses, tax credits for contributions to assist fundraising, and the allocation of free and paid broadcast advertising (Fletcher and Blais 2012, 155). The amendments to the Canada Elections Act in 2004 and 2007 included the banning of contributions to political parties and candidates by corporations, associations, and unions; a maximum contribution of $1,000 in any calendar year to each registered party or to entities of a registered party; only Canadian citizens or permanent residents could make contributions; the prohibition of cash donations of more than $20.00; the registration of constituency associations; and quarterly allowances for political parties (ibid.).

The previously noted growing role of third party-advertising during an election period that promoted or opposed a registered party or candidate garnered specific rules that were partially clarified in a Supreme Court test case under the Charter of Rights and Freedoms. These included the registration of such groups if spending more than $500 during an election campaign, the provision that all election advertising must identify the third party that is paying for it, limits on election advertising spending (per constituency and nationally) during the formal election period, and a prohibition on setting up multiple organizations or pooling/colluding with another group (Fletcher and Blais 2012, 158).

The issue of third-party involvement eventually confronts broader notions of interest group pluralism, civil society, and also direct democracy and how to limit third parties during election periods. Moreover, this issue confronts the growing practices of permanent campaigning. Nonetheless, one recent empirical study of the 2004, 2006, and 2008 Canadian federal elections concluded that "third parties are not spending large amounts relative to spending limits ... and that current third party spending limits therefore appear to be situated comfortably within the expectations of the egalitarian model" (Lawlor and Crandall 2011, 1). The issue of permanent campaigning is linked to practical issues of when campaigns begin and end in minority government versus majority government contexts and of the party practices of continuous campaigning, aided by a tactical belief in the value of attack politics and by the reduced costs of conducting continuous campaigning by parties, individual MPs, and candidates and by third parties via burgeoning social networks. As Fletcher and Blais (2012) succinctly observe:

> Regulatory regimes must balance fairness and the freedom to participate. That balance is difficult to achieve and is rarely free from challenge. Regimes of campaign regulation face continuous challenges from social and technological change, participants seeking loopholes, and the unintended consequences of other reforms. Now that we have something close to permanent election campaigns it is imperative to consider the best rules of engagement for the never-ending rhetorical wars that have emerged in representative democracies. (150)

Permanent campaigning is being aided by the growth of funding by political party riding associations. Much of this is not governed by accountability rules or reporting (Bryden and Rennie 2013). This combined change in the Canadian political culture has led to new regulatory challenges and to new realms of unruliness as both political parties and third parties test the limits of regulatory boundaries and regulatory agency capacities. For example, government advertising paid by taxpayers during an election campaign or, indeed, in the immediate run-up to an election, can be seen as partisan. Governments need to inform citizens but the arts of advertising can easily be shifted or reworded to be messages of persuasion for the governing party. There are no federal election–related rules on such an issue, although there are in some provinces (Fletcher and Blais 2012, 161–2).

In his report on the 2011 federal election, Canada's Chief Electoral Officer and head of Elections Canada suggested to Parliament the need review and change aspects of federal law (Chief Electoral Officer of Canada 2011). The 2011 election was what one commentator referred to as Canada's first full-scale "social media election" (Minsky 2011, 1). In the report, the Chief Electoral Officer observed that a key development was "the greater use of communications tools by candidates during the election" and "the use of Facebook, Twitter, YouTube videos, automated telephone messages, email and Web sites is on the rise and raises the question of whether these messages amount to election advertising" (2011, 43). Third-party advertising also continued to shift from traditional to new means of media.

Historically and in recent prime ministerial eras, both the Liberal Party and Conservative Party (formerly the Progressive Conservative

Party) have had their share of election law misbehaviour, loophole experimentation, and non-compliance. The Harper Conservatives, however, both during elections and in between elections, have tested the edges of legality and propriety more visibly and even stridently. In part, this behaviour and even the perception of such behaviour flowed initially from the aggressive and continuous attack politics strategy preferred from the outset of Prime Minister Stephen Harper's coming to power in 2006, and then in his government's first two minority government contexts from 2006 to 2008 and 2008 to 2011, and its majority government since 2011. Three cases showed the Conservatives' edgy search for advantage.

The first case was the "in and out" election overspending affair. Following the 2011 election, the Conservative Party and its fund-raising arm, the Conservative Fund of Canada, pleaded guilty. But prior to that, since the 2006 election, they had denied any wrongdoing. The offending "in and out" practice consisted of moving national party funds into local constituency funds and then partly back out in such a way that this broke election rules and funding limits.

The second, and more serious and intriguing case centred on the use of so-called robo-calls, whereby automated calls in several federal constituencies during the 2011 federal election were directed at providing deliberately misleading information regarding when and where to vote. The Conservative Party's election team denied such practices, as did the prime minister, and even suggested that it was carried out by a rogue supporter or supporter of an opposition party. The jury is still out in the robo-calls case, but it gained credibility as a Conservative Party election offence precisely because of the earlier Harper-era politics as continuous warfare strategies.

Following a court decision in 2012 to declare one Tory seat victory null and void and to call for a by-election, the politics of the robo-calls fight escalated further. Nine individuals are seeking new ballots in seven further close federal Conservative-held ridings where the alleged robo-calls and related offences are said to have occurred. The Conservatives then launched a court case against these legal bids by alleging that the seven individuals are, in fact, fronted and funded by the left-wing Council of Canadians, a long-time third-party NGO which, the Conservatives argue, has had a long-term goal of seeing an NDP government win power (Chase 2012). The larger policy and political battle over robo-calls was also tied to concerns by the federal Privacy Commissioner that political parties are completely outside privacy laws. These concerns relate to political party data systems, which "amass huge amounts of personal information about citizens" (Cheadle 2012, 7). We return to these and other privacy issues in our discussion later in the chapter on Parliament's watchdog agencies.

The third case was the Senate expenses scandal of 2013, which was centred on expense excesses regarding several Senators but eventually focused on Conservative Senator Mike Duffy, a well-known former television journalist. When Duffy had to pay back expenses of over $90,000, in order to do so he was given a personal cheque from Nigel Wright, Prime Minister Harper's chief of staff. Wright was forced to resign, and the accountability issues were brought directly to the door of the prime minister and the Prime Minister's Office (Walkom 2013; Southey 2013).

Rules and Conventions Regarding Responsible Government in Parliamentary Democracy

Political parties and elections, each governed by the laws and rules already examined above, produce an elected House of Commons that is then expected to function according to the rules and conventions of responsible government, which centre on the winning political party (with a majority or minority of MPs) producing a prime minister and Cabinet that governs for up to five years. Responsible government requires a government that has the confidence of the House of Commons and that is accountable to Parliament, and whose policies, laws, spending, and tax decisions are the subject of legitimate scrutiny by a loyal opposition consisting of the Official Opposition party and other political parties, as well as all MPs as representatives of individual constituencies or ridings (Malloy 2004; Franks 1997). The prime minister is not technically elected directly as in presidential political systems but, rather, is the leader of the party that wins the most seats. Canadian responsible government also involves the role of the governor general of Canada as the Queen's representative in Canada. Clearly, though, the prime minister has a dominant role in voter intentions and actual voting, and the prime minister appoints a Cabinet (of thirty to forty ministers), which functions under the doctrine of collective and individual ministerial responsibility for all policies and decisions by a Cabinet (Sutherland 1991). The Cabinet deliberates under the equally strong norms of executive secrecy regarding Cabinet proceedings and debate (D'Ombrain 2004; Doern 1977; Galnoor 1977).

Many diverse aspects of responsible government and related parliamentary reform are addressed in the published literature (Franks 1997; D'Aquino, Doern, and Blair 1983; Van Loon and Whittington 1981; Stewart 1977). Various other aspects have already been referred to in previous chapters including Throne Speeches and Budget Speeches, aspects of the role of parliamentary committees, private members' bills, and of course, the extended development of various kinds and degrees of delegated government and their accountability challenges for both the Cabinet as political executive and for Parliament.

Our focus here is on the evolution and nature of the core rules and conventions that lie at the heart of responsible government in an era of expanded prime ministerial power (Aucoin, Jarvis, Turnbull 2011; Aucoin 2008; Malloy 2010). This is because they are a part of the triage of institutional power and legitimacy that political parties, elections, and Parliament constitute. Parliament's ability to be the focal point for effective responsible government after elections depends on rule- and convention-based junctures regarding when Parliament is convened or meets, when it is prorogued (between parliamentary sessions), and in ways that trigger elections (Hicks 2012; Aucoin, Jarvis, and Turnbull 2011; Russell and Sossin 2009). Recently, it has also involved renewed intense debates about the rules or the lack thereof regarding coalition governments and related possible transfers of power without a new election.

The exemplary analysis by Aucoin, Jarvis, and Turnbull (2011) of Canadian responsible government and of the need to democratize the constitution argues:

The Canadian problem has two dimensions. One dimension is constitutional; the other is is a matter of parliamentary government. The constitutional dimension concerns the capacity of the prime minister's constitutional powers to summon, prorogue and dissolve the House of Commons to advance the partisan interests of the governing party. For example, there are no firm rules for the governor general to refer to when the prime minister has lost the confidence of the House of Commons and wants to dissolve it ...

The parliamentary government dimension concerns the capacity of the prime minister to abuse the rules and procedures of the

House of Commons that are meant to allow the government
to manage the business of the House in an orderly and efficient
manner ...
In both of these ways the prime minister governs in bad faith,
allowing the government's partisan interests to subvert the
opportunities for backbench government MPs and opposition
MPs to perform their basic parliamentary responsibilities. (3–4)

A central feature of their analysis is that some key provisions in
Canada are weaker regarding core rules than in other countries with
systems of responsible government including Great Britain, Australia,
and New Zealand.

Although prime ministerial excesses are a strong focus of concern
in the last decade, and even earlier, this does not mean that prime
ministers reject agendas for parliamentary reform. However, these
agendas tend to occur before they come into office and weaken once
they themselves have control. Thus, for example, Paul Martin in his
run-up battle to succeed Jean Chrétien as Liberal leader and prime
minister advocated reforms to deal with what he called Parliament's
democratic deficit. So did Stephen Harper in the 2006 election campaign advocate a plan for "better democracy" including the adoption of legislation requiring a fixed election date every four years and
also increased powers for Parliament and its committees to review
departmental spending. Even earlier, reflecting Reform Party concerns about democratic weakness, Harper and political scientist and
party adviser Tom Flanagan co-authored a paper referring to the
system as a "benign dictatorship" (Harper and Flanagan 1997).

The Aucoin, Jarvis, and Turnbull agenda of responsible government reforms are worth noting for their responsible government
logic and values and for the reason that they raise normal historic
issues about more rules and clearer rules, and how this affects the
other central aspect of responsible government, namely, that prime
ministerial power, political parties, and democratic mandates provide a needed disciplining core for effective democracy and governance. This is because of the implicit and explicit need to not have a
political system based on a US-style more rampant "separation of
powers" and "checks and balances" system. With respect to *constitutional reform*, they suggest proposals that would:

• Establish a deadline requiring the House of Commons to be summoned within thirty days after a general election

- Establish fixed election dates every four years on a specific date, binding both the prime minister and the governor general unless a majority of two-thirds of MPs approve a motion to dissolve Parliament for an early election
- Adopt a "constructive non-confidence" procedure
- Require the consent of a two-thirds majority of the House of Commons in order to prorogue Parliament. (Aucoin, Jarvis and Turnbull 2011, 119)

With respect to *parliamentary governance reform*, Aucoin, Jarvis, and Turnbull (2011, 231), suggest proposals that would:

- Adopt legislation limiting the size of ministries to a maximum of twenty-five individuals and the number of parliamentary secretaries to eight at any given time
- Use secret preferential ballots by committee members to select House of Commons committee chairs for the duration of the parliamentary session
- Adopt a set schedule for opposition days in the House of Commons that cannot be altered by the government unilaterally
- Reduce, by 50 percent, the partisan political staff complement on Parliament Hill.

The mix of rules, conventions, and flexible discretion are inherent in the above kinds of reforms and ranges of potential change. A recent study argued for the need for, essentially, "guidelines on government formation" (Public Policy Forum 2012, 2). Many authors have referred to increased prime ministerial power and control of cabinets and Parliament and its growing presence in both Liberal and Conservative prime ministerial eras (Savoie 2010; Simpson 2010). However, particular concerns have emerged about the Harper era in terms of how systematic and extensive the detailed control levers have become (Martin 2010).

For example, and going beyond the above kinds of reform items, the Harper majority government has been severely criticized for its practice of using massive budget implementation legislation of five hundred or so pages within which are contained major and minor changes to dozens of laws and regulations, many or most of which have little or nothing to do with the budget and its taxing and spending focus (Coyne 2012). Ordinarily, in terms of parliamentary democracy and responsible government, such bills would be presented to

Parliament as separate bills and then sent for scrutiny both in the House and its committees. Various kinds of omnibus bills have certainly been deployed by federal Liberal and Conservative governments as they practise the sometimes needed but more normally still dubious arts of managing the legislative agenda in Parliament and also scheming their way through strategies for avoiding and limiting debate particularly regarding contentious bills and policies.

REGIME CHANGE AND INERTIA II: PARLIAMENTARY WATCHDOG REGULATORS AND COMPLEX "GOTCHA" FUNCTIONS

The second aspect of regime change centres on the emergence and growth of parliamentary watchdog regulatory agencies. We have already referred to one of them, the Chief Electoral Officer of Canada as head of Elections Canada. Table 9.1 shows a list of these agencies.

Space does not allow us to examine all of them in this section. For example, the Parliamentary Budget Officer (PBO) is not included. It functions as an arm of the Parliamentary Library and is not a regulator per se. However, through conducting research studies, making appearances before parliamentary committees, holding press conferences, and issuing media statements, the PBO does aim to shape the actions and discourse of MPs and the federal government on matters of public budgeting. In that sense, the PBO operates through soft tools of information and suasion.

In the rest of this section of the chapter, we look first at the watchdog agencies as a group and then illustrate briefly some of the individual agencies' development, challenges, and aspects of unruliness including the Access to Information Commissioner, the Privacy Commissioner, the Commissioner of Lobbying, and the Public Sector Integrity Commissioner. Each of these selected sample agencies has separate unique mandates, values, and functional trajectories. They also increasingly have challenges in both mandate and operational cooperation and collision.

The Parliamentary Watchdog Agencies as a Group

In the above Table 9.1, the first four agencies are, in order, the oldest arms of Parliament's watchdog bureaucracy, with the next two emerging in the 1980s and the last three since 2006, although emerging as

Table 9.1 Parliamentary Watchdog Officers and Agencies

• Auditor General	• Access to Information Commissioner
• Chief Electoral Officer	• Conflict of Interest and Ethics
• Public Service Commission	Commissioner
• Official Languages Commissioner	• Commissioner of Lobbying
• Privacy Commissioner	• Public Sector Integrity Commissioner

reformed agencies from earlier entities. Both official studies and academic analyses over the past forty years have agreed on many of the key questions and issues about their roles but also expressed them in changing kinds of analytical discourse partly in response to changing concerns about parliamentary democracy, responsible government (and, indeed, other kinds and arenas of democracy), and public management (Sutherland 2010).

A mid-1980s assessment by Sutherland and Doern (1985) of the watchdog agencies in place at that time initially referred to them as "public service bureaucracy III." This differentiated them as a "new control bureaucracy" to be distinguished from I (traditional government departments) and II (non-departmental, arm's-length agencies). The study concluded:

> With the parliamentary control agencies ... we see cabinet almost washing its hands of both individual and collective policy responsibility: it has given the organization an act, and attached it to "Parliament" – the details can work themselves out. Yet Parliament has few sustained mechanisms through which it monitors its own watchdogs and the issues they raise. Some of its own bodies, justified as extensions of Parliament, can be left to float, the outcome of the lack of political control or even interest being left to the contingencies of the leadership of the various bodies. (54)

The reality is, therefore, "much more dubious" because there is a need to continuously address and answer the following three important questions:

1 What is "Parliament" or the "House of Commons" in relation to the "government" and the doctrine of ministerial responsibility?
2 What is "Parliament" or the "House of Commons" in terms of its capacity to to fight for the concerns of such agencies?

3 What is "Parliament" or the "House of Commons" in terms of its capacity to oversee and direct the actions of such agencies? (Ibid.)

In a later article, Sutherland (1991) wisely warned and advised that "every reform is its own problem" (91).

A more recent study by Stilborn (2010) recalibrated and extended the above kinds of questions by exploring three key issues and questions:

1 Are the officers of Parliament actually supporting Parliament, or are they instead sidelining Parliament by holding governments directly accountable before the public?
2 Do their single-issue mandates foster standards that governments are unlikely to meet, and thus bias the officers in favour of criticism?
3 Is there a danger that the exceptional independence of the officers insulates them from the need to be accountable, either for their internal practices or for responsiveness to broader public interest considerations and priorities? (243)

A further 2012 study contracted by the federal government to the Institute on Governance, eschews the watchdog nomenclature in favour of the concept of oversight bodies or *guardians* functioning "within the Government of Canada" (Pastre and Cain 2012, 4). This study is a part of a larger examination that includes the "cumulative impact of their scrutiny on government departments" (3). Media commentators have related these cumulative impact issues to a growing sense that senior civil servants in departments were being bombarded by these agencies and that, among other things, it was giving the opposition a field day.. There are now more meetings among the watchdog agency heads and staffs given the need for better coordination.

Finally, it is crucial to draw attention to recent analysis by political scientist Paul Thomas whose latest look at Parliament's watchdog agencies builds on his earlier work (Thomas 2003) but explicitly focuses on the concept of trust regarding the role of these agencies (Thomas 2012). The analysis looks first at the often elusive and multidimensional nature of trust, a feature we have already seen in chapter 1's theoretical account of regulatory behaviour, especially in the context of co-regulation and networked governance. Thomas argues that trust is of great importance for the "successful operation of parliamentary agencies … (regarding) both external public trust in government as an institution and … internal trust among and within the numerous organizations which comprise government" (2012, 1).

Overall, these kinds of analyses of parliamentary watchdogs show that they are still not often viewed or reformed as a group of agencies, although greater concerns may be emerging, some being raised in the context of the recession and budget cuts. The media's focus on the "gotcha" function is understandable given twenty-four-hour media reporting cycles but rarely with much follow-up on the question of, now that agency has "gotcha," what does it or the public or the media or Parliament "do with ya"? Moreover, both watchdog and gotcha nomenclature is used to sum up the discovery of sins and omissions of virtually any federal regulatory body in addition to those of Parliament.

Nonetheless, as Stilborn points out, the agencies as a group have budgets and staff that in total exceed the budget of the Privy Council Office, and their staff complement is greater than the Treasury Board Secretariat (2010, 246). In addition, building on several of the questions posed above, there remains the crucial dilemma of whether watchdogs as a group actually reinforce Parliament and its committees and debates or are seen and are in reality a very separate regulatory governance and democratic arena. To probe some of these and other underlying issues raised above, we need to look illustratively at the above-mentioned four individual watchdog agencies (keeping in mind as well the analysis above of the Chief Electoral Officer and Elections Canada).

Four Selected Individual Watchdog Agencies: Scope, Trajectories, and Dilemmas

The Access to Information Commissioner was established in 1983 under the Access to Information Act. The Commissioner reviews the complaints of individuals and organizations who believe that federal institutions have not respected their rights under the act (Information Commissioner of Canada 2011). The Commissioner also promotes access to information. Regarding disputes, the Commissioner uses mediation and persuasion but also can appeal to the Federal Court of Canada when cases/disputes involve important principles of law and interpretation. Complaints can relate to administrative matters such as delays in departmental responses and the fees they charge and also to exemptions where institutions withheld the records under specific sections of the act. Such exceptions are, therefore, matters of secrecy including Cabinet secrecy and can relate to communications with foreign governments, national security, commercial secrets, and personal privacy (Gingras 2012; D'Ombrain 2004). There is also parliamentary secrecy as the 2013 scandal regarding the expenses of some Senators highlighted (Bronskill 2013). With these statutory exceptions, therefore, the Information Commissioner of Canada is clearly not the only official or regulator regarding access to government records. And the complex nature of players and access brokers is changing rapidly under information and communication technology (ICT) and in the context of recent technology- centred open government policies such as the Harper government's Action Plan on Open Government in 2012 (Craft 2013; Larsen and Walby 2012).

The Information Commissioner's 2010–11 annual report looked back at developments and trends in the past decade and found significant deterioration in performance. Among her observations and expressed concerns are:

- In terms of timeliness, slightly more than half of all access requests made to federal institutions are now completed within the thirty-day limit.
- In terms of disclosure, fewer than one-fifth of all requests currently result in all information being released.
- The exercise of discretion in determining which information to disclose has been skewed towards greater protection of information.
- The percentage of exemptions claimed for national security has increased three-fold since 2002–03. (Information Commissioner of Canada 2011, 2)

Overall, the Commissioner also stresses how out of date Canada's 1980s access to information legislation is:

I believe the way forward must include the review and modernization of Canada's access legislation. This statement has been reiterated countless times in Canada and in international studies. Developed in the pre-digital era, the Act is out of touch with

today's information technology, common practices and expectations. It is out of step with more progressive standards adopted
by other jurisdictions ... the legislation needs to clarify what
could constitute ministerial records as opposed to departmental
records. It also needs to introduce a duty to document information so that there is an official record of important decisions
made on behalf of Canadians. (3)

These weaknesses in performance and in legislation have, indeed,
been borne out by other comparative studies including a recent one
that ranked Canada in fortieth position among eighty-nine countries
(Centre for Law and Democracy 2011; Woods 2011).

The Privacy Commissioner of Canada functions under the Privacy
Act of 1983 and under the later Personal Information and Electronic
Documents Act and amendments passed during the period 2001 to
2004. The Commissioner acts as an independent parliamentary
officer to advocate for the privacy rights of Canadians related to the
federal public sector and the private sector (within defined federal
jurisdiction). The Commissioner's powers include the following:
investigating complaints and issuing reports; pursuing legal action
where matters remain unresolved; assessing compliance with obligations under the legislation through the conduct of audit and review
activities and publicly report on findings; advising on, and reviewing, privacy impact assessments of new and existing government initiatives; and providing legal and policy analyses and expertise (Office
of the Privacy Commissioner of Canada 2012a, 2).

Privacy regulation has been a concern for many decades and, of
course, extends to many statutory and regulatory realms from policing to health care and drugs and to modern genomics, and so despite
some references to the Privacy Commissioner as a privacy czar, it is
obvious, as with the Information Commissioner, that the privacy regulator is not alone in the practice of her or his craft (Levin and
Nicholson 2005; Bennett and Raab 2003; Bennett 1999; Flaherty
1989). Given the diverse and changing views about privacy in a liberal political society and in relation to concerns about a growing surveillance society, not to mention privacy merchants, the issues about
how to define abuses and to deal with them are genuinely difficult and
potentially impossible (Etzioni 2012; Centre for Digital Democracy
2012). These concerns were renewed in 2013 following revelations
about the extent to which the US National Security Agency was

collecting and monitoring massive amounts of personal data on Americans and citizens of other countries via data from the big Internet companies including Google, Facebook, Apple, and YouTube (*Economist* 2013). The implications for Canada and Canadians were immediately recognized (Geist 2013).

In view of its private sector mandate, the Privacy Commissioner has a broader socio-economic scope than the Information Commissioner and, not surprisingly, the two mandates are, to a significant extent, the polar opposites of each other. The 2011 annual report of the Privacy Commissioner illustrates the scope and tensions in its mandate via its discussion of both privacy as it relates to children and youth but also in regard to the growing presence of online behavioural advertising (Office of the Privacy Commissioner of Canada 2012b). On the former, the report shows that the current Facebook generation of young people communicates continuously online but

> All of that online communication creates a permanent record – and that could carry risks to their privacy and to their reputations. Not just today but perhaps even more in the future. Teenagers are expected to make mistakes – it's a natural part of growing up. The fact that electronic records of many of the mistakes of today's youth will persist for decades to come is cause for deep concern. (1)

With regard to online behavioural advertising, "the practice of tracking a consumer's online activities in order to deliver advertising geared to that consumer's inferred interests," the Commissioner again stressed both concerns and pointed to the regulatory challenges and gaps (3). The Commisioner noted that "what it means in practice is that Internet ad networks follow you around online, watching what you do so that they can serve you targeted ads … [and] we have specifically pointed out that organizations engaged in online behavioural advertising should avoid tracking children – or tracking on websites aimed at children – since meaningful consent may be difficult to obtain" (3).

A related crucial privacy regulation debate in 2012 followed the federal Public Safety Minister Vic Toews' introduction and defence of the Harper government's lawful access legislation, Bill C-10, which has been given the title of Protecting Children from Online

Predators Act. The bill would allow police, without a warrant from the courts, to access basic personal information about Internet users as a way to track and catch persons who prey on children. The minister initially bombastically labelled any critics of his bill as being on the side of the child predators, a belligerent discourse which then generated a fierce counter-attack from any number of civil liberties advocates including critics in normally conservative media such as the *National Post* (Selley 2012). Some commentators also saw the counter-attack as itself over the top because some of the provisions in the legislation had been in a similar 2004 Martin Liberal government bill that was later withdrawn (Coyne 2012).

Even earlier, however, the Privacy Commissioner had written Toews, in October 2011, and in her letter stated that "my provincial and territorial privacy colleagues ... have called upon the federal government in 2009 and 2011 to take a cautious approach to legislative proposals to create an expanded surveillance regime that would have serious repercussions for privacy rights" (Office of the Privacy Commissioner of Canada 2011, 1).

The Commissioner of Lobbying of Canada inherited a mandate parts of which go back to the late 1980s when the initial system of lobby registration was begun and carried out by the then existing Ethics Counsellor. The Commissioner's current mandate was a centre-piece of the Lobbying Act that came into force in 2008 as a Harper-era initiative in its larger accountability package (Shepherd 2009). The Commissioner's three-fold mandate deals with maintaining a registry of lobbyists that is accessible to Canadians, fostering greater awareness of the requirements of the act through education and outreach, and ensuring compliance with the legislation and the Lobbyists' Code of Conduct (Office of the Commissioner of Lobbying in Canada 2011a, 1). The following four overriding principles underpin the lobbying registration system:

1 Free and open access to government is an important matter of public interest.
2 Lobbying public office holders is a legitimate activity.
3 It is desirable that public office holders and the public be able to know who is engaged in lobbying activities.
4 A system for the registration of paid lobbyists should not impede free and open access to government. (Ibid., i.)

Initially focused on lobbying of the political executive branch of the federal government, the Designated Public Office Holder Regulations under the Lobbying Act were amended in 2010 to include members of Parliament and senators as designated public office holders. Interpretative issues have also arisen regarding the Lobbyists' Code of Conduct, such as its Rule 8 provisions regarding improper influence. This followed a Federal Court of Appeal decision that had broadened the scope of circumstances in which this rule applies (ibid., 1–2). In addition to its compliance and outreach functions, the Commissioner issues interpretation bulletins and advisory opinions – soft regulatory tools, in effect – with the former broader and more comprehensive and the latter directed to specific groups (Office of the Commissioner of Lobbying in Canada 2011b, 24).

Overall, the Commissioner of Lobbying has functioned without huge controversy. But within its mandate, there are necessarily embedded its own twinned trade-offs between public *information* (such as the need to register and to reveal lobbyist meetings with ministers and officials on a monthly basis) and *privacy* (the right not to have to reveal what was discussed).

Of considerable and related interest historically are the extended tentacles of broader impacts of lobbying and of the scrutiny of lobbyists. For example, in 1989, a private publication, the *Lobby Monitor*, emerged under the leadership of John Chenier and Sean Moore. It reported on the activities of lobbyists, in part, as they were revealed by lobby registration information. Not surprisingly, the lobby industry and the lobbied wanted to know more about who was lobbying whom. In 2011, the *Lobby Monitor* was purchased by Hill Times Publishing and, thus, had a closer commercial link to the *Hill Times* newspaper, the paper that focuses closely and in detail on activities and controversies on Parliament Hill and with regard to the political executive (*Lobby Monitor* 2012).

In its essential focus, the regulation of lobbying, of course, strives to regulate aspects of another arena of democracy: interest group pluralism and the wider realms of civil society democracy and NGO politics. The key word here is "aspects" because, as we have seen in earlier regime chapters, other regulatory bodies routinely affect the conduct of lobby groups and entities variously defined. It is also essential in an even larger context to relate Canada's system of lobby registration to that of other countries and jurisdictions.

Canada's system compares relatively well against the US system of lobby registration. In fact, Canada and the United States were among the earliest reformers in this regulatory field. Nevertheless, authors such as Holman and Luneburg (2012) point out that it "was only in the late 1980s and early 1990s that Canada and the United States learned from mistakes made in the past and finally began to institute effective transparency regimes" (76). These authors also show changes in the past two decades in EU countries and in Eastern Europe and note, in contrast with North American developments, that early "European lobbyist regulations focused not on transparency as a means to gain public confidence in government, but on providing business interests with *access* to law makers as a means to bolster fledgling economies" (75). International developments or inaction on the lobbying registration front are also important in the sense that some states have such rules, but most still do not. This situation internationally affects business strategies in trade and NGO lobbying amid complex rules in some countries and unregulated lobbying in others (Hogan, Murphy, Chari 2008).

Among parliamentary watchdog agencies, the Public Sector Integrity Commissioner of Canada is, arguably, the agency that has had the most peculiar history and the worst start among the regulators being examined. It was one of the three main Harper-era Accountability Act agencies and was established in 2007 to replace and strengthen the previous Public Service Integrity Commissioner, a Treasury Board Secretariat–based office created in 2001 to protect public service whistle blowers. The Commissioner's mandate is to "establish a safe confidential and independent mechanism for public servants or members of the public to disclose potential wrongdoing in the federal public sector" (Office of the Public Sector Integrity Commissioner of Canada 2011, 3). Under the provisions of the Public Servants Disclosure Protection Act, public servants are also protected from reprisals for making such disclosures or for cooperating in investigations under the act.

Influenced strongly by the Chrétien-era sponsorship scandal, where officials were seen as ineffective on blowing the whistle on ministers and senior players, the Martin Liberal government proposed the new legislation with its new parliamentary agency as a key feature. At the time, scholars such as Paul Thomas (2005) examined the issues "based on the premise that whistle blowing is most appropriately regarded as morally ambiguous activity" (1) and stressed, based on comparative analysis, that the "benefits of such laws in terms of promoting 'right-doing' and correcting wrongdoing have been oversold" (1). The Harper government's endorsement of the new parliamentary watch-dog proceeded into law even though the new Commissioner's work would relate, thereafter, mainly to actions and complaints on its watch.

In the event, it is unlikely that an accountability-seeking government could have anticipated the early debacle that accompanied the new commissioner. In its first five years, and over four hundred complaints having been submitted, no wrongdoing was found until an announced single case early in 2012. Prior to that, the agency had been the subject of a high-profile report by the Office of the Auditor General of Canada (2010). During the Auditor General's investigation, the first commissioner, Christiane Ouimet, resigned amid the already well-known failed record of the agency (Brennan 2012). As her successor put it in the agency's 2010–11 annual report, "the sudden retirement of my predecessor ... followed by the tabling of the Auditor General's report ... were two events that had a profound impact on the members of my team and on the reputation of the young office" (Office of the Public Sector Integrity Commissioner of Canada 2011, 4).

Interestingly, one of the first things said in the foreword to the Auditor General's report were two related gaps in the parent legislation regarding the Commissioner. The first "is the inability to pursue information outside the public sector during an investigation under the Act" and the second is "the lack of an independent mechanism for addressing allegations of reprisal within PSIC," in other words, within the Office of the Public Sector Integrity Commissioner of Canada itself (Office of the Auditor General of Canada 2010, 1). In its 2011–12 annual report, entitled *Tell Us: You Are Protected*, the Commissioner indicated that more new cases were now emerging, and work had also begun on the earlier backlog (Office of the Public Sector Integrity Commissioner of Canada 2012).

THE THREE REGIME ATTRIBUTES

We now look across the two realms of the regulation of parliamentary democracy regime in relation to the three regime attributes in our analytical framework. They help us understand change and inertia in this often understudied regime by traditional regulatory scholars.

Ideas, Discourse, and Agendas

With respect to ideas, discourse, and agendas, it is possible to see across the four decades modes of discussion that are both reinforcing but also contradictory and that have yielded complex standards of rule-based behaviour and also unruliness of the policy and mandate conflict kind. While the core regulatory ideas relate to parliamentary democracy and responsible government, the discourse of responsible government has not enjoyed pre-eminence. Indeed, over the period as a whole, it has often been sublimated as attention shifted to prime ministerial–led notions of efficient and controlling government. Even related notions of ministerial responsibility (collective and individual) have lost currency in political discourse, even though, in an everyday operational sense, they sit at the heart of this regulatory and governance regime (Malloy 2004).

Although parliamentary democracy is the overarching value, the boundaries of the regime have increasingly been difficult to keep watertight in terms of discourse and practice. The regulatory scope spills over necessarily into democracy seen as pluralist, civil society, and direct democracy, be it in rules about elections and third-party pluralist group involvement in campaigns or the rules about lobbying by interest groups, professional lobbyists, and companies.

With respect to political parties, ideas that have accompanied their slow-moving inertia-driven regulation have included massive amounts of self-regulation – they are, arguably, the ultimate political oligopoly – as well as minimalist notions of regulated public utilities, and fund-receiving agents, but still not legally cast as central political institutions even though they demonstrably are.

A bundle of permanently conflictual and, arguably, ever more complex ideas and discourses abound within responsible government, prime ministerial, Cabinet-parliamentary relations, and across the watchdog agencies. Much of this complex policy and mandate conflict derives from tangled and contested notions of access to information and privacy as revealed in watchdog commissioners of that name and mandate and also in different ways in other watchdogs without such names (e.g., lobbying and public sector integrity). And, of course, Cabinet secrecy (privacy of a different kind) sits at the heart of this regulatory regime, since such secrecy is said to be crucial to encouraging frank debate within Cabinet and among ministers and then after decisions are made, to all ministers supporting such decisions including those that in private Cabinet deliberations, some may have ardently opposed (D'Ombrain 2004).

Crucially, Cabinet government and responsible government are also informational government of both the selective and statutorily required kinds. The former is the world of periodic ministerial off-the-record meetings and briefings with selected/preferred journalists; spin and communications strategies that brand policies and rules and that now use the entire array of Internet and social network technologies; and often obligatory "non-answer" answers or attack answers in parliamentary Question Period and before parliamentary committees. The statutory kinds of information provision consist of the tabling of numerous reports by both the government (across all of its departments and agencies) and Parliament's own watchdogs.

Public and Private Power in Regulation Making and Compliance

This second attribute of regime evolution indicates that some quite strong forces of power shape change and inertia in this regulatory regime. Regarding both responsible government and political parties, there is no doubt that prime ministers have deliberately, strategically, and tactically worked to expand their control relative to earlier periods. Both the Chrétien and Harper eras reveal this power play in relation to Parliament, internal Cabinet control, and governing from the centre of the federal government. Prime ministerial power is constrained somewhat by differences between minority and majority government, but the Harper era is especially noteworthy because its control strategies were noticeably augmented by the arts and excesses of attack politics and permanent campaigning.

Public power in regulation making and compliance, in other senses, had some familiar features. This is apparent in regard to the growing range of rules, codes, advisory opinions, and guidance mechanisms both to enforce and educate and ensure awareness of the changing watchdog values across the growing set of Parliament's mandate requirements. We have seen that responsible government is still governed by constitutional and parliamentary conventions dealing with the calling of Parliament after an election, with prorogation and dissolution, and with what constitute legitimate processes for establishing formal coalition governments (Hicks 2012).

Although the watchdog agencies are agents of Parliament and governed through laws passed by Parliament, in fact, it is prime ministerial and executive power that decided when to establish them, when to amend mandates, and when to refuse to change them even when change was needed. Some of these watchdog agencies could just as easily not have been created as agents of Parliament and, instead, could have been agencies lodged in the executive structure of government. Regarding private power, this regulatory regime seems, at first glance, not influenced as much as others by private power, corporate or otherwise. However, this is misleading in some ways because of varied kinds of interest group, N G O, and direct democracy pressures and advocacy. Thus, we have seen that on the corporate and commercial side, Internet-based firms and privacy merchants as an industry have sought to limit regulation, to define the Internet as democracy incarnate, or to confine it to a form of guidance as its powers to monitor and collect data on consumers and citizens have grown exponentially. Of course, historically, N G O lobbies, often in alliance with their preferred political party allies, have been key advocates of regulatory reform that led to new access to information, privacy, and lobbying laws in the first place.

Science, Evidence, and Knowledge

The evolution of the parliamentary democracy regime, not surprisingly, is rarely cast as a science-based regime or one based on science-based changes and developments, where science is usually understood as the natural sciences. But the regime and its current and future challenges and aspects of unruliness are definitely influenced by the nature of changing communication and Internet technologies and, therefore, inter-regime regulatory unruliness because telecom and Internet regulators are always playing catch-up. This is evident in privacy concerns related to the so-called Facebook generation and issues related to new technology-centred data manipulation and abuse as revealed in the robo-call issues from the 2011 federal election. Genuine concerns arise here, as they have in earlier chapters, regarding regulatory agency policy and mandate conflicts.

Other broader forms of analytical evidence and knowledge have been and continue to be a part of the forces of change and of the status quo. In the regulation of political parties and elections, we have shown how research and study by the Barbeau Committee in the 1960s, and the Lortie Commission in the early 1990s, led to some regulatory change and recrafted how to think about and act on the problems at hand. Nonetheless, governments and politicians were also often sluggish in their response to suggested reforms. Through their annual and periodic analytical reports, some of Parliament's watchdog bodies also became part of the underlying knowledge base and narrative about what was working, what was not, and what was only barely being glimpsed let alone understood. Some academics and think tanks whose work we have cited are part of this underbelly of knowledge and advocacy including Canadian and international centres on democracy, information access, lobbying, and privacy.

CONCLUSIONS

The regulatory regime for parliamentary democracy and responsible government is not normally a part of the academic mainstream coverage of regulatory governance in Canada or elsewhere. Parliamentary democracy evokes many images and reactions, some positive but many negative, where Parliament as a set of political parties and MPs often seems to voters like an unregulated conspiracy against the electorate. Responsible government as a constitutional and democratic principle is, arguably, less fully understood by voters and citizens – all the more so when growing prime ministerial government and a world of continuous attack politics is evident. Moreover, in real political and democratic terms, Canada has a federal system of democracy where parliamentary democracy and responsible government are also central in each province and territory.

The need to understand the federal regulatory regime for parliamentary democracy and responsible government is important in its own terms as the apex of democracy as well as in the larger indirect sense that, if this regime is not performing well or is subject to the unruliness discussed above, then Canadians may have markedly less interest in, and knowledge about the efficacy of the other five regulatory regimes and their multiple regulatory bodies.

Hence, we have mapped the two realms that constitute the regulation of parliamentary democracy regime and analysed both change and inertia across the past forty to fifty years. The first realm, political parties and elections, and responsible Cabinet-parliamentary government sits at the apex of this regime with the power of the prime minister assuming ever greater governing control. The focus here is the regulation of political parties and elections and in the rules and conventions regarding how Parliament functions vis-à-vi the Cabinet and prime minister in crucial areas such as the convening, prorogation, and dissolution of Parliament and what the modern meanings of responsible government are or ought to be. The second realm of parliamentary watchdog agencies has required an analysis of the evolution of these agencies as a group of watchdog entities and also, illustratively, of the broad trajectories of development regarding a sample of these individual agencies. They constitute Parliament's own "civil service" and, thus, the agencies' mandates raise issues regarding the role of expertise and experts linked to traditional practices of elected MPs as watchdogs themselves on both sides of the parliamentary divide.

The analysis has shown the increased potential for policy and mandate clashes and, hence, unruliness among agencies overall and in particular situations, such as cases involving access to information versus privacy as well within lobbying regulation and rules regarding whistle blowing. There are high levels of potential unruliness when government departments face what may look and feel like regulatory overload as they seek to implement and change both their core departmental statutory, regulatory, and policy mandates and, in addition, the varied parliamentary watchdog values and mandates.

Parliamentary democracy anchored in political parties, elections, and ultimately, responsible parliamentary government has been weakened by forms of unruliness. Political parties still retain narrow forms of regulatory coverage even though they are absolutely central to parliamentary government. This includes major gaps in rules regarding the functioning of Parliament itself related to prorogation and the formation of coalition governments. In the analysis of the regulation of political parties and elections, centred partly on the Chief Electoral Officer, we have seen the often slow progress of this aspect of regulation, an arena dominated by political parties themselves but also by changing Internet and social network technologies in relation to the role of third parties and, hence, more pluralist notions of democracy. The tactical and often dark arts of permanent campaigning have also been shown – with possibly no ostensible regulatory solutions in sight or workable.

The chapter's look at Parliament's watchdog agencies as a group showed that across the past forty years, although we have more of them, the ultimate question of whether they are a boon to parliamentary democracy and responsible government or a distraction remains unanswered in a convincing way and is, possibly, unanswerable. Unruliness is evident here both of the regulatory agency–related and regulatory regime complexity kinds. In part, this is because, as we have seen, it requires the testing of watch dogs against questions such as, what is "Parliament" or the "House of Commons" in relation to the "government" and the doctrine of ministerial responsibility? what is "Parliament" or the "House of Commons" in terms of capacity to fight for the concerns of such agencies? and what is "Parliament" or the "House of Commons" in terms of capacity to oversee and direct the actions of such agencies? Moreover, the real or alleged failures of the agencies or of Parliament can rarely be separated from those of the government in office which had the power, ultimately, to create and fund them and to establish and amend their legal and regulatory mandates and, partly, also to ignore them when convenient. These questions are easily a part of unruliness of the agenda-setting kind, in that watchdog agencies have seemingly just been "add-ons" without having an agenda about them or about how they are to be governed as a group.

The closer illustrative examination of a selection of watchdog agencies shows how, centrally or even indirectly, they were caught in the twinned worlds of access to information, on the one hand, and privacy/secrecy, on the other, and hence, unruly growing agency mandate clashes and huge grey zones. Thus, the Information Commissioner reports show much slower responses to information requests and many more exceptions to information that is ultimately granted. The Privacy Commissioner, whose scope extends well beyond the state, sees a growing need for both privacy rules and enforcement but also education regarding the awareness of privacy threats and issues in a world where commercial privacy merchants are in the ascendancy.

In general, the chapter reveals all three types of unruliness, including where regulatory policy and mandates continuously collide and where rules are slow or even impossible to get established in the first place. The interstices and spaces among and between laws, rules, regulations, conventions, codes, and statements of guidance also emerge as they have in other regulatory regimes.

10

Rules and Unruliness in Canadian Regulatory Democracy and Governance

The core academic focus and contribution of *Rules and Unruliness* has been three-fold in nature. First, scholars, students, and practitioners of regulation need a deeper appreciation of a fundamental characteristic of contemporary and historical regulation, namely, the inability to effectively develop and enforce both parent laws and delegated regulations given policy conflicts over mandates and an inability to develop effective policy, as well other related gaps, complexities, and challenges in a Canadian regulatory system that is more complex than it was in earlier times. We have labelled these regulatory inabilities and impairments as *unruliness*. Understanding this unruliness and the nature of rule making necessitates an extended mapping of multiple regulatory regimes and their key attributes, concepts that are central to our analytical framework. Second, academics and practitioners require a systematic extension of the analysis of regulation to include regulatory welfarism, hence, our examination of both the societal framework regulatory regime and the regime of social sectors. Aspects of these regimes have been previously referred to as *civic regulation*; however, they extend even more broadly as key features of Canadian societal, social, and community life. Third, the book includes a crucially needed discussion of the regulatory regime for Canadian parliamentary democracy itself, a regime that comprises rules regarding political parties and elections, the practice of responsible government, and Cabinet secrecy, as well as Parliament's various watchdog agencies that deal with access to information, privacy, lobbying, ethics, and other accountability values and political ideas.

These academic focal points contribute analytically and historically to grasping how Canadian regulatory democracy and governance have evolved during the current Harper government era and the preceding Trudeau, Mulroney, and Chrétien-Martin prime ministerial eras. The analytical framework we developed and deployed helped to address our central questions: (1) What kinds of regulatory unruliness have been evident or addressed in the Canadian regulatory system overall? (2) How has Canadian regulatory democracy and governance changed in the past four decades? (3) How does Canada's system of public regulatory democracy and governance need to be reformed to deal democratically with rule making, compliance, and unruliness in a globalized context? (4) How and why has Canadian regulatory capitalism emerged in the past two decades, in particular, and is it different from regulatory capitalism in other competitor countries? (5) Why does regulatory welfarism in social policy need a greater presence and understanding in mainstream regulatory scholarship? (6) Can Canada achieve an effective adherence to regulatory agendas and to a multiple-points-in-time full-life cycle system of regulatory governance as envisaged in the federal Cabinet Directive on Regulatory Management (CDRM), the main set of macro-rules about federal rule making and in related health and environmental regulatory policy positions? We offer concluding answers to these questions below through a linked discussion of our main arguments.

Examining the basic regulatory regime map shows the sectoral and framework regimes to have different basic initial focal points and distinctive inherent ranges and directions of coverage, the first more vertical and the second more horizontal. The economic sectoral regime and the marketplace framework regime examined in chapters 5 and 7, respectively, are the paradigmatic heartland of basic academic regulatory analysis. The regulatory regime of social sectors and the societal framework regulatory regime explored in chapters 6 and 8, respectively, have typically not been a focal point in academic regulatory analysis; indeed, they have often been peripheral despite their historic and contemporary importance in Canadian affairs and in the life chances of individuals, families, and communities. The two regimes regarding overall policy and governance are both of the framework variety. The macro-regulatory governance regime, which sets out rules about rule making, has been included in basic regulatory scholarship in the past but the parliamentary democracy regime has not, hence, the latter's crucial inclusion in this book.

Analysis in the chapters in Part II was conducted in terms of our three regime attributes: (1) ideas, discourse, and agendas; (2) public and private power in regulation making and compliance; and (3) science, evidence, and knowledge. These attributes shed valuable light on both change and inertia as we examined each regime's evolution over four to five decades and through eighteen selected illustrative case study industries, social sectors, and framework realms.

Regarding the attribute of ideas, discourse, and agendas, the analysis has shown a wide range of ideas, most separately desirable and valued but rarely stated on their own, and how they circulate and compete in the structure of regulatory mandates. These ideas include the paired social and economic values at the centre of the CDRM but now extended in the CDRM to include other ideas, as shown in chapter 4. The ideas, discourse, and agendas attribute also includes an array of combined, more particular, although rarely narrow ideas such as prudential banking, invention and innovation, privacy and secrecy versus access to information, varied yet often strongly held values and notions of morality and law and order, modal and inter-modal transportation safety versus security goals, and the prevention of terrorism. Official mandate ideas, in addition, change and co-mingle with changing discourse as revealed in different ways of debating red tape reduction, streamlining, smart regulation, responsible regulation, and reframed versions of the nanny state.

Public and private power as an explanatory attribute is demonstrated in diverse ways. Public power within the state varies greatly in different regimes and in different realms within each regime. In the framework realm of banking and financial services, power is concentrated in the Department of Finance and the Bank of Canada. In the regulatory regime for parliamentary democracy, public power still centres on political parties and the governing party and its prime ministr, especially. In the two social regimes, sectoral and societal framework, power is at first glance more diffused among social ministers and departments but in a larger sense of priorities and resource allocation, it is increasingly located in, and deployed by the Department of Finance and also, in the Harper era, in Justice Canada and in Citizenship and Immigration Canada.

Regarding science, evidence, and knowledge as an explanatory attribute, our analysis of several regulatory regimes shows obvious inertia, subtle shifts, and evident change. Notions of science-based regulation have, certainly, been the focus of trade policy and regulation but they have had to battle with concepts of precaution where broader forms of evidence, uncertainty, and knowledge are argued as being essential. Evidence-based and diverse knowledge-based features of regulation are present in environmental regulation and patent regulation as well in efforts to practise enhanced post-market product and project monitoring. We have also seen, in an era of attack politics and permanent campaigning, growing concerns about the absence and rejection of evidence with ministers, interests and lobby groups saying that values alone should justify change or the status quo, and both state and non-state actors engaged in processes of conjuring up their own facts.

Canada's regulatory system, we have argued, is rife with unruliness. The unruliness examined conceptually and empirically in the regime chapters included the following three basic types: unruliness related to regulatory agencies; unruliness related to regulatory regime complexity; and unruliness related to regulatory agenda setting. The main kinds of unruliness, actual and potential, need to be better understood in regulatory scholarship and practise, so that Canadians can appreciate why unruliness is occurring and how and to what extent it is being addressed. This means recognizing that some rules and even regimes of rules are focused on securing compliance regarding undesirable behaviour that has already occurred, whereas other rules are focused more on preventative missions to ensure that various kinds of undesirable behaviour do not occur in the first place. And still other rules involve regulations that establishing positive goals for the regulated to meet. There are, in addition, diverse perceptions and reactions of particular constituencies to existing laws or to planned regulations. Reactions may range from eager acceptance through passive compliance, civil dissent, and judicial challenges to aggressive resistance and conflicts. Issues of evaluating regulatory performance need to have an appreciation of these varied contexts and realities of regulation.

Our analysis underscores the central political and temporal realities of rules: that public regulation involves decisions by state authorities about *regulatory flows*, that is, the most recent regulatory measures, which typically are more visible and often publicly contentious. But the management of these flows is still not informed by an explicit government-wide agenda-setting process and debate. Public regulation involves the continuing existing *regulatory stock* of rules and policies made by previous governments, sustained by popular support and interest group support, and the institutional inertia and the power of the status quo. Rules are also made (and unmade) in decisions by the courts and tribunals. The story of new regulation and some deregulation has definitely emerged in our review of the four prime ministerial eras, where initiatives ranging from wage and price controls and the Charter of Rights and Freedoms have later been joined by free trade agreements, post-9/11 security state rules, and border thickening measures, as well as efforts to weaken some aspects of Canadian environmental assessment rules in the name of economically driven responsible regulation to facilitate energy exports. The story of the existing regulatory stock requires more detective work both within and across regimes. To be sure, there have been exercises in reducing red tape and reducing the paper burden, although paradoxically, some of these regulatory cleansing processes have involved new rules and procedures to determine what is excessive red tape – defined as undue and unnecessary compliance and reporting costs. Red tape, at its political core, is a set of rules that some interests and governments have fought to establish.

Additionally, crucial to both rules and unruliness and regime complexity has been the contextual account, described in chapter 3, of the changing overall ecosystem of regulatory governance and interests. This regulatory environment includes foundational concepts in economic regulation linked to policing versus planning modes and aspirations in regulation; the relationship between independent regulators and elected, especially Cabinet authorities; the much more complicated nature of the structure of interests involved in regulatory politics and power; and, finally, frequent exogenous factors and forces including technological changes and periodic crises.

OUR ARGUMENTS IN RELATION TO THE QUESTIONS POSED

Several main arguments have been advanced, which we now draw out in a final concluding way and discuss with regard to the related questions posed by the authors as well as their links to explanations of change and inertia within and across regulatory regimes.

Regulatory Unruliness Is Growing

Our first overall argument is that regulatory unruliness is growing in Canada and internationally. In answering the question of what kinds of unruliness have been evident or addressed in Canada, we have identified and examined three types: (1) unruliness related to regulatory agencies,

(2) unruliness related to the complexity of regulatory regimes, and (3) unruliness related to regulatory agenda-setting dynamics and processes. But it is not at all clear that these types of unruliness are being addressed or even recognized as such. The core regulatory reform ideas of the past four to five decades have not so much replaced or succeeded each other, as being placed beside or layered on top of each other. For example, command-and-control regulation is, arguably, in decline in economic sectoral and marketplace framework regulation but its remnants are still aligned partially with the reforming kinds of co-regulation, management-based regulation, and risk-benefit regulation. In contrast, in the regulatory regime of social sectors and in the societal framework regulatory regime, command and control is alive and well. This mix of change and inertia contributes to unruliness of the three types. Table 10.1 provides some final summary examples from the book.

Unruliness related to regulatory agencies was demonstrated in chapter 5's account of the economic sectoral regime, where examples include an inability to get policies established or agreed upon, policy mandate conflicts, and conflicts between appointed regulators and elected ministers. The latter occurred in telecommunications regulation, where regulatory mandates and complexity were unworkable and often ignored in the face of changing economic and social realities. Unruliness related to regulatory agencies was also presented in chapter 7's analysis of the marketplace framework regime. Patent regulation of intellectual property and linked drug and genomic regulation has seen large rapid increases in the volume of product approval processing, and in the wider global system, in the rent-seeking abuses of patent trolls that litigate and feed off the massively more complex and often dubious nature of many modern patents. Our examination of the watchdog agencies in chapter 9's account of the parliamentary democracy regulatory regime exposed both sharp and growing conflicts among agencies, especially in dealing with access to information versus secrecy and privacy. Unruliness related to regulatory regime complexity and unruliness related to agenda setting also emerge more strongly, as we see in other arguments advanced in this book.

Regulatory Democracy and Its Multiple Changing Arenas and Criteria

Second, Canadian regulatory democracy needs to be seen in the context of all of its many forms and arenas of democracy. We asked how Canadian regulatory democracy and governance changed in the past four decades, and we have shown the growing array of democratic

Table 10.1 Examples of Unruliness Examined

1 UNRULINESS RELATED TO REGULATORY AGENCIES
• CRTC policy conflicts as well as rivalries between appointed regulators and elected ministers
• The NEB's virtual exclusion during two key periods of energy regulatory change: the 1980–84 National Energy Program and federal climate change policy
• Banking and financial services regulatory agencies playing a massive catch-up game trying but often failing to stay ahead of diverse new and complex risk products and computerized trading, and of outright but hard to enforce criminal behaviour
• Growing collisions between Parliament's watchdog agencies for access to information versus privacy and also in relation to Cabinet secrecy
• Impacts and uncertainties regarding crises, e.g., BSE, SARS, listeriosis, *E. coli*, and post-9/11 Canada-US border controls
• Linked regulatory processes and gaps for drugs, biotechnology, and patents because of hugely increased volume of applications and approvals by multiple regulatory bodies.

2 UNRULINESS RELATED TO THE COMPLEXITY OF REGULATORY REGIMES
• Constant uncertain trade-offs in the now extended overall purposes of the overarching CDRM across the six regimes
• Serious democratic and regulatory gaps in the regulatory regime for parliamentary democracy, including those related to prorogation and coalition government but also regarding the conduct of elections in an Internet and social network age
• Contradictions and massive complexity in the rules in the societal framework regulatory regime and in the regulatory regime of social sectors that increasingly are within taxation and public spending such as via tax-centred or administered rules regarding charities, and any number of new levered spending programs in areas of research, infrastructure, and contracting, and also in law and order and morality rule making and enforcement
• Intense and changing discourse needed to sell and characterize battles between environmental and economic development goals as applied to different industries, regions, spatial domains, and projects in Canada and internationally
• Greater complexity in what competition means as a framework regulatory value given diverse kinds of actual and potential regulatory offences as they relate to innovation, sustainable development, and consumption, as well as consumer-centred fair markets
• Complex aggregate international and Canadian links and uncertainties between regulating banking and financial services and sovereign debt regulation and, therefore, taxation and spending internationally, and in fiscal federalism within Canada.

3 UNRULINESS RELATED TO AGENDA SETTING
• Ongoing inability to develop and debate regulatory agendas and priorities in a public manner despite the aspirations of the CDRM
• Slowness in getting the Assisted Human Reproduction Agency established but then its rapid demise in 2012 following a Supreme Court of Canada ruling
• Inability to come close to meeting the lofty and desirable goals of the life cycle approach to regulation as set out in CDRM and in Health Canada and other policy announcements (all non-statutory); such more than "single point in time" temporal regulation involves both enhanced capacities and intricate post-market monitoring by complex networks of players
• Diverse regulatory evaluation practices, e.g., regular five-year reviews of the Bank Act; uncertain, unplanned, and episodic reviews of competition, health care, environmental, and intellectual property systems of rules.

criteria and arenas. We contend that there is a compelling need for greater democratic governance of regulation, in all of its actual and potential arenas of debate and accountability, in a way that more readily scrutinizes regulatory programs over longer time frames. These democratic reforms should relate to internal Cabinet debate in an era of excessive prime ministerial power, and to parliamentary scrutiny, including wider reporting by Parliament's regulatory watchdogs. In this context, it is especially crucial that the regulation of parliamentary democracy achieves renewed and urgent attention academically and in mainstream regulatory debate. This is a case of rule making being empowering for the citizenry. If the regulation of parliamentary democracy does not garner fundamental democratic trust, then the legitimacy of other regulatory regimes in terms of public trust will suffer consequently.

Parliamentary democracy – anchored in organized political parties, fair and regular elections, and ultimately, responsible government – has been weakened by forms of unruliness. For example, political parties still retain narrow forms of regulatory coverage even though regulatory coverage is absolutely central to parliamentary government. This narrowness includes major gaps in rules regarding the functioning of Parliament itself related, for example, to prorogation and the formation of coalition governments.

At the same time, however, it must be emphasized that regulatory democracy is not simple; ultimately, democracy in Canada relates to all five democratic arenas and their differently expressed and ranked forms of governance: parliamentary, federalist, interest group pluralist, civil society, and direct democracy. Given these five arenas, claims to democracy or to the lack of democracy must meet multiple, conflicting tests and evidence. These tests are often relaxed and smoothed over by the discourse of engagement and consultation, where some democratic values are fudged rather than practised. These forms of democratic battle can also be, as we have seen, among the causes of all three of the basic types of unruliness that we have identified and explored.

Regulatory Governance and the Need to Defend
Independent Regulators

Third, in considering how it needs to be reformed, we have shown that Canada's system of regulatory governance exhibits complex forms of delegated governance and degrees of independence. Our contention is that, in many ways, regulatory independence by arm's-length commissions and watchdog agencies needs democratic reinforcement. As a constitutional convention in our parliamentary Cabinet system of government, regulatory independence has been harmed unnecessarily and unwisely by ministerial incursions on specific decisions by boards and commissions and, perhaps more seriously, by weakening the scientific and evidence-based resources that crucially underpin such delegated governance. These ministerial excursions have been present regarding decisions of the regulators of nuclear energy (that included the dismissal of the agency head), telecommunications and broadcasting, and foreign investment. Arguably, the greatest threat of this kind has come from efforts to muzzle scientists in regulatory departments by subsuming the public advice they provide under the shackles of government communications strategies. As we have shown, while independent regulators need credible and earned reputations and legitimacy, some have been weakened in recent years rather than strengthened.

There are grey zones on these issues and practices that go straight to competing claims to democracy. Ministers are elected MPs and, thus, can lay claim directly to the values of responsible parliamentary government. And, both in the past and under present laws, there are processes whereby room is left for ministers or the Cabinet to make individual decisions under proscribed procedures or appeal mechanisms. At the same time, the independence of many regulatory agencies is grounded in the need for expertise, science, evidence, and transparent procedures, not to mention various notions of democracy centred on interest group pluralism, and direct democracy, including the role of social networks. If Cabinet and ministerial forays look and feel like small "p" versions of politics, partisan or otherwise, then there can easily be a loss of independence and the reputation of independence coveted by most arm's-length regulatory bodies.

The Emergence of Canadian Regulatory Capitalism

Fourth, we asked how and why Canadian regulatory capitalism has emerged and whether it is different from that in other countries. Our analysis indicates that a Canadian version of regulatory capitalism has, indeed, emerged – in concert with countries elsewhere – and that regulatory capitalism is fast overlaying the earlier deregulatory and market liberalism era of the late1970s and1980s, which was itself considerably overplayed during that period as an accurate descriptor of what was happening to regulation overall. Market liberalism is advancing in some respects, but it has not yielded fewer rules; rather, market liberalism is proceeding by more rules and more complex and often colliding kinds of interwoven rules under both Liberal and Conservative governments, at times mandated by the growing number of international agreements to which Canada is a signatory.

Significant examples emerge in chapter 5 from the analysis of underlying changes in the energy, transportation, and telecommunications sectoral regulatory agencies, and in related changes in the approaches taken in the past decade by their parent departments. Canadian regulatory capitalism exhibits some particular differences with other trading partners, including the United States, because of the natural resource endowments in different regions versus manufacturing focal points in others. The role of Canadian federalism and federalist democracy is relevant here, including aspects of the division of powers in such fields as agriculture and immigration where there is concurrent jurisdiction, and realms such as trade and commerce where federal powers seem to be strong but are accompanied in areas such as competition policy by a reluctance to exercise them.

Regulatory capitalism, the modern Canadian version, emerged under the discourse and regulatory processes advocated and changed under concepts of innovation-related "smart regulation" strategies during the Chrétien-Martin era, some of which was later absorbed into the Harper-era Cabinet Directive on Regulatory Management. This smart regulation approach has yielded new forms of co-regulation relating to drugs, patents, research ethics, and research funding by arm's-length granting bodies and new independent foundations. Forms of regulatory capitalism have increasingly materialized via voluntary codes initiated by non-governmental organizations, and these and other triggering processes have led to numerous public-private certification codes, standards, and agreements in diverse realms of environmental, health, and safety policy.

Fifth, we inquired into why social welfarism in public policy needs a greater presence in mainstream regulatory scholarship. Compared with regulatory capitalism, which fundamentally has international and global dimensions, regulatory welfarism is primarily anchored in domestic relations of power – in the Canadian federation, most notably in national and subnational governance arrangements in the realms of both the state and civil society. Furthermore, regulatory welfarism does not necessarily signify a decentering of the state itself. There is no single fulcrum for managing society, no central designer to engineer society. In liberal market societies, social entities and civic and economic relationships have always been fundamental shapers of most people's everyday existence.

For regulation of the social, there are several different sites that shift over time and restructure within and across jurisdictions. These sites include the federal and provincial states and local public bodies; professions, health disciplines, and occupational associations; myriad NGOs, civil society interests, and entities; and individuals and families. Corresponding in exemplar form with these sites is command-and-control regulation, delegated regulation, co-regulation, and self-regulation or governance of the self.

Societal Framework and Social Sectoral Regulation
and Their Centrality to Regulatory Scholarship

Our sixth main argument is that Canada's regulatory governance system needs a far greater focus on democratic and policy needs related to social and civic regulation in both a sectoral sense and in terms of societal framework regulation. This incorporates social welfare state program spending embedded with more and more rules in areas such as health care, education, housing, charities, immigration, and assisted human reproduction, to mention only a few examples. As we have seen in chapter 8 and elsewhere, it also ultimately includes regulation related historically and in the present day to law and order, morality and sexuality, and extended national security in the age of heightened terrorism and fears of terrorism. The case for the full inclusion of both the social sector and societal framework regulatory regimes in the mapping of Canadian rules and in the architecture of Canadian regulatory democracy and governance is a compelling one.

The analysis in chapters 6 and 8 implies a different although complementary way of thinking about increased command-and-control regulation and how red tape is viewed in regulatory discourse. Notably, an array of new social sectoral and societal framework laws and regulations has emerged. New laws contain new red tape; red tape not for business, but for various actors and interests ranging from judges to many individuals in diverse circumstances facing complex practical human situations that may or may not be criminal in nature or that require large amounts of wise discretion. All red tape analysis is caught up in the fact that many laws and rules produce good rules or aspects of good rule making; nevertheless, the focus, in practical terms, is on *excessive* red tape built into the very definition of actual red tape. In short, on almost a daily regulation-making basis, there is more red tape for some people, less red tape for others.

Tackling Regulatory Agendas and Life Cycles:
From Aspiration to Practice

Can Canada achieve an effective adherence to developing regulatory agendas and to a multiple-points-in-time full-life cycle regulatory governance, as set out in the CDRM? In relation to this final question, our argument is that Canada's regulatory system as a system still focuses primarily on a "one regulation at a time" approach, as discussed in chapter 4, and consequently, has reduced chances of dealing successfully with many contemporary regulatory challenges. Unless it moves towards a regulatory agenda–centred approach that addresses broader notions and groups of rules with common risk, uncertainty, and risk-benefit characteristics, Canada's system of regulatory governance will remain both deficient and unruly. Aspects of a regulatory agenda–centred approach do happen within independent regulatory agencies and their periodic changes in mandate, as shown in chapters 5 and 7, but not in the federal regulatory system as a whole through a focused public democratic debate on regulatory priorities. Chapter 4 showed how the CDRM has elevated the idea of regulatory plans and priorities to a higher aspirational level than in the past. This planning and priority setting on rules remains at the departmental level and is not a call for an overall cross-governmental regulatory agenda. At present, it is more nudgelike than policy or rulelike.

Also largely aspirational is the desirable overall policy for more comprehensive life cycle regulation, from pre-market to post-market, in many regulatory regimes and product, project, and process activities. A higher probability of achieving such multiple points in time and often extended intergenerational regulatory capacities will depend on all the elements of Canadian regulatory democracy. This will require extended investments in regulatory capacity, including science, evidence, and knowledge development in a much more networked set of players, especially regarding post-market monitoring.

To probe and understand Canadian regulatory democracy and governance, unruliness is a valuable and necessary complementary analytical entry point. It is complementary because unruliness can only be defined and appreciated in relation to the larger world of rules and regulation, hence, our focus on rules *and* unruliness. Our larger analytical framework helps tell a modern story about six regulatory regimes and rule making, compliance, and prevention across a forty- to fifty-year period, a period of rules and unruliness during which Canada changed a great deal in concert with ever more complex global and international economic, social, and political developments across all of the main fields of regulation.

Glossary of Major Terms

CABINET DIRECTIVE ON REGULATORY MANAGEMENT
(CDRM) is the overall federal policy directive on regulation making
and the evaluation of regulatory programs. Announced in 2012 by
the Harper Conservative government, the policy built on earlier overall policy documents, including the Cabinet Directive on Streamlining
Regulation (CDSR) adopted in 2006. It includes requirements for
departments to submit regulatory plans and priorities, and it also
contains provisions for a more explicit life cycle approach to regulation. The CDRM also complements statutes such as the Statutory
Instruments Act.

CANADA GAZETTE PROCESSES are information and consultation processes whereby federal departments and agencies demonstrate that Canadians have been consulted and that they have had an
opportunity to participate in developing or modifying regulations
and regulatory programs. Part I of the *Canada Gazette* process
involves a pre-publication stage, where interested parties, including
stakeholders previously consulted at the beginning of the regulatory
process, are given the opportunity to see how the final draft proposal
is in keeping with previous consultation drafts. Part II involves the
enactment and publication stage.

CAP AND TRADE REGULATION is an incentive-based approach
to environmental and related kinds of regulation whereby a cap on
a given type of emission is set by the government but then good and
efficient complying firms are allowed to trade/sell their assigned
emission permits to firms which are not good and efficient.

CIVIC REGULATION, a term formulated by Prince (1999a), refers to rule making with respect to numerous social aspects of human behaviour and needs, moral conduct and standards, intergovernmental relations, and human rights and civil liberties.

COMMAND-AND-CONTROL REGULATION is a term given to a regulatory approach that involves detailed procedures and controls that are largely input-focused rather than output- or outcome-focused. It was and is criticized by those who advocate more flexible and incentive-based approaches to economic regulation in recognition of the different situations that regulated entities face where a one-size-fits-all approach simply does not work. Although said to be in decline in economic and marketplace regulatory regimes, it remains quite central in the regulatory regime of social sectors and in the societal framework regulatory regime.

CONSTITUTIONAL AND QUASI-CONSTITUTIONAL PROVISIONS govern the substance and processes of regulation. Constitutional provisions refer to the federal-provincial constitutional division of powers and the provisions of the Canadian Charter of Rights and Freedoms. Quasi-constitutional provisions refer to rules governing rule making in free trade agreements such as the North America Free Trade Agreement (NAFTA) and also the federal-provincial agreements such as the Agreement on Internal Trade (AIT). The Canadian Human Rights Act is relevant as well.

CO-REGULATION is a process whereby both the state and businesses, interest groups, and non-governmental organizations (NGOS) make rules jointly and also assist in a coordinated system of monitoring and enforcement. Co-regulation relates to ideas and practices of partnerships and networked governance arrangements. Co-regulation is a key part of the concept of regulatory capitalism.

DEREGULATION refers to major steps being taken to eliminate rules so as to allow more competition. The late 1970s and in the 1980s were in Canada a major era of deregulation in previously monopoly or oligopolistic utility industries such as telecommunications, energy, airlines, and railways. The purpose was to allow new entrants to compete on the basis of both price and quality. In more recent years, deregulation has been revived as a topic of debate in regard to the effects of previous efforts and to the moves towards new forms of deregulation in areas such as environmental assessment.

ECONOMIC REGULATION is the term initially used to encompass the regulation of key industrial sectors characterized by public utility or monopoly features. It involves state efforts to control the economic behaviour of individuals and firms. There need be no assumption in such a restricted definition of a public interest goal. Nor is it limited, which is particularly germane to the Canadian case, to private actors because in most Canadian regulated sectors, at least until the wave of privatizations that occurred in the 1980s, publicly owned firms – such as CN Rail, the CBC, and Air Canada – were major actors. It is equally important that the definition of economic regulation is not confined to regulated firms. Under certain circumstances, the economic behaviour of customers and not just firms is regulated and such regulation is crucial.

ECONOMIC SECTORAL REGULATORY REGIME, historically refers to public utility regulation but the regime has shifted and been reshaped by technology and other forces that reconfigured sectoral mandates across the past forty years. Core regulators in the energy, transportation, and telecommunications sectors are the National Energy Board (NEB), the Canadian Transportation Agency (CTA), and the Canadian Radio-television Telecommunications Commission (CRTC). In regulatory terms, economic sectors are fluid with changing boundaries, issues, participants, and relationships.

EVIDENCE-BASED REGULATION refers to a broadening of the concept of science-based regulation by including more diverse kinds of knowledge and expertise including the social sciences, the theory and practice of cost-benefit analysis, law, the medical and health professions, but also certain kinds of front-line knowledge possessed by people such as birdwatchers functioning as citizen scientists. Increasingly, the concept of evidence-based regulation and its advocates have expressed growing deep concerns about regulation based on little or no evidence and knowledge where individuals and interests have argued that their values and ideologies were reasons enough for taking regulatory action or denying the need for regulation.

EXTERNALITIES are the costs or benefits resulting from a program (regulatory, spending, or tax) or project that accrue to third parties which may or may not be explicitly addressed by public authorities.

FEDERAL SPENDING POWER means the power of Parliament to make payments to people or institutions or governments for purposes on which it (Parliament) does not necessarily have power to legislate. Under the authority of the spending power of Parliament, several federal-provincial programs have been funded by the federal government. Essentially, the spending power of the federal government has been used to institute conditional grant programs which are, in effect, spending with rules of eligibility.

FINANCIAL ADMINISTRATION ACT is federal legislation that establishes the rules and regulations for the handling of public funds. It sets out the procedures for the collection and expenditure of monies and the kind of reporting system to be used.

GOVERNANCE is a conceptual construct to recognize more explicitly that governance is more than government, more than the state, and more than public policy pronounced and implemented by the state and its bureaucracies. Governance also implies the state playing a role characterized at times more by steering than rowing, and also employing softer instruments of governing rather than harder command-and-control regulatory ones. At its core, governance is a set of interacting policies, decisions, policy instruments, processes, laws, and values involving joint action by the state and its agencies, business interests, NGOs, and civil society interests and entities.

GOVERNMENTALITY is a concept inspired by Michel Foucault on the government of one's self and of governing at a distance. The governmentality literature examines changes in the role of the state and for tracing changes in state-society relationships in contemporary politics. In particular, governmentality relates the diverse and delegated forms of governance in regulation as well as in the shape shifting of regulatory regimes, especially in the public and private relations of power in rule making and compliance.

GOVERNMENTS IN MINIATURE is a term coined by Schultz and Alexandroff (1985), and used in this book, too, to describe regulatory agencies created to be the primary governmental institutions for directing and influencing economic and related social impacts of vital infrastructural, public utility, and networked industries. Historically, in the Canadian context, governments in miniature referred to federal sectoral economic regulatory agencies, the NEB, the CTA, and the CRTC.

LAISSEZ-FAIRE is an economic doctrine that asserts that the best way to achieve strong economic growth and a high standard of living is to limit strictly all government intervention in the economy to maintaining the value of the currency and to protecting private property. This includes regulatory intervention of some kinds. The doctrine of laissez-faire is derived from the writings of Adam Smith.

LEVERED MONEY refers to spending where those seeking public funds will only receive such funding if they bring other money (public or private) as well to the total funding of a given project or program. Levered money involves funding with many kinds of rules about eligibility, co-funding, and reporting and accountability requirements within and among participating and networked partner entities.

LIFE CYCLE REGULATION is an approach to regulation that advocates the need to regulate and monitor the complete cycle of behaviour in temporal and spatial terms. Such full cycles can include the later formal evaluation of regulatory programs; regulating the full life of a given physical asset such as a mine or energy facility from cradle to grave; and engaging in both pre-market assessments of products prior to approval for use and then extensive post-market assessments of the actual use of the products once they are on the market.

MACRO-REGULATORY GOVERNANCE REGIME is the regime that makes rules about rule making. Centred at present on the Cabinet Directive on Regulatory Management, it also extends to other key pillars of constitutional and Cabinet-parliamentary government. Life cycle aspirations of regulatory policy operate in this macro-regime as does the issue of regulatory agendas.

MANAGEMENT-BASED REGULATION is an approach to regulation that more explicitly recognizes that regulation is increasingly a matter of de facto co-governance with private firms and related interests and organizations. Thus, it deploys regulatory authority in a way that utilizes the private sector's knowledge about its particular circumstances and engages with firms in developing their own internal procedures and monitoring practices to regulate and respond to risks.

MARGINAL BENEFIT is the extra satisfaction or benefit that results from the production of an extra unit of a particular good or service.

MARGINAL COST is the extra cost incurred in producing an additional unit of output.

THE CONCEPT OF MARGINAL COST is central to the determination of the optimal prices and quantities of goods and services.

MARKETPLACE FRAMEWORK REGULATION is a regime of regulation that reaches across sectors of the economy to ensure that the commercial marketplace of producers, sellers, and buyers/consumers of goods and services are functioning in competitive free and fair market arrangements. Examples of marketplace framework regulation include laws regarding competition, consumers, intellectual property, bankruptcy, and corporations.

MINIATURIZATION is a process in which the policy-making mandates and rule-making and enforcement powers of a regulatory agency have been radically redefined, shared out, and reduced over time. Examples of miniaturization include the federal sectoral economic regulatory agencies, the NEB, and the CTA. The result is that such agencies have diminished independent decision-making capacity and no longer are they the primary governmental institutions to influence and direct activities in a given sector or realm.

MULTILEVEL REGULATION refers to rule-making and compliance coordination and monitoring involving international, regional, national, subnational (provinces, cities and local government) authorities. Multilevel regulation can be cooperative but also conflictual in nature.

NANNY STATE is a British-centred term and discourse used to express opposition to excessive and unnecessary rules in the economy and society. The metaphorical reference is to the tough discipline deployed by nannies hired by the rich to ensure that children behave. Related terms in the North American context are *big brother* and *social engineering* by the state.

NIGHT WATCHMAN STATE refers to the state's rule making regarding law and order, morality, and various kinds of surveillance. Often seen as the original purposes of the state before eras such as the welfare state and later notions of the regulatory state, the night watchman idea is still a crucial realm of rule making and enforcement.

NUDGE as a governance theory developed by Thaler and Sunstein (2012) does not really refer to regulation as such. Instead, nudge favours softer approaches geared psychologically to how people think and then to design "choice environments" that make it easier for people to choose for themselves and their societies, by nudging them through the provision of appropriate information to appropriate viable and accepted better forms of behaviour. Nudge techniques have been recommended with regard to issues such as organ transplant donations, smoking, obesity, and neighbourhood electricity and water conservation.

PARLIAMENTARY DEMOCRACY REGULATORY REGIME refers to the rules, laws, regulations, and conventions governing political parties and elections and the practices of responsible government. It includes, as well, Parliament's many watchdog agencies dealing with access to information, privacy, lobbying, and ethics and other accountability values and ideas.

PERFORMANCE-BASED REGULATION is a form of rule making and compliance where the focus is on achieving and reporting on agreed stated performance outcomes/results without heavy prior prescriptive requirements as to how they are to be achieved. This approach to regulation obviously contains many of the implicit features of flexibility and incentive-based regulation but is even more outcome-focused. It is dependent on complex accountability and transparency requirements for periodic reporting about performance claims and outcomes.

POLITICAL ECONOMY OF REGULATION literature offers broad interpretations of stages in regulatory development with a focus on the macro-relations of regulatory power between the state and capitalism and between the state and society.

POST-MARKET REGULATION refers to more recent approaches to regulation that focus beyond the one point in time, i.e., pre-market notions of regulation to the longer and broader post-market uses of products and processes in diverse individual, sectoral, social, and spatial settings and networks. Post-market regulation involves a much larger set of actual and potential players, citizens, patients, and knowledge experts in the post-market monitoring process.

PRE-MARKET REGULATION involves processes for the safety and risk assessment of products and production processes before they are allowed to be sold on the market. In areas such as drug regulation in the wake of the thalidomide crisis in the 1960s, for example, pre-market safety regulation became the dominant model of safety regulation in many product realms.

PRIME MINSITERIAL ERAS refers here to the main federal prime ministerial and governing political party and partisan eras, i.e., the Trudeau Liberals from 1968 to the early 1980s, the Mulroney Conservatives from 1984 to 1992, the Chrétien and then Martin Liberals in the 1993 to 2005 period, and the Harper Conservatives from 2006 to the present.

RED TAPE is the term and discourse used to discuss excessive regulation either in parent rules or in the procedures and paperwork involved. Red tape initially referred simply to the colour of the tape used to bind files and folders of statutes. This could simply mean that all rules are red tape. But in a contemporary sense, red tape reduction involves identifying excessive red tape typically linked by business interests to concepts of unreasonable or undue costs of compliance.

RED TAPE ANALYSIS relates to how red tape is thought about and examined empirically and who is doing the analysis and in whose interests. All red-tape analysis is caught up in the fact that many laws and rules produce good rules or aspects of good rule making; nevertheless, the focus, in practical terms, is on *excessive* red tape or undue compliance costs built into the very definition of actual red tape. In short, on almost a daily regulation-making basis, there can be and is more red tape for some, less red tape for others. Thus, an array of new social sectoral and societal framework laws and regulations has emerged, but red tape in this context is not red tape for business but for various actors and interests ranging from judges, to many individuals in diverse circumstances facing complex practical social and human situations which may or may not be criminal in nature or which require large amounts of wise discretion.

RED FLAGS refers to a term and discourse where new hazards, risks, and harms are flagged or brought to public attention and that imply the need or potential need for more regulation or new kinds of regulation.

REGULATION refers broadly to rules of behaviour backed up by the sanctions of the state. Such rules include mainly delegated law or the "regs," but in a larger sense regulation refers also to rule making in the parent statute. The Statutory Instruments Act defines regulation as a "statutory instrument made in the exercise of a legislative power conferred by or under an Act of Parliament, or for the contravention of which a penalty, fine or imprisonment is prescribed by or under an Act of Parliament."

REGULATION THEORY emerged in France and was reflected and modified in other European countries depending, in part, on particular systems of capitalism in different countries. Regulation in this theoretical tradition did not refer to the particular policy instrument notion of regulation (where regulation is just one instrument of governing) but rather something that, in today's terminology, is much more akin to broad governance structures. Regulation theory concentrates on systemic features of power in systems of capitalism and at different stages of capitalism such as the Fordist and post-Fordist eras.

REGULATORY AGENDA refers to processes whereby departments and agencies are required to indicate their regulatory priorities for a given period. Regulatory agendas may be simply in the form of lists of rather explicit rankings whereby some proposed new regulations will proceed and others will not. To date, regulatory agendas have not emerged or been required at a cross-government level.

REGULATORY ATTRIBUTES refer to basic important features regulating change and inertia and that also provide further insights into
unruliness. The main regulatory attributes examined are (1) ideas,
discourse, and agendas; (2) public and private power in regulation
making and compliance; and (3) science, evidence, and knowledge.

REGULATORY BUDGET is the notional concept that argues that
regulations impose state-mandated private sector costs for businesses and individuals that need to be more explicitly seen and
aggregated as a part of public sector budgets and budgeting including through the setting of regulatory agendas analogous to tax and
spending budgets.

REGULATORY CAPITALISM is a characterization and era of regulation that seeks to differentiate it from the 1970s and 1980s era of
neo-liberalism. Regulatory capitalism seeks to capture the fact that
regulation is growing markedly but is less a feature of state rule and
enforcement and much more a system of co-regulation and compliance between the state and business interests and firms but also
other non-state interests and networks. Regulatory capitalism is,
thus, a crucial feature needed to understand both regulation and
modern capitalism.

REGULATORY CAPTURE is both a theory and set of frequently
expressed views that regulatory agencies tend to be captured by the
interests they are regulating. Such capture dynamics occur gradually
or are built in from the outset through political-industrial collusion.

REGULATORY GOVERNANCE is a subset of the broader concept
of overall governance that emerged in the literature on politics, policy, and public administration over the past thirty years. Thus, regulatory governance refers to the deployment of softer instruments of
governing such as guidelines and codes of behaviour rather than just
harder command-and-control direct regulatory instruments, in part
out of recognition of the need to regulate and serve different kinds
of entities being regulated but also other clients who are the beneficiaries of regulation. But regulatory governance theory has always to
some significant extent recognized that state-centred regulatory bodies almost always do more than regulate. They are typically multifunctional in nature. In addition to regulation per se, state-centred

regulatory bodies are planning entities; they exhort, persuade, and provide information; they adjudicate, negotiate, network, conduct research, and utilize different kinds of science, evidence, and knowledge; and the rules they deploy mandate large amounts of mainly private spending by businesses and citizens.

REGULATORY HARMONIZATION is the process whereby nation states or subnational governments in federations agree to adopt rules that are virtually identical.

REGULATORY IMPACT ASSESSMENT SYSTEM (RIAS) is the formal analytical process and methodology required under regulatory policy to identify regulatory impacts and to ensure, where appropriate, that new regulations only proceed where regulatory risk-management benefits exceed regulatory costs.

REGULATORY POLICY is the overall policy of a government regarding its approach and processes for rule making, especially regarding delegated law (the "regs").

REGULATORY REGIME is a set of interacting agencies, statutes, rules, processes, and values in a defined large realm of regulation. Examples include the economic sectoral regime, the marketplace framework regime, and the four others examined in this book. The notion of a regime can also be used to characterize a smaller realm such as the intellectual property regime or the food regulatory regime.

REGULATORY REGIME OF SOCIAL SECTORS refers to the policies, rules, institutions, and processes governing particular social groups or constituencies. Three sample sectors are profiled in this book: registered charities, citizenship and immigration, and assisted human reproduction technologies. The regulatory regime of social sectorsis given relatively little recognition among traditional regulatory scholars.

REGULATORY SHIFT is a concept that refers to a range of other related regulatory changes and needs. These can include re-regulation (as defined below) but also the use of new regulatory techniques (such as price caps), or user fees, transitional measures, and regulatory cost reductions, and red tape and paper burden reductions.

REGULATORY STATE refers, in part, to a particular way of theorizing and characterizing the state by identifying particular countries or jurisdictions that were weaker or less developed welfare states. Both the European Union and the United States have been cast in this way. In practice, of course, all modern states are regulatory states in significant ways.

REGULATORY WATCHDOGS is a general term to describe the basic role of all regulatory agencies and regulatory departments. In the Canadian case, regulatory watchdogs is also used as a descriptor of Parliament's own regulatory agencies that report to Parliament and whose number has grown in recent years.

REGULATORY WELFARISM has its own historical elements and relatively distinct relationships among institutions and actors for managing social sectors and societies. In economic affairs, political developments, and social trends, regulatory welfarism spans centuries, not just recent decades. There is a continual pattern of change and inertia in formal and informal rules coupled with hybrid networks of regulatory setting, implementation, and compliance. Regulatory welfarism is primarily anchored in domestic relations of power; in the Canadian federation, most notably in national and subnational governance arrangements in the realms of both the state and civil society.

RELATED SCIENCE ACTIVITIES (RSA) are actions that complement and extend R&D by contributing to the generation, dissemination, and application of scientific and technological knowledge. RSA is often crucially embodied in the education, training, and experience of scientific and technical personnel working on the front lines of regulatory monitoring activity and of various kinds of regulatory product approvals in key federal regulatory departments and agencies.

RE-REGULATION relates to new rules and regulatory agencies established in the era of 1980s deregulation to meet new or changed public interest needs related to sectors such as telecommunications, transportation, and energy, but also trade law, which had been deregulated in significant ways. In countries such as the United Kingdom, re-regulation was also deemed essential because of the privatization of state-owned industries that were a part of liberalized market strategies.

RESEARCH AND DEVELOPMENT (R&D) is scientific, engineering, and design activities that result in new or improved products and production processes. R&D spending is considered a significant indicator of a country's capacity for innovation and economic growth.

RISK-BENEFIT REGULATION refers to views and discourse that seeks to draw more applied attention to the belief that most areas of safety regulation are rarely only about safety in some absolute sense but, increasingly, about complex kinds of risk-benefit regarding rule making, pre-market product and process approvals, and post-market monitoring.

SCIENCE-BASED REGULATION is the term applied to the need for regulation to be underpinned by independent science-based causal knowledge, especially science in the natural sciences and engineering. Related discourse also emerged in trade agreements where rules and product approvals had to be based on so-called sound science. Later and other regulatory mandates have extended these notions by referring to evidence-based regulation and knowledge-based regulation where knowledge expertise can include various social sciences, including interdisciplinary science.

SECTORAL REGULATION refers to a regime of diverse regulatory rules and agencies that focus on particular sectors of the economy such as telecommunications, airlines, railways, shipping, and energy (oil, gas, nuclear, electricity). Sectoral regulation emerged, in part, to deal with monopoly public utilities but, increasingly, has sought to ensure that new entrants can enter such markets and reduce prices through competition and improved product quality.

SELF-REGULATION historically relates to processes by which the state allowed key professions such as law and medicine to regulate themselves. Thus, in exchange for their delegated control of entry to the profession and basic qualifications, these two dominant professions had to maintain core professional legal and medical values anchored as well around lawyer-client and doctor-patient privilege and confidentiality. Few, if any, later professions have matched the power structure won by doctors and lawyers historically, but many subsequent knowledge groups and occupations have sought and partially achieved similar but more limited powers. The notion of self-regulation has also been used as a descriptor where other particular kinds of partial self-regulation by businesses and NGOs emerge in concert with regulation by the state.

SOCIAL REGULATION is the name conferred on early forms of public interest–focused consumer, health, safety, and environmental regulation, especially in the 1960s and 1970s. Other concepts of regulation with basic social goals and intent have also been characterized as civic regulation and, in this book, as social sectoral regulation and social framework regulation linked to the social welfare state.

SOCIETAL FRAMEWORK REGULATORY REGIME refers to broad horizontal societal coverage or the social management and steering of society. Three realms are examined: law and order, morality and sexuality, and the welfare state. Regarding the welfare state, rules are often embedded in taxation, in public spending conditions, and levered spending related to health care, employment, pensions, and education, and also in other aspects of detailed governance in these combined yet diverse social welfare areas. In many respects, this regime includes the oldest kind of state regulation begun under historic notions of the night watchman state and their modern variants, reinvented with new vigour.

STATUTORY INSTRUMENTS ACT governs the regulatory process in that it defines a regulation as a statutory instrument made in the exercise of a legislative power conferred by or under an act of Parliament, or for the contravention of which a penalty, fine, or imprisonment is prescribed by or under an act of Parliament. This definition of regulation includes a rule, an order, or regulation governing proceedings before a judicial or quasi-judicial body established by an act of Parliament, and any instrument described as a regulation in any other act of Parliament. However, as regulatory governance and instrument types have become more varied, it would appear that related instruments such as guidelines, codes, and standards may or may not be captured by this statutory definition.

SYSTEMIC RISK denotes the risks of widespread failure and, thus, potentially significant harm across entire systems of economic institutions as opposed to particular risks caused by individual firms or constituent members, or particular products and processes.

TOO BIG TO FAIL is an idea, centred mainly in banking policy, that identifies a particular financial institution as being one that cannot be allowed by the state to fail via bankruptcy or through a fear that it will, through contagion, lead to other bank failures. The state intervenes through bailout funding by the state.

TRIAGE PROCESS was established to differentiate medium/high impact from low impact regulatory proposals with the possible implication that the low impact ones could proceed directly to the stage II *Canada Gazette* process. The triage process, which requires departments and agencies to develop a statement that reveals a number of possible impacts, is in its own way, a system of agenda setting and also potential red tape reduction.

UNRULINESS refers to inabilities to effectively develop and enforce rules because of conflicts that make it impossible to establish policies and rules or because any number of policy and mandate conflicts, democratic gaps, and governance challenges. The three main types are (1) unruliness related to regulatory agencies, (2) unruliness related to the complexity of regulatory regimes, and (3) unruliness related to agenda setting. The term unruliness is also used to designate the mood of the contemporary age of national and subnational states, economic interests, and social actors.

References

Abele, Frances, and Michael J. Prince. 2006. "Four Pathways to Aboriginal Self-Government in Canada." *American Review of Canadian Studies* 36(4): 568–95.

Agranoff, Robert. 2007. *Managing within Networks: Adding Value to Public Organizations*. Washington, DC: Georgetown University Press

Alberta. 2010. *Enhancing Assurance: Report and Recommendations of the Regulatory Enhancement Task Force to the Ministry of Energy*. Edmonton: Alberta Ministry of Energy.

– 2011. *Enhancing Assurance: Developing an Integrated Energy Resource Regulator: A Discussion Document*. Edmonton: Alberta Ministry of Energy.

Alemanno, Alberto. 2012. "Nudging Smokers: The Behavioural Turn of Tobacco Risk Regulation." *European Journal of Risk Regulation*, Special Issue on Nudge, 7(3): 22–33.

Alieweiwi, Jehad, and Rachel Laforest. 2009. "Citizenship, Immigration and the Conservative Agenda," in *The New Federal Policy Agenda and the Voluntary Sector: On the Cutting Edge*, edited by Rachel Laforest, 137–53. Montreal and Kingston: McGill-Queen's University Press.

Anderson, M., and R.U. Sprenger (eds.). 2000. *Market-Based Instruments for Environmental Management*. Cheltenham: Edward Elgar.

Anderson, Robert D. 1980. "The Federal Regulation-Making Process and Regulatory Reform, 1969–1979," in *Government Regulation: Scope, Growth, Process*, edited by W.T. Stanbury, 66–78. Montreal: Institute for Research on Public Policy.

Applebaum, Bunyamin, and Eric Dash. 2011. "S&P Downgrades Debt Rating of U.S. for the First Time." *New York Times*, 5 Aug. 1.

Armstrong, Christopher, and H.V. Nelles. 1986. *Monopoly's Moment: The Organization and Regulation of Canadian Utilities 1830–1930.* Philadelphia: Temple University Press.

Aronson, J.D., and P.F. Cowhey. 1988. *When Countries Talk: The International Trade in Communications Services.* Cambridge, MA: Ballinger.

Ascah, Bob. 1999. *Politics and Public Debt: The Dominion, the Banks, and Alberta's Social Credit.* Edmonton: University of Alberta Press.

Assisted Human Reproduction Agency of Canada (AHRC). 2011. *2011–12 Estimates*, Part III, *Report on Plans and Priorities.* Ottawa: Public Works and Government Services Canada.

Atkinson, Michael M. 2011. "Lindblom's Lament: Incrementalism and the Consistent Pull of the Status Quo." *Policy and Society* 30(1): 9–18.

Aucoin, Peter. 1997. *The New Public Management: Canada in Comparative Perspective.* Montreal and Kingston: McGill-Queen's University Press.

– 2008. "New Public Management and New Public Governance: Finding the Balance," in *Professionalism and Public Service: Essays in Honour of Kenneth Kernaghan*, edited by David Siegel and Ken Rasmussen, 16–33. Toronto: University of Toronto Press.

Aucoin, Peter, Mark D. Jarvis, and Lori Turnbull. 2011. *Democratizing the Constitution: Reforming Responsible Government.* Toronto: Edmond Montgomery.

Ayres, Ian, and John Braithwaite. 1992. *Responsive Regulation: Transcending the Deregulation Debate.* Oxford: Oxford University Press.

Bache, Ian, and Matthew Flinders (eds.). 2004. *Multi-level Governance.* Oxford: Oxford University Press.

Baker, Andrew. 2013. "The Gradual Transformation? The Incremental Dynamics of Macroprudential Regulation." *Regulation and Governance* 7(3): 22–34.

Bakvis, Herman, and Mark D. Jarvis (eds.). 2012. *From New Public Management to New Political Governance.* Montreal and Kingston: McGill-Queen's University Press.

Baldwin, Robert. 2008. "Regulation Lite." *Regulation and Governance* 2: 193–215.

Baldwin, Robert, Colin Scott, and Christopher Hood (eds.). 1998. *A Reader on Regulation.* Oxford: Oxford University Press.

Bank of Canada. 2011. *Regulation of the Canadian Financial System.* Ottawa: Author.

Barron, Christie. 2011. *Governing Girls: Rehabilitation and the Age of Risk*. Halifax: Fernwood.

Bell, S., and Andrew Hindmoor. 2009. *Rethinking Governance: The Centrality of the State in Modern Society*. Cambridge: Cambridge University Press.

Benkler, Yochai. 2006. *The Wealth of Networks*. New Haven: Yale University Press.

Bennear, Lori S. 2007. "Are Management-Based Regulations Effective?" *Journal of Policy Analysis and Management* 26: 327–48.

Bennett, Colin J. 1999. "Where the Regulated Are the Regulators: Privacy Protection within the Contemporary Canadian State," in *Changing the Rules: Canadian Regulatory Regimes and Institutions*, edited by G. Bruce Doern, Margaret M. Hill, Michael J. Prince, and Richard J. Schultz, 293–316. Toronto: University of Toronto Press.

Bennett, Colin J., and Charles D. Raab. 2003. *The Governance of Privacy: Policy Instruments in Global Perspective*. Aldershot: Ashgate.

Bernstein, Marver. 1955. *Regulating Business by Independent Commission*. Princeton: Princeton University Press.

Berthiaume, Lee. 2013. "Anger Erupts over Harper's 'Enemy' List as Dismissed Minister Peter Kent Draws Watergate Comparison." *Postmedia News*, 17 July.

Bessen, James, and Michael A. Meurer. 2008. *Patent Failure*. Princeton: Princeton University Press.

Bickerton, James, and Alain-G. Gagnon. 2009. *Canadian Politics*. (5th ed.). Toronto: University of Toronto Press.

Bird, Malcolm, and Christopher Stoney. 2006. "Government Approaches to the Regulation of 'Sin,'" in *How Ottawa Spends 2006–2007: In from the Cold – The Tory Rise and the Liberal Demise*, edited by G. Bruce Doern, 247–65. Montreal and Kingston: McGill-Queen's University Press.

Bird, Roger (ed.). 1988. *Documents of Canadian Broadcasting*. Ottawa: Carleton University Press.

Bishop, Grant. 2013. "After Lac-Megantic, How Should We Regulate Risk?" *Globe and Mail*, 16 July.

Blackwell, Tom. 2012. "The Fertility Industry Is Left Unregulated." *National Post*, 31 March, A8.

Blais, Andre. 1986. *Industrial Policy*. Toronto: University of Toronto Press.

Blidook, Kelly. 2012. *Constituency Influence in Parliament: Countering the Centre*. Vancouver: UBC Press.

Bloemraad, Irene. 2006. *Becoming a Citizen: Incorporating Immigrants and Refugees in the United States and Canada*. Berkeley: University of California Press.

Borins, Sandford, and David Brown. 2008. "E-consultation: Technology at the Interface between Civil Society and Government," in *Professionalism and Public Service: Essays in Honour of Kenneth Kernaghan*, edited by David Siegel and Ken Rasmussen, 178–206. Toronto: University of Toronto Press.

Bouckaert, Geert, Guy Peters, and Koen Verhoest. 2010. *Shifting Patterns of Public Management*. London: Palgrave.

Boyer, Robert. 2001. "The Origins of Regulation Theory," in *Regulation Theory: The State of the Art*, edited by Robert Boyer and Yves Saillard, 78–91. London: Taylor and Francis.

Boyle, James. 2008. *The Public Domain: Enclosing the Commons of the Mind*. New Haven: Yale University Press.

Bradford, Neil, and Caroline Andrew. 2011. "The Harper Immigration Agenda: Policy and Politics in Historical Context," in *How Ottawa Spends 2011–2012: Trimming Fat or Slicing Pork?* edited by Christopher Stoney and G. Bruce Doern, 262–79. Montreal and Kingston: McGill-Queen's University Press.

Braithwaite, John. 2000. "The New Regulatory State and the Transformation of Criminology." *British Journal of Criminology* 40(2): 222–38.

– 2005. *Neoliberalism or Regulatory Capitalism*. Canberra: Regulatory Institutions Network, Australian National University.

– 2008. *Regulatory Capitalism*. Cheltenham: Edward Elgar.

Braithwaite, John, and Peter Drahos. 2000. *Global Business Regulation*. Cambridge: Cambridge University Press.

Bratt, Duane. 2008. *Prairie Atoms: The Opportunities and Challenges of Nuclear Power in Alberta and Saskatchewan*. Calgary: Canada West Foundation.

Bregha, Francois. 2011. "How to Get Serious about the Strategic Environmental Assessment of Policies and Plans," in *How Ottawa Spends 2011–2012: Trimming Fat or Slicing Pork?* edited by Christopher Stoney and G. Bruce Doern, 144–62. Montreal and Kingston: McGill-Queen's University Press.

Brennan, Richard J. 2012. "Federal Public Sector Integrity Commissioner Finally Finds Wrongdoing." *Toronto Star*, 9 March, 12.

Bronskill, Jim. 2013. "Canada's Access to Information Law Is still Full of Holes after 30 Years." *Toronto Star*, 1 July, 3.

Brooks, Stephen. 1994. "How Ottawa Bends: Plastic Words and the Politics of Morality," in *How Ottawa Spends 1994–1995: Making Change*, edited by Susan D. Phillips, 71–90. Ottawa: Carleton University Press.

Brown-John, C. Lloyd. 1981. *Canadian Regulatory Agencies*. Toronto: Butterworths.

Brownsey, Keith. 2005. "Alberta's Oil and Gas Industry in the Era of the Kyoto Protocol," in *Canadian Energy Policy and the Struggle for Sustainable Development*, edited by G. Bruce Doern, 200–22. Toronto: University of Toronto Press.

– 2006. "The Alberta Oilpatch: Multilevel Regulation Transformed," in *Rules, Rules, Rules, Rules: Multilevel Regulatory Governance*, edited by G. Bruce Doern and Robert Johnson, 283–304. Toronto: University of Toronto Press.

Brunnermeier, Markus, Charles Goodhart, Martin Hellwig, A.D. Persaud, and Hyun Shin. 2009. *The Fundamental Principles of Financial Regulation*. Geneva: International Center for Monetary and Banking Studies.

Bryden, Joan, and Steve Rennie. 2013. "Political Party Riding Associations Spend Millions with Little Accountability." *Toronto Star*, 18 July, 5.

Burchell, Gordon, Colin Gordon, and Peter Miller (eds.). 1991. *The Foucault Effect: Studies in Governmentality*. London: Harvester Wheatsheaf.

Burgess, Michael. 2000. *Federalism and European Union: The Building of Europe, 1950– 2000*. London: Routledge.

Buthe, Tim (ed.). 2011. "Private Regulation in the Global Economy." *Business and Politics* 12: 38–52.

Buthe, Tim, and Walter Mattli. 2013. *The New Global Rulers: The Privatization of Regulation in the World Economy*. Princeton: Princeton University Press.

Cairncross, F. 1997. *The Death of Distance: How the Communications Revolution Will Change Our Lives*. Cambridge, MA: Harvard Business School.

Cairns, Alan, and Cynthia Williams. 1985. "Constitutionalism, Citizenship and Society in Canada," in *Constitutionalism, Citizenship and Society in Canada*, edited by Alan Cairns and Cynthia Williams, 1–50. Toronto: University of Toronto Press.

Calmes, Christian. 2004. *Regulatory Changes and Financial Structure: The Case of Canada*. Bank of Canada Working Paper 2004–26. Ottawa: Bank of Canada.

Canada. 1964. *Report of the Royal Commission on Banking and Finance*. Ottawa: Queen's Printer.

- 1985a. *Report of the Royal Commission on the Economic Union and Development Prospects for Canada*, vol. 1. Ottawa: Minister of Supply and Services Canada.
- 1985b. *Freedom to Move: A Framework for Transportation Reform.* Ottawa: Minister of Transport.
- 1999. *Speech From The Throne.* Ottawa: Parliament of Canada, 12 Oct.
- 2002. *Achieving Excellence.* Ottawa: Public Works and Government Services Canada.
- 2003. *Options for Amending the Competition Act: Fostering a Competitive Marketplace.* Ottawa: Government of Canada.
- 2006. *Canada's Access to Medicines Regime: Consultation Paper.* Ottawa: Health Canada.
- 2007. *Cabinet Directive on Streamlining Regulation* (CDSR). Ottawa: Government of Canada.
- 2008. *Compete to Win.* Report of the Competition Policy Review Panel. Ottawa: Industry Canada.
- 2009. *Final Report of the Independent Investigator into the 2008 Listerosis Outbreak.* Ottawa: Government of Canada. (The Weatherill Report).
- 2011a. *Cutting Red Tape and Freeing Business to Grow.* Red Tape Reduction Commission. Consultation Discussion Paper. Ottawa: Treasury Board of Canada Secretariat.
- 2011b. *Budget Speech 2011.* Ottawa: Government of Canada, 22 March.
Canada Revenue Agency (CRA). 2011. *2011–12 Estimates*, Part III, *Report on Plans and Priorities.* Ottawa: Public Works and Government Services Canada.
Canadian Environmental Assessment Agency. 2010. *Annual Report 2009–2010.* Ottawa: Author.
Canadian Federation of Independent Business (CFIB). 2010. *Prosperity Restricted by Red Tape.* http://www.cfib–fcei.ca/cfib–documents/rr3104.pdf
Canadian Intellectual Property Office (CIPO). 2007. *Strategic Plan 2007–2012.* Ottawa: Author.
- 2011a. *Business Plan 2011–2012.* Ottawa: Author.
- 2011b. *Legislation.* Ottawa: Author.
- 2011c. *Consultations and Discussions.* Ottawa: Author.
Canadian International Council. 2011. *Rights and Rents: Why Canada Must Harness Its Intellectual Property Resources.* Ottawa: Author.
Canadian Radio and Television Commission (CRTC). 1970. "Press Release on Canadian Content Proposals for Television and AM Radio ..." 12 Feb. Ottawa: Author.

– 1971. "Canadian Broadcasting 'a Single System'– Policy Statement on Cable Television," 16 July. Ottawa: Author.

Canadian Radio-television and Telecommunications Commission (CRTC). 1976. "Telecommunications Regulation – Procedures and Practices." Ottawa: Ottawa: Author, 20 July.

– 1978. "Report on Pay Television." Ottawa: Author.

– 1979. *CNCP Telecommunications, Interconnection with Bell Canada.* Telecom Regulatory Policy CRTC Decision 79-11. Ottawa: Author.

– 1983. "Decision 82-240 on Pay Television," 18 March. Ottawa: Author

– 1985. *Interexchange Competition and Related Issues.* Telecom Regulatory Policy CRTC Decision 85–19. Ottawa: Author.

– 1992. *Competition in the Provision of Public Long Distance Voice Telephone Services and Related Resale and Sharing Issues.* Telecom Regulatory Policy CRTC Decision 92–12. Ottawa: Author.

– 1993. "Structural Public Hearing Public Notice." CRTC 1993-94. Ottawa: Author.

– 1994a. "Call for Comments – Proposed Exemption Order Respecting Direct-to-Home Satellite Undertakings." Public Notice 1994-19. Ottawa: Author.

– 1994b. *Review of Regulatory Framework.* Telecom Regulatory Policy CRTC Decision 1994-19. Ottawa: Author.

– 1997. *From Vision to Results at the CRTC.* Ottawa: Author.

– 2005. "Regulatory Framework for Voice Communications Services Using Internet Protocol." Telecom Regulatory Policy CRTC Decision 2005-28. Ottawa: Author, 12 May.

– 2011a. "Usage-Based Billing for Gateway Access and Third Party Internet Access Services." Telecom Regulatory Policy CRTC Decision 2011-44. Ottawa: Author, 25 Jan.

– 2011b. "Billing Practices for Wholesale Residential High-Speed Access Services." Telecom Regulatory Policy CRTC Decision 2011-703." Ottawa: Author, 15 Nov.

Canadian Transportation Agency (CTA). 2011. *Annual Report 2010–2011.* Ottawa: Author.

– 2012. *Role and Structure.* Ottawa: Author. http:www.cta-otc.gc.ca/eng/process

Caplan, Gerald L., and Florian Sauvageau. 1986. *Report of the Task Force on Broadcasting Policy.* Ottawa: Minister of Supply and Services Canada.

Carmel, Jonathan (ed.). 2009. "Financial Market Regulatory Reform," Special Issue, *Economist's Voice* 6(2): 8–11.

Carolan, Michael. 2010. "The Mutability of Biotechnology Patents: From Unwieldy Products of Nature to Independent 'Objects.'" *Theory, Culture and Society* 27: 110–29.

Carpenter, Daniel. 2010. *Reputation and Power: Organizational Image and Pharmaceutical Regulation at the FDA*. Princeton: Princeton University Press.

Carty, Kenneth, and Lisa Young. 2012. "The Lortie Commission and the Place of Political Parties as Agents of Responsible Government," in *From New Public Management to New Political Governance*, edited by Herman Bakvis and Mark D. Jarvis, 105–27. Montreal and Kingston: McGill-Queen's University Press.

Castells, M. 1996. *The Information Age: Economy, Society and Culture*, vol. 1, *The Rise of Network Society*. London: Blackwell.

Castle, David (ed.). 2009. *The Role of Intellectual Property Rights in Biotechnology Innovation*. Cheltenham: Edward Elgar.

Caulfield, Timothy. 2003. "Human Cloning Laws, Human Dignity, and the Poverty of Policy Making Dialogue." *BMC Medical Ethics* 4(3): 1–7.

– 2009. "Biotechnology Patents, Public Trust and Patent Pools: The Need for Governance," in *The Role of Intellectual Property Rights in Biotechnology Innovation*, edited by David Castle, 357–68. Cheltenham: Edward Elgar.

Centre for Digital Democracy. 2012. *Protecting Privacy, Promoting Consumer Rights and Ensuring Corporate Accountability*. Washington, DC: Author.

Centre for Law and Democracy. 2011. *Rating of Legal Framework for Right to Information in 89 Countries*. Halifax: Author.

Chase, Steven. 2012. "Tories Say Professional Agitators behind Robo-calls Legal Fight." *Globe and Mail*, 24 May, 11.

Cheadle, Bruce. 2012. "Robo-calls Scandal Lays Bare Privacy Concerns around Voter Databases." *Globe and Mail*, 24 May, 12.

Chief Electoral Officer of Canada. 2011. *Report of the Chief Electoral Officer of Canada On the 41st General Election of May 2, 2011*. Ottawa: Author.

Chunn, Dorothy E., and Shelley A.M. Gavigan. 2004. "Welfare Law, Welfare Fraud, and the Moral Regulation of the 'Never Deserving' Poor." *Social and Legal Studies* 13(2): 219–43.

Citizenship and Immigration Canada. 2011. *2011–12 Estimates*, Part III, *Report on Plans and Priorities*. Ottawa: Public Works and Government Services Canada.

– 2012. "Protecting Vulnerable Foreign Workers from the Risk of Abuse and Exploitation in Sex Trade Related Businesses." *Canada Gazette* 146(28), 14 July.

Clancy, Peter. 2011. *Offshore Petroleum Politics: Regulation and Risk in the Scotian Basin*. Vancouver: UBC Press.

Clarke, John. 2007. "Subordinating the Social? Neo-liberalism and the Remaking of Welfare Capitalism." *Culture Studies* 21(6): 974–87.

Clarkson, Stephen. 2009. "The Governance of Energy in North America: The United States and Its Continental Periphery," in *Governing the Energy Challenge: Canada and Germany in a Multilevel Regional and Global Context*, edited by Burkhard Eberlein and G. Bruce Doern, 99–121. Toronto: University of Toronto Press.

Coglianese, Cary. 2008. "The Rhetoric and Reality of Regulatory Reform." *Yale Journal of Regulation* 25(1): 117–30.

– 2010. "Management-Based Regulation: Implications for Public Policy," in *Risk and Regulatory Policy: Improving the Governance of Risk*, edited by the OECD, 159–84. Paris: OECD.

Coglianese, Cary (ed.). 2012. *Regulatory Breakdown: The Crisis of Confidence in U.S. Regulation*. Philadelphia: University of Pennsylvania Press.

Coleman, William. 1998. *Financial Services, Globalization and Domestic Policy Change*. Toronto: Macmillan.

Coleman, William, and Grace Skogstad. 1990. *Policy Communities and Public Policy in Canada*. Toronto: Copp Clark Pitman.

Commissioner of Competition. 2008. "A Synthesis and Review of Recent Reform Proposals Regarding Canada's Competition Act." Paper prepared for the Competition Policy Review Panel. Ottawa: Competition Bureau.

Competition Bureau. 2007. *Self-regulated Professions: Balancing Competition and Regulation*. Ottawa: Author.

– 2010. *Regulated Conduct*. Ottawa: Author.

– 2011a. *Our Legislation*. Ottawa: Author.

– 2011b. *Closed Consultations: 2000 to 2011*. Ottawa: Author.

– 2011c. *Our Organization*. Ottawa: Author.

– 2011d. *Final Merger Enforcement Guidelines*. Ottawa: Author.

– 2011e. *List of Updated Publications and Guidance Documents*. Ottawa: Author.

Competition Tribunal. 2011. *The Competition Tribunal*. Ottawa: Author.

Conference Board of Canada. 2002. *Including Innovation in Regulatory Frameworks*. Ottawa: Author.

– 2006. *Death by a Thousand Paper Cuts: The Effect of Barriers to Competition on Canadian Productivity*. Ottawa: Author.

– 2008. *Making Canada More Competitive: Improving Major Project Regulation in Canada*. Ottawa: Author.

– 2010a. *Conflicting Forces for Canadian Prosperity: Examining the Interplay between Regulation and Innovation*. Ottawa: Author.

– 2010b. *Intellectual Property in the 21st Century*. Ottawa: Author.
– 2011. *Governing Food: Policies, Laws, and Regulations for Food in Canada*. Ottawa: Author.
Conklin, David (ed.). 2001. *Canadian Competition Policy: Preparing for the Future*. Toronto: Pearson Education.
Cooney, R., and B. Dickson. 2005. *Biodiversity and the Precautionary Principle*. London: Routledge.
Corbett, David. 1965. *Politics and the Airlines*. Toronto: University of Toronto Press.
Corrigan, Philip. 2006. "On Moral Regulation: Some Preliminary Remarks," in *Moral Regulation and Governance in Canada: History, Context, and Critical Issues*, edited by Amanda Glasbeek, 57–73. Toronto: Canadian Scholars' Press.
Cowhey, P.F. 1990. "The International Telecommunications Regime: The Political Roots of Regimes for High Technology." *International Organization* 44(2): 55–68.
Coyne, Andrew. 2012. "Same Old Bill, New Hysteria." *National Post*, 20 Feb., 1.
Craft, Jonathan. 2013. "The Promise and Paradox of Open Government in the Harper Era," in *How Ottawa Spends 2013–2014*, edited by Christopher Stoney and G. Bruce Doern, chapter 7. Montreal and Toronto: McGill-Queen's University Press.
Crane, David A. 2008. "Report on Best Competition Advocacy Practices." Paper prepared for the Competition Policy Review Panel. Ottawa: Competition Bureau.
Crawford, Adam. 2006. "Networked Governance and the Post-regulatory State? Steering, Rowing and Anchoring the Provision of Policing and Security." *Theoretical Criminology* 10(4): 449–79.
Crews, Jr, C.W. 1998. "Promise and Peril: Implementing a Regulatory Budget." *Policy Sciences* 31: 343–69.
Currie, A.W. 1960. "The Board of Transport Commissioners as an Administrative Body," in *Canadian Public Administration*, edited by J.E. Hodgetts and D.C. Corbett, 220–34. Toronto: Macmillan.
Curry, Bill. 2012. "Watchdogs of Parliament Forge Closer Ties." *Globe and Mail*, 12 May.
Dalfen, C. 1989. "Competition and Interconnection in the Canadian Telecommunications Industry," in *Kommunikation ohne Monopole*, edited by E.-J. Mestmacker, 121–34. Baden-Baden: Nomos.
– 2006. "Regulation Is as Much an Art as a Science." *Globe and Mail*, 26 April, A19.

Daniel, Fred, Charles Freedman, and Clyde Goodlet. 1992. "Restructuring the Canadian Financial Industry." *Bank of Canada Review* (Winter): 21–45.

D'Aquino, Thomas, G. Bruce Doern, and Cassandra Blair. 1985. *Parliamentary Democracy in Canada: Issues for Reform.* Toronto: Methuen.

Darling, Howard. 1980. *The Politics of Freight Rates: The Railway Freight Rate Issue in Canada.* Toronto: McClelland and Stewart.

Dauda, Carol L. 2010. "Sex, Gender, and Generation: Age of Consent and Moral Regulation in Canada." *Politics and Policy* 38(6): 1159–85.

Davidson, Roger, and Gayle Davis. 2012. *The Sexual State: Sexuality and Scottish Governance, 1950–80.* Edinburgh: Edinburgh University Press.

Davies, Howard. 2010. *The Financial Crisis: Who Is to Blame?* London: Polity Press.

Dean, Mitchell. 1994. "'A Social Structure of Many Souls': Moral Regulation, Government, and Self-Formation." *Canadian Journal of Sociology* 19(3): 145–68.

de Beer, Jeremy, Richard Gold, and Mauricio Guaranga. 2011. *Intellectual Property Management: Issues and Options.* Ottawa: Genome Canada.

Delacourt, Susan. 2013. "Conservatives Won't Say Who Is on 'Enemy List.'" *Toronto Star,* 16 July.

DeLong, Bradford. 2011. "Economics in Crisis." *Economist's Voice* 8(2): 14–18.

Department of Finance. 2010a. *Canada's Economic Action Plan: Fourth Report to Canadians – Improving Access to Financing and Strengthening Canada's Financial System.* Ottawa: Author.

– 2010b. *Minister of Finance Announces Review of Financial Institutions Legislation.* Ottawa: Author, 20 Sept.

Dewees, Donald (ed.). 1983. *The Regulation of Quality.* Toronto: Butterworths.

Dobrowolsky, A., and Jane Jensen. 1993. "Reforming the Parties: Prescriptions for Democracy," in *How Ottawa Spends 1993–1994: A More Democratic Canada,* edited by Susan Phillips, 72–87. Ottawa: Carleton University Press.

Docherty, David C. 2005. *Legislatures.* Vancouver: UBC Press.

Dodge, David. 2011. "Public Policy for the Canadian Financial System: From Porter to the Present and Beyond," in *New Directions for Intelligent Government in Canada: Papers in Honour of Ian Stewart,* edited by Andrew Sharpe. Ottawa: Centre for the Study of Living Standards.

Doern, G. Bruce. 1977. "Government Secrecy in Canada," in *Government Secrecy in Democracies,* edited by Itzhak Galnoor, 143–56. New York: Harper Colophon Books.

- 1978. *The Regulatory Process in Canada*. Toronto: Macmillan.
- 1988. "Consumer and Corporate Affairs: The Dilemmas of Influencing without Spending," in *How Ottawa Spends 1988–1989*, edited by Katherine Graham, 233–68. Ottawa: Carleton University Press.
- 1995a. *The Regulation of Patent and Trade-Mark Agent Qualifications: Institutional Issues and Options*. Ottawa: Canadian Intellectual Property Office.
- 1995b. *Fairer Play: Canadian Competition Policy Institutions in a Global Market*. Toronto: C.D. Howe Institute.
- 1996a. "Canadian Competition Policy Institutions and Decision Processes," *Comparative Competition Policy*, edited by G. Bruce Doern and Stephen Wilks, 68–101. Oxford: Clarendon Press.
- 1996b. "Looking for the Core: Industry Canada and Program Review," in *How Ottawa Spends 1996–1997: Life under the Knife*, edited by Gene Swimmer, 73–98. Ottawa: Carleton University Press.
- 1997. "Regulating on the Run: The Transformation of the CRTC as a Regulatory Institution." *Canadian Public Administration* 40(3): 516–38.
- 1998a. "The Interplay among Regimes: Mapping Regulatory Institutions in Britain and North America," in *Changing Regulatory Institutions in Britain and North America*, edited by G. Bruce Doern and Stephen Wilks, 29–50. Toronto: University of Toronto Press.
- 1998b. "The Canadian Radio-television and Telecommunications Commission: Transformation in the 1990s," in *Changing Regulatory Institutions in Britain and North America*, edited by G. Bruce Doern and Stephen Wilks, 354–75. Toronto: University of Toronto Press.
- 1999a. "Moved Out and Moving On: The National Energy Board as a Reinvented Regulatory Agency," in *Changing the Rules: Canada's Changing Regulatory Regimes and Institutions*, edited by G. Bruce Doern, Margaret M. Hill, Michael J. Prince, and Richard J. Schultz, 82–98. Toronto: University of Toronto Press.
- 1999b. *Global Change and Intellectual Property Agencies*. London: Pinter.
- 2003. "Improving Regulatory Relations in Multi-level Governance: Principles and Mechanisms." Paper prepared for an OECD workshop on Multi-level Regulation, Paris, 1 July.
- 2004a. "Federal Competition Policy, Competitiveness, and the Canadian Pulp and Paper Industry." Paper prepared for Natural Resources Canada and Industry Canada, Ottawa, Feb.
- 2004b. "The Agri-Food Sector and Federal Policies and Priorities: A Public Policy Framework Discussion Framework." Paper prepared for Agriculture and Agri-Food Canada, Ottawa.

- 2004c. "'Smart Regulation,' Regulatory Congestion, and Natural Resources Regulatory Governance," in *How Ottawa Spends 2004–2005: Mandate Change in the Paul Martin Era*, edited by G. Bruce Doern, 245–76. Montreal and Kingston: McGill-Queen's University Press.
- 2005. "The Governance of Effective Regulatory Cooperation: A Framework, Case Studies and 'Best Practice.'" Paper prepared for the Policy Research Initiative, Privy Council Office, Ottawa.
- 2006. "The Adequacy of Consumer Input in Federal Policy Processes." Paper prepared for the Office of Consumer Affairs, Industry Canada, Ottawa.
- 2007. *Red-Tape, Red-Flags: Regulation for the Innovation Age*. Ottawa: Conference Board of Canada.
- 2009. "An Idea Whose Time Has Come: A Regulatory Budget and Strategic Regulatory Agenda." *Regulatory Strategy, Horizons* 10(3): 22–30.
  2010a. "The Governance and Reform of Food Safety Systems: Canada in a Comparative Context." Paper prepared for Agriculture and Agri-Food Canada, Ottawa.
- 2010b. "The Relationships between Regulation and Innovation in the Transport Canada Context." Paper prepared for Transport Canada, Ottawa.
- 2011a. "Strengthening the Governance Oversight of Regulation and Red Tape Reduction: Improving Transparency, Predictability and Accountability." Paper prepared for the Red Tape Reduction Commission, Government of Canada, Ottawa, Sept.
- 2011b. "Regulatory Budgets and Agendas: So Close but Yet so Far as a Macro Regulatory Reform Idea." Presentation to International Regulatory Reform Conference, Amsterdam, 11–12 March.
Doern, G. Bruce, and Tom Conway. 1995. *The Greening of Canada*. Toronto: University of Toronto Press.
Doern, G. Bruce, Arslan Dorman, and Robert Morrison (eds.). 2001. *Canadian Nuclear Energy Policy: Changing Ideas, Interests, and Institutions*. Toronto: University of Toronto Press, 2001.
Doern, G. Bruce, and Monica Gattinger. 2003. *Power Switch: Energy Regulatory Governance in the 21st Century*. Toronto: University of Toronto Press.
Doern, G. Bruce, Margaret M. Hill, Michael J. Prince, and Richard J. Schultz (eds.). 1999. *Changing the Rules: Canada's Changing Regulatory Regimes and Institutions*. Toronto: University of Toronto Press.

Doern, G. Bruce, and Robert Johnson (eds.). 2006. *Rules, Rules, Rules, Rules: Multilevel Regulatory Governance*. Toronto: University of Toronto Press.

Doern, G. Bruce, and Kenneth Kernaghan. 2012. "New Public Management and New Public Governance: Reflections on the Aucoin Legacy," in *From New Public Management to New Political Governance*, edited by Herman Bakvis and Mark D. Jarvis, 380–90. Montreal and Kingston: McGill-Queen's University Press.

Doern, G. Bruce, and Jeffrey S. Kinder. 2007. *Strategic Science in the Public Interest: Canada's Government Laboratories and Science-Based Agencies*. Toronto: University of Toronto Press.

Doern, G. Bruce, and Mark MacDonald. 1999. *Free Trade Federalism: Negotiating the Canadian Agreement on Internal Trade*. Toronto: University of Toronto Press.

Doern, G. Bruce, and Robert Morrison. 2009. "Canada's Nuclear Crossroads: Steps to a Viable Nuclear Energy Industry." *C.D. Howe Institute Commentary 290*. Toronto: C.D. Howe Institute.

Doern, G. Bruce, Leslie A. Pal, and Brian W. Tomlin (eds.). 1996. *Border Crossings: The Internationalization of Canadian Public Policy*. Toronto: Oxford University Press.

Doern, G. Bruce, and Richard Phidd. 1983. *Canadian Public Policy: Ideas, Structure, Process*. Toronto: Methuen.

– 1992. *Canadian Public Policy: Ideas, Structure, Process*. (2nd ed.). Toronto: Nelson.

Doern, G. Bruce, and Michael J. Prince. 2012. *Three Bio-Realms: Biotechnology and the Governance of Food, Health, and Life in Canada*. Toronto: University of Toronto Press.

Doern, G. Bruce, and Ted Reed (eds.). 2000. *Risky Business: Canada's Changing Science-Based Policy and Regulatory Regime*. Toronto: University of Toronto Press.

Doern, G. Bruce, and Markus Sharaput. 2000. *Canadian Intellectual Property: The Politics of Innovating Institutions and Interests*. Toronto: University of Toronto Press.

Doern, G. Bruce, and Chris Stoney (eds.). 2009. *Research and Innovation Policy: Changing Federal Government–University Relations*. Toronto: University of Toronto Press.

– 2012. *How Ottawa Spends 2012–2013: The Harper Majority, Budget Cuts, and the New Opposition*. Montreal and Kingston: McGill-Queen's University Press.

Doern, G. Bruce, and Brian Tomlin. 1991. *Faith and Fear: The Free Trade Story*. Toronto: Stoddart.

Doern, G. Bruce, and Glen Toner. 1985. *The Politics of Energy.* Toronto: Methuen.

Doern, G. Bruce, and Stephen Wilks (eds.). 1996a. *National Competition Policy Institutions in a Global Market.* Oxford: Clarendon Press.

– 1996b. *Comparative Competition Policy.* Oxford: Clarendon Press.

– 1998. *Changing Regulatory Institutions in Britain and North America.* Toronto: University of Toronto Press.

D'Ombrain, Nicholas. 2004. "Cabinet Secrecy." *Canadian Public Administration* 47(3): 332–59.

Drahos, P., and R. Mayne. 2002. *Global Intellectual Property Rights: Knowledge, Access and Development.* London: Palgrave.

Dryzek, John, and Patrick Dunleavy. 2009. *Theories of the Democratic State.* London: Palgrave.

Duhamel, Marc. 2003. "On the Social Welfare Objectives of Canada's Antitrust Statute." *Canadian Public Policy* 29(3): 301–18.

Dupre, S. 1987. "The Workability of Executive Federalism in Canada," in *Federalism and the Role of the State,* edited by Herman Bakvis and William Chandler, 122–37. Toronto: University of Toronto Press.

Dutfield, Graham. 2003. *Intellectual Property and the Life Science Industries.* Aldershot: Ashgate.

Eberlein, Burkard, and G. Bruce Doern (eds.). 2009. *Governing the Energy Challenge.* Toronto: University of Toronto Press.

Eberlein, Burkhard, and Edgar Grande. 2005. "Reconstituting Political Authority in Europe," in *Complex Sovereignty,* edited by Edgar Grande and Louis Pauly, 146–67. Toronto: University of Toronto Press.

Economic Council of Canada. 1979. *Responsible Regulation.* Ottawa: Author.

– 1981. *Reforming Regulation.* Ottawa: Author.

Economist. 2010. "Sovereign Debt Wiggle Room: The IMF Offers Indebted Governments Some Reassurance." 4 Sept., 84.

– 2013. "Look Who's Listening." 15 June, 24–6.

Eatwell, John, and Murray Milgate. 2011. *The Fall and Rise of Keynesian Economics.* Oxford: Oxford University Press.

Eisner, M.A. 1993. *Regulatory Politics in Transition.* Baltimore: Johns Hopkins University Press.

Eliadis, P., Margaret Hill, and Michael Howlett (eds.). 2005. *Designing Government: From Instruments to Governance.* Montreal and Kingston: McGill-Queen's University Press.

Elections Canada. 2012. *About Us.* Ottawa: Author.

Ellis, D. 1992. *Split Screen: Home Entertainment and the New Technologies.* Toronto: Friends of Canadian Broadcasting.

Elson, Peter R. 2011. *High Ideals and Noble Intentions: Voluntary Sector–Government Relations in Canada*. Toronto: University of Toronto Press.

Environment Canada and National Energy Board. 2012. "Letter Amending Joint Review Panel Agreement on Northern Gateway Pipeline Project." Ottawa: Author, 3 Aug.

Ernst, John. 1994. *Whose Utility? The Social Impact of Public Utility Privatization and Regulation*. London: Open University Press.

Etzioni, Amitai . 2012a. "Legislation in the Public Interest: Regulatory Capture and Campaign Reform." *Agenda for Social Justice: Solutions 2012*: 11–19.

– 2012b. "The Privacy Merchants: What Is to Be Done?" *University of Pennsylvania Journal of Constitutional Law* 14(4): 929–51.

Evans, Barbara. 2009. "Seven Pillars of a New Evidentiary Paradigm: The Food, Drug and Cosmetic Act Enters the Genomic Era." *Notre Dame Law Review* 85: 22–36.

External Advisory Committee on Smart Regulation. 2004. *Smart Regulation: A Regulatory Strategy for Canada*. Ottawa: Author.

Flaherty, David H. 1989. *Protecting Privacy in Surveillance Societies*. Chapel Hill: University of North Carolina Press.

Fletcher, Fred, and Andre Blais. 2012. "New Media, Old Media, Campaigns, and Canadian Democracy," in *From New Public Management to New Political Governance*, edited by Herman Bakvis and Mark D. Jarvis, 151–78. Montreal and Kingston: McGill-Queen's University Press.

Flinders, Matthew. 2001. *The Politics of Accountability in the Modern State*. Aldershot: Ashgate.

– 2008. *Delegated Governance and the British State: Walking without Order*. Oxford: Oxford University Press.

– 2012. *Defending Politics: Why Democracy Matters in the Twenty-First Century*. Oxford: Oxford University Press.

Forbes, J.D., R.D. Hughes, and T.K. Varley. 1982. *Economic Intervention and Regulation in Canadian Agriculture*. Ottawa: Economic Council of Canada.

Forest Products Association of Canada (FPAC). 2003a. "Promoting Efficiency and Adaptability in Canada's Open Economy." Submission to the Public Policy Forum in response to the Discussion Paper, *Options for Amending the Competition Act: Fostering a Competitive Marketplace*. Ottawa: Author, Sept.

– 2003b. " Efficiencies in a Canadian Context: Fostering Continual Advancement." Submission to the Senate Standing Committee on Banking, Trade and Commerce, Ottawa: Author, Oct.

- 2003c. "Competition Policy in a Small Open Economy: The Canadian Experience." Ottawa: Author, Oct.
- 2008. "FPAC Submission to Competition Policy Review Panel." Ottawa: Author, Jan.

Fox, Dov. 2008. "The Regulation of Biotechnologies: Four Recommendations." *Perspectives* 38(2): 111–26.

Franks, C.E.S. 1997. *The Parliament of Canada*. Toronto: University of Toronto Press.

Franks, C.E.S., and David E. Smith. 2012. "The Canadian House of Commons under Stress: Reform and Adaptation," in *From New Public Management to New Political Governance*, edited by Herman Bakvis and Mark D. Jarvis, 70–104. Montreal and Kingston: McGill-Queen's University Press.

Fraser, Matthew. 1999. *Free-for-All: The Struggle for Dominance on the Digital Frontier*. Toronto: Stoddart.

French, Richard. 2011. "Second-Guessing the CRTC Comes at a Price." *Globe and Mail*, 2 Feb.

Friesen, Arthur, Alessandro Alasia, and Ray Bollam. 2010. *The Social Economy across the Rural to Urban Gradient: Evidence from Registered Charities*. Ottawa: Statistics Canada.

Gal, Michal S. 2001. "Size Does Matter: The Effects of Market Size on Optimal Competition Policy." *Southern California Law Review* 74: 1450–70.

Galnoor, Itzhak (ed.). 1977. *Government Secrecy in Democracies*. New York: Harper Colophon Books.

Geist, Michael. 2011. "Why Canada's New Copyright Law Remains Flawed." *Toronto Star*, 1 Oct., 5.
- 2013. "Surveillance Laws Can't Handle Modern Snooping Technologies." *Toronto Star*, 14 June, 9.

Gingras, Anne-Marie. 2012. "Access to Information: An Asset for Democracy or Ammunition for Political Conflict, or Both?" *Canadian Public Administration* 55(2): 221–46.

Glanz, James. 2012. "Power, Pollution and the Internet." *New York Times*, 23 Sept. http://www.nytimes.com/2012/09/23/technology/data-centers-waste

Glasbeek, Amanda (ed.). 2006. *Moral Regulation and Governance in Canada: History, Context, and Critical Issues*. Toronto: Canadian Scholars' Press.

Globe and Mail. 1995. 7 June, B1, B14.

Globerman, S.H., H.N. Janisch, and W.T. Stanbury. 1996a. "Convergence, Competition and Canadian Content," in *Perspectives on the New*

Economics and Regulation of Telecommunications, edited by W.T. Stanbury, 55–73. Montreal: Institute for Research on Public Policy.

– 1996b. "Moving toward Local Distribution Network Competition in Canada." *Telecommunications Policy* 20(2): 141–57.

Globerman, S.H., H. Oum Tae, and W.T. Stanbury. 1993. "Competition in Public Long Distance Markets in Canada." *Telecommunications in Canada* 17 (May/June): 297–310.

Goldacre, Ben. 2012. *Bad Pharma: How Drug Companies Mislead Doctors and Harm Patients*. London: Fourth Estate.

Goldberg, Susan, and Chloe Brushwood Rose (eds.). 2009. *And Baby Makes More: Known Donors, Queer Parents and Our Unexpected Families*. London, ON: Insomniac Press.

Goode, William J. 1969. "The Theoretical Limits of Professionalism," in *The Semi-Professions and Their Organization*, edited by Amitai Etzioni, 77–94. New York: Free Press.

Gotell, Lise. 1996. "Policing Desire: Obscenity, Law, Pornography Politics, and Feminism in Canada," in *Women and Canadian Public Policy*, edited by Janine Brodie, 279–317. Toronto: Harcourt Brace.

Grabosky, Peter. 1995. "Using Non-governmental Resources to Foster Regulatory Compliance." *Governance* 8(4): 527–50.

– 2012. "Beyond Responsive Regulation: The Expanding Role of Non-state Actors in the Regulatory Process." *Regulation and Governance* 6(3): 44–56.

Grande, Edgar, and Louis W. Pauley (eds.). 2005. *Complex Sovereignty*. Toronto: University of Toronto Press.

Grant, Peter S., Anthony H.A. Keenleyside, and Michel Racicot. 1993. *Canadian Broadcast and Cable Regulatory Handbook*. Toronto: McCarthy Tetrault.

Guadamuz, Andres. 2011. *Networks, Complexity and Internet Regulation*. Cheltenham: Edward Elgar.

Gilder, G. 2000. *Telecosm: How Infinite Bandwidth Will Revolutionize Our World*. New York: Free Press.

Gwyn, Richard. 2008. *John A.: The Man Who Made Us*. Toronto: Vintage.

– 2011. *Nation Maker Sir John A. MacDonald: His Life, Our Times*. Toronto: Random House.

Haines, Fiona. 2011. *The Paradox of Regulation: What Regulation Can Achieve and What It Cannot*. Cheltenham: Edward Elgar.

Hale, Geoffrey. 2012. "Toward a Perimeter: Incremental Adaptation or a New Paradigm For Canada–U.S. Security and Trade Relations," in *How Ottawa Spends 2012–2013: The Harper Majority, Budget Cuts, and the*

New Opposition, edited by G. Bruce Doern and Christopher Stoney, 106–26. Montreal and Kingston: McGill-Queen's University Press.

Hall, Peter, and M. Soskice. 2001. *The Institutional Foundations of Comparative Advantage*. Oxford: Oxford University Press.

Hall, R. 1990. *The CRTC as Policy Maker: 1968–1992*. Ph.D. dissertation, Graduate Program on Communications, McGill University.

Hallsworth, Simon, and John Lea. 2011. "Reconstructing Leviathan: Emerging Contours of the Security State." *Theoretical Criminology* 15(2): 141–57.

Hancher, Leigh, and Michael Moran. 1986. *Capitalism, Culture and Regulation*. London: Clarendon Press.

Hancock, D. 1992. "Regulated Competition: Resale and Sharing in Telecommunications." *Media and Communications Law Review* 2: 251–96.

Hardin, Herschel. 1985. *Closed Circuits: The Sellout of Canadian Television*. Vancouver: Douglas and McIntyre.

Harris, C. 2012. "Civil Warrior." *Walrus* (Oct.): 24–32.

Harris, R.A., and S.M. Milkis. 1989. *The Politics of Regulatory Change*. New York: Oxford University Press.

Harris, Stephen L. 1995. *The Political Economy of the Liberalization of Entry and Ownership in the Canadian Investment Dealer Industry*. Ph.D. dissertation, Department of Political Science, Carleton University.

– 1999. "The Globalization of Finance and the Regulation of the Canadian Financial Services Industry," in *Changing the Rules: Canadian Regulatory Regimes and Institutions*, edited by G. Bruce Doern, Margaret M. Hill, Michael J. Prince, and Richard J. Schultz, 361–88. Toronto: University of Toronto Press.

– 2010. "The Global Financial Meltdown and Financial Regulation: Shirking and Learning – Canada in an International Context," in *How Ottawa Spends 2010–2011: Recession, Realignment and the New Deficit Era*, edited by G. Bruce Doern and Christopher Stoney, 68–86. Montreal and Kingston: McGill-Queen's University Press.

Harrison, Trevor. 1996. "Class, Citizenship, and Global Migration: The Case of the Canadian Immigration Business Program, 1978–1992." *Canadian Public Policy* 21(1): 7–23.

Harper, Stephen, and Tom Flanagan. 1997. "Our Benign Dictatorship." *Next City* (Winter): 22–8.

Hart, H.L.A. 1963. *Law, Liberty and Morality*. Oxford: Oxford University Press.

Haseler, Stephen. 2010. *Meltdown UK: There Is Another Way*. London: Forumpress.

Health Canada. 2006. *Blueprint for Renewal: Transforming Canada's Approach to Regulating Health Products and Food*. Ottawa: Author.

– 2007a. *Blueprint for Renewal II: Modernizing Canada's Regulatory System for Health Products and Food*. Ottawa: Author.

– 2007b. *Food, Health and Consumer Safety Action Plan*. Ottawa: Author.

Heaver, Trevor D., and James C. Nelson. 1977. *Railway Pricing under Commercial Freedom: The Canadian Experience*. Vancouver: Centre for Transportation Studies, University of British Columbia.

– 1978. "The Roles of Competition and Regulation in Transport Markets: An Examination of Bill C–33," in *Studies on Regulation in Canada*, edited by W.T. Stanbury, 66–79. Toronto: Butterworths for the Institute for Research on Public Policy.

Heaver, Trevor D., and William G. Waters II. 2005. "Transportation Policy in Canada," in *Handbook of Transport Strategy, Policy and Institutions*, edited by K.J. Button and D.A. Hensher, 122–36. Amsterdam: Elsevier.

Held, D., A. McGrew, D. Goldblatt, and J. Perraton. 1999. *Global Transformations: Politics, Economics, and Culture*. London: Polity Press, and Stanford: Stanford University Press.

Hemphill, Thomas. 2003. "The Role of Competition Policy in the US Innovation System." *Science and Public Policy* 30(4): 285–94.

Henderson, J. 1989. *Decade of Denial: The CRTC, the Public Interest and Pay Television*. M.A. thesis, Graduate Communications Program, McGill University.

Henman, Paul. 2011. "Conditional Citizenship? Electronic Networks and the New Conditionality in Public Policy." *Policy and Internet* 3(3): 76–86.

Hermer, Joe, and Janet Mosher (eds.). 2002. *Disorderly People: Law and Politics of Exclusion in Ontario*. Halifax: Fernwood.

Hicks, Bruce M. 2012. "The Westminster Approach to Prorogation, Dissolution and Fixed Election Dates." *Canadian Parliamentary Review* (Summer): 20–7.

Hill, Margaret M. 1988. "Freedom to Move: Explaining the Decision to Deregulate Canadian Air and Rail Transportation." Unpublished research paper, School of Public Administration, Carleton University.

– 1999a. "Recasting the Federal Transport Regulator: The Thirty Years' War," in *Changing the Rules: Canadian Regulatory Regimes and Institutions*, edited by G. Bruce Doern, Margaret M. Hill, Michael J. Prince, and Richard J. Schultz, 57–81. Toronto: University of Toronto Press.

– 1999b. "Managing the Regulatory State: From 'Up' to 'In and Down' to 'Out and Across,'" in *Changing the Rules: Canada's Changing*

Regulatory Regimes and Institutions, edited by G. Bruce Doern, Margaret M. Hill, Michael J. Prince, and Richard J. Schultz, 259–76. Toronto: University of Toronto Press.

Hiltz, Robert. 2011. "Opposition Critics Slam Immigration Fraud Line." *Postmedia News*, 9 Sept.

Hirshman, A. 1970. *Exit, Voice, and Loyalty: Responses to Decline in Firms, Organizations and States*. Cambridge, MA: Harvard University Press.

HM Treasury. 2008. *Budget 2008*. London: Author.

HM Treasury and Department for Business Enterprise and Regulatory Reform. 2008. *Regulatory Budgets: A Consultation Document*. London: Author, Aug.

Hoberg, George (ed.). 2002. *Capacity for Choice: Canada in a New North America*. Toronto: University of Toronto Press.

Hodgetts, J.E. 1973. *The Canadian Public Service: The Physiology of Government 1867–1970*. Toronto: University of Toronto Press.

Hogan, John, Gary Murphy, and Raj Chari. 2008. "Next Door They Have Regulation, but Not Here: Assessing the Opinions of Actors in the Opaque World of Unregulated Lobbying. *Canadian Political Science Review* 2(3): 125–51.

Holman, Craig, and William Luneberg. 2012. "Lobbying and Transparency: A Comparative Analysis of Regulatory Reform." *Interest Groups and Advocacy* 1(1): 75–104.

Hood, Christopher. 2011. *The Blame Game: Spin, Bureaucracy, and Self-Preservation in Government*. Princeton: Princeton University Press.

Hood, Christopher, Henry Rothstein, and Robert Baldwin. 2001. *The Government of Risk: Understanding Risk Regulation Regimes*. Oxford: Oxford University Press.

House of Commons Committee on Election Expenses. 1966. *Report of the Committee on Election Expenses*. (The Barbeau Report). Ottawa: Queen's Printer.

House of Commons Standing Committee on Industry, Science and Technology. 2002. *A Plan to Modernize Canada's Competition Regime*. Ottawa: Author, April.

Hooghe, Liesbet, and Gary Marks. 2003. "Unravelling the Central State, but How?" *American Political Science Review* 97(2): 233–43.

Howlett, Michael. 2004. "Administrative Styles and Regulatory Reform." *International Public Management Journal* 7(3): 110–24.

Howlett, Michael, and M. Ramesh. 2003. *Studying Public Policy: Policy Cycles and Policy Subsystems*. Oxford: Oxford University Press.

Hubbard, Ruth, and Gilles Paquet. 2007. "Public-Private Partnerships: P3 and the 'Porcupine Problem,'" in *How Ottawa Spends 2007–2008: The Harper Conservatives – Climate of Change*, edited by G. Bruce Doern, 254–72. Montreal and Kingston: McGill-Queen's University Press.

Hufbauer, Gary, and Jeffrey Schott. 2005. *NAFTA Revisited: Achievements and Challenges*. Washington, DC: Institute for International Economics.

Human Resources and Skills Development Canada (HRSDC). 2011. *2011–12 Estimates*, Part III, *Report on Plans and Priorities*. Ottawa: Public Works and Government Services Canada.

Hunt, Alan. 1999. *Governing Morals: A Social History of Moral Regulation*. Cambridge: Cambridge University Press.

Immigration and Refugee Board (IRBD). 2011. *2011–12 Estimates*, Part III, *Report on Plans and Priorities*. Ottawa: Public Works and Government Services Canada.

Industry Canada. 2011. *Intellectual Property Policy*. Ottawa: Author.

Information Commissioner of Canada. 2011. *Paving the Access Ramp to Transparency: Annual Report 2010–2011*. Ottawa: Author.

Ireland, Derek, Eric Milligan, Kernaghan Webb, and Wei Xie. 2012. "The Rise and Fall of Regulatory Regimes: Extending the Life-Cycle Approach," in *How Ottawa Spends 2012–2013: The Harper Majority, Budget Cuts, and the New Opposition*, edited by G. Bruce Doern and Christopher Stoney, 127–44. Montreal and Kingston: McGill-Queen's University Press.

Ireland, Derek, and Kernaghan Webb. 2010. "The Canadian Escape from the Subprime Crisis? Comparing US and Canadian Approaches," in *How Ottawa Spends 2010–2011: Recession, Realignment and the New Deficit Era*, edited by G. Bruce Doern and Christopher Stoney, 87–108. Montreal and Kingston: McGill-Queen's University Press.

Jaccard, Mark. 2006. "Mobilizing Producers toward Sustainability: The Prospects for Sector-Specific, Market-Oriented Regulations," in *Sustainable Production: Building Canadian Capacity*, edited by Glen Toner, 154–77. Vancouver: UBC Press.

Jackman, Martha. 2000. "Constitutional Jurisdiction over Health Care in Canada." *Health Law Journal* 8: 95–117.

Jacobs, Scott. 1999. *Regulatory Reform in the United States*. Paris: OECD.

Jakobi, Tobias. 2012. "Regulating Regulation? The Regulatory Policy of the OECD." Paper presented at the Conference on New Perspectives on Regulation, Governance and Learning, University of Exeter, 27–9 June.

James, Jr., H.S. 1998. "Implementing a Regulatory Budget: Estimating the Mandated Private Expenditure of the Clean Air Act and Safe Drinking Water Act." *Policy Sciences* 31(4): 279–300.

Janisch, H.N. 1978. *The Regulatory Process of the Canadian Transport Commission.* Ottawa: Law Reform Commission of Canada, Administrative Law Series.

– 1979. "Policy-Making in Regulation: Towards a New Definition of the Status of Independent Agencies in Canada." *Osgoode Hall Law Journal* 17(1): 46–106.

– 1985. Independence of Administrative Tribunals: In Praise of 'Structural Heretics.'" *Canadian Journal of Administrative Law and Practice* 1(1): 1–19.

Janisch, Hudson. 1978a. "The Role of the Independent Regulatory Agency in Canada." *University of New Brunswick Law Journal* 27 (Jan.): 92–109.

– 1978b. "The Canadian Transport Commission," in *The Regulatory Process in Canada,* edited by G. Bruce Doern, 128–46. Toronto: Macmillan.

– 1999. "Competition Policy Institutions: What Role in the Face of Continued Sectoral Regulation?" in *Changing the Rules: Canada's Changing Regulatory Regimes and Institutions,* edited by G. Bruce Doern, Margaret M. Hill, Michael J. Prince, and Richard J. Schultz, 101–21. Toronto: University of Toronto Press.

– 2012. "The Relationship between Governments and Independent Regulatory Agencies: Will We Ever Get It Right?" *Alberta Law Review* 40(4): 46–58.

Jenson, Jane. 1990. "Representations in Crisis: The Roots of Canada's Permeable Fordism." *Canadian Journal of Political Science* 23(4): 653–84.

Jenson, Jane, and Denis Saint-Martin. 2003. "New Routes to Social Cohesion? Citizenship and the Social Investment State." *Canadian Journal of Sociology* 28(1): 77–99.

Jessop, Robert. 1999. "The Changing Governance of Welfare: Recent Trends in Its Primary Functions, Scale, and Modes of Coordination." *Social Policy and Administration* 33(4): 348–59.

– 2002. *The Future of the Capitalist State.* London: Polity Press.

Jochelson, Richard, and Kirsten Kramar. 2011. *Sex and the Supreme Court: Obscenity and Indecency Law in Canada.* Halifax: Fernwood.

Johnson, Robert. 2006. "Regulatory Policy: The Potential for Common Federal-Provincial-Territorial Policies on Regulation," in *Rules, Rules, Rules, Rules: Multilevel Regulatory Governance,* edited by G. Bruce Doern and Robert Johnson, 52–79. Toronto: University of Toronto Press.

Jones, David P., and Anne S. de Villars. 1999. *Principles of Administrative Law.* (3rd ed.). Toronto: Carswell.

Jones, M., and B. Salter. 2009. "Proceeding Carefully: Assisted Human Reproduction Policy in Canada." *Public Understanding of Science* 9(2): 1–15.

Jordana, J., and David Levi-Faur (eds.). 2004. *The Politics of Regulation: Examining Regulatory Institutions and Instruments in the Governance Age*. Cheltenham: Edward Elgar.

Justice Canada. 2011. *2011–12 Estimates*, Part III, *Report on Plans and Priorities*. Ottawa: Public Works and Government Services Canada.

Kaiser, Gordon E. 1986. "Developments in Canadian Telecommunications Regulation," in *Marketplace for Telecommunications*, edited by Marcellus S. Snow, 173–200. New York: Longman.

Kane, T.G. 1980. *Consumers and the Regulators*. Montreal: Institute for Research on Public Policy.

Kay, John. 2003. *The Truth about Markets*. London: Penguin Allen Lane.

– 2011. *Obliquity: Why Our Goals Are Best Achieved Indirectly*. London: Profile Books.

Kelly, James. 1999. "Bureaucratic Activism and the Charter of Rights and Freedoms: The Department of Justice and Its Entry into the Centre of Government." *Canadian Public Administration* 42: 476–511.

Khemani, R.S., and W.T. Stanbury (eds.). 1991. *Canadian Competition Policy Law and Policy at the Centenary*. Halifax: Institute for Research on Public Policy.

Kiewiet, Roderick. 2006. "The Regulatory Budget." Paper presented at the Conference on Fiscal Challenges: An Interdisciplinary Approach to Budgetary Policy, University of California, 10–11 Feb.

Kinder, Jeffrey S. 2010. *Government Laboratories: Institutional Variety, Change and Design Space*. Ph.D. dissertation, School of Public Policy and Administration, Carleton University.

Kinsman, Gary, and Patrizia Gentile. 2010. *The Canadian War on Queers: National Security and Sexual Regulations*. Vancouver: UBC Press.

KPMG International (ed.). 2008. *Holy Grail or Achievable Quest? International Perspectives on Public Sector Performance Management*. London: Author.

Krasner, David (ed.). 1983. *International Regimes*. Ithaca: Cornell University Press.

Kravis, Marie-Josee. 2009. "Regulation Didn't Save Canada's Banks." *Wall Street Journal*, 7 May, 7.

Krawchenko, Tamara. 2012. "New Directions for Regulatory Practice." Paper for Regulatory Governance Initiative, School of Public Policy and Administration, Carleton University.

Krugman, Paul. 2008. *Return of Depression Economics and the Crisis of 2008.* London: Penguin.

– 2010. "Appeasing the Bond Gods." *New York Times*, 19 Aug. http://www.nytimes.com/2010/08/20/opinion/20krugman.html

Labrosse, John R., R. Olivares-Caminal, and Dalvinder Singh (eds.). 2011. *Managing Risk in the Financial System.* Cheltenham: Edward Elgar.

Laforest, Rachel. 2009a. "Introduction," in *The New Federal Policy Agenda and the Voluntary Sector: On the Cutting Edge*, edited by R. Laforest, 1–6. Montreal and Kingston: McGill-Queen's University Press.

– 2009b. "Policy Currents and the Conservative Undertow," in *The New Federal Policy Agenda and the Voluntary Sector: On the Cutting Edge*, edited by R. Laforest, 155–67. Montreal and Kingston: McGill-Queen's University Press.

Langford, John. 1976. *Transport in Transition.* Montreal and Kingston: McGill-Queen's University Press.

Larsen, Mike, and Kevin Walby (eds.). 2012. *Brokering Access: Power, Politics and Freedom of Information.* Vancouver: UBC Press.

Laurance, Jeremy. 2012. "Drug Giants Fined $11bn for Criminal Wrongdoing." *Independent*, 20 Sept., 3.

Lawlor, Andrea, and Erin Crandall. 2011. "Understanding Third-Party Advertising: An Analysis of the 2004, 2006, and 2008 Canadian Elections." *Canadian Public Administration* 54: 509–29.

Lee, Ian. 2007. "Righting Wrongs: Locking Them Up without Losing the Key – Tory Reforms to Crime and Punishment," in *How Ottawa Spends 2007–2008: The Harper Conservatives – Climate of Change*, edited by G. Bruce Doern, 220–53. Montreal and Kingston: McGill-Queen's University Press.

Lemmens, Trudo, and Ron A. Bouchard. 2007. "The Regulation of Pharmaceuticals in Canada," in *Canadian Health Law and Policy* (3rd ed.), edited by J. Downie, T. Caulfield, and C. Flood, 121–36. Toronto: Butterworths.

Leiss, William. 2000. "Between Expertise and Bureaucracy: Risk Management Trapped at the Science-Policy Interface," in *Risky Business: Canada's Changing Science-Based Policy and Regulatory Regime*, edited by G. Bruce Doern and Ted Reed, 49–74. Toronto: University of Toronto Press.

Lenihan, Don. 2012. *Rescuing Policy: The Case for Public Engagement.* Toronto: Public Policy Forum.

Leroux, Darryle. 2010. "Québec Nationalism and the Production of Difference: The Bouchard-Taylor Commission, the Herouxville Code of Conduct, and Québec's Integration Policy." *Québec Studies* 49: 107–26.

Levasseur, Karine. 2012. "In the Name of Charity: Institutional Support
for and Resistance to Redefining the Meaning of Charity in Canada."
Canadian Public Administration 55(2): 181–202.
Levi-Faur, David. 2005. "The Global Diffusion of Regulatory Capitalism."
Annals of the American Academy of Political and Social Science 598:
12–32.
– 2012a. "The Regulatory Rescue of the Welfare State." Paper presented
at the Conference on New Perspectives on Regulation, Governance and
Learning, University of Exeter, 27–9 June.
– 2012b. "The Developmental State versus the Regulatory State." Paper
presented at the Conference on New Perspectives on Regulation,
Governance and Learning, University of Exeter, 27–9 June.
Levi-Faur, David (ed.). 2011. *Handbook on the Politics of Regulation*.
Cheltenham: Edward Elgar.
Levin, Avner, and Mary Jo Nicholson. 2005. "Privacy Law in the United
States, the EU and Canada: The Allure of the Middle Ground." *Law and
Technology Journal* 2(2): 357–95.
Lindblom, Charles E. 1992. *Inquiry and Change*. New Haven: Yale
University Press.
Lindblom, Charles E., and Edward J. Woodhouse. 1993. *The Policy
Making Process*. (3rd ed.). New York: Prentice-Hall.
Lipsey, R.G., and C. Baker. 1995. "A Structuralist View of Technical
Change and Economic Growth," in *Technology, Information
and Public Policy*, edited by T.J. Courchene, 13–26. Kingston: John
Deutsch Institute for the Study of Economic Policy, Queen's
University.
Little, Margaret, and Jane Hillyard. 1998. *No Car, No Radio, No Liquor
Permit: The Moral Regulation of Single Mothers in Ontario, 1920–1997*.
Toronto: Oxford University Press.
Lobby Monitor. 2012. *About Us*. Ottawa: Author. http://www.
lobbymonitor.ca/about
Locke, Stephen. 1998. "Modelling the Consumer Interest," in *Changing
Regulatory Institutions in Britain and North America*, edited by G. Bruce
Doern and Stephen Wilks, 162–86. Toronto: University of Toronto Press.
Lodge, Martin, and Christopher Hood. 2011. "Into an Age of Multiple
Austerities? Public Management and Public Service Bargains across
OECD Countries." *Governance* 25(1): 79–101.
Lortie Commission. 1991. Royal Commission on Electoral Reform and
Party Financing. *Reforming Electoral Democracy*. Ottawa: Minister of
Supply and Services.

Lucas, A.R. 1977. *The National Energy Board.* Ottawa: Law Reform Commission.

– 1978. "The National Energy Board," in *The Regulatory Process in Canada*, edited by G. Bruce Doern, 259–313. Toronto: Macmillan.

Lucas, A.R., and Trevor Bell. 1978. *The National Energy Board: Policy, Procedures, Practice.* Ottawa: National Energy Board.

Luckert, Martin, David Haley, and George Hoberg. 2012. *Policies for Sustainably Managing Canada's Forests.* Vancouver: UBC Press.

Mabbett, Deborah. 2011. "The Regulatory Rescue of the Welfare State," in *Handbook o n the Politics of Regulation*, edited by David Levi-Faur, 88–100. Cheltenham: Edward Elgar.

Mackrael, Kim. 2013. "Safety Board Warns against Blaming One Person for Lac-Megantic Disaster." *Globe and Mail*, 13 July.

Majone, Giandomenico. 1994. "The Rise of the Regulatory State." *West European Politics* 17(3): 77–101.

– 1997. "From the Positive to the Regulatory State: Causes and Consequences of Changes in the Mode of Governance." *Journal of Public Policy* 17(2): 139–67.

Mallea, Paula. 2011. *Fearmonger: Stephen Harper's Tough-on-Crime Agenda.* Toronto: James Lorimer.

Malloy, Jonathan. 2004. "The Executive and Parliament in Canada." *Journal of Legislative Studies* 10(2/3): 206–17.

– 2010. "The Drama of Parliament under Minority Government," in *How Ottawa Spends 2010–2011: Recession, Realignment and the New Deficit Era*, edited by G. Bruce Doern and Christopher Stoney, 31–47. Montreal and Kingston: McGill-Queen's University Press.

Marcellin, Sherry S. 2010. *The Political Economy of Pharmaceutical Patents.* Aldershot: Ashgate.

Marks, Gary, L. Hooghe, and K. Blank. 1996. "European Integration from the 1980s: State-Centric versus Multi-level Governance." *Journal of Common Market Studies* 34: 343–77.

Martin, James K. 2011. "Options for Reducing the Cost of Compliance with Rules for Small Business." Paper prepared for the Red Tape Reduction Commission, Ottawa.

Martin, Lawrence. 2010. *Harperland: The Politics of Control.* Toronto: Viking.

Marx, Axel, M. Maertens, Johan Swinnen, and Jan Wouters (eds.). 2012. *Private Standards and Global Governance.* Cheltenham: Edward Elgar.

Masters, Brooke, and Phillip Stafford. 2012. "Libor Rejig to Foil Manipulation." *Financial Times*, 28 Sept., 2.

May, Peter J. 2007. "Regulatory Regimes and Accountability." *Regulation and Governance* 1(1): 8–26.

McCreath, Graeme. 2011. *The Politics of Blindness: From Charity to Parity.* Vancouver: Granville Island Publishing.

McDougall, John N. 1982. *Fuels and the National Policy.* Toronto: McClelland and Stewart.

McFarland, Janet. 2012. "Flaherty Not Giving Up on National Securities Regulator." *Globe and Mail,* 29 March, 12.

McLaren, Angus, and Arlene T. McLaren. 1986. *Bedroom and the State: The Changing Practices and Politics of Contraception and Abortion in Canada, 1880–1980.* Toronto: University of Toronto Press.

McManus, John C. 1978. "On the 'New' Transportation Policy after Ten Years," in *Studies on Regulation in Canada*, edited by W.T. Stanbury, 122–33. Toronto: Butterworths for the Institute for Research on Public Policy.

Mendelsohn, M. 2003. "A Public Opinion Perspective on Regulation." Paper prepared for the External Advisory Committee on Smart Regulation, Ottawa, Dec.

Meuleman, L. 2008. *Public Management and the Meta-Governance of Hierarchies, Networks and Markets.* Berlin: Phisica-Verlag.

Meyers, R.T. 1998. "Regulatory Budgeting: A Bad Idea Whose Time Has Come?" *Policy Sciences* 31: 371–84.

Mihlar, Fazil. 1999. "The Federal Government and the RIAS Process: Origins, Need and Non-Complaince," in *Changing the Rules: Canadian Regulatory Regimes and Institutions*, edited by G. Bruce Doern, Margaret M. Hill, Michael J. Prince, and Richard J. Schultz, 277–92. Toronto: University of Toronto Press.

Miki, Roy. 2005. *Redress: Inside the Japanese Canadian Call for Justice.* Vancouver: Raincoast Books.

Mills, Lisa, and Ashley Weber. 2006. "Access to Medicines: How Canada Amends the Patent Act," in *How Ottawa Spends 2006–2007: In from The Cold – The Tory Rise and the Liberal Demise*, edited by G. Bruce Doern, 229–46. Montreal and Kingston: McGill-Queen's University Press.

Minister of Transport, Canada. 2013. *Railway Service Performance.* http://www.tc.gc.ca/eng/mediaroom. Releases-2013-h084e-7234.html

Minsky, Amy. 2011. "Election Laws Must Consider Online Tools: Electoral Officer."

Postmedia News, *National Post,* 18 Aug, 12.

Mishra, Ramesh. 1990. *The Welfare State in Capitalist Society: Policies of Retrenchment and Maintenance in Europe, North America and Australia.* Toronto: University of Toronto Press.

Mitchell, Graeme G. 2011. "Not a General Regulatory Power – A Comment on *Reference re Assisted Human Reproduction Act.*" *Supreme Court Law Review* 54: 633–70.

Mitnick, B. 1980. *The Political Economy of Regulation.* New York: Columbia University Press.

Montpetit, E. 2003. "Public Consultations in Policy Network Environments: The Case of Assisted Human Technology Policy in Canada." *Canadian Public Policy* 29(1): 95–110.

– 2004. "Policy Networks, Federalism and Managerial Ideas: How ART Non-decision in Canada Safeguards the Autonomy of the Medical Profession," in *Comparative Biomedical Policy: Governing Assisted Reproductive Technologies*, edited by I. Bleiklie, M. Goggin, and C. Rothmayr, 64 81. London: Routledge.

– 2009. "Has the European Union Made Europe More or Less Democratic? Elections, Network Deliberations and Advocacy Groups." Paper presented to the Conference on Bringing Civil Society in the European Union and the Rise of Representative Government, European University Institute, Florence, 13 March.

Murray, Brian C., Richard G. Newell, and William A. Pizer. 2008. *Balancing Cost and Emissions Certainty: An Allowance Reserve for Cap-and-Trade.* Washington, DC: Resources for the Future.

National Energy Board (NEB). 2001. *2001–2002 Estimates*, Part III, *Report on Plans and Priorities.* Ottawa: Author.

– 2005. *Annual Report 2004.* Ottawa: Author.

– 2008. *2007 Annual Report to Parliament.* Ottawa: Author.

– 2011. *The National Energy Board Filing Requirements for Offshore Drilling in the Canadian Arctic.* Ottawa: Author.

– 2012a. *Annual Report 2011 to Parliament.* Ottawa: Author.

– 2012b. *Section 58 Streamlining Order.* Ottawa: Author.

National Roundtable on the Environment and the Economy. 2011. *Canada's Opportunity: Adopting Life Cycle Approaches for Sustainable Development.* Ottawa: Author.

Niklasson, Lars. 2012. "The Regulatory State versus the Developmental State: The Case of the EU." Paper presented at the Conference on New Perspectives on Regulation, Governance and Learning, University of Exeter, 27–9 June.

Nivola, Pietro S., and John C. Courtney. 2011. *Know Thy Neighbour: What Canada Can Tell Us about Financial Regulation*. Washington, D C: Brookings Institution.

Nocera, Joe. 2012. "Frankenstein Takes Over the Market." *New York Times*, 3 Aug., 1.

Organization of Economic Cooperation and Development (OECD). 2001. *Businesses' Views on Red Tape*. Paris: Author.

– 2002a. OECD *Reviews of Regulatory Reform: Canada 2002*. Paris: Author.

– 2002b. *Regulatory Reform in Canada: Government Capacity to Assure High Quality Regulation*. Paris: Author.

– 2002c. *Report on the Role of Competition Policy in Regulatory Reform in Canada*. Paris: Author.

– 2004. *Canada – Updated Report*. Paris: Author.

– 2010. *Risk and Regulatory Policy: Improving the Governance of Risk*. Paris: Author.

Office of the Auditor General of Canada. 2010. *The Public Sector Integrity Commissioner of Canada*. Ottawa: Author.

– 2011. *What We Do*. Ottawa: Author.

Office of the Commissioner of Lobbying of Canada. 2011a. *Annual Report 2010–2011*. Ottawa: Author.

– 2011b. *Administering the Lobbying Act: Observations and Recommendations Based on the Experience of the Last Five Years*. Ottawa: Author.

Office of the Privacy Commissioner of Canada. 2011. "Letter to Minister of Public Safety Vic Toews." Ottawa: Author, 26 Oct.

– 2012a. *About Us*. Ottawa: Author.

– 2012b. *Annual Report to Parliament*. Ottawa: Author.

Office of the Public Sector Integrity Commissioner of Canada. 2011. *Learning and Growing: 2010–2011 Annual Report*. Ottawa: Author.

– 2012. *Tell Us: You Are Protected, 2011–2012 Annual Report*. Ottawa: Author.

Omidvar, Ratna, and Ted Richmond (eds.). 2003. *Perspectives on Social Inclusion: Immigrant Settlement and Social Inclusion in Canada*. Toronto: Laidlaw Foundation.

O'Riordan, Timothy, and James Cameron. 1994. *Interpreting the Precautionary Principle*. London: Earthscan.

Owen, B. 1999. *The Internet Challenge to Television*. Cambridge, MA: Harvard University Press.

Paehlke, Robert C. 2003. *Democracy's Dilemma*. Cambridge, MA: MIT Press.

Pager, Sean A., and Adam Candeub (eds.). 2012. *Transnational Culture in the Internet Age*. Cheltenham: Edward Elgar.

Pal, Leslie A. 2011a. "Assessing Incrementalism: Formative Assumptions, Contemporary Realities." *Policy and Society* 30(1): 29–39.

– 2011b. "Into the Wild: The Politics of Economic Stimulus," in *How Ottawa Spends 2011–2012: Trimming Fat or Slicing Pork?* edited by Christopher Stoney and G. Bruce Doern, 39–59. Montreal and Kingston: McGill-Queen's University Press.

– 2012. *The Frontiers of Governance: The OECD and Global Public Management Reform*. London: Palgrave Macmillan.

– 2013. *Beyond Policy Analysis: Public Issue Management in Turbulent Times* (5th ed.). Toronto: Nelson.

Pal, Leslie A., and Judith Maxwell. 2003. "Assessing the Public Interest in the 21st Century: A Framework." Paper prepared for the External Advisory Committee on Smart Regulation, Ottawa.

Palast, Greg, Jerrold Oppenheim, and Theo MacGregor. 2003. *Democracy and Regulation: How the Public Can Govern Essential Services*. London: Pluto Press.

Pastre, Antoine, and Todd Cain. 2012. *The Role of Independent Guardians: Description and Synthesis*. Ottawa: Institute on Governance.

Peck, Jamie. 2001. *Workfare States*. New York: Guilford Press.

Peers, F.W. 1979. *The Public Eye: Television and the Politics of Canadian Broadcasting 1952–1968*. Toronto: University of Toronto Press.

Peltzman, S. 1976. "Towards a More General Theory of Regulations." *Journal of Law and Economics* 19: 211–40.

Peters, B. Guy. 1996. "United States Competition Policy Institutions: Structural Constraints and Opportunities," in *Comparative Competition Policy*, edited by G. Bruce Doern and Stephen Wilks, 40–67. Oxford: Clarendon Press.

Phillips, Peter W.B. 2007. *Governing Transformative Technological Innovation: Who's in Charge?* London: Edward Elgar.

Phillips, Susan D. 2001. "More than Stakeholders: Reforming State-Voluntary Sector Relations." *Journal of Canadian Studies* 35(4): 182–202.

– 2009. "The Harper Government and the Voluntary Sector: Wither a Policy Agenda?" in *The New Federal Policy Agenda and the Voluntary Sector: On the Cutting Edge*, edited by Rachel Laforest, 7–34. Montreal and Kingston: McGill-Queen's University Press.

Phillips, Susan D., and Karine Levasseur. 2004. "The Snakes and Ladders of Accountability: Contradictions between Contracting and Collaboration for Canada's Voluntary Sector." *Canadian Public Administration* 47(4): 451–74.

Phillips, Susan D., and Steven Rathgeb Smith. 2011. "Between Governance and Regulation: Evolving Government–Third Sector Relationships," in *Governance and Regulation in the Third Sector: International Perspectives*, edited by Susan D. Phillips and Steven Rathgeb Smith, 1–13. London: Routledge.

Picard, André. 2012. "Fertility Law Needs a Reset." *Globe and Mail*, 3 April, L5.

Pierre, Jon, and B. Guy Peters. 2000. *Governance, Politics and the State*. London: Palgrave Macmillan.

Pinker, Robert. 1971. *Social Theory and Social Policy*. London: Heinemann.

Piven, Frances Fox, and Richard A. Cloward. 1971. *Regulating the Poor: The Functions of Public Welfare*. New York: Pantheon.

Porter, Michael. 2001. "Competition and Anti-trust: Towards a Productivity-Based Approach to Evaluating Mergers," in *Canadian Competition Policy: Preparing for the Future*, edited by David Conklin, 10–24. Toronto: Pearson Education.

Preston, Alex. 2012. " From Scandal to Catastrophe: The Rise and Fall of Investment Banking." *New Statesman*, 28 Sept. to 4 Oct., 23–35.

Prince, Michael J. 1999a. "Civic Regulation: Regulating Citizenship, Morality, Social Order, and the Welfare State," in *Changing the Rules: Canadian Regulatory Regimes and Institutions*, edited by G. Bruce Doern, Margaret M. Hill, Michael J. Prince, and Richard J. Schultz, 201–27. Toronto: University of Toronto Press.

– 1999b. "Aristotle's Benchmarks: Institutions and Accountabilities of the Canadian Regulatory State," in *Changing the Rules: Canadian Regulatory Regimes and Institutions*, edited by G. Bruce Doern, Margaret M. Hill, Michael J. Prince, and Richard J. Schultz, 228–56. Toronto: University of Toronto Press.

– 1999c. "From Health and Welfare to Stealth and Farewell: Federal Social Policy, 1980 to 2000," in *How Ottawa Spends 1999–2000: Shape Shifting – Canadian Governance toward the 21st Century*, edited by Leslie A. Pal, 151–96. Toronto: Oxford University Press.

– 2001. "How Social Is Social Policy? Fiscal and Market Discourse in North American Welfare States." *Social Policy and Administration* 35(1): 2–13.

– 2003. "Taking Stock: Governance Practices and Portfolio Performance of the Canada Pension Plan Investment Board," in *How Ottawa Spends 2003–2004: Regime Change and Policy Shift*, edited by G. Bruce Doern, 134–54. Oxford: Oxford University Press.

– 2004. "La Petite Vision, Les Grands Decisions: Chrétien's Paradoxical Record in Social Policy." *Review of Constitutional Studies* 9(1/2): 199–219.

– 2005. "From Welfare State to Social Union: Shifting Choices of Governing Instruments, Intervention Rationales, and Governance Rules in Canadian Social Policy," in *Designing Government: From Instruments to Governance*, edited by Pearl Eliadis, Margaret M. Hill, and Michael Howlett, 281–302. Kingston and Montreal: McGill-Queen's University Press.

– 2008. "Claiming a Disability Benefit as Contesting Social Citizenship," in *Contesting Illness: Processes and Practice*, edited by Pamela Moss and Katherine Teghtsoonian, 28–46. Toronto: University of Toronto Press.

– 2009. *Absent Citizens: Disability Politics and Policy in Canada.* Toronto: University of Toronto Press.

– 2010a. "Self–Regulation, Exhortation, and Symbolic Politics: Gently Coercive Governing?" in *Policy: From Ideas to Implementation*, edited by Glen Toner, Leslie A. Pal, and Michael J. Prince, 77–108. Montreal and Kingston: McGill-Queen's University Press.

– 2010b. "What about a Disability Rights Act for Canada? Practices and Lessons from America, Australia, and the United Kingdom." *Canadian Public Policy* 36(2): 199–214.

– 2012. "A Hobbesian Prime Minister and the Night Watchman State: Social Policy under the Harper Conservatives," in *How Ottawa Spends 2012–2013*, edited by Christopher Stoney and G. Bruce Doern. Montreal and Kingston: McGill-Queen's University Press, 53-70.

Prince, Michael J., E. Mopfu, T. Hawkins, and P. Devlieger. 2010. "Social Safety Nets and Assessments," in *Rehabilitation and Health Assessments*, edited by E. Mopfu and T. Oakland, 591–620. New York: Springer.

Princen, Thomas, Michael Maniates, and Ken Comca. 2002. *Confronting Consumption.* Cambridge, MA: MIT Press.

Pross, A. Paul, and Iain S. Stewart. 1994. "Breaking the Habit: Attentive Publics and Tobacco Regulation," in *How Ottawa Spends 1994–95: Making Change*, edited by Susan D. Phillips, 129–64. Ottawa: Carleton University Press.

Prosser, Tony. 2010. *The Regulatory Enterprise: Government, Regulation and Legitimacy.* Oxford: Oxford University Press.

Public Policy Forum. 2012. *Towards Guidelines on Government Formation: Facilitating Openness and Efficiency in Canada's Governance*. Ottawa: Author.

Public Safety Canada. 2008. *2008–09 Estimates*, Part III, *Report on Plans and Priorities*. Ottawa: Public Works and Government Services Canada.

– 2011. *2011–12 Estimates*, Part III, *Report on Plans and Priorities*. Ottawa: Public Works and Government Services Canada.

Radaelli, Claudio. 2004. "The Puzzle of Regulatory Competition." *Journal of Public Policy* 24 Part I (Jan.–Apr.): 1–24.

– 2009. "Desperately Seeking Regulatory Impact Assessment: Diary of a Reflective Researcher." *Evaluation* 15(1): 31–48.

Radaelli, Claudio, and F. DeFrancesco. 2007. *Regulatory Quality in Europe: Concepts, Measures, and Policy Processes*. Manchester: Manchester University Press.

Radaelli, Claudio, and A.C. Meuwese. 2010. "Hard Questions, and Equally Hard Solutions in Impact Assessment." *West European Politics* 33(1): 136–53.

Rainie, Lee, and Barry Wellman. 2012. *Networked: The New Social Operating System*. Cambridge, MA: MIT Press.

Ralston Saul, John. 2008. *A Fair Country: Telling Truths about Canada*. Toronto: Viking.

– 2010. *Louis-Hippolyte La Fontaine and Robert Baldwin*. Toronto: Penguin.

Ranger, Louis. 2010. "In Search of Innovation Policies in the Transport Sector." Paper presented to the International Transport Forum, Leipzig, Germany, 26–8 May.

Ratnovski, Lev, and Rocco Huang. 2009. *Why Are Canadian Banks More Resilient?* IMF Working Paper No. 09/152, 1–19. Washington, DC: International Monetary Fund.

Rayside, David. 2008. *Queer Inclusions, Continental Divisions: Public Recognition of Sexual Diversity in Canada and the United States*. Toronto: University of Toronto Press.

Redden, Candace Johnson. 2002. *Health Care, Entitlement, and Citizenship*. Toronto: University of Toronto Press.

Redford, E. 1969. *Democracy in the Administrative State*. Oxford: Oxford University Press.

Regulatory Policy Committee (UK). 2011a. *What the RPC Does*. Regulatory Policy Committee. http://regulatorypolicycommittee. independent.gov.uk/what–the–rpc–does

– 2011b. *Rating Regulation.* Regulatory Policy Committee. http://
regulatorypolicycomittee.independent.gov.uk/ratingregulation
Reference re Assisted Human Reproduction Act. 2010. SCC 61.
Reschenthaler, G.B. 1978. "Direct Regulation in Canada: Some Policies
and Problems," in *Studies on Regulation in Canada,* edited by W.T.
Stanbury, 22–31. Toronto: Butterworths for the Institute on Research
on Public Policy.
Reschenthaler, G.B., and B. Roberts. 1978. *Perspectives on Canadian
Airline Regulation.* Toronto: Butterworths for the Institute for Research
on Public Policy.
Rhodes, R.A.W. 1997. *Understanding Governance.* London: Open
University Press.
Rice, James J., and Michael J. Prince. 2013. *Changing Politics of Canadian
Social Policy.* Toronto: University of Toronto Press.
Rideout, V. 2003. *Continentalizing Canadian Telecom: The Politics of Regu-
latory Reform.* Montreal and Kingston: McGill-Queen's University Press.
Rivers, Nic, and Mark Jaccard. 2009. "Talking without Walking: Canada's
Ineffective Climate Effort," in *Governing the Energy Challenge,* edited
by Burkard Eberlein and G. Bruce Doern, 285–313. Toronto: University
of Toronto Press.
Rixen, Thomas. 2013. "Why Regulation after the Crisis Is Feeble: Shadow
Banking, Offshore Financial Centers, and Jurisdictional Competition."
Regulation and Governance 7(2): 26–37.
Roche, Maurice. 1992. *Rethinking Citizenship: Welfare, Ideology and
Change in Modern Society.* Cambridge: Polity Press.
Rodger, John J. 2008. *Criminalising Social Policy: Anti-social Behaviour
and Welfare in a De-civilised Society.* Cullompton: Willan.
Rogoff, Kenneth. 2011. "The Second Great Contraction." *Bloomberg
News,* 13 Aug.
Roman, Andrew J. 1978. "Regulatory Law and Procedure," in *The
Regulatory Process in Canada,* edited by G. Bruce Doern, 68–93.
Toronto: Macmillan.
Rose, Nikolas. 1996. "The Death of the Social? Re-figuring the Territory
of Government." *Economy and Society* 25(3): 327–56.
Rose, Nikolas, and Peter Miller. 1992. "Political Power beyond the State:
Problematics of Government." *British Journal of Sociology* 43(2):
172–205.
Rosenau, James N. 2007. "Governing the Ungovernable: The Challenge of
a Global Disaggregation of Authority." *Regulation and Governance*
1(1): 88–97.

Rousseau, Stephane. 2012. *A Question of Credibility: Enhancing the Accountability and Effectiveness of Credit Rating Agencies.* Toronto: C.D. Howe Institute.

Royal Commission on Aboriginal Peoples. 1996. *Final Report.* Ottawa: Royal Commission on Aboriginal Peoples.

Royal Society of Canada. 2001. *Elements of Precaution: Recommendations for the Regulation of Food Biotechnology in Canada.* Ottawa: Author.

Russell, Peter H., and Lorne Sossin. 2009. *Parliamentary Democracy in Crisis.* Toronto: University of Toronto Press.

Ryan, Phil. 2010. *Multicultiphobia.* Toronto: University of Toronto Press.

Sabatier, Paul A. 1988. "An Advocacy Coalition Framework of Policy Change." *Policy Sciences* 21: 129–68.

Salomon, Lester M. (ed.). 2002. *The Tools of Government: A Guide to the New Governance.* Oxford: Oxford University Press.

Sandel, Michael J. 2009. *Justice: What's the Right Thing to Do?* New York: Farrar, Straus and Giroux.

Saner, Marc A. 2002. "An Ethical Analysis of the Precautionary Principle." *International Journal of Biotechnology* 4(1): 81–95.

Savoie, Donald. 1999. *Governing from the Centre: The Concentration of Power in Canadian Politics.* Toronto: University of Toronto Press.

– 2010. *Power: Where Is It?* Montreal and Kingston: McGill-Queen's University Press.

– 2013. *Whatever Happened to the Music Teacher? How Government Decides and Why.* Montreal and Kingston: McGill-Queen's University Press.

Schultz, Richard J. 1977. "Regulatory Agencies and the Canadian Political System," in *Public Administration in Canada: Selected Readings*, edited by Kenneth Kernaghan, 48–60. Toronto: Methuen.

– 1980. *Federalism, Bureaucracy and Public Policy: The Politics of Highway Transportation Regulation.* Montreal and Kingston: McGill-Queen's University Press.

– 1988. "Regulating Conservatively: The Mulroney Record 1984–1988," in *Canada under Mulroney*, edited by Andrew B. Gollner and Daniel Salee, 186–205. Montreal: Vehicule Press.

– "New Domestic and International Bedfellows in Telecommunications." *Media and Communications Law Review* 1: 55–70.

– 1995. "Paradigm Lost: Explaining the Canadian Politics of Deregulation," in *Canada's Century: Governance in a Maturing Society – Essays in Honour of John Meisel*, edited by C.E.S. Franks et al, 110–23. Montreal and Kingston: McGill-Queen's University Press.

– 1999a. "Still Standing: The CRTC, 1976–1996," in *Changing the Rules: Canadian Regulatory Regimes and Institutions*, edited by G. Bruce Doern, Margaret M. Hill, Michael J. Prince, and Richard J. Schultz, 29–56. Toronto: University of Toronto Press.
– 1999b. "Governing in a Gale: Overview of Regulatory and Policy Setting for Canadian Telecommunications." in *The Electronic Village: Policy Issues of the Information Age*, edited by D. Orr and T.H. Wilson. Toronto: C.D. Howe Institute.
– 1999c. "Winning and Losing: The Consumers' Association of Canada and the Telecommunications Regulatory System" in *Changing the Rules: Canadian Regulatory Regimes and Institutions*, edited by G. Bruce Doern, Margaret M. Hills, Michael J. Prince, and Richard J. Schultz, 174–200. Toronto: University of Toronto Press.
– 2000. *The Consumers' Association of Canada and the Federal Regulatory System, 1973–1992*. Vancouver: SFU-UBC Centre for the Study of Government and Business.
– 2008 "Telecommunications: What a Difference a Minister Can Make," in *How Ottawa Spends 2008–2009*, edited by Allan M. Maslove, 155–71. Montreal and Kingston: McGill Queen's University Press.
– 2011. "Industry Canada as Economic Regulator: Globealive and the Lessons of Political Licensing," in *How Ottawa Spends 2011–2012: Trimming Fat or Slicing Pork?* edited by Christopher Stoney and G. Bruce Doern, 198–217. Montreal and Kingston: McGill-Queen's University Press.
Schultz, Richard J., and Alan Alexandroff. 1985. *Economic Regulation and the Federal System*. Toronto: University of Toronto Press.
Schultz, Richard, and Mark R. Brawley. 1996. "Telecommunications Policy," in *Border Crossings: The Internationalization of Canadian Public Policy*, edited by G. Bruce Doern, Leslie A. Pal, and Brian W. Tomlin, 82–107. Toronto: Oxford University Press.
Schultz, Richard J., and G. Bruce Doern. 1998. "No Longer Governments in Miniature: Canadian Sectoral Regulatory Institutions in a North American Context," in *Changing Regulatory Institutions in Britain and North America*, edited by G. Bruce Doern and Stephen Wilks, 108–32. Toronto: University of Toronto Press.
Scott, S. 1992. *The Continuing Debate over the Independence of Regulatory Tribunals*. Special Lectures of the Law Society of Upper Canada (Administrative Law). Toronto: Law Society of Upper Canada.
Sell, Susan. 1998. *Power and Ideas: The North-South Politics of Intellectual Property and Antitrust*. Albany: State University of New York Press.

– 2010. "The Rise and Role of Trade-Based Strategy: Historical Institutionalism and the International Regulation of Intellectual Property." *Review of International Political Economy* 17(4): 762–90.

Selley, Chris. 2012. "We Won't Let C-30 Limit Our Freedom without a Fight." *National Post*, 22 Feb., 12.

Senate of Canada, Standing Committee on Transport and Communications. 1992. *Report on the Subject Matter of Bill-62, An Act Respecting Telecommunications*. Third Session, Thirty-Fourth Parliament, June.

Shepherd, Robert. 2009. "Evaluating the Rationale of the New Federal Lobbying Act: Making Lobbying Transparent or Regulating the Industry?" in *How Ottawa Spends 2009–2010: Economic Upheaval and Political Dysfunction*, edited by Allan Maslove, 115–50. Montreal and Kingston: McGill-Queen's University Press.

Shepherd, Robert, and Christopher Stoney. 2010. "Do Institutions for Parliamentary Oversight Offer Better Tools for Scrutinizing and Improving Governance?" in *Approaching Public Administration: Core Debates and Emerging Issues*, edited by Roberto Leone and Frank Ohemeng, chapter 7. Toronto: Edmond Montgomery.

Shields, John, and B. Mitchell Evans. 1998. *Shrinking the State: Globalization and Public Administration "Reform."* Halifax: Fernwood.

Simpson, Jeffrey. 2010. *The Friendly Dictatorship: Reflections on Canadian Democracy*. Toronto: McClelland and Stewart.

Smith, David. 2007. *The Peoples's House of Commons: Theories of Democracy in Contention*. Toronto: University of Toronto Press.

Smith, Jason, Preston Rhea, and Sascha Meinrath. 2012. "Promoting Digital Equality: The Internet as a Public Good and Commons," in Society for the Study of Social Problems, *Agenda for Social Justice: Solutions 2012*, chapter 6.

Smith, Jennifer, and Gerald Baier. 2012. "Fixed Election Dates, the Continuous Campaign, and Campaign Advertising Restrictions," in *From New Public Management to New Political Governance*, edited by Herman Bakvis and Mark D. Jarvis, 128–49. Montreal and Kingston: McGill-Queen's University Press.

Sinclair, Peter R. 2011. *Energy in Canada*. Toronto: Oxford University Press.

Southey, Tabatha. 2013. "Duffy the Empire Slayer: How the PMO Created a Big, Big, Problem." *Globe and Mail*, 7 July, 7.

Sparrow, Malcolm K. 2000. *The Regulatory Craft*. Washington, DC: Brookings Institution.

– 2008. *The Character of Harms: Operational Challenges in Control.* Cambridge: Cambridge University Press.

Spicer, K. 1992. "Responses to Globalization of Telecommunications." *Telecommunications Policy* 16(9): 717–21.

Squires, Peter. 1990. *Anti-social Policy: Welfare, Ideology and the Disciplinary State.* London: Harvester Wheatsheaf.

Stanbury, William T. 1980. *Government Regulation: Scope, Growth, Process.* Montreal: Institute for Research on Public Policy.

– 1988. *Telecommunications Policy and Regulation.* Montreal. Institute for Research on Public Policy.

– 1992. "Reforming the Federal Regulatory Process in Canada, 1971–1992." House of Commons Standing Committee on Finance, Appendix SREC-2 to *Regulations and Competitiveness.*

Standing Senate Committee on Energy, the Environment and Natural Resources. 2012. *Now or Never.* Ottawa: Author.

Statistics Canada. 2011. *About Us.* Ottawa· Author.

Stavins, Robert. 2008. "A Meaningful U.S. Cap and Trade System to Address Climate Change." Working Paper for the Fondazione Eni Enrico Mattei, Paper 241. Rome: Fondazione Eni Enrico Mattei.

Stemshorn, Barry, and Robert W. Slater. 2008. "Potential for a Regulatory Breakthrough? Regulatory Governance and Human Resource Initiatives," in *How Ottawa Spends 2008–2009: A More Orderly Federalism?* edited by Allan M. Maslove, 59–81. Montreal and Kingston: McGill-Queen's University Press.

Stevenson, Garth. 1987. *The Politics of Canadian Airlines: From Diefenbaker to Mulroney.* Toronto: University of Toronto Press.

Stewart, A., and W.H.N. Hull. 1994. *Canadian Television Policy and the Board of Broadcast Governors 1958–1968.* Edmonton: University of Alberta Press.

Stewart, John B. 1977. *The Canadian House of Commons.* Montreal and Kingston: McGill-Queen's University Press.

Stigler, George J. 1971. "The Theory of Economic Regulation." *Bell Journal of Economics and Management Science* 2: 41–60.

Stigler, Joseph E. 2011. "The IMF's Switch in Time." *Economist's Voice* 8(2): 1–3.

Stilborn, John A. 2010. "The Officers of Parliament: More Watchdogs, More Teeth, Better Governance," in *How Ottawa Spends 2010–2011: Recession, Realignment, and the New Deficit Era,* edited by G. Bruce Doern and Christopher Stoney, 243–60. Montreal and Kingston: McGill-Queen's University Press.

Strange, Carolyn, and Tina Loo. 1997. *Making Good: Law and Moral Regulation in Canada, 1867–1939*. Toronto: University of Toronto Press.

Strick, John (1990) *The Economics of Government Regulation: Theory and Canadian Practice*. Toronto: Thompson.

Sunstein, Cass R. 2013. *Simpler: The Future of Government*. New York: Simon and Schuster.

Surtees, L. 1994. *Wire Wars*. New York: Prentice-Hall.

Sutherland, Sharon. 1983. "The Justice Portfolio: Social Policy through Regulation," in *How Ottawa Spends 1983: The Liberals, the Opposition and Federal Priorities*, edited by G. Bruce Doern, 173–207. Toronto: Lorimer.

– 1991. "Responsible Government and Ministerial Responsibility: Every Reform Is Its Own Problem." *Canadian Journal of Political Science* 24 (March): 91–120.

– 2010. "The State of Research on Canada's Parliament." *Canadian Parliamentary Review* (Autumn): 49–55.

Sutherland, Sharon, and G. Bruce Doern. 1985. *Bureaucracy in Canada: Control and Reform*. Toronto: University of Toronto Press.

Svantesson, Dan J.B. 2011. "Fundamental Policy Considerations for the Regulation of Internet Cross-Border Privacy Issues." *Policy and the Internet* 3(3): 66–76.

Swimmer, Gene (ed.). 1996. *How Ottawa Spends 1996–1997: Life under the Knife*. Ottawa: Carleton University Press.

Taylor, Mark C. 2001. *The Moment of Complexity: Emerging Network Culture*. Chicago: University of Chicago Press.

Taylor-Gooby, Peter. 1991. *Social Change, Social Welfare and Social Science*. London: Harvester Wheatsheaf.

Telecommunications Policy Review Panel (TPR Panel). 2006. *Final Report*. Ottawa: Industry Canada.

Thaler, Richard H., and Cass R. Sunstein. 2008. *Nudge*. New Haven: Yale University Press.

Thomas, Paul. 2003. "The Past, Present and Future of Officers of Parliament." *Canadian Public Administration* 46(3): 287–314.

– 2005. "Debating a Whistle-Blower Protection Act for Employees of the Government of Canada." *Canadian Public Administration* 48: 147–84.

– 2012. "Trust and the Role of Independent Parliamentary Agencies." Paper prepared for the Office of the Public Sector Integrity Commission, Ottawa.

Thompson, Fred. 1997. "Toward a Regulatory Budget." *Public Budgeting and Finance* 17: 89–98.

Thompson, G., J. Frances, R. Levacic, and J. Mitchell (eds.). 1991. *Markets, Hierarchies and Networks: The Coordination of Social Life.* London: Sage.

Thompson, Grahame F. 2004. "Is All the World a Complex Network?" *Economy and Society* 33(3): 411–24.

Toner, Glen. 1986. "Stardust: The Tory Energy Program," in *How Ottawa Spends 1986–1987*, edited by Michael J. Prince, 119–48. Toronto: Methuen.

– 2000. "Canada: From Early Frontrunner to Plodding Anchorman," in *Canadian Environmental Policy: Context and Cases*, edited by Debora VanNijnatten and Robert Boardman (2nd ed.), 59–80. Toronto: Oxford University Press.

Toner, Glen (ed.). 2006. *Sustainable Production: Building Canadian Capacity.* Vancouver: UBC Press.

– 2008. *Innovation, Science, Environment: Canadian Policies and Performance: 2008–2009.* Montreal and Kingston: McGill-Queen's University Press.

Tozzi, Jim. 1979. *Towards a Regulatory Budget: A Working Paper on the Cost of Federal Regulation.* Washington, DC: Office of Management and the Budget.

Transport Canada. 2007. *Moving Forward: Changing the Safety and Security Culture.* Ottawa: Transport Canada.

Transportation Safety Board of Canada (TSB). 2013. *Mandate.* Ottawa: Author.

Treasury Board Secretariat (TBS). 2011a. *Policy on Evaluation.* Ottawa: Author.

– 2011b. *Management Accountability Framework.* Ottawa: Author.

– 2011c. *Reports on Plans and Priorities.* Ottawa: Author.

– 2011d. *The Programs and Activities of the Secretariat.* Ottawa: Author.

– 2011e. *A Guide to the Regulatory Process.* Ottawa: Author.

– 2011f. *Triage Statement.* Ottawa: Author.

– 2011g. *Regulatory Affairs Sector.* Ottawa: Author.

– 2011h. *Centre for Regulatory Expertise (CORE).* Ottawa: Author.

– 2011i. *Guide to the Federal Regulatory Development Process.* Ottawa: Author.

– 2011j. *2010 Annual Report on the Health of the Evaluation Function.* Ottawa: Author.

– 2011k. "The Cabinet Directive on Streamlining Regulation." Presentation to Red Tape Reduction Commission and Regulatory Cooperation Council, 3 and 10 June. Ottawa: Author.

- 2013. "The Cabinet Directive on Regulatory Management." Ottawa: Author.

Trebilcock, Michael. 1978. "Winners and Losers in the Modern Regulatory State: Must the Consumers Always Lose?" *Osgoode Hall Law Journal* 13(3): 619–47.

Trebilcock, Michael, and Robert Howse. 1995. *The Regulation of International Trade*. London: Routledge.

Trebilcock, Michael, Ralph Winter, Paul Collins, and Edward Iacobucci. 2002. *The Law and Economics of Canadian Competition Policy*. Toronto: University of Toronto Press.

Turner, Bryan S. 1988. *Status*. Minneapolis: University of Minnesota Press.

Valverde, Mariana, and Lorna Weir. 2006. "The Struggle of the Immoral: Preliminary Remarks on Moral Regulation," in *Moral Regulation and Governance in Canada: History, Context, and Critical Issues*, edited by Amanda Glasbeek, 75–84. Toronto: Canadian Scholars' Press.

VanAudenrode, Marc, Jim Royer, Lisa Pinheiro, and Anne Faye. 2008. "Adapting Competition Policy to a Global Economic Environment." Paper prepared for the Competition Policy Review Panel.

Vandervort, Lucinda. 1979. *Political Control of Independent Administrative Agencies*. Ottawa: Law Reform Commission of Canada.

Van Loon, Richard, and Michael Whittington. 1981. *The Canadian Political System*. (3rd ed.). Toronto: McGraw-Hill Ryerson.

VanNijnatten, Debora. 2002. "Getting Greener in the Third Mandate? in *How Ottawa Spends 2002–2003: The Security Aftermath and National Priorities*, edited by G. Bruce Doern, 216–33. Toronto: Oxford University Press.

Vass, Peter (ed.). 2007. *Regulatory Review 2006–2007*. Bath, UK: Centre for the Study of Regulated Industries, University of Bath.

Vogel, David. 2012. *The Politics of Precaution: Regulating Health, Safety, and Environmental Risks in Europe and the United States*. Princeton: Princeton University Press.

Vogel, Stephen K. 1996. *Freer Markets, More Rules: Regulatory Reform in Advanced Industrial Countries*. Ithaca: Cornell University Press.

von Finckenstein, Konrad. 2007. "Notes for an Address to the 2007 Telecommunications Invitation Forum," Montebello, QC, 26 April.

Wacquant, Loïc. 2009. *Prison of Poverty*. Minnesota: University of Minnesota Press.

Walkom, Thomas. 2013. "Mike Duffy Senate Scandal Inches Closer to Stephen Harper." *Toronto Star*, 5 July, 4.

Waters, W.G., and W.T. Stanbury. 1999. "Deregulation, Pressures for Re-regulation and Regulatory Shifts: The Case of Telecommunications and Transportation," in *Changing the Rules: Canadian Regulatory Regimes and Institutions*, edited by G. Bruce Doern, Margaret M. Hill, Michael J. Prince, and Richard J. Schultz, 143–73. Toronto: University of Toronto Press.

Webb, Kernaghan (ed.). 2004. *Voluntary Codes: Private Governance, the Public Interest and Innovation*. Ottawa: Carleton Research Unit on Innovation, Science and Environment.

Weiss, Linda. 1998. *The Myth of the Powerless State*. Cambridge: Polity Press.

Whitaker, Reg. 2003. "More or Less than Meets the Eye? The New National Security Agenda," in *How Ottawa Spends 2003–2004: Regime Change and Policy Shift*, edited by G. Bruce Doern, 44–58. Montreal and Kingston: McGill-Queen's University Press.

– 2005. "Made in Canada? The New Public Safety Paradigm," in *How Ottawa Spends 2005–2006: Managing the Minority*, edited by G. Bruce Doern, 77–95. Montreal and Kingston: McGill-Queen's University Press.

White, B.W. 1981. "Proposals for a Regulatory Budget." *Public Budgeting and Finance* 1(3): 46–55.

White, Graham. 2006. *Cabinets and First Ministers*. Vancouver: UBC Press.

Whyte, John D. 2011. "Federalism and Moral Regulation: A Comment on *Reference re Assisted Human Reproduction Act*." *Saskatchewan Law Review* 74(1): 45–57.

Wiles, Anne. 2007. *Strategically Natural: Nature, Social Trust and Risk Regulation of Genetically Modified Foods and Natural Health Products in Canada*. Ph.D. dissertation, Department of Geography, Carleton University.

Wilks, Stephen. 1999. *In the Public Interest: Competition Policy and the Monopolies and Mergers Commission*. Manchester: Manchester University Press.

Wilks, Stephen, and G. Bruce Doern. 2007. "Accountability and Multi-level Governance in UK Regulation," in *Regulatory Review 2006–2007*, edited by Peter Vass, 341–72. Bath, UK: Centre for the Study of Regulated Industries, University of Bath.

Williams, Glen. 2009. *Canadian Politics in the 21st Century*. (7th ed.). Toronto: Nelson.

Wilson, James Q. (ed.). 1980. *The Politics of Regulation*. New York: Basic Books.

Wincott, Daniel. 2012. "The Regulatory State versus the Welfare State." Presentation to Conference on New Perspectives on Learning, Regulation and Governance, University of Exeter, 27–9 June.

Woodrow, R. Brian, and Kenneth Woodside. 1982. *The Introduction of Pay Television in Canada*. Montreal: Institute for Research on Public Policy.

Woodrow, R. Brian, Kenneth Woodside, Henry Wiseman, and John B. Black. 1980. *Conflict over Communications Policy: A Study of Federal-Provincial Relations and Public Policy*. Toronto: C.D. Howe Institute.

Woods, Michael. 2011. "Canada Mediocre in Access to Information Rankings." *Toronto Star*, 29 Sept., 6.

Wright, John. 2012. "Theorizing the Regulatory State for the Post-Crisis Era." Paper presented at the Conference on New Perspectives on Regulation, Governance and Learning, University of Exeter, 27–9 June.

Yeh, Stuart S. 2010. "Financial Sector Incentives, Bailouts: Moral Hazard, Systemic Risk and Reforms." *Risk, Hazards and Crisis in Public Policy* 1(2): 97–130.

Index